# OUR FATHER ABRAHAM

## CENTER FOR JUDAIC-CHRISTIAN STUDIES

*To explore and to understand the Jewish roots of our faith is to expand and to enrich our Christian experience. This premise is at the heart of the educational endeavors of the Center for Judaic-Christian Studies, a non-profit organization that is restoring to the Church an appreciation of its full Hebrew heritage.*

*The cornerstone of the Center's biblical research is the innovative work of Christian and Jewish scholars in Israel, collectively known as the "Jerusalem School for the Study of the Synoptic Gospels." Building upon twenty-five years of fruitful collaboration between Dr. Robert Lindsey of the Narkis Street Baptist Church and Prof. David Flusser of the Hebrew University, a team of distinguished scholars in Jerusalem is continuing to document the life and times of Jesus from a Hebrew perspective. They are clarifying the challenging words of Jesus and illuminating his mission and message by drawing upon the disciplines of archeology, history, linguistics, and biblical and rabbinic studies. A free sample issue of* Jerusalem Perspective, *a monthly report from Israel on Gospel research, is available upon request.*

*The Center for Judaic-Christian Studies wants the Christian public to share in the adventure of returning to the foundations of our faith. Toward this end, it has promoted a wide range of educational programs (including lectures, seminars, and national conferences), has produced a television series and audio and video tapes, and has published several books and co-published others, including this outstanding volume by Dr. Marvin R. Wilson.*

*To learn more about the Center for Judaic-Christian Studies, write and request a free copy of the Center's catalog of educational materials.*

> *Dwight A. Pryor, President*
> *Center for Judaic-Christian Studies*
> *P. O. Box 293040*
> *Dayton, Ohio 45429*

# OUR FATHER ABRAHAM

## Jewish Roots of the Christian Faith

Marvin R. Wilson

WILLIAM B. EERDMANS PUBLISHING COMPANY
GRAND RAPIDS, MICHIGAN
AND
CENTER FOR JUDAIC-CHRISTIAN STUDIES
DAYTON, OHIO

Copyright © 1989 by Marvin R. Wilson
Published by Wm. B. Eerdmans Publishing Company
255 Jefferson Ave., S.E., Grand Rapids, MI 49503
and
Center for Judaic-Christian Studies
P.O. Box 293040, Dayton, OH 45429

*Reprinted, March 1991*

**Library of Congress Cataloging-in-Publication Data**

Wilson, Marvin R.
Our father Abraham.

Bibliography: p. 338
Includes index.
1. Judaism—Relations—Christianity. 2. Christianity and other religions—Judaism.
3.   Christianity—Origin.
I. Title.
BM535.W55  1989   261.2'6   88-33512
ISBN 0-8028-0423-3

*To my wife Polly,*
*without whose love, encouragement, and support*
*this book would never have come to be.*

*A wife of noble character who can find?*
*She is worth far more than rubies.*

*Proverbs 31:10*

# Contents

## II Church and Synagogue in the Light of History

# CONTENTS

CONTENTS

# CONTENTS

# CONTENTS

## V  Toward Restoring Jewish Roots

# Pronunciation Key
## for Transliterated Hebrew Words

### Vowels

| | |
|---|---|
| *a* as in *father* | *(dabar, shalom, lappidim)* |
| *e* as in *red* | *(ha-zeh, mishteh)* |
| *i* as in *machine* | *(li, dodi)* |
| *o* as in *cold* | *(torah, kenegdo, zimrot)* |
| *u* as in *tune* | *(ketubah, nissu'in, galut)* |

### Consonants

*ḥ* represents the harsh guttural sound of Hebrew *ḥet (yiḥus, mishpaḥah, orḥim, ḥokhmah)*

*kh* represents the spirantized sound of Hebrew *kaph* as in the German word *Bach (shadkhan, hakhnasat)*

*tz* represents the Hebrew *tsadhe (mitzvah, matzot)*

*b* after a vowel is pronounced *v (dabar, ketubah)*

' represents the separation of sounds of Hebrew *aleph (nebi'im, nissu'in)*

' represents the separation of sounds of Hebrew *ayin (da'at, me'at)*

### Hyphen

- the hyphen in Hebrew words is a grammatical indicator to separate an article from the word which follows *(ha-zeh, ha-ba)*, or an indicator which connects the conjunction "and" to the word which follows *(ve-nitḥazeq, u-she'on, ve-hagita)*

# Preface

The roots of Christianity run deep into Hebrew soil. Though the Hebrew heritage of the Church is rich and extensive, many Christians are regrettably uninformed about it. Most of it has been treated either passively and superficially, or more often, it has simply been left unexplored.

Christian seminaries, colleges, and other educational institutions have been largely responsible for this lack. Many have not produced professional clergy, teachers, and lay leaders with a well-rounded, balanced education. Christian educators have frequently stressed the origins, impact, and contributions of Western civilization on the Church and modern society. But study of both the Hebrew world of the east Mediterranean and the modern Jewish community of the Diaspora has often been superficial or deemed optional or even irrelevant. Consequently, the crop of our knowledge about Hebrew heritage and Christian-Jewish relations that we continue to reap within the Church is quite lean. Time has come for the Church to have a renewed biblical vision. It has sown the seeds of neglect long enough.

"Heritage" implies something which has been conveyed or handed down from generation to generation. It means the transference of a legacy. If it is to be *our* Judeo-Christian heritage it is important to understand what our predecessors in the faith have delivered over to us. Unfortunately, few Christians have had the tools and encouragement to familiarize themselves with this vast heritage. Indeed, currently there is a notable lack of textbooks and other study materials suitable for classroom use written by Christians who are active in the field of Jewish studies and Christian-Jewish relations. This volume is an attempt to help bridge this educational gap.

*Our Father Abraham* is an introduction to the world of Hebrew thought. It is intended primarily for Christians, but it is hoped that Jews may benefit from much of this book as well. I have sought to write with a wide readership in mind. The primary objective of this volume, however, is to serve as a text for Christian seminarians and collegians, clergy and church leaders, and laypersons who are serious students of Scripture, theology, and history.

Although this work is a biblical, historical, and cultural study, the reader will quickly find out that it is concerned with more than exploring the past. Learning to think Hebraically is only the start. These pages also have a contemporary application; they are a call for Christians to reexamine their Jewish roots so as to effect a more authentically biblical lifestyle. This priceless legacy of the Jewish people must be made useful; it must affect not only Christian theory but also experience.

This quest for Jewish roots may be unsettling to some. We all tend to be creatures of habit. No one likes to have long-held viewpoints challenged or established practices questioned. Change is often disturbing. In this connection, the exact relation between Christianity and Judaism is, in many ways, complex. Admittedly, many areas lack clear and definitive answers. Nevertheless, the goal of this investigation is to strengthen the Church's understanding of its foundations through both thought and action. Our concern is to demonstrate why the Church cannot afford to be passive about the Jewish experience in history—whether ancient or modern.

The title of this work, *Our Father Abraham*, is a biblical expression (see Luke 1:73; John 8:53; Acts 7:2; etc.) that epitomizes the deep spiritual link every Christian has with the Jewish people. As we will point out particularly in the first two chapters, gentile Christians are grafted by faith into Israel (Rom. 11:17-24), and through this faith commitment come to know Israel's father as their father too. Elsewhere Paul says that "those who believe are children of Abraham" (Gal. 3:7); indeed, through faith, "Abraham is the father of us all" (Rom. 4:16). Although Abraham himself is not the principal focus of this volume, the title *Our Father Abraham* describes its main thrust: an exposition on what it means for today's Church to be part of Abraham's spiritual family (cf. Gal. 3:29).

In large measure, this volume reflects my own spiritual pilgrimage. My strong impression is, however, that I am not alone in this regard. Many of the issues and emphases that I have chosen to include are those which I wish had been part of my own formal education as a Christian but were not; yet today, as a result of my own quest, they have come to be greatly valued. Thus this work does not pretend to present a comprehensive treatment of the Jewish roots of Christianity, much less a standard systematic text on basic Judaism. Rather, it deals with some of the more relevant aspects of Hebrew heritage bearing on the life of the Church. Not every topic dealt with will be equally valuable for, or directly applicable to, all readers. The Christian community is diverse, gifts and abilities differ from person to person, and each comes to this subject area from a different starting point. My overall aim, however, is to challenge all readers to a deeper appreciation of our Hebrew heritage.

In broad outline, this book reflects a variety of emphases. The opening chapters develop an historical perspective on the Jewish origin of the Church and the centuries of de-Judaization to follow. Next, we set forth the importance and nature of Hebrew heritage, and some of the negative consequences that have resulted from the Church being severed from its Jewish roots. Then we consider several major themes by which today's Church can directly benefit from a study of Hebrew heritage. The book concludes with a discussion of some of the practical ways the Church may become more attuned to the Hebraic mind-set of Scripture.

In more specific detail, we have implemented the above emphases by dividing the manuscript into five main sections. Part I deals with what it means for Gentiles to be spiritual Semites, grafted into and supported by Israel (Rom. 11). Here we also deal with certain influences or problems such as Hellenism, Judaizing, Paul and the Law, and what is encompassed in this work by the term *Hebrew* or *Jewish heritage.*

Part II is mainly diachronic in approach. It focuses on Christian-Jewish relations throughout two thousand years of history. Here we trace the Jewish beginnings of the Church and the various factors which led to its split from the Synagogue. We also trace the history of contempt between Church and Synagogue, showing how the de-Judaization of the Church led to anti-Judaism and anti-Semitism.

In Part III we seek to establish the importance of the Old Testament and other early Jewish sources as foundational for understanding the background and teachings of the New Testament. Furthermore, some of the more important characteristics of Hebrew thought are set forth in order to help the reader get inside the Jewish mind-set of the biblical authors. This section concludes with an examination of three main areas where the Church has deviated from its Jewish roots and found its theology distorted in the process. In each case, a biblical (Hebraic) corrective is offered so as to bring the Church back into theological balance.

Part IV contains a number of selected studies where Hebrew heritage heavily influences the Church. Here we treat at considerable length teaching on marriage and the family and the concept of learning. We also include a chapter on Passover to provide the Jewish background to the Last Supper, and a fourth chapter which stresses the ongoing relevance of the ancestral homeland of the Jewish people to Christians today.

Part V is a practical chapter. It explores a number of channels which Christians can follow with profit to become more firmly attached to their

Jewish roots. It also explains how Christians can reach out and build productive relations with today's Jewish community.

Several features enhance the usability of this book as a text. As an introductory study for Christians of various denominational and educational backgrounds, we have sought to define or translate virtually all Hebrew terms and to explain all technical vocabulary. In addition, the book is closely outlined, allowing the student to follow easily the flow of discussion and to note points of major transition. Furthermore, there are study and discussion questions at the end of each chapter. These questions draw the reader back to review important points developed in the chapter and serve as appropriate examination questions for those wishing to use this material for testing purposes. The questions may also be utilized by interfaith dialogue groups for preparatory homework and as a catalyst for in-group discussion. The various indexes and the selective bibliography found at the end of the book will assist students desiring to do additional research and personal study.

For several decades the subject of this volume has been a particular interest of mine in regard to research, teaching, and publication. Portions of *Our Father Abraham* are based on previous articles I have written. The publications which bear on certain chapters of this manuscript are as follows: Chapter two—"Judaizers," in *Evangelical Dictionary of Theology,* ed. Walter A. Elwell (Grand Rapids: Baker Book House, 1984), p. 590. Chapter seven—"Anti-Semitism," ibid., pp. 60-61. Chapter eight—"Shema, The," in *International Standard Bible Encyclopedia,* 4 vols., ed. G. W. Bromiley, et al. (Grand Rapids: William B. Eerdmans Publishing Co., 1979-88), 4:469-70. Chapter ten—"Hebrew Thought in the Life of the Church," in *The Living and Active Word of God,* ed. Morris Inch and Ronald Youngblood (Winona Lake, IN: Eisenbrauns, 1983), pp. 123-35. Chapter twelve—"Passover," in *International Standard Bible Encyclopedia,* 3:675-79. Chapter thirteen—"'Real Estate' Theology: Zionism and Biblical Claims" in *Christianity and the Arab/Israeli Conflict,* The Evangelical Round Table (Princeton: Princeton University Press, 1986), 1:87-99. Chapter fourteen—"The Jewish Concept of Learning: A Christian Appreciation," *Christian Scholar's Review* 5/4 (1976): 350-63. Furthermore, unless otherwise noted, all biblical quotations throughout this volume are taken from the *New International Version* (Grand Rapids: Zondervan Publishing House).

This manuscript would not have been a reality without the influence, encouragement, and help of many along the way. Early in my career, two Jewish scholars began to have a very significant impact on my thinking; they planted the seed from which this book eventually grew. First, my graduate-school mentor, Cyrus Gordon, former chairman of the Department of Mediterranean Studies at Brandeis University, imparted to me a profound love for the Hebrew Bible and its impact upon the world. Second, over the years, the writings of the late Abraham Joshua Heschel have deeply stimulated my appreciation of the relation of Judaism to Christianity. Both of these giants lit a fire within me during the 1960s which has never gone out.

I owe a special word of thanks to my good friend, Dwight Pryor, president of the Center for Judaic-Christian Studies, co-publisher of this volume. Dwight's persistent vision and strong encouragement were responsible for getting this project officially launched. I am most grateful for the helpfulness of the Center's office staff—especially Georgia Clifton, Robert Morris, and David Wharton—each of whom read significant portions of the manuscript in its earliest stage and offered many useful comments throughout.

Over the past decade or more, a number of knowledgeable and gracious friends, each intimately familiar with the land of the Bible and its people and culture, have personally provided input into this book through their expertise in such areas as Hebraica, bibliography, Jewish history, modern Israel, and Christian-Jewish relations. Accordingly, I wish to acknowledge with gratitude my debt to the following scholars from the Jerusalem School for the Study of the Synoptic Gospels: the director David Bivin, Robert Lindsey, Halvor Ronning, Miriam Ronning, and Bradford Young. It is also fitting that I recognize three others, all residents of Jerusalem, who have in various yet important ways encouraged the writing of this book: the late G. Douglas Young, founder and long-time president of the Institute of Holy Land Studies; Clarence Wagner, Jr., president of Bridges for Peace; and James Monson, biblical geographer and historian.

Furthermore, I am grateful for the impetus and insights provided toward the accomplishing of this work by several other kind friends, each a recognized specialist in one or more subject areas dealt with in this manuscript. These include Roy Blizzard, Jr., president of Yavo Incorporated, Austin, Texas; Frank Eiklor, president of Shalom International, Costa Mesa, California; Rabbi Yechiel Eckstein, president of The Holyland Fellowship of Christians and Jews, Chicago, Illinois; and Sonia Schreiber Weitz, founder and co-director of the Holocaust Center, Jewish Federation of the Northshore, Peabody, Massachusetts.

One particular scholar-teacher, however, I must single out. Rabbi A. James Rudin, national interreligious affairs director, the American Jewish Committee, New York, New York, has greatly enlarged my understanding of Judaism and the Jewish people. With this cherished and esteemed friend, I have had the rare privilege of co-editing three volumes on Christian-Jewish relations between 1978 and 1987. Few have contributed as much as Jim Rudin, a tireless pioneer and educator in the world of interfaith dialogue. I and numerous other Christians respect his ability to communicate the heart of the Jewish experience with clarity, sensitivity, and warmth. Jim Rudin has made an indelible mark upon my thinking.

With kind thanks I also wish to recognize the following institutions whose libraries provided me access for research and writing: First, my own institution, Gordon College (Wenham, Massachusetts), also the American Jewish Committee (New York, New York), Gordon-Conwell Theological Seminary (South Hamilton, Massachusetts), Harvard Divinity School (Cambridge, Massachusetts), Tyndale House (Cambridge, England), and Cambridge University (Cambridge, England).

My deep gratitude also goes to Gordon College (the United College of Gordon and Barrington) where I continue to enjoy the privilege of teaching the Jewish Scriptures, Judaism, and classical Hebrew. For a period of several years Gordon College tangibly encouraged the research and writing of this volume with grants through its faculty development program. Also I am very thankful to this same institution for providing me a sabbatical leave, spring term, 1987. The time was profitably spent in Cambridge, England, where I completed the first draft of this manuscript. I am indebted in a special way to my former and present Gordon students, however. Through class lectures and discussions—especially those held in my Modern Jewish Culture course—Gordon students have given me considerable feedback on much of the material touched upon in this book. It is primarily because of the changes I have witnessed in these and other students that I am more firmly convinced than ever in the value of Christian study of Hebrew heritage and the importance of Christian-Jewish relations.

Last, but far from least in importance, I am most grateful for the skill and support of several other key individuals directly involved in this project. My faculty colleague, William Buehler, read several lengthy portions of the manuscript and made valuable comments. My capable teaching assistant, Ann Droppers, was responsible for the tedious task of indexing. Jane Dunfee, assistant director of academic computer services at Gordon College, provided valuable assistance at several important places. Mary Jasper Cate deserves a special word of deep appreciation on my part. Mary's skill on the word processor, her keen editorial advice, and her sensitive and faithful support throughout have been major factors in the accomplishment of this work. I am also deeply indebted to Gary Lee, editor at William B. Eerdmans Publishing Company. In a host of helpful ways Gary adeptly and enthusiastically moved this publication on to completion.

This manuscript goes forth with the hope that it will prove instrumental in pointing Christians of every denomination and ethnic background to the importance and richness of their Hebrew heritage. But more than this, my deepest desire is to convey through these pages an attitude, not merely information. For Christian-Jewish relations that are rooted today in a new sense of appreciation and trust between both communities will have even greater potential for growth tomorrow.

*Marvin R. Wilson*
*Wenham, Massachusetts*

*Part I*

# A New People: Abraham's Spiritual Children

*Chapter One*

# The Root and Branches

*Consider this: You do not support the root, but the root sup-
ports you*

Romans 11:18b

Since their beginning, the people of God have stressed the importance of
understanding their uniqueness, of knowing from whom they have come.
Roots were always important, for Israel's faith was deeply imbedded in
history. Thus knowledge of beginnings is central to biblical thought. The
Old Testament opens with the book of Genesis, which in Hebrew is entitled *bere'shit,* "in the beginning" or "by way of beginning." This foundational source contains many genealogical tables that fix the beginnings
of the Jewish people within a specific ancient Near Eastern setting.
Likewise, the New Testament begins with the Gospel of Matthew tracing
the line of Jesus. Matthew introduces his account with these words: "A
record of the genealogy of Jesus Christ the son of David, the son of
Abraham" (1:1). To be cognizant of one's past was essential for establishing confidence about the future.

## "Look to Abraham Your Father"

God's sovereign plan in history was to establish his covenant through a
man called Abraham (or Abram, as he was originally known). Abraham
was a Semite, a descendant of Noah's son Shem (Gen. 11:10-32). The
patriarch Abraham was the first person in the Bible to be called a "He-

3

brew" (Gen. 14:13). All Jews trace their ancestry to Abraham as father of the Hebrew nation.[1] Accordingly, the Lord proclaimed through his prophet, "Look to the rock from which you were cut . . . look to Abraham, your father" (Isa. 51:1-2).

Genesis 12 records the call of Abraham. God told him that his offspring would inherit the land of Canaan (v. 7; cf. 13:15; 17:8) and that he would have numerous descendants (12:2; cf. 13:16; 15:5). God also promised Abraham, "all peoples on earth will be blessed through you" (12:3; cf. 18:18; 22:18). In the New Testament, Peter's speech to his fellow Jews gathered near the Temple indicates that they, as physical descendants of Abraham, are heirs of this promised blessing (Acts 3:25; cf. 3:12). But the New Testament also indicates that gentile believers—those who are spiritual rather than lineal descendants of Abraham—likewise share in this Abrahamic kinship (cf. Gal. 3:8). Indeed, all Christians find their origin in Abraham the Hebrew, for, as Paul states, "If you belong to Christ, then you are Abraham's seed" (Gal. 3:29).

The biblical phrase "our father Abraham" (John 8:53; Acts 7:2) thus expresses the family relationship that every person of faith has with "the man of faith" (Gal. 3:9). The New Testament writers argue that those who display Abraham's faith and deeds are Abraham's true offspring (John 8:31-41). James reminds his readers that Abraham, as father of the faithful, is called "God's friend" (Jas. 2:23; cf. 2 Chr. 20:7). Furthermore, James links all Christians to this exemplary patriarch by speaking of him as "our ancestor Abraham" (2:21), a man whose "faith was made complete by what he did" (v. 22). Indeed, the New Testament emphasizes that before Abraham was circumcised, he believed God and acted upon that belief (Rom. 4:9-12). In sum, according to the book of Hebrews, Abraham's faithful obedience, from the moment God called him (Heb. 11:8ff.), serves as an inspiring witness to the Church (12:1), that new people of God both rooted in Abraham and numbered among his children.

The question of origins is a question of roots. Since the American public became absorbed with a moving television documentary called "Roots" a number of years ago, many people have been more conscious about their own roots. Considerable interest in tracing family, ethnic, and national ties has resulted in a recent flood of literature on this subject.

At the same time, however, many Christians seem to have little knowledge about their biblical roots. They have never really penetrated

---

1. Here, and elsewhere throughout this book, the words *Jew* and *Jewish* are sometimes used rather than *Hebrew* and *Hebraic*. Whereas the latter terms are often utilized to stress the linguistic and cultural dimensions of the Israelite people, *Jew* and *Jewish* normally carry a more extensive and contemporary connotation.

the inner world of biblical thought. Christians can converse intelligently about the latest automobiles, fashions, music, and sports, but too few give evidence of a deep understanding of their spiritual heritage. At best, their grounding in biblical soil is both shallow and shaky. Hence, they usually embrace an uncritical conformity to the prevailing spirit of today's world. As children of Abraham, Christians should be asking, "What does it mean to claim spiritual kinship with Abraham and the Jewish people?"

God's people are called to be different from the world, through the "renewing of the mind" (Rom. 12:2). Every Christian must seriously heed Paul's warning, "Don't let the world around you squeeze you into its own mould" (Rom. 12:2, Phillips). Thus a Christian mind is one in the process of being renewed according to divinely revealed thought patterns and values.

A Christian's frame of reference must be constructed of sound building blocks derived from Scripture. But God's people can scarcely be expected to heed Paul's admonition to "work out" their salvation (Phil. 2:12) within that biblical frame of reference unless they know how that frame is constructed. How does today's Christian learn to think and approach life as Abraham, Moses, David, and the prophets did, and as Jesus, Paul, and the apostles did? This knowledge comes only by uncovering the overarching mind-set that the writers of Scripture reflect. We must enter their world and become conversant with their culture. We too must "look to Abraham our father."

## Athens or Jerusalem?

What is the inner world of biblical thought? What is the cultural mind-set of the authors of Holy Writ? Are we to understand the Bible chiefly through the eyes of Hellenism (Greek thought and culture) or through the eyes of Judaism (Hebrew thought and culture)? Obviously, the last question focuses on the New Testament. Most scholars affirm an essentially strong Jewish background to Gospel studies and to the life and teachings of Jesus.[2] But scholars debate widely the background of the writings of Paul, "apostle to the Gentiles" (Rom. 11:13).

2. Note the evidence discussed in the following works: David Bivin and Roy B. Blizzard, *Understanding the Difficult Words of Jesus* (Austin, TX: Center for Judaic-Christian Studies, 1984); Pinchas E. Lapide, *Hebrew in the Church*, trans. Erroll F. Rhodes (Grand Rapids: William B. Eerdmans Publishing Co., 1984); Harvey Falk, *Jesus the Pharisee: A New Look at the Jewishness of Jesus* (New York: Paulist Press, 1985); and David Flusser, *Judaism and the Origins of Christianity* (Jerusalem: Magnes Press, 1988).

Some, such as the late Jewish scholar Samuel Sandmel, stress the importance of Hellenism in grasping the key to Pauline thought.[3] While recognizing Hellenistic elements in Paul, however, W. D. Davies views the apostle differently. In his monumental work *Paul and Rabbinic Judaism,* Davies argues that Paul must be understood as one who belonged to the mainstream of first-century Rabbinic Judaism, and that he was thus "primarily governed both in life and thought by Pharisaic concepts."[4] In his widely discussed volume *Paul and Palestinian Judaism,* E. P. Sanders finds yet a different clue for interpreting Paul. Sanders calls for a radical separation of Judaism from Pauline Christianity, considering the latter as a distinct religion in opposition to Judaism. In short, in Sanders's view, Paul "converted" to Christianity from Judaism.[5]

From yet another angle—primarily that of linguistics—James Barr has added further stimulus to the "Athens versus Jerusalem" discussion. In a substantive and controversial volume, *The Semantics of Biblical Language,* Barr rejects the idea that the basic characteristics of a culture (e.g., Greek or Hebrew) are traceable through the words, grammar, and syntax of the language of that culture.[6] He challenges the approach of a number of works in this field, including Thorleif Boman, *Hebrew Thought Compared with Greek,* and the widely acclaimed, multivolume work edited by Gerhard Kittel and Gerhard Friedrich, *The Theological Dictionary of the New Testament.*[7] Barr maintains that words cannot express concepts and that language and mentality cannot be easily correlated. Accordingly, he downplays the value of lexicons and theological dictionaries. In short, Barr believes it is questionable—if not precarious—to make distinctions between Greek and Hebrew views of life.

The world of biblical scholarship owes a great debt to Barr for the many useful insights he has articulated. These focus particularly on the use of linguistic methods such as etymologizing; Barr correctly observes

3. See Samuel Sandmel, *Judaism and Christian Beginnings* (New York: Oxford University Press, 1978). Also note my review of Sandmel's work in *Westminster Theological Journal* 42/2 (Spring, 1979): 443-48.

4. W. D. Davies, *Paul and Rabbinic Judaism,* 4th ed. (Philadelphia: Fortress Press, 1980), pp. 1, 16.

5. E. P. Sanders, *Paul and Palestinian Judaism* (Philadelphia: Fortress Press, 1977).

6. See James Barr, *The Semantics of Biblical Language* (New York: Oxford University Press, 1961).

7. Barr referred to the earlier German editions of both works, which were subsequently translated: Thorleif Boman, *Hebrew Thought Compared with Greek,* trans. Jules L. Moreau (repr. New York: W. W. Norton & Co., 1970); *The Theological Dictionary of the New Testament,* ed. Gerhard Kittel and Gerhard Friedrich, trans. Geoffrey W. Bromiley, 10 vols. (Grand Rapids: William B. Eerdmans Publishing Co., 1964-76).

that the meaning of a root is not necessarily part of the meaning of a derived form. Also welcome is his emphasis on the laws of language, contextual analysis, and the study of the larger linguistic complex. But Barr's position fails to be fully convincing. By downplaying any distinction between Greek and Hebrew manners of thinking, Barr does not take into adequate consideration such nonverbal aspects as the historical, cultural, and social-psychological setting from which the respective thought derives. Furthermore, he gives the impression that one may translate from one language to another without any major loss. This is not necessarily the case, however, for words may have a particular cultural and historical development within their own language. For example, while it would be normal to expect that the Hebraic idea behind the Greek term *nómos*, "law," would be readily communicated to the minds of Jewish readers (i.e., they would take the term in the sense of *torah*, "teaching"), the same word *(nómos)* may be initially understood differently (i.e., in its customary Hellenistic sense) by Greek readers. Some of the dimensions of this broader question of the contrast of Greek and Hebrew thought, raised by Barr, will be discussed further in later chapters.[8]

In reference to the above discussion it must be recognized that some scholars have displayed a tendency to overemphasize the opposition between Athens and Jerusalem,[9] particularly when it comes to Paul's writings, which evince a strong continuity with Judaism as well as a discontinuity. We must be careful to define what is meant by *discontinuity* here. One must certainly recognize that Paul used Greek to aid communication (e.g., his extensive use of the Septuagint, the Greek translation of the Old Testament), and he employed certain stylistic devices (e.g., Greek rhetorical forms and phrases) so as to present material in a manner the audience would understand.[10] But some claim that discontinuity extends to the source of Paul's religious thought in pagan Hellenistic beliefs. However, scholars have marshalled considerable material to oppose the popular position that early Christianity was a syncretistic faith which borrowed its essential beliefs from Hellenistic philosophy or religion.[11]

8. For further comment and critical evaluation on many of the above issues, see the work of David Hill, *Greek Words and Hebrew Meanings* (Cambridge: Cambridge University Press, 1967), especially pp. 1-22, 294-300; also Moises Silva, *Biblical Words and Their Meaning* (Grand Rapids: Zondervan Publishing House, 1983).

9. This imbalance has been pointed out by Robert Martin-Achard, *An Approach to the Old Testament,* trans. J. C. G. Greig (Edinburgh: Oliver & Boyd, 1965), p. 46.

10. Davies, *Paul and Rabbinic Judaism,* pp. xxiii, xxiv.

11. For example, see the evidence set forth by Ronald H. Nash, *Christianity and the Hellenistic World* (Grand Rapids: Zondervan Publishing House, 1984). Note especially pp. 57-65, 81-112, 263-70.

Indeed, today convincing evidence challenges the earlier widespread belief that Paul's writings bear the distinctive mark of Platonism. In sum, contemporary Christians have strong reasons to question any approach to Paul which finds the primary roots of his theology in Hellenism, Gnosticism, or mystery religions.

As we will develop in greater detail in the next chapter, Paul upheld the goodness of the Jewish tradition of *torah*. Indeed, Paul "came to understand the Christian life as patterned after that of Judaism: it was for him not the antithesis but the full flowering of that Faith."[12] This meant for Paul, Diaspora Jew that he was, a deep rooting in the Hebrew Scriptures and rabbinic thought. Paul was proud of being a Jew (2 Cor. 11:22), in his words, "a Hebrew of Hebrews . . . a Pharisee" (Phil. 3:5). As in the case of ancient Israel, so with Paul, God channeled "His Word thought by Hebrew minds, even when their lips spoke and their hands wrote Greek."[13]

If one is to interpret the teaching of Paul—and, indeed, all of Scripture—correctly, one must understand his background and the context in which he wrote. Krister Stendahl has wisely observed that "the task of biblical studies, even of biblical theology is to *describe,* to relive and relate, in terms of presuppositions of the period of the texts, what they meant to their authors and their contemporaries."[14] Paul wrote in Greek, the lingua franca of his day. But his inner world of the spirit reflects primarily his Hebrew heritage, fed from sources which originally flowed from Jerusalem. So at the core, Paul's theology was essentially Hebraic, albeit in his letters dressed in Greek words. This was the spiritual mind-set of Paul, the Jewish scholar of Tarsus. Accordingly, the great Jewish theologian Abraham Heschel has correctly observed that "geographically and historically Jerusalem and Athens, the age of the prophets and the age of Pericles, are not too far removed from each other. Spiritually they are worlds apart."[15]

Let us return then to the original question, "Athens or Jerusalem?" Not simply for the writings of Paul, but for the entire Scriptures, the primary cultural context is that of the Semitic world of the Hebrew people.

12. Davies, *Paul and Rabbinic Judaism,* p. xxx.

13. Claude Tresmontant, *A Study of Hebrew Thought,* trans. M. F. Gibson (New York: Desclee Co., 1960), p. x.

14. Krister Stendahl, "Implications of Form-Criticism for Biblical Interpretation," *Journal of Biblical Literature* 77 (1958): 38. Cf. David Hill, *Greek Words and Hebrew Meanings,* p. 22.

15. Abraham J. Heschel, *God in Search of Man* (New York: Farrar, Straus & Giroux, 1955), p. 15.

Consequently, the authors of God's Word—virtually every one of them a Jew—have a profoundly Hebraic perspective on life and the world. If we are to interpret the Bible correctly, we must become attuned to this Hebraic setting in the ancient Near East. Thus we must look primarily not to Athens but to Jerusalem for the biblical view of reality. For the prophets and apostles produced a Book that is, without question, Hebraic in composition and orientation. Succinctly stated, "The Old Testament is the foundation for the New. The message of the New Testament is in the Hebrew tradition as against the Greek tradition. Our tutors to Christ are Moses and the Prophets, and not Plato and the Academies."[16]

The implications of this context for developing a Christian mind are immense. We are driven to realize that the theological vocabulary and linguistic idioms behind much of the Greek New Testament are Hebraic to the very core. David Noel Freedman affirms the Hebraic foundation of New Testament thought: "The thought pattern of biblical religion was firmly fixed in the Hebrew language by long centuries of usage. . . . The language of biblical religion is Hebrew, as the Dead Sea Scrolls have shown, not only for sectarian Judaism of the 1st century B.C., but also for New Testament Christianity of the 1st century A.D."[17] The Hebraic origins of Christianity find strong support in the witness of the New Testament itself. Paul states that "the Gentiles are heirs together with Israel, members together of one body" (Eph. 3:6b). Hence Gentiles have a new history—Israel's history is now their history. In writing to the predominantly gentile church of Corinth, Paul states that the ancient Israelites were the forebears of the Corinthians: "our forefathers were all under the cloud, and . . . they all passed through the sea" (1 Cor. 10:1). In the early Church, therefore, Jew and Gentile claimed a common spiritual ancestry with the Hebrews of old.

## The World of the Bible

The biblical scholar and theologian G. A. F. Knight has observed that "if God chose Israel, then he also chose to use the Hebrew language. If we accept that obvious fact, then we must proceed to accept more. The Hebrews had their own peculiar manner of thinking about most things in

16. Norman H. Snaith, *The Distinctive Ideas of the Old Testament* (New York: Schocken Books, 1964), p. 159.

17. David Noel Freedman, "The Scrolls and the New Testament," *Journal of Biblical Literature* 78 (1959): 331. Cf. James Barr, *Semantics of Biblical Language*, pp. 18-19.

heaven and earth."[18] Now we agree generally with this statement, but would like to emphasize the word *most*. That is, the Hebrews did have a particular or separate approach to life in *most* areas, but not in every area. The Hebrews—though called to live distinct lives apart from the rest of the world—still were very much part of the world. They were joint partakers of the human experience. As such, the Hebrews shared many of the institutions, cultural practices, and practical everyday patterns of life and wisdom that were common to other ancient peoples. In sum, the Hebrews lived, moved about, and participated within the same East Mediterranean cultural continuum as their neighbors.

Several brief examples are useful to note. The Egyptians practiced circumcision before the Hebrews began to employ this rite. The wisdom literature of the Old Testament reveals some form of literary interdependence with the same genre of poetry in Egypt and Mesopotamia. The Canaanites offered animal sacrifices in the promised land even before God instituted this priestly ritual under Moses. The literary structure of the Mosaic Law Code—in particular, the book of Deuteronomy—reflects the direct influence of the suzerain treaty formulas of the Hittites, Israel's neighbor to the north. The Hebrews used a Phoenician architect, Huram (or Hiram) of Tyre, to design the Temple of Solomon (1 Kgs. 7:13). Canaanite linguistic material from Ugarit is vital to our understanding of many Psalms. In the New Testament, we observe that Paul shows familiarity with non-Jewish sources. In Athens he debates the Epicurean and Stoic philosophers, who appear to hear him gladly up to his discussion of the resurrection (Acts 17:16-33). In Titus 1:12, Paul cites Epimenides, a pagan Cretan poet. These examples are representative in showing that cross-cultural influence or borrowing was taking place on a number of different levels among several peoples of the ancient world. The Hebrews were part of this open environment of cultural sharing.

But in this matter of borrowing the Hebrews did differ from their neighbors in one significant area: the origin of their religion was rooted in divine revelation rather than pagan sources. Dependence upon or borrowing from another people did not necessarily mean agreement; the intention behind the borrowing or use of material from another people was crucial. There is a profound difference between the use of Aaron's golden calf—an idea borrowed from the Egyptians—and the use of certain names of the months on the Hebrews' calendar—an obvious borrowing from the Babylonians. Further-

---

18. G. A. F. Knight, *A Biblical Approach to the Doctrine of the Trinity,* Scottish Journal of Theology Occasional Papers, no. 1 (Edinburgh: Oliver & Boyd, 1953), p. 6. Cf. also Barr, *Semantics of Biblical Language,* pp. 8-20.

more, the Hebrews' borrowing was not a kind of acculturation or syncretism which derived from some fortuitous, indiscriminate cross-fertilization of ideas. Rather, when they did engage in cross-cultural interchange, the practices and concepts which they borrowed were characteristically cast in a different mold. This mold often resulted in the shattering of pagan myths, as in Psalm 68:4, where David declares that it is the God of Israel, not Baal (as in Canaanite mythology), "who rides on the clouds." Thus, the Hebrews placed all thought and every aspect of life, wherever derived, in and under the full theistic context of covenant responsibility—baptized, as it were, into Yahwistic faith. Perhaps, in a similar way, we may understand Paul's use of oral traditions and familiar rabbinic concepts from his day, along with the Hebrew Scriptures, which were baptized "unto Christ."[19]

In the preceding paragraphs we have sought to show that the world of the Bible embraced a variety of cultures and peoples. The Greek, Roman, Canaanite, Mesopotamian, and Egyptian cultural backgrounds are important in understanding certain aspects of the biblical text. By the findings of archeology we know that throughout hundreds of years of biblical history, Jews lived within or rubbed shoulders with many of these civilizations. Since the Bible—in a magnificent and yet mysterious way—is God's voice (divinely inspired) in human words (culturally conditioned language), it is absolutely essential to understand the various peoples and religions of the biblical world. Without entering the Mesopotamian world of the patriarchs, the Egyptian world of the Exodus, the Babylonian world of Daniel, and the Persian world of Esther—to name but a few—knowledge of the commonalities as well as the differences which the Hebrews experienced in relation to their neighbors, each so vital to the process of biblical interpretation, will be lost.

Nevertheless, we must still return to what we emphasized at the beginning of this section. For with all these ancient cultures affecting the history of God's chosen people, one should never forget that the writers of Scripture were Jews who did have "their own peculiar manner of thinking." Because they were an intimate part of the religious world of Israel they reflected, primarily and fundamentally, a Hebraic way of looking at life. Though their larger environment was often pagan, the Hebrews, as bearers of God's Torah to the world, stood in distinct contrast to their neighbors. As a community of faith, responsible to their Redeemer who had summoned them to a life of holiness set apart unto him, their lifestyle was expected to be different from the polytheistic culture around them. In style of dress, in eating habits, in manner of worship, and in ethical values

19. Cf. Davies, *Paul and Rabbinic Judaism,* p. 16.

the Hebrews were God's "treasured possession," a living "kingdom of priests" (Exod. 19:5-6).

Herein lies the uniqueness of the Israelite faith. Their understanding of God and his relation to their lives and to history as a whole gave meaning to sustain them amidst an often hostile environment. The significance of this fact has been accurately summed up in these words: "The Hebrews were located geographically in the ancient Middle East, and during most of their long history were under the sovereignty of powers greater than themselves. Yet, remarkably, they were the only one of those peoples to succeed in maintaining themselves through the centuries as a culture. It was primarily their unique religion which sustained them, making them capable of withstanding those forces of absorption and disintegration which would have removed them as a people from the stage of history."[20]

## The Olive Root and Branches

Thus far, we have emphasized this main point: the Bible reflects a view of reality which is essentially Hebraic. Indeed, for the earliest Church, to think "Christianly" was to think Hebraically. It should not be surprising that the understructure and matrix of much of the New Testament is Hebraic. After all, Jesus was a Jew, not a Christian of gentile origin. His teachings, like those of his followers, reflect a distinct ethnicity and culture. The evidence found in the New Testament is abundantly clear: as a mother gives birth to and nourishes a child, so Hebrew culture and language gave birth to and nourished Christianity.

In Romans 9–11, Paul discusses the present and future of Jew and Gentile in the plan of God. His stress on justification by faith rather than the works of the Law leads some scholars to argue that Paul sees the Jew and Torah permanently set aside. But the apostle himself says, "By no means!" (Rom. 11:1). As Krister Stendahl rightly points out, "Romans 9–11 is not an appendix to chapters 1–8, but the climax of the letter."[21]

In Romans 11, Paul warns those who have come to faith out of gentile backgrounds not to "boast" (v. 18) or become "arrogant" (v. 20). They are but wild olive branches grafted into the olive tree (Israel, v. 24), allowed by God's goodness to "share in the nourishing sap from the olive root" (v. 17). Here Paul points to a unity between Israel (the tree) and the

20. Eugene G. Bewkes, et al., *The Western Heritage of Faith and Reason*, ed. J. Calvin Keene (New York: Harper & Row, 1963), p. 4.
21. Krister Stendahl, *Paul Among Jews and Gentiles* (Philadelphia: Fortress Press, 1976), p. 85.

Gentiles (the ingrafted branches) by drawing upon a horticultural meta-phor familiar from the Old Testament. It is Hebraic through and through. Of Israel Jeremiah writes, "The LORD called you a thriving olive tree, with fruit beautiful in form" (Jer. 11:16). Also concerning Israel Hosea states, "His splendor will be like an olive tree" (Hos. 14:6). David refers to himself by saying, "I am like an olive tree flourishing in the house of God" (Ps. 52:8). Paul uses this symbol of the living and growing olive tree to show that the destinies of faithful Jews and Gentiles are inextri-cably bound together. Thus the Church, firmly planted in Hebraic soil, finds its true identity in connection with Israel. The Church is fed, sus-tained, and supported by this relationship.

It is important, at this point, that we explore more fully the back-ground and nature of this olive-tree imagery. It depicts beautifully how Jew and Gentile relate to each other. The olive tree was well-known in the Mediterranean world of New Testament times. The important place the olive has had in Rome's economy from Bible times until now is indicated by Italy's being the leading olive-growing country in the world today. Thus it should not seem strange that the apostle, when writing to the church at Rome, would use the figure of the olive tree. To those from the Occident (West), the olive tree, with its gnarled trunk and soft, gray-green leaves, does not appear to be an especially beautiful tree. But to those from the Orient (East), the olive tree has an artistic appearance that has been ad-mired for ages. So it is quite clear why Paul, a Jew with Roman citizen-ship (Acts 22:25), selected the olive tree to illustrate a central theological point. Many readers of his letter to the church at Rome were Roman Jews who knew the olive well from both Scripture and everyday life.

Today, however, most people living in North America or in certain parts of Western Europe are far less acquainted with this remarkable tree of Bible times. So it is important that we emphasize some of its features. Olive trees were famous for their longevity, outliving most other fruit trees. Today, one may visit the Garden of Gethsemane (*Gethsemane* means lit-erally "olive press") on the Mount of Olives and view a venerable grove of olive trees, many of which are hundreds of years old. Well did Moses describe Canaan as a "land with olive oil" (Deut. 8:8). The roots of the olive tree (cf. Rom. 11:18) are remarkably sturdy, thriving in the rocky soil and the hot, dry climate of the land. Very old olive trees often have tender young shoots which spring up around the roots. This sight doubtless prompted the psalmist to speak of children being "like olive shoots" around the table of the home (Ps. 128:3).

Further insight into Paul's theological metaphor may be gained by recognizing that olive trees were prized for their fruitfulness, which usually lasted for centuries. The rich fruit was either eaten or used for the making of olive oil. Olive oil was considered a major source of wealth as early as the time of Solomon (see 1 Kgs. 5:11; 2 Chr. 2:10), approximately one thousand years before the time of Paul. Olive oil was also used for cooking, for lamps, for ceremonial anointing, and for healing the sick. Olive wood was used for construction purposes, including part of the Solomonic Temple (1 Kgs. 6:23-33). Today, Bethlehem still attracts thousands of visitors each week to its olive-wood factories and stores.

## Grafted into Israel

Against the above background on the importance of the olive tree, we now return to Paul's figure of the olive root and branches. We shall focus on some of the significant details of Paul's teaching and their implications for us today. First, Paul depicts Gentiles as branches from a wild olive tree which have been grafted into a cultivated olive tree (Rom. 11:17, 24). Elsewhere Paul describes Gentiles as those who were "uncircumcised," "excluded from citizenship in Israel," "foreigners to the covenants of the promise," "without hope," and "far away" (see Eph. 2:11-13). This terminology could not be more vivid in expressing God's mercy to the Gentiles. They were pagan idol-worshipers (1 Cor. 12:2), those who, in and of themselves, had little to offer. In contrast, being a Jew had an advantage: "Jews were entrusted with the very words of God" (Rom. 3:2). So, the unusual type of ingrafting portrayed here—taking that which is wild by nature and joining it in intimate association with choice cultivated stock—underscores the point that what is worthless, with nothing of which to boast, suddenly receives value through its new connection. The marvel of God's grace to those outside redemptive history is here illustrated. The Gentiles, those who simply "stand by faith" (Rom. 11:20) with no claim to human merit or superiority, are now infused with full life and vigor through the Jewish people.

Second, one must accurately identify the root of the olive tree (Rom. 11:16-18). Some have argued that the root represents the Messiah or the messianic movement. But this view confuses the expression "root of Jesse" (Isa. 11:1; cf. also 53:2) or "Root of David" (Rev. 5:5) with "root of the olive tree."[22] The flow of the context supports the conclusion that the root

22. For an extensive discussion on the distinction of these terms see David Bivin, "The Identity of the Root of the Olive Tree in Romans 11" (unpublished manuscript; Jerusalem: Jerusalem School for the Study of the Synoptic Gospels, 1987). It should be noted that some of the Church Fathers and, more recently, Karl Barth interpreted the root

represents the patriarchs: Abraham, Isaac, and Jacob, the faithful fore-fathers of the Jews, the stalwart founders of that original people of God. It is they who possessed an enduring faith, never decayed or uprooted through the years of time. Through this faith-filled, deep-rooted, Jewish channel, God promised that salvation and blessing would some day come to the Gentiles (see Gen. 12:3). In Paul's day, that time had fully come. Gentiles were now grafted into Israel, that mysterious remnant which walked in loving obedience with the living God.

Third, one should note that the root brings support to the newly in-grafted branches (Rom. 11:18). The Greek term Paul uses here is *bastázō*, meaning "bear," "carry," "lift up," "support." Elsewhere in the New Testament it is used of a person who bears a burden (Matt. 20:12) and of a beast which supports a person (Rev. 17:7). In Luke 11:27, it refers to a womb which bears a child, suggesting the nuance of nourishment, life-support, or that upon which one is utterly dependent. Indeed, a study of various contexts in which *bastázō* occurs shows that this verb "implies the constant attitude of submission."[23] This nuance, then, suggests the proper attitude required of the gentile believer in regard to his place in the family of God. Firmly supported by the fatness of the olive root, Israel, Gentiles have no room for a spirit of arrogance, pride, or self-sufficiency (Rom. 11:20). They are dependent upon the Jews for their salvation and spiritual existence. Dan Johnson has effectively noted this relationship: "From Paul's time until the present, the church has tended to view its existence independently of Israel. . . . In Paul's view any church which exists independently of Israel ceases therein to be the church as a part of God's salvation plan and becomes simply another religious society."[24]

The olive branch has long symbolized peace (cf. Gen. 8:11). It is both ironic and tragic, however, that while the figure Paul uses in Romans 11 depicts the unity of two peoples, Jews and Gentiles, their relationship has proved historically to be the opposite. The Church never seriously heeded Paul's warning to stand in awe, to "be afraid" (Rom. 11:20). As we pointed out above, it was purely God's grace and mercy that brought the gentile world into this olive-tree connection with Israel, the faithful of God's ancient covenant people. Yet, as we will later see in more detail, as early as

---

as Christ (see Barth, *Church Dogmatics,* trans. Geoffrey W. Bromiley, et al. [Edinburgh: T. & T. Clark, 1957], 2/2:285-87).

23. F. Büchsel, *Theological Dictionary of the New Testament* (Grand Rapids: William B. Eerdmans Publishing Co., 1964), 1:596.

24. Dan G. Johnson, "The Structure and Meaning of Romans 11," *Catholic Biblical Quarterly* 46 (1984): 100.

the middle of the second century the Church had arrogated to itself the very position of the olive tree.[25] The story of this arrogant takeover, with the severing of Jewish roots and the long history of anti-Judaism to follow, will be discussed in chapters three through seven below.

Like the church at Rome, we who are from gentile stock must be ever reminded that neither does the "nourishing sap" (v. 17) of the olive tree find its source in us, nor do we support the root of that same tree. Rather, Paul says, the reverse is true. Israel is "the root that supports you" (v. 18). One may say that for a Gentile to have a right relation to God he must humbly accept and appreciate a Jewish Book, believe in a Jewish Lord, and be grafted into a Jewish people, thereby taking on their likeness through a commonly shared stock.

This initial chapter has sought to open up the larger context of Hebrew thought in the life of the Church. But before drawing it to a close, we are driven back to Paul's poignant metaphor of the root and branches. In particular, such graphic imagery ought to give every Christian reason to pause and respond to this challenging question posed by Abraham Heschel: "The vital issue for the Church is to decide whether to look for roots in Judaism and consider itself an extension of Judaism, or to look for roots in pagan Hellenism and consider itself as an antithesis to Judaism."[26] In brief, the central matter is our ability to come to grips with whether "we who once were not his people, and who have become his people only through his grace, can learn nothing from those who from of old have been his people."[27]

## UNDERSTANDING CHAPTER ONE

1. In the first verse of the New Testament (Matt. 1:1), what two Old Testament characters are linked to the Jewish genealogy of Jesus? Why do you think these names are placed first in Matthew's list of descendants?

2. From what biblical person does the word *Semite* derive?

3. Who was the first person in the Bible to be called a "Hebrew"?

4. Every Christian finds his spiritual origin in Abraham. How does Galatians 3:29 explain this kinship?

25. Peter Richardson, *Israel in the Apostolic Church* (Cambridge: Cambridge University Press, 1969), pp. 9-14.

26. Abraham J. Heschel, *The Insecurity of Freedom* (New York: Schocken Books, 1972), pp. 169-70.

27. William S. LaSor, "The Messiah: An Evangelical Christian View," in *Evangelicals and Jews in Conversation,* ed. Marc H. Tanenbaum, Marvin R. Wilson, and A. James Rudin (Grand Rapids: Baker Book House, 1978), p. 93.

5. Give a brief definition of Hellenism. Check some additional works in order to understand why Hellenism spread so rapidly throughout the Mediterranean world.

6. How does E. P. Sanders differ from W. D. Davies in his understanding of Paul's Christianity in relation to Judaism?

7. In what way has James Barr contributed to the "Athens versus Jerusalem" discussion? Discuss and evaluate his position.

8. One popular belief states that the roots of Paul's theology are primarily in pagan, non-Jewish religious thought. For those who argue for a non-Hebraic origin of Paul's religion, name three common sources from which Paul's theology is thought to derive.

9. In the New Testament, who describes himself as "a Hebrew of Hebrews . . . a Pharisee"?

10. Define "lingua franca." What was the lingua franca in New Testament times? How did this influence the Jewish community of the first century?

11. Discuss the observation of Heschel that "geographically and historically Jerusalem and Athens, the age of the prophets and the age of Pericles, are not too far removed from each other. Spiritually they are worlds apart."

12. What insight do texts such as Ephesians 3:6 and 1 Corinthians 10:1 give us as to how Gentiles within the early Church understood their history?

13. Give five or six examples of how the Bible reflects cross-cultural influence or borrowing between the Hebrew people and their neighbors.

14. How did cross-cultural borrowing by the Hebrews differ from the borrowing practiced by other ancient peoples? What implications does this subject carry for our understanding of biblical inspiration and authority?

15. How is it that when David proclaims that the God of Israel "rides on the clouds" (Ps. 68:4) he is in effect shattering a pagan myth?

16. Jesus was not a Christian. Agree or disagree with this statement. Discuss.

17. In the opinion of Krister Stendahl, what is the climax of Paul's letter to the Romans?

18. How do Jeremiah and Hosea shed light on Paul's use of the olive tree in the book of Romans?

19. Why was the olive tree a valuable commodity in Bible times?

20. According to Paul's metaphor in Romans 11, what do the wild olive branches represent?

21. From Paul's point of view, why is the "ingrafting" of Gentiles into the people of Israel an illustration of God's mercy and grace?

22. Briefly set forth two main interpretations for the root of the olive tree in Romans 11. Which view seems to be correct? Discuss.

23. From a study of the meaning of the verb *bastázō,* tell what the usage of this word in Romans 11:18 implies in regard to the relation of Gentiles to Jews.

24. Discuss the conclusion of Dan Johnson that "in Paul's view any church

*17*

which exists independently of Israel ceases therein to be the church as a part of God's salvation plan and becomes simply another religious society."

25. "For a Gentile to have a right relation to God he must humbly accept and appreciate a Jewish Book, believe in a Jewish Lord, and be grafted into a Jewish people, thereby taking on their likeness." Do you agree or disagree? Discuss.

26. Abraham Heschel says that the vital issue the Church must decide is where to look for its roots. He poses two options for today's Church. What are these options?

*Chapter Two*

# Gentiles, Jews, and Jewish Heritage

*You are no longer foreigners and aliens, but fellow citizens with
God's people and members of God's household*

Ephesians 2:19

In the previous chapter we emphasized one major theme: the roots of
Christianity run deep into the soil of Judaism. Gentile believers depend
upon or are supported by Israel, as illustrated through Paul's metaphor of
the olive tree. Connected to Israel as Abraham's spiritual seed, Christians
are debtors to Jews for their vast religious heritage. As child is bonded to
mother, Christianity could not exist without Judaism.[1] In the words of
W. D. Davies, "the very matrix of Christianity is Judaism: Christianity is
the very bone of Judaism."[2] Throughout this volume we will explore in
greater depth the biblical implications of this Christian-Jewish relationship. In this chapter we will specially focus on the problems of Judaizing,
Paul and the Law, and the place of the Jewish heritage in today's Church.

## A New Spiritual Family

Pope Pius XI once made the striking observation that "spiritually, we are
all Semites." For Christians who correctly understand the nature of their

1. See John Shelby Spong, "The Continuing Christian Need for Judaism," *Christian Century* (September 26, 1979): 918-22.
2. W. D. Davies, *The Gospel and the Land* (Berkeley: University of California Press,
1974), p. 382.

spiritual heritage and biblical roots, this statement is a truism. The purpose of studying the Bible is to acquire a biblical mentality, that is, "to become spiritual Semites in the midst of a generation which feels and even thinks outwith [sic] the biblical categories."[3] Indeed, the more biblical one becomes, the more Semitic one will be. It is impossible to be anti-Semitic or anti-Judaic and take the Bible seriously; otherwise one engages in a form of self-hatred. For the Christian, the Old and New Testaments are simply divisions of the same Book.

Though scholars are not agreed about the etymology of the name *Abraham,* the name seems to mean "father of many" or "father of multitudes." In the book of Genesis, God stresses the destiny associated with Abraham's name by stating, "I have made you a father of many nations. I will make you very fruitful; I will make nations of you, and kings will come from you" (Gen. 17:5-6). The Hebrew word here translated "nations" is *goyim,* which can also be translated "Gentiles." Here is an indication that God's covenant sphere would be enlarged, and that non-Jews would one day name Abraham as their father. Paul says that Abraham's spiritual family includes those who share the faith of Abraham, for "he is the father of all who believe" (Rom. 4:11).

Paul further stresses the importance of Abraham's faith: "Abraham believed God, and it was credited to him as righteousness" (Rom. 4:3). The thrust of Paul's argument is that there is no new way of joining God's family now that "time had fully come" (Gal. 4:4). Rather, people in the New Testament age must come into a right relationship with God the same way people did during the Old Testament age. Thus salvation, whether for Abraham or for the gentile community at Rome in Paul's day, was not by human attainment but by faith. Spiritually melded into Israel, the Church was built upon a Hebraic foundation of Jewish apostles and prophets, with a Jewish Lord as its chief cornerstone (see Eph. 2:20).

## Salvation by Grace or Works?

There is a common belief in today's Church that Judaism—whether in Paul's day or our own—teaches salvation by works of the Law, whereas Christianity is a religion of grace. Such an understanding of Judaism is in reality far more a caricature or misrepresentation than the truth. Indeed, as

---

3. Robert Martin-Achard, *An Approach to the Old Testament,* trans. J. C. G. Greig (Edinburgh: Oliver & Boyd, 1965), p. 79.

one Christian scholar explains, "to the extent that we propagate this view in our preaching and our teaching, we are guilty of bearing false witness."[4]

Paul emphasizes that the true sign of belonging to the seed of Abraham is not physical but spiritual (Rom. 2:28-29). It involves circumcision of the heart rather than earning one's way into his family through personal achievement. This teaching of Paul is nothing new, however; Moses and the prophets taught the same thing (Deut. 10:16; Jer. 4:4). Likewise, Paul says, "For it is by grace you have been saved, through faith —and this not from yourselves, it is the gift of God—not by works, so that no one can boast" (Eph. 2:8-9). Furthermore, "he saved us, not because of righteous things we had done, but because of his mercy" (Tit. 3:5). These emphases again were not strange to Paul's Jewish upbringing, for they are deeply imbedded in the Jewish Scriptures.

The common teaching of first-century Judaism—although one might not always get this impression by reading certain sections of Paul's letters —was that "election and ultimately salvation are considered to be by God's mercy rather than human achievement."[5] Pinchas Lapide, a Jewish scholar of New Testament studies, concurs: "The rabbinate has never considered the Torah as a way of salvation to God . . . [we Jews] regard salvation as God's exclusive prerogative, so we Jews are the advocates of 'pure grace.'" He concludes by stressing that all masters of the Talmud teach that salvation could be attained "only through God's gracious love."[6] Historically, it is true that Judaism has not placed the same emphasis upon faith that Christianity has. It is important for today's Christian community to understand, however, that Judaism does not teach that participation in the *olam ha-ba*, "the coming world," is achieved by works, but through the gratuitous mercy of God.

## A New Terminology

The New Testament uses a larger set of theological terms to describe the new relationship of Gentiles who have been "grafted into" Abraham's spiritual family.[7] Most Christians today tend to consider themselves "Gentiles."

---

4. Carl D. Evans, "The Church's False Witness Against Jews," *Christian Century* (May 5, 1982): 531.

5. E. P. Sanders, *Paul and Palestinian Judaism* (Philadelphia: Fortress Press, 1977), p. 422.

6. Pinchas Lapide and Peter Stuhlmacher, *Paul: Rabbi and Apostle*, trans. Lawrence W. Denef (Minneapolis: Augsburg Publishing House, 1984), pp. 37-39.

7. I am indebted to Robert Lindsey for his stimulating discussion of this theme: "Jewish-Christian Identity," *Hayahad Digest* 3/15 (Petach Tikvah, Israel, 1963): 1, 2, 7, 8.

Yet the Scriptures often make a sharp dichotomy or distinction between those of the faith of Israel and Gentiles. The *goyim,* "Gentiles," are variously described as those who sacrifice to demons (1 Cor. 10:19, 20), those who worship idols, and those of a pagan sexual ethic (Acts 15:23-29). But once Gentiles come to faith in the living God of Israel, they no longer stand on the side of those whose lives revolve around heathen, idolatrous practices. Proselyte baptism was a graphic reminder of this fact. The candidate, fully naked, immersed himself in the waters, symbolically cleansing himself from antecedent defilement. His past behind him, he emerged to take his stand with the people of Israel.

Now it is to be recognized that the New Testament often retains the historical or popular term *Gentile* for a non-Jew who has already come to believe the gospel message. But this common or popular method of reference may be due primarily to the writer's need to communicate effectively with an audience. Thus, the writer likely refrained from introducing—and making exclusive use of—a new (and potentially confusing) set of theological terms.

Whether of Jewish or pagan background, New Testament believers are related positively to the Old Testament community of faith. As emphasized above, they are the spiritual children of Abraham. Accordingly, when we let the New Testament speak for itself, we begin to hear a group of theological terms used for all Christians—non-Jewish and Jewish—which reflects this rich Hebraic connection. For example, Peter calls his readers—largely a non-Jewish audience—a "chosen people, a royal priesthood, a holy nation, a people belonging to God" (1 Pet. 2:9). They are even said to belong to the Diaspora (Greek *diasporá;* 1 Pet. 1:1). In addition, the terms *saints, disciples, heirs, fellow-partakers,* and members of the *ekklēsía* (those "called out," i.e., the Church) are found elsewhere. Finally, the term *believers* is very common in the New Testament (especially in Johannine literature), and today Christians in Israel frequently use the corresponding Hebrew term *ma'aminim* to designate their fellow believers.

## Gentile and Christian Are Not Synonymous

Great confusion exists in the Jewish community today over the word *Gentile.* It is commonly assumed that *Gentile* and *Christian* are equivalent terms. But in fact millions of Gentiles do not make any Christian profession. In today's Church, everyone understands what is meant by *gentile Christian.* This understanding derives in part from the unspoken assumption—created largely by historical factors—that the church is for Gentiles and the synagogue for Jews. From another point of view, however, the term *gentile*

*Christian* is misleading. It is tantamount to saying *pagan Christian.* When one becomes a Christian, one takes on a new identity, by no means a pagan identity. Even *non-Jew* or *non-Jewish* would seem to be a more appropriate title (at least from the above point of view) for a gentile believer. But this terminology also creates a disadvantage: it puts some distance—likely too much—from those whose origins one ought thankfully to embrace.

For obvious reasons, we have not eliminated the word *Gentiles,* in the sense of believers, from this book. The New Testament is not consistent here, and neither are we. Nevertheless, a serious effort to return to some of the more biblically rooted, theologically descriptive terms discussed above which were used by the early Church would be a significant step in making today's Church more aware of its Jewish roots.

## A Western World with an Eastern Book

Our Judeo-Christian heritage is both multifaceted and rich.[8] This fact is memorably encapsulated in the words of William Lecky: "Hebraic mortar cemented the foundations of American democracy."[9] It is unfortunate, however, that modern Christianity has too often laid claim to a vast heritage from the past about which it has remained largely ignorant.[10] In this

8. For a discussion of the origin of this term, see Luther H. Harshbarger and John A Mourant, *Judaism and Christianity: Perspectives and Traditions* (Boston: Allyn and Bacon, 1968), pp. 447-50. The authors point out that the expression "Judeo-Christian heritage" has come into popular usage only in the modern period and has gained wider currency in this century. Matthew Arnold was the first to popularize the idea that Hebraism and Hellenism were the two sources of Western culture. What modern scholarship has not sufficiently stressed, however, is that the "Christian" side of the term "Judeo-Christian heritage" represents primarily Hebraic and not Hellenistic roots.

9. Quoted in David de Sola Pool, *Why I Am a Jew* (Boston: Beacon Press, 1957), p. 185.

10. The question is often raised, "Can we rightly say there is a 'Judeo-Christian tradition'?" See Fred Berthold, et al., eds., *Basic Sources of the Judeo-Christian Tradition* (Englewood Cliffs: Prentice-Hall, 1962), p. 1. In *The Myth of the Judeo-Christian Tradition* (New York: Harper & Row, 1970), Arthur A. Cohen takes a dissenting position and argues that there is no Judeo-Christian tradition, but a tradition of "theological enmity" (pp. 189-223). While we must recognize decisive elements of difference between Judaism and Christianity, particularly in the theological realm, the use of the expression "Judeo-Christian heritage" is, in my opinion, acceptable to describe the elements mutually shared —especially in the broad areas of culture and religion—that have vitally affected the institutions and ideas of Western civilization. It should not seem strange that the Church claims a "Judeo-Christian heritage" in the light of the fact that the Church is, in a tangible sense, the outgrowth of Judaism. In New Testament thought, the history of the Church is an extension of Israel's history.

vein, Stuart Rosenberg poignantly reminds the Christian community that before one can be "fully Christian," one must also "know what it means to be a Jew." Furthermore, he points out that "the stronger a man's Christian faith, the more Jewish will he regard himself."[11]

It seems especially difficult for Christians living in the United States, Canada, and the British Isles to get inside the Hebrew mind. This difficulty results from most people in this area of the world having their roots in the West, whereas the homeland of the Hebrew people is the ancient Near East, a world strange to Westerners. It is understandable, therefore, why Westerners have usually been more exposed to, and influenced by, the philosophical culture of the ancient Greeks, especially Platonic thought. A colossal cultural curtain has separated the West from the East.

During the early Christian centuries, a Western worldview began to reshape many religious concepts and institutions of the Church which had originated in a thoroughly Hebrew culture. Episcopal Bishop John Spong has clearly stated the nature of this problem and the road to its solution: "The Bible is a Hebrew book, telling the story of the Hebrew people. Jesus was a Hebrew Lord. We, on the other hand, are Western people sharing a very diverse and sometimes controversial heritage that comes from many sources." He concludes incisively: "If the Bible is going to be understood in our day, we must develop 'Hebrew eyes' and 'Hebrew attitudes' toward life."[12] "Western eyes" must be replaced by "Eastern eyes" if modern Christians intend to read the Bible the way it was written. The Bible can make sense only when it is viewed and studied in the light of its own distinctive Near Eastern setting and cultural context. Such a challenge to today's Church has been issued nowhere more emphatically than in the words of the late Swiss Protestant theologian Karl Barth: "The Bible . . . is a Jewish book. It cannot be read and understood and expounded unless we are prepared to become Jews with the Jews."[13]

## The Problem of Judaizing

Some Christians protest when any call is made for non-Jewish believers to return to the Jewish roots of early Christianity, for such a return seems

11. Stuart E. Rosenberg, *The Christian Problem: A Jewish View* (New York: Hippocrene Books, 1986), pp. 222-23. Cf. also idem, *Judaism* (Glen Rock, NJ: Paulist Press, 1966), pp. 16-17.

12. John Shelby Spong, *This Hebrew Lord* (New York: Seabury Press, 1974), p. 31.

13. Karl Barth, *Church Dogmatics,* trans. Geoffrey W. Bromiley, et al. (Edinburgh: T. & T. Clark, 1956), 1/2:511.

like Judaizing, which Paul battled. In Bible times, Judaizers were gentile converts who followed the religious practices and customs of Judaism. Let us look at this allegation more closely and seek to sort out some of its implications.

## Diversity among Early Believers

Believers in the early Church had no one position on the precise relation of Jewish Law to gentile believers. Some early converts held to antinomianism (literally "against law"). But Paul, especially in the book of Romans, refutes the notion that once a person comes to a right standing with God by faith he no longer has an obligation to the Law but is free to live as he pleases. Other gentile converts held to the moral code of Judaism but were not bound to any ceremonial laws. These believers were most likely influenced by the Greek-speaking Hellenistic Jews from the Diaspora who were of a more liberal spirit and persuasion. A third, even stricter group, from the Jerusalem church, appears to have upheld the whole teaching of the Law except for circumcision. But the strictest group of gentile converts in the upholding of Jewish Law were the so-called Judaizers. Unquestionably influenced by the party of the Pharisees, these Gentiles submitted to the entire Law, including circumcision (cf. Acts 15:5). The Ebionites, a Jewish-Christian sect which flourished for several centuries after A.D. 70, are most likely a continuing reflection of the Judaizing movement. An ascetic group, committed to poverty as a life-style, the Ebionites upheld the whole Jewish Law but rejected Paul's letters on the grounds that he was an apostate from the Law.

## Not Bound but Free

Today, it is one thing for a non-Jew to be bound by *halakhah* (Jewish law) —to observe certain rituals, ceremonies, and customs. For example, one may feel compelled or obligated, as a necessary part of one's Christian experience, to observe Sabbath, dietary laws, or the practice of circumcision. But the early Church never imposed any of these Jewish ritual practices on non-Jews. Thus if a non-Jew does feel compelled to observe certain Jewish practices, that compulsion may be interpreted as Judaizing.

It is another thing, however, for one to be free as a Christian and not subject to bearing responsibility for the "yoke of the law" (cf. Gal. 5:1), yet to observe some Jewish practices. For example, when a non-Jew adopts moral and ethical values, social and spiritual ideals, and an overall orientation toward life and the world that is Hebraic, this is not Judaizing. Or a

non-Jew may choose voluntarily to conform to certain observances, celebrations, or customs which are both Jewish and rooted in Scripture. Such
practice is not necessarily Judaizing. Following a meaningful biblical custom is far different from being bound by a required practice.

To those in the modern Church concerned about the dangers of
Judaizing after nineteen hundred years of de-Judaizing, we would pose
these questions: Is it Judaizing to seek to reconstruct certain aspects of
the first-century Jewish context of the New Testament and early Church?
Is it Judaizing to investigate the life and teachings of Jesus through Jewish
eyes? Is it Judaizing to find personal fulfillment by adopting a perspective on God and one's neighbor that emerges from the teachings of the
Hebrew prophets? Is it Judaizing to resonate positively to a Jewish pattern of worship, music, and celebration of special events in life? Is it
Judaizing to find in modern Israel—within its people and the historic land
itself—that for which you deeply care, a veritable laboratory filled with
spiritual and historical meaning? To each of the above questions we would
answer an emphatic no!

## Judaizing in Bible Times

The Bible itself has little to say about Judaizing. The only Old Testament
reference to Judaizing is found in Esther 8:17. Here the Hebrew verb
*yahad,* "to become a Jew" or "to profess oneself to be a Jew," is used of
those Gentiles in Persia who adopted the Jewish way of life out of fear
for Esther's decree which permitted the Jews to avenge themselves on
their enemies (Esth. 8:13). The Septuagint (the ancient, authorized Greek
translation of the Hebrew Scriptures) uses *Ioudaízō,* "to Judaize," in this
passage, and adds that they became circumcised, which would normally
imply conversion. In this circumstance, however, they may only have pre-
tended to be Jews in order to save their own lives by identification with
the Jewish cause.

In the New Testament, the verb *Ioudaízō* (RSV "live like Jews"; NIV
"follow Jewish customs"), occurs only in Galatians 2:14. In this passage,
Paul relates how he opposed Peter at Antioch because Peter refused to eat
with the Gentiles in the church there. By practicing social separation, Peter
was in effect saying to these non-Jewish believers, "Unless you conform
to Jewish dietary laws and a Jewish life-style, we cannot maintain fellowship with you." By his withdrawal, Peter, a Jew, was compelling these Gentiles to Judaize—that is, to follow Jewish customs.

Jesus, however, had already instituted a change with regard to Old
Testament regulations on clean and unclean foods (Mark 7:1-23; cf.

Lev. 11 and Deut. 14). As "apostle to the Gentiles" (Rom. 11:13), Paul was against imposing a strict Jewish dietary code on non-Jews. Such a requirement might have implied that the belief of non-Jews was defective in comparison with that of Jewish believers, that something else (i.e., conformity to Jewish custom) had to be added to their commitment of faith (cf. Acts 15:1, 5). Thus Paul was opposed to Judaizing, for it had the potential of distorting salvation by grace alone and of being an argument for developing two separate assemblies—one for Jews and one for non-Jews.

Furthermore, in the coming of Jesus of Nazareth and through the new covenant set in motion by his death, the ritual and ceremonial aspects of Mosaic Law were no longer technically binding. Yet they could have been of spiritual value for the gentile believers. That is, although they were not mandatory for a right relationship with God, they could have helped the Gentiles to understand their faith properly. But again, it is important to stress that these laws were not prescriptive or obligatory. Rather, they were but shadows of the better things to come. Thus Christians were now free from the responsibility of Jewish ceremonial ordinances (Acts 15:10; Gal. 4:3; 5:1).

## Paul and the Law

Paul's understanding of the Law has remained a subject of much debate. In reading Paul, one may gain a feeling of personal struggle—even ambivalence—within the apostle concerning his relation to the Law. We shall therefore seek to put this issue in clearer perspective.

If one accepts the thesis that Paul "converted" from Judaism to Christianity, then Paul becomes one who stands primarily in opposition to the Law. As we have previously pointed out, however, Paul did not view Christianity as a religion distinct from Judaism. Rather, in W. D. Davies's words, Paul understood Christianity "as a form of his ancestral religion or as a further stage of its development, however 'new.'"[14] Paul's theology was not essentially new, for "he had integrated and reinterpreted (not ignored) the rich traditions—Old Testament, Apocalyptic, Pharisaic—of his people in the light of Christ."[15] In the same vein, Pinchas Lapide states forcefully: "Throughout his [Paul's] lifetime his people remained Israel. His Bible was the *Tanak*, his God was the God of his fathers, his Messiah was a Jew,

14. W. D. Davies, *Paul and Rabbinic Judaism,* 4th ed. (Philadelphia: Fortress Press, 1980), p. xxxvi.
15. Ibid.

and from Jews alone emerged his mother church. . . . Despite all of his Christocentricity, the Israelites remained his beloved brethren and blood relatives even after Easter."[16] About Paul's identity Lapide concludes that "he is neither an anti-Semite nor an anti-Judaist. He is not even an apostate, much less an antinomian—expressions that would have horrified him. In his own way he remained a believing Jew and missionary, but above all else he is a hero of the faith—not of the lukewarm rational *pistis* of the philosophers, but of the incandescent Hebraic *emuna*."[17]

Just as Jesus, "born under law" (Gal. 4:4), recognized its authority throughout his life (cf. Rom. 15:8), so Paul upheld the validity of the Law. In his terms, "Do we, then, nullify the law by this faith? Not at all! Rather, we uphold the law" (Rom. 3:31). Some eighty times Paul quotes from the Law to establish the authority of his arguments. He emphasizes that "the law is holy, and the commandment is holy, righteous and good" (7:12). He also says "I delight in God's law" (7:22). He recognizes the Law as "good" (1 Tim. 1:8) and "spiritual" (Rom. 7:14), and he builds his theology by drawing heavily on the Old Testament Decalogue (13:8-10).

Though Paul affirms the goodness of the Law in such passages, he seems overly negative about the Law elsewhere in the New Testament (e.g., 2 Cor. 3:6; Gal. 3:25; 5:1). But, as Walter Kaiser has astutely pointed out, "That is not where the problem ever existed, for Israel or the Church: the problem always was with people, not the law."[18] If Paul appears negative, therefore, it is usually in the context of those who tried to use conformity to the Law as a basis of self-righteousness. To Paul, Christ alone was God's gift of righteousness to the sinner. Compared to this gift, all else was considered worthless. In Paul's words, "Whatever was to my profit I now consider loss for the sake of Christ . . . not having a righteousness of my own that comes from the law, but that which is through faith in Christ" (Phil. 3:7, 9).

The Protestant tradition, especially Lutheranism, has tended to see the leitmotif for Paul's understanding of the gospel in the emphasis on justification by faith as opposed to the works of the Law. Though this theme is certainly important to Paul, we are in essential agreement with Davies, who finds the locus of Paul elsewhere, namely, in his "subordination of the Law to Christ as in Himself a New Torah—new not in the sense that He contravened the old but that He revealed its true character, or put

16. Pinchas Lapide and Peter Stuhlmacher, *Paul: Rabbi and Apostle*, p. 43.
17. Ibid., p. 54.
18. Walter C. Kaiser, Jr., "The Place of Law and Good Works in Evangelical Christianity," in *A Time to Speak: The Evangelical-Jewish Encounter*, ed. A. James Rudin and Marvin R. Wilson (Grand Rapids: William B. Eerdmans Publishing Co., 1987), p. 132.

it in a new light."[19] Christ was central to all of Paul's teaching, preaching, and living (Gal. 2:20-21; Phil. 1:21). For Paul, not simply the words of Jesus constituted the New Torah; rather, it was "the totality of his life, death, and resurrection, the Living Person, who constituted the New Torah."[20]

Did this mean that Paul threw out his Jewishness and became as those from the non-Jewish world who had become believers in Jesus of Nazareth? Not at all! Though Paul declared himself to be "free and belong to no man" (i.e., he was not bound by the standards of others, 1 Cor. 9:19), he was free to act "like a Jew," becoming "like one under the law" (9:20). That is, Paul felt at liberty to adhere to the regulations of the Mosaic Law in matters such as circumcision (Acts 16:3), the Nazirite vow (18:18), and purification ritual (21:20-26). Furthermore, toward the end of his third missionary journey, Paul, still faithful to Judaism, wanted to get to Jerusalem by Pentecost (20:16). Paul adhered personally to such Jewish practices as the above apparently to show the people that by becoming a Christian he had not forsaken the Law but remained a faithful Jew, firmly committed to his ancestral Scriptures and traditions.[21] Likewise, Paul seems to have no objection in his writings to Jewish Christians continuing to keep various ceremonies of the Law, since this was a way of demonstrating their solidarity with their kinsmen in the Jewish community at large.[22] It is likely that Paul allowed his Jewish hearers and the recipients of his letters to decide for themselves as to what he really thought about continuing the practice of circumcision and other basic Jewish customs.[23] In any case, Paul was not unconditionally bound, except to his Lord. For, like Moses, the prophets, and Jesus, right standing before God was not something mechanically achieved by human effort (Rom. 3:21, 28). Rather, it was walking with God by faith, in obedience and love.

## Jewish Heritage and Today's Church

In this chapter we have emphasized the importance of understanding the Bible through Hebrew eyes. "The writers are Hebrew, the culture is He-

19. Davies, *Paul and Rabbinic Judaism,* p. xxxiv.
20. Ibid., p. xxxiii.
21. James D. Smart, *Doorway to a New Age* (Philadelphia: Westminster Press, 1972), p. 122.
22. Kaiser, "The Place of Law and Good Works," p. 125.
23. Richard N. Longenecker, *Paul: Apostle of Liberty* (New York: Harper & Row, 1964), p. 223.

brew, the religion is Hebrew, the traditions are Hebrew, and the concepts are Hebrew."[24] If on this point we are essentially agreed, the next step is to define the sources and scope of this biblical heritage, and to think about the ongoing relevance of Judaism in the Church today. In what sense ought gentile believers to become "Jewish" in identity and life-style through being spiritually "grafted" into Israel? What can be done to begin to restore the loss of Jewish perspective in today's Church? These questions are not simple to answer. The grass roots of the Church—not to speak of the scholarly community—thinks little about these matters, and thus has reached no consensus of opinion. However complex some of these questions are, we hope that this book will provide some direction and shed specific light on these and other related issues. In this connection, we shall conclude this chapter by giving a brief, preliminary response to some of the above issues and a broad outline of the remainder of this volume.

First, those in the Christian community who may feel the olive tree died about two thousand years ago and thus the root has no life now left in it must read Romans 11 again. There Paul emphatically says that God has not rejected his people (v. 1). And though "some" (not all) of the branches of the olive tree have been broken off through unbelief (v. 17), "God is able to graft them in again" (v. 23). Israel, however, remains a "holy" people, for "the root is holy" (v. 16). Israel is yet "loved on account of the patriarchs" (v. 28), "for God's gifts and his call are irrevocable" (v. 29). The common belief today that Gentiles have replaced the Jewish tree, rather than being grafted into it, is a position of post-New Testament Christian triumphalism that finds no support in Romans 11.

In order to uncover the Jewish heritage of the Church one must be familiar with the main Jewish sources relating to the thought, language, and life of the early Christian community. It is generally accepted that the New Testament writings (twenty-seven documents produced from ca. A.D. 50 to 100) constitute the authoritative foundational bases of Christian thought. The most important single source for understanding the New Testament is the Jewish Scriptures, the Old Testament. The early Church appealed widely to both the Hebrew Bible and its Greek translation, the

---

24. David Bivin and Roy B. Blizzard, *Understanding the Difficult Words of Jesus* (Austin, TX: Center for Judaic-Christian Studies, 1984), p. 22. In relating the above perspective to a section from the Gospels, David Bivin, director of the Jerusalem School for the Study of the Synoptic Gospels (a group of Jewish and Christian scholars engaged in translating the Greek Gospels back into what the School believes was an original Hebrew life of Jesus), states: "When you read Jesus' Sermon on the Mount [in Hebrew], you feel you are right back there, hearing a rabbi speaking. Anything we can't translate back into Hebrew is suspect for us" (interview reported in "Who Was Jesus?" *Time Magazine* [August 15, 1988], p. 40).

Septuagint. Another valuable source is Jewish apocalyptic literature, produced between 200 B.C. and A.D. 100. Apocalyptic works such as 1 Enoch, Testaments of the Twelve Patriarchs, and Psalms of Solomon have an important bearing on the Jewish theological background to the New Testament. A third useful source for New Testament thought is the Dead Sea Scrolls. Documents such as the Manual of Discipline, The War of the Sons of Light Against the Sons of Darkness, and the Temple Scroll have particular relevance. A fourth group of writings is the Apocrypha. Works such as 1 and 2 Maccabees and Sirach (Ecclesiasticus) are valuable intertestamental sources that shed historical and religious light on the Judaism of New Testament times. A fifth source is the Targums, Aramaic paraphrases of books (or passages) of the Hebrew Bible, produced from about the third century B.C. to the third century A.D. (cf. Neh. 8:8). A sixth source is the works of Josephus, a first-century Jewish historian.

Rabbinic literature constitutes another major collection of Jewish sources useful to New Testament research. One may gain considerable insight into early Christian thought through a study of the Talmud, which comprises the Mishnah, or Oral Law, composed about A.D. 200, and the Gemara, a commentary on the Mishnah, compiled about A.D. 500. Much of the Talmud was likely circulated for several centuries by word of mouth before being formally reduced to writing; unfortunately, it is often difficult to ascertain the precise date of each rabbinic tradition. Other useful rabbinic writings are the *Midrashim* (singular *Midrash*), homiletical commentaries (e.g., parables, allegories, didactic stories, or other types of practical exposition) on the Hebrew Scriptures. These were passed on orally for generations and began to be written down in the second and third centuries A.D.

Unlike historic Christianity, modern Judaism does not embrace *one* authoritative source, but many; and all reach back to the Torah as the bedrock. Thus, other later Jewish sources which build on the Hebrew Bible and Talmud (e.g., the Codes, the Responsa, the commentaries of Rashi, and the works of Maimonides and other noted rabbis) are also of vital importance in reflecting how the essence of Judaism has been understood over the centuries. Consequently, in seeking to define Jewish heritage, Christians must recognize the great breadth and depth of the tradition and —perhaps most important of all—that it is a living tradition. In sum, therefore, we must emphasize with Davies that "the whole complex of Judaism is meant by 'the Jewish heritage.' That is, Judaism as well as the Old Testament constitutes the heritage of Christianity."[25]

It is important that we seek to clarify the term *Judaism* before going

25. Davies, *The Gospel and the Land,* p. 378.

further. Judaism may be defined as the religion and culture of the Jewish people. Jewish civilization includes historical, social, and political dimensions in addition to the religious. The word *Judaism* derives from the Greek *Ioudaismós*, a term first used in the intertestamental period by Greek-speaking Jews to distinguish their religion from Hellenism (see 2 Macc. 2:21; 8:1; 14:38). In the New Testament the word appears twice (Gal. 1:13-14) in reference to Paul's prior consuming devotion to Jewish faith and life.

Hebrew religion began to give rise to Judaism after the destruction of the Temple and the Exile of Judah in 586 B.C. The term *Jew,* in its biblical use, is almost exclusively postexilic. The Jewish religion of the biblical period evolved through such historical stages as the intertestamental, rabbinic, and medieval to the modern period of the nineteenth century with Orthodox, Conservative, and Reform Judaism.

Throughout its history, Jewish religion took on new teachings and practices. But the lengthy development of Judaism and its many changes make it incorrect to posit, as some have done, that Jewish history produced two separate religions: an Old Testament religion of Israel and the postexilic religion of Judaism. Despite the shifting phases of its history, the essence of the religious teaching of Judaism has remained remarkably constant, firmly rooted in the Hebrew Scriptures (Old Testament).[26]

How may we define more precisely the conceptual framework or makeup of this Jewish heritage under discussion in this section? In large measure, this is the subject of the present volume, an area we touched on briefly (from a slightly different angle) in the preface. For broad organizational purposes, however, we have chosen to view Judaism in the context of covenant. These opening chapters have introduced us to the concept of covenant through our study of Abraham, man of the covenant and spiritual father of both Jews and Christians. The next five chapters (Part II) will primarily take a diachronic approach, thereby emphasizing the history of how Church and Synagogue, each laying claim to covenant promises, have related to one another over the past nineteen hundred years.

Within the biblical concept of covenant, Judaism sees at least four pillars upon which it rests: God, Torah, the people of Israel, and the land of Israel, each one depending on and interacting with the others.[27] Using

---

26. For further discussion, see my "Judaism," in *Evangelical Dictionary of Theology,* ed. Walter A. Elwell (Baker Book House, 1984), pp. 588-90; also my "Branches of Judaism" and "The Influence of Judaism," in *Eerdmans' Handbook to the World's Religions,* ed. R. Pierce Beaver, et al. (Grand Rapids: William B. Eerdmans Publishing Co., 1982), pp. 292-95, 301-302.

27. Abraham J. Heschel, "The Nation and the Individual," *Conservative Judaism* 15 (Spring, 1961): 26.

this frame of reference we may now spell out the dimensions of Jewish heritage to be addressed in the pages which follow.

The revelation or teaching of the living God, who gave guidance and instruction for the benefit of his people, will be our main emphasis on Jewish heritage. (Since he revealed the truth of his Word primarily through Hebraic concepts, significant Hebrew terms will be emphasized throughout this work.) Many chapters will focus on the Jewish background and understanding of various institutions and theological or ethical themes vital to the Christian faith, including worship, prayer, meditation, the use of Scripture, the Lord's Supper, and the Church as community. We will study the nature of salvation, faith, and spirituality. We will also give attention to the Jewish concept of history, work as worship, and the importance of wisdom, knowledge, and learning. In addition, we will emphasize the importance of understanding the Jewishness of Jesus. Furthermore, the reader will find extensive teaching on marriage and the family, because these topics are so foundational to the Church's Jewish heritage and of contemporary relevance to most Christians.

The remaining two pillars of Judaism, the people of Israel and the land of Israel, remind us that "the promises are tied to earth, life, land."[28] Thus one chapter will deal with the Church's Jerusalem connection, showing the importance of the Holy Land, a very tangible dimension of Jewish heritage. The final chapter of this book will largely focus on the Jewish people. The contemporary Jewish community not only embodies for the Church a rich repository of Jewish thought, but also provides a major link and resource to aid in the search for, and recovery of, Jewish roots.

At the outset of this study, the question is surely to be asked whether this volume is a call to turn the clock back to the first century and restore the full Jewish roots of the early Church. Not at all! Such a wide-sweeping reform would not only be impractical but also impossible to perform. It would not even be advisable. Why? The Church has become so de-Judaized over the centuries—even before Paul's day the Hellenizing of Judaism had begun—and today is so much a product of our modern world and culture, that such a radical move would hardly take hold on any large scale. Certainly, few in the modern Church of the Western world would opt to remove stained-glass windows, organs, choir robes, Sunday school superintendents, and the mixing of sexes in worship on the grounds that these are non-scriptural (i.e., non-Jewish) intrusions into the structure and life of the

28. Seymour Siegel, "The Meaning of Israel in Jewish Thought," in *Evangelicals and Jews in Conversation,* ed. Marc H. Tanenbaum, Marvin R. Wilson, and A. James Rudin (Grand Rapids: Baker Book House, 1978), p. 105.

Church. Certain institutions and practices are followed, and with good reason, because they are matters of tradition, expediency, or practical accommodations to our present culture.

But, in full recognition of the above, our primary purpose is to point out certain areas where the Church has neglected its Jewish heritage to its own detriment. Also, we desire to help the Church to learn to think Hebraically. In addition, on the basis of Hebrew thought we intend to point to some new directions for the Church in the areas of worship and lifestyle. The final chapter below presents some concrete ideas to consider for those seeking renewal in this area. For if there is a biblical mind-set, and if that mind-set is fundamentally Hebraic, then what we can learn from a study of the Hebraic "root that supports us" ought to be far more important than a passing theological fad.

## UNDERSTANDING CHAPTER TWO

1. "It is impossible to be anti-Semitic or anti-Judaic and take the Bible seriously; otherwise one engages in a form of self-hatred." Do you agree with what is implied in this statement? Discuss.

2. What is the apparent meaning of Abraham's name? In the plan of God, how does this meaning relate not only to Jews but also Gentiles?

3. What Hebrew term is translated both "nations" and "Gentiles"? Discuss how this term has evolved today into a pejorative expression in the context of Christian-Jewish relations.

4. From Bible times to the present day, the mainstream teaching of Judaism —contrary to common misunderstanding—is that salvation is not ultimately based upon works of the Law or human achievement. Instead, what does Judaism teach in this regard?

5. The New Testament associates the term *Gentile* with at least three practices common in the pagan world but not sanctioned by Judaism. What are these "gentile" practices?

6. List some of the theological terms the New Testament uses for Gentiles who have become part of the Church. When viewed in their first-century setting, why were these terms often preferred for non-Jewish members of the Church?

7. In Israel today, who are known by the Hebrew term *ma'aminim*? What is the English translation of this word? From what New Testament book(s) is this Hebrew concept derived (cf. Greek *pisteúontes*)?

8. Are the words *Gentile* and *Christian* synonymous? Why or why not? What limitations does use of the term *gentile Christian* present?

9. In William Lecky's words, what "cemented the foundations of American democracy"?

10. In the words of Rabbi Stuart Rosenberg, before a person can be "fully Christian," what must he also know?

11. Karl Barth has stated that the Bible cannot be understood and expounded until Christians are prepared to become changed, as it were, into something different. What must they become?

12. Define the following: Judaizers, antinomians, Ebionites. Briefly describe the diversity of positions in the early Church in regard to the application of Jewish Law to gentile believers.

13. Is there a fine line for a non-Jew who chooses to observe certain Jewish practices out of his Christian liberty as opposed to being bound to these practices by those who are Judaizing? Discuss how one may know when he has crossed the line.

14. Discuss the different contexts for the one Old Testament passage (Esther) and the one New Testament passage (Galatians) that refer specifically to Judaizing.

15. Why was Paul opposed to Judaizing? What two likely reasons are presented in this chapter?

16. Give New Testament evidence that Paul upheld the validity and goodness of the Law.

17. Why does Paul seem overly negative about the Law in certain New Testament passages? Explain.

18. What New Testament evidence may be cited to show that Paul felt at liberty to adhere to the regulations of the Mosaic Law even after he became a believer in Jesus?

19. List at least six of the more important ancient Jewish sources for understanding the New Testament.

20. Define Targum, Mishnah, Gemara, Talmud, and Midrash with approximate dates for each compilation.

21. Discuss the meaning of the word *Judaism*. When was this term first used?

22. What is encompassed by the expression "the Jewish heritage"?

23. The biblical concept of covenant rests upon four foundational pillars, each depending on the other. Name these four intermingling dimensions of covenant.

*Part II*

# Church and Synagogue in the Light of History

## Chapter Three

# The Earliest Church and Judaism

*Do not leave Jerusalem, but wait for the gift my Father promised*

Acts 1:4

The context for our study of Judaic heritage and the Church was set in the opening two chapters. There we sought to show from the New Testament that Jew and Gentile are seen to be inextricably bound together in the plan of God. Gentiles who had come to faith within the early Church joined themselves to God's ancient people. They had to adjust to Israel, not the reverse.

By way of brief review, concerning Paul's teaching about the olive tree, Israel (Rom. 11), we observed that the root and branches of that tree are holy (v. 16). In the verses which follow (17-24), we established that the root of Israel is the patriarchs (Abraham and his immediate descendants). The branches represent individual Israelites who are nourished by the sap which flows upward to them from those roots.

Gentiles are depicted as not being by nature part of the cultivated olive tree, Israel. Rather, they are branches from a wild olive tree, who are grafted in among the others to share in the nourishing sap from the olive root (vv. 17, 24). As a new people of God, non-Jewish believers are now nourished by a rich heritage, with roots extending back to Abraham, father of the faithful. It must be emphasized that there is but one olive tree. It represents one people of God, Jew and non-Jew, fed by the same life-giving sap. A spirit of arrogance, triumphalism, or boasting is excluded. Gentiles —those who once served idols—do not support that ancient root, Israel, but Israel is the root that supports them (v. 18).

*39*

Little did Paul realize, however, that his words of warning to the non-Jewish world about boastfulness and superiority would go largely unheeded. As we will point out in the next few chapters, after Paul's time the Church would be virtually severed from its Jewish roots. How did an all-Jewish movement become detached from its original milieu, and then flourish as a new, separate faith community? In order to understand the appalling rootlessness of today's Church in regard to its Jewish origins, we must turn to the New Testament to see how the Church began. By tracing briefly the early history of the Church, we will be able to pinpoint some of the factors which contributed to this breaking off from the root.

## Jesus and His Followers

The life and teachings of Jesus reveal a deep commitment to the Jewish beliefs and practices of his day. He was born of Jewish parents (Matt. 1:16) and circumcised on the eighth day in accord with Jewish Law (Luke 2:21). As a boy he celebrated Passover (Luke 2:41-43), and as a youth he learned by interacting with various Jewish teachers, all of whom were amazed at his understanding (Luke 2:46-47). Frequenting the synagogue from Sabbath to Sabbath as was his custom at the start of his adult ministry (Luke 4:16), Jesus was exposed to a wide range of Jewish thought. To be sure, first-century Judaism was far from monolithic. Pharisees, Sadducees, Essenes, Zealots, and other sects dotted the religious landscape. It would appear, however, that the teachings of Jesus show closest affinity to that of the Pharisees. To a certain degree—but not exclusively—the rabbinic teachings of the Talmud reflect this Pharisaic teaching. It has been estimated that one can find parallels in rabbinic literature to perhaps as much as ninety percent of Jesus' teachings.[1] Though this estimate is doubtless excessive, current research on the Synoptic Gospels is revealing in increasing measure a profoundly Jewish setting for the words of Jesus.

Furthermore, Jesus' early followers were Jews. Less than three scant years after Jesus launched his public ministry, a nucleus among them would found the primitive Christian assembly. Jesus discipled his followers in the fashion of a typical first-century itinerant teacher of Judaism. Not in synagogue classrooms but on hillsides, in fields, and in remote locations this Galilean carpenter's son clustered many pupils about him.

---

1. The above figure by Herford is questionable. Nonetheless, one cannot dispute that a high percentage of material in the Gospel narratives may be paralleled in rabbinic literature. See R. Travers Herford, *Judaism in the New Testament Period* (London: Lindsey Press, 1928), p. 187.

Jesus was articulate, and he drew much of his rich teaching material from the Hebrew Scriptures and from rabbinic traditions familiar in his day. But he also taught directly, on his own authority, which sometimes resulted in the inability of his disciples to understand (Mark 4:10-13). Though the company was often wider than the Twelve (Luke 6:13; 10:1), Peter, James, and John, an inner circle of three, become most prominent in the Gospel narratives. But in addition to the common people Jesus discipled, some of his chief followers were Jewish leaders (John 12:42; 19:38-39). In sum, the ministry of Jesus was focused; in his words, he came to find the "lost sheep of Israel" (Matt. 15:24).

## Beginnings: A Jewish Church

A cursory look at the beginnings of Christianity reveals a Church that was made up exclusively of Jews. Indeed, the Church was viewed as a sect within Judaism, as the book of Acts makes clear in referring to early followers of Jesus as "the sect of the Nazarenes" (Acts 24:5).[2] They seemed to function easily within Judaism in that they were described as "enjoying the favor of all the people" (2:47).

The Church was born in Jerusalem, King David's royal abode. A city with a history of prophets, priests, and kings, Jerusalem, with its sanctuary, had been the focus of Jewish religious life for over a millennium. After Jesus departed into heaven, his followers remained continually at the Temple, praising God (Luke 24:53). Jesus had instructed them to stay in Jerusalem to await the coming of the Spirit (Acts 1:4-5). A group of about a hundred and twenty Jewish believers came together in an upper room for prayer (1:14-15). Among them were the Twelve from Galilee (1:11, 13).

---

2. The term *Nazarenes* is used only here in the New Testament for the followers of Jesus; elsewhere it is used of Jesus (e.g., Acts 2:22). F. F. Bruce states that the term is puzzling, but it would seem the New Testament writers understood the expression to mean "belonging to Nazareth." The Greek *Nazōraíoi* (Acts 24:5), "Nazarenes," was likely used as a designation for Jewish Christians from a very early date. It was apparently retained in Hebrew conversation (and later in Hebrew literature) by the term *Notzrim,* designating "Christians" (literally "Nazarenes") and *Notzri,* "Christian" (literally "Nazarene"). In the Talmud, Jesus and the Christians are called *Notzrim.* Furthermore, the Jews may have linked the word *Notzrim* with the "branch [Hebrew *notzer*] of violence" of Sir. 40:15, which has "no tender twig," a figure for "lasting prosperity." In a similar way, Christians associated *Notzrim* with the messianic Branch *(netzer)* found in Isa. 11:1 (probably the text upon which Matt. 2:23 is based). See F. F. Bruce, *The Book of the Acts,* New International Commentary on the New Testament, rev. ed. (Grand Rapids: William B. Eerdmans Publishing Co., 1988), pp. 63 n. 72, 440-41.

*41*

The Church had begun in embryonic form with the Twelve (cf. John 20:22). But in the miraculous coming of the Holy Spirit (Acts 2), it experienced a dramatic birth. Jews from Jerusalem and from regions near and far had assembled to celebrate *Shabuot.* This late spring festival occurred fifty days after Passover. Shabu'ot was the Jewish Feast of Weeks ("weeks" is the meaning of Hebrew *shabu'ot;* cf. Deut. 16:10), or Feast of Harvest (Exod. 23:16). After New Testament times, the Jewish community came to associate this holiday with the anniversary of the giving of the Law at Mount Sinai. This great revelation at Sinai occurred in the third month after the Israelites left Egypt (cf. Exod. 19:1). A special feature of Shabuot was the offering of two loaves of leavened, salted bread, baked from the freshly ripened grain (Lev. 23:16-21; Num. 28:26). Throughout Bible times Shabuot was a required pilgrim festival (Exod. 23:14-17). Annually, it brought thousands of Jews to dwell in Jerusalem at the time when the fields were ready for harvest (note the spring ingathering of barley in the book of Ruth). In Jesus' day, they came "from every nation under heaven" (Acts 2:5). Luke lists fifteen of these by name (Acts 2:9-11). In his first sermon, delivered on the day of Pentecost (Shabuot), Peter addressed his audience as "fellow Jews" (2:14) and "men of Israel" (2:22). And he quoted to them from Joel, their own Hebrew prophet (Acts 2:17-21).

In Peter's second sermon (Acts 3), he referred to "the God of Abraham, Isaac and Jacob, the God of our fathers" (v. 13). He also said to his Jewish hearers, "You are heirs of the prophets and of the covenant God made with your fathers" (v. 25). In a style reminiscent of the ancient Hebrew prophets (cf. Ezek. 18:30, 32), he called upon his Jerusalem audience to "repent" (Acts 3:19). This term has a rich background in biblical Judaism. In the Hebrew Bible, the verb often used to express "repent" is *shub,* which means "to turn around, return, renounce." It suggests a spiritual about-face. A person turns away from his sin and goes back to the living God of Israel. Maimonides (12th century), the greatest medieval Jewish philosopher-theologian, provides further insight into this key biblical concept. He explains that the Hebrew noun for repentance, *teshubah,* involves several specific steps. The first is confession or acknowledgment of guilt. The second is regret or expressing shame and sorrow over committing the wrong. The third step involves a strong resolution not to commit the sin again. The final step is reconciliation with God, whereby alienation has been overcome and fellowship restored.[3] Against this background, it is clear that Judaism has never understood conversion to

---

3. See S. Schechter, *Some Aspects of Rabbinic Theology* (London: Adam and Charles Black, 1909), p. 337.

mean the abandoning of one's ancestral people and ancestral Jewish faith. Rather, it was to become renewed and restored in God's forgiveness and love within that same community.

The activities and speeches of the apostles, as recorded in the book of Acts, give abundant evidence for the Jewishness of the earliest Church. The apostle Simon (his Greek name was Peter) prayed at the Temple in Jerusalem (3:1); made a defense before the Sanhedrin, the Jewish supreme court (4:5-12); and protested when asked to "kill and eat" nonkosher food (10:13-14). Furthermore, the Jewish apostles taught daily in the Jerusalem Temple (5:42), had contact with the high priest (7:1), and interacted with the teachers of Hebrew Law, such as Gamaliel (5:34). The apostle Paul (referred to by his Hebrew name, Saul, until Acts 13, the time of his first missionary venture into the gentile world) comments on his Jewish pedigree by stating, "I am a Jew, born in Tarsus of Cilicia, but brought up in this city [i.e., Jerusalem]. Under [literally 'at the feet of'; cf. Mishnah Abot 1:4] Gamaliel I was thoroughly trained in the law of our fathers and was just as zealous for God as any of you are today" (22:3). Paul also records that he was "circumcised on the eighth day, of the people of Israel, of the tribe of Benjamin, a Hebrew of Hebrews; in regard to the law, a Pharisee" (Phil. 3:5). Paul was also "a son of Pharisees [plural]" according to Acts 23:6. The plural here implies that even beyond his own immediate father his forebears were Pharisees. In addition, Paul spoke in Hebrew (Acts 21:40; Greek *Hebraíos*, which here could also mean the Aramaic vernacular), his own ethnic tongue.

At the time of Peter, James, John, and Paul, a major question confronted the primitive Church. The question was not whether Jews could belong to this new, Spirit-born community (cf. Joel 2:28-29); instead, the issue was whether Gentiles could, upon repentance of sin, belong to a totally Jewish community. The New Testament evidence is irrefutable about the beginnings of the Church: in its origin, Christianity was Jewish to the very core. The essentially non-Jewish character of today's Church is a matter of history, not a question of origins.

## The Hebraists and the Hellenists

Though the beginnings of the Jerusalem church were thoroughly Jewish, this community of earliest Christians was far from monolithic. In the first part of the book of Acts two diverse groups of Jewish Christians appear. One group was the Hebraists, or "Hebrews." These were Hebrew- and/or Aramaic-speaking Jews, most of whom were native to Palestine.

The Hebraists kept a firm commitment to their Jewish faith and ancestral customs. With a concerned eye focused upon those non-Jewish cultural influences around them, the Hebraists maintained close ties to the Jerusalem Temple.

The Hellenists were the other category of Jewish Christians. These "Grecian Jews" were—with varying degrees of strictness—Jewish in matters of faith, but adopted the Greek language and customs. Most of these Hellenistic Jews had roots in, or affinities with, the Greco-Roman world of the Diaspora. Generally they were more free-thinking and open to change than the Hebraists. In dress and thought, the Hellenists gave evidence of their daily contact with the gentile world about them. They had to balance traditional loyalty with new challenges from life in the Diaspora. But Jerusalem provided the Hellenists with a "venerable center . . . peculiarly their own."[4]

## Stephen and the Hellenists

Stephen was one of the leaders of the Hellenistic group in the Jerusalem church. He and six other Hellenists—all seven have Greek names—were chosen to oversee a problem which had arisen between the Hellenistic Jewish Christians and the Hebraists. Hellenistic Jews complained that their widows had been overlooked in the daily distribution of food (Acts 6:1). The problem was solved by the seven, and the whole church was pleased (6:3-5). This gracious and cooperative spirit shown by the Hebraists to the Hellenists was a vote cast in favor of maintaining a pluralistic unity within the Jerusalem church.

Tensions soon mounted, however, as Stephen engaged in an argument over the messiahship of Jesus in one of the synagogues of Jerusalem. Stephen was eventually brought before the Sanhedrin and charged with speaking against the Temple and Mosaic religion (Acts 6:12-13). The speech of Stephen to the Sanhedrin (Acts 7) is a moving example of a Jewish Christian delivering a Hellenistic apologetic against Jews who object to the gospel.[5] The thrust of the speech was threatening to the Jewish religious leadership, who venerated the Temple as the ultimate and final expression of true religion, for Stephen emphasized that God does not dwell in a structure (7:48; cf. Jer. 7:4). Furthermore, Stephen accused his

4. John J. Collins, *Between Athens and Jerusalem* (New York: Crossroad, 1983), p. 245.

5. See the discussion by F. F. Bruce, *The Defense of the Gospel*, rev. ed. (Grand Rapids: William B. Eerdmans Publishing Co., 1977), pp. 23-31.

Jewish brothers of rejecting the "Righteous One" (Jesus) whose coming the prophets had predicted (Acts 7:52). In sum, this provocative messenger announced that a new order had already arrived with the Messiah; he is more important than all ancestral religion.

Over this in-house Jewish disagreement, Stephen was seized and stoned to death. His martyrdom triggered a great persecution against the Jerusalem church. The apostles remained in Jerusalem, but the rest of the Jewish Christians were scattered throughout Judea and Samaria (8:1). The persecution and consequent dispersion was directed mainly toward the Hellenists of the Jerusalem church, the group within which Stephen had been prominent. From this point on—at least until the end of the Second Jewish Revolt in A.D. 135—the Jerusalem church appears to have been made up almost exclusively of Hebraists.[6]

## Outreach to Gentiles

In his providence, God used the stoning of Stephen to propel the early Christian witness beyond the confines of the mother congregation. Before his ascension, Jesus had instructed his disciples that they were to begin witnessing to him in Jerusalem, and then move to "all Judea and Samaria, and to the ends of the earth" (Acts 1:8). The book of Acts—particularly from chapter 8 onward—chronicles these events.

The first Jew to take the gospel outside Jerusalem was Philip. As one of the Hellenist leaders in the Jerusalem church (6:5), he was doubtless prepared to move with greater ease in broader cultural settings. His travels took him northward to Samaria, then to Gaza, and then along the coastal road to Azotus (Ashdod) and Caesarea. When the Jerusalem church learned how the Samaritans had accepted Philip's message, they sent Peter and John—two Hebraists—to minister there (8:12-14). This vanguard outreach by Philip paved the way so that Peter and John might be able to preach the gospel in many Samaritan villages (8:25). Thus the Jerusalem church was starting to confirm the ministry of the Hellenists. The Hebraists and Hellenists would still have to resolve other problems and tensions, but it was clear that God was sovereignly working through both groups to further effect his plan to "declare his glory among the nations" (Ps. 96:3). Yet, in the course of daily events each group was being true to its own vision.

6. F. F. Bruce, *The Book of the Acts,* p. 162.

## The Special Calling of Paul

The next recorded event in the outworking of God's purpose to reach the gentile world was the radical redirection of Saul (Paul) while on the road to Damascus (Acts 9). Though scholars typically describe this life-changing experience as a conversion, it would be more correctly labeled a "call." In this vein, Krister Stendahl has shrewdly observed: "Here is not that change of 'religion' that we commonly associate with the word *conversion*. Serving the one and the same God, Paul receives a new and special calling in God's service. God's Messiah asks him as a Jew to bring God's message to the Gentiles."[7] As we have emphasized, at no point in his life did Paul leave Judaism; rather, he understood his relationship to the Messiah as the full blooming of his Jewish faith.

A Diaspora Jew from Tarsus, Paul was uniquely equipped for this gentile mission. He was knowledgeable in the rich legacy of his people through his Pharisaic training under the famous Jewish teacher Gamaliel. But being a Roman citizen (Acts 22:25-29) from a Mediterranean seaport, he was also thoroughly acquainted with the prevailing customs of the Greco-Roman world. Furthermore, many of Paul's letters reveal an intimate knowledge of the Septuagint. This Greek translation of the Hebrew Scriptures, originating around 250 B.C. and written in the lingua franca of Paul's day, was an enormous asset in making Paul's message understandable throughout the non-Jewish world. Before his call, Paul sought to root out—even as far as Damascus—any believers he had driven out of the Jerusalem church (Acts 9:1-3). But his heavenly commission turned him into a fiery apostle to the Gentiles, the most influential single voice in the early Church.

## Further Success among the Gentiles

After Paul's call, Peter brought the gospel to Cornelius, a centurion in the Roman army who lived in the major port city of Caesarea. Through Peter's preaching and the action of the Holy Spirit, Cornelius came to faith (Acts 10:44-48). The text states that Cornelius was a "God-fearer" (10:2). A God-fearer was a Gentile who followed certain Jewish religious practices but stopped short of the circumcision required of all full proselytes. At this point in the early history of the Church, in a remarkable yet logical way, God set about to accomplish the furthering of His word in various cities

---

7. Krister Stendahl, *Paul Among Jews and Gentiles* (Philadelphia: Fortress Press, 1976), p. 7.

through these God-fearers, who carried with them an attraction and love for synagogue worship and the Jewish way of life. Because they were sensitive and open to Jewish teaching, God-fearers served as a natural bridge between Hebraic and Hellenistic cultures. Thus they became the foundational core for many of the churches Paul visited on his journeys (cf. Acts 13:16, 43; 16:14; 17:4, 17; 18:7). Indeed, this was "the Christian starting-point of the Gentile mission as compared to Jewish reserve with reference to god-fearers; . . . [In] the missionary practice of Paul [he] always preaches at synagogue worship and can thus address the 'god-fearers' better than the Jews themselves."[8] Thus, in the initial spread of Christianity from its Jewish womb in Jerusalem throughout the Mediterranean world, we see a Jewish orientation to worship and life already being practiced by this God-fearing nucleus of non-Jews. God-fearers are important for our present study, for they provide a further line of evidence that churches founded in major cities of the gentile world were not necessarily prone to de-Judaization from the very start.

When word reached the Jerusalem church that Cornelius had responded positively to the gospel, a controversy broke out about Peter (Acts 11:1-3). The Cornelius incident underscored some of the obstacles that the Jerusalem church had to face if Gentiles were to be brought into the Church. At the start, Peter was very reluctant to associate with a Gentile or visit one (10:28). Furthermore, the Jewish followers of Jesus at first did not know how to handle the fact (i.e., "they were astonished") that the Holy Spirit was poured out even on the Gentiles (10:45). In addition, certain of the Hebraists ("the circumcised") in the Jerusalem congregation—separatistic and overly zealous for the Law—objected that Peter would eat with "uncircumcised" men (11:3). But the early Church had no blueprint to follow to resolve such difficulties. For the time being, therefore, they were content to accept non-Jewish believers, primarily on experiential grounds—God had done it (11:17-18; cf. 15:8-12).

The Gentiles continued to accept the gospel, especially from the preaching of Paul and Barnabas. Syrian Antioch, located on the Orontes River several hundred miles north of Jerusalem, became one of the first thriving centers of Christian outreach (Acts 11:19-30). From Antioch, which had easy access to the Mediterranean coast, Paul and Barnabas set sail on a missionary tour. Traveling through Cyprus to Asia Minor (modern-day southern Turkey), they preached in Pisidian Antioch (13:13-52), in Iconium (14:1-7), in Lystra, and in Derbe (14:8-20). Then

---

8. H. Balz, *Theological Dictionary of the New Testament* (Grand Rapids: William B. Eerdmans Publishing Co., 1974), 9:213.

they returned to Syrian Antioch to report to the church which had sent them out (13:3; 14:27).

The gospel was now beginning to penetrate westward into the gentile world. Soon Paul would eye even Spain ambitiously (Rom. 15:24). For the immediate future, however, a crisis arose in the church at Antioch. It was an issue that Paul and the other apostles would have to face head-on: the place of Jewish Law in a church which had become increasingly populated by non-Jews.

## The Council of Jerusalem

The Council of Jerusalem in Acts 15 is the watershed for the entire book of Acts. The council was called because certain men had come from Judea to Antioch and insisted that circumcision and adherence to the Law of Moses were essential for salvation. Paul and Barnabas debated the issue with them. Then the Antioch assembly sent Paul and Barnabas as delegates to Jerusalem to discuss the issue with the apostles there. James, the brother of the Lord, enjoyed a position of leadership and respect in the Jerusalem church. He presided over the council, which convened about A.D. 49. Jews from the Pharisaic or circumcision party who believed in Jesus presented the issue for discussion. Their position—essentially that of the Judaizers discussed in chapter two above—required non-Jews to enter the Church in the same manner that gentile proselytes entered Judaism.

Peter addressed the council first. A number of years earlier he had witnessed Cornelius and his household receiving the Holy Spirit, followed by water baptism, much like the Jerusalem believers on Shabuot (Acts 2). Peter apparently had not insisted that circumcision be an essential element in the salvation of the Gentile Cornelius (the text is silent on this point). Accordingly, in the presence of the council, Peter argued that non-Jewish believers bear no heavy "yoke" of Jewish Law (see Acts 15:10).

The council handed down its decision: Non-Jews entering the Church should not have the Jewish rite of circumcision imposed on them. In its decision the council emphasized the principle of God's free grace in Christ. Gentiles were to know that to stand in the liberty of Christ meant no preconditions or potentially entangling qualifications. So stated, the council ruled out any "theological necessity of circumcision for righteousness."[9] Gentiles should be clear on this point: Salvation was

9. Richard N. Longenecker, *Paul: Apostle of Liberty* (New York: Harper & Row, 1964), p. 259.

a gift of God; one could not procure or obtain it by mere conformity to any ceremonial ritual.

While Gentiles were not subject to the ceremonial law, the council did request that they support Jewish-Gentile fellowship in the Church, that is, that they respect and honor the conscience of their Jewish brothers and sisters. Accordingly, the Jerusalem apostles specified four areas—most of which were associated with pagan or idolatrous practices—Gentiles should avoid: (1) food polluted by idols, (2) eating blood or meat from which the blood had not been drained in a kosher manner, (3) the meat of strangled animals (a guideline similar to the preceding), and (4) fornication—that is, pagan standards concerning sex (see Acts 15:20, 29). Furthermore, in this apostolic declaration it is probably correct to see "a version of the Noachian commandments possibly abbreviated or in the form current in the first century."[10] The rabbis defined the Noachian commandments as seven commandments binding on the descendants of Noah (Gentiles), that is, on all mankind.[11]

Richard Longenecker, a scholar of early Christianity, sums up the significance of the Jerusalem Council: "The decision reached by the council must be considered one of the boldest and magnanimous in the annals of church history." He concludes further, "While still attempting to minister exclusively to Jews themselves, Jewish Christians in Jerusalem refused to impede the progress of that other branch of the Christian mission whose every success inevitably meant only further difficulty and oppression for them."[12] We must emphasize, however, that the sins of triumphalism, arrogance, and pride manifest through a future gentilized church—not the decision of the Jerusalem Council—created Jewish oppression. The Church failed to "remember . . . the root [Israel]" (Rom. 11:18).[13]

The council communicated their decision by letter to the gentile

10. W. D. Davies, *Paul and Rabbinic Judaism,* 4th ed. (Philadelphia: Fortress Press, 1980), p. 118.

11. The seven Noachian laws deal with: (1) prohibition of the worship of other gods, (2) blaspheming the name of God, (3) cursing judges, (4) murder, (5) incest and adultery, (6) robbery, and (7) the prohibition of eating flesh with the blood of life in it (see Genesis Rabbah 16:6). Cf. George Foot Moore, *Judaism in the First Centuries of the Christian Era* (Cambridge: Harvard University Press, 1927), 1:274ff. The Talmud declares that under duress, to save his life, a Jew is permitted to violate any commandment of the law but idolatry, adultery, and murder (Sanhedrin 74a). The striking resemblance to both the Noachian laws and the areas proscribed by the Jerusalem Council is to be noted.

12. Richard N. Longenecker, *New Testament Social Ethics for Today* (Grand Rapids: William B. Eerdmans Publishing Co., 1984), p. 39.

13. See Terrance Callan, *Forgetting the Root: The Emergence of Christianity from Judaism* (New York: Paulist Press, 1986).

believers in Antioch, Syria, and Cilicia. It spoke clearly to the question provoked by those who were seeking to Judaize. Simply stated, that question was, Does a Gentile have to observe all the laws of the Jews in order to be a Christian? The council gave a definitive answer; it said no.

## UNDERSTANDING CHAPTER THREE

1. What evidence is there in the Gospels that Jesus had a Jewish upbringing?

2. Many Jewish religious sects existed at the time of Jesus. To which sect do the teachings of Jesus seem to show closest affinity?

3. Briefly describe the teaching ministry of Jesus in regard to (a) where and how he taught, (b) the content of his teaching, and (c) the various types of people he taught.

4. At first the Church was viewed as a sect within Judaism. What term does the book of Acts use for this sect? By consulting the appropriate footnote on this chapter, indicate (a) the possible derivation of the above term, and (b) what the Hebrew expressions *Notzrim* and *Notzri* mean.

5. One might argue that before the Church was born through the coming of the Holy Spirit (Acts 2), it had its start elsewhere in embryonic form. What occasion was this?

6. Be able to answer the following questions about Shabuot, the Jewish festival marking the birth of the Church: (a) What is the literal meaning of Shabuot? (b) Give two other names in biblical literature by which this holiday is called. (c) What special offering was made on Shabuot, and how did the substance offered relate to the agricultural season? (d) After the New Testament period when many Jews were living outside the land in nonagriculturally centered communities, how did the meaning of Shabuot change from its original agricultural significance?

7. What Hebrew prophet formed the basis of Peter's sermon on Shabuot (Acts 2)?

8. What concrete meaning stands behind the Hebrew verb *shub,* "repent"? According to Maimonides, repentance involves four specific steps. What are they?

9. Why is the word *conversion* an inaccurate or misleading English translation for the Hebrew term *teshubah,* "repentance"?

10. According to Acts 22:3, what Jewish sage trained the apostle Paul? With which Jewish sect did Paul claim identity (Phil. 3:5)? According to the Greek text of Acts 21:40, in what language did Paul address the crowd? What other possible meaning could be applied to this Greek word?

11. Carefully distinguish the Hellenists from the Hebraists in the Jerusalem church. To which group did Stephen belong?

12. Why did the speech of Stephen before the Sanhedrin prove threatening to the Jewish religious leadership? The consequent martyrdom of Stephen trig-

gered a great persecution. Against whom was it mainly directed? What impact did this persecution have upon the future makeup of the Jerusalem church?

13. Who was the first Jew to take the gospel outside Jerusalem? How was this person prepared to move with greater ease in the broader cultural settings of Samaria, Gaza, and Caesarea? Explain how the above events were a significant step toward greater unity between the two main groups within the Jerusalem fellowship.

14. Did Paul have a "conversion" on the road to Damascus? What term(s) is (are) preferable to use in describing this life-changing experience? Why? Did Paul have any contact with the Jerusalem church prior to his Damascus road experience? Explain.

15. Who were the "God-fearers" in New Testament times? Explain how the God-fearers served as a natural bridge to link both Hebraic and Hellenistic elements within the Church. What place did the God-fearers have in various churches visited by Paul?

16. Why did Peter have opposition from the Jerusalem church concerning his visit to the house of Cornelius? How was this controversy resolved—at least for the moment?

17. From what city did Paul and Barnabas set sail on the first major westward penetration of the Christian message into the gentile world? Locate this city on a map.

18. What issue provoked the calling of the apostolic council in Jerusalem? Who presided over the council? What year was it likely held?

19. Summarize the decision of the council. What four questionable areas or practices did the council specify that Gentiles should avoid? This list of prohibitions seems to be an early formulation of what is known today in Judaism as the seven Noachian (Noachide) commandments. What are these seven laws incumbent upon all non-Jews (see footnotes)?

20. This watershed decision of the council has been described by one scholar as "one of the boldest and magnanimous in the annals of church history." Explore the implications of this statement in the light of both ancient and modern history.

# Chapter Four

# Theological Conflict and Persecution

*They called the apostles in and had them flogged. Then they ordered them not to speak in the name of Jesus, and let them go*

Acts 5:40

The Jerusalem Council (Acts 15), discussed in the previous chapter, was an alpine event. Its decision would have profound implications for both Church and Synagogue in the years to come. By calling this council, the Church took a clear stand on the issue of gentile circumcision (Acts 15:5, 28-29). This most ancient of all covenant rites would not be a prerequisite to join the still fledgling messianic community which had rapidly expanded into the gentile world.

The picture of the Church which we are able to draw at this mid-century juncture is composite. It comprised essentially three main groups. One segment was made up of traditionalists from the circumcision party. They were conservative Jewish believers, most likely from the sect of the Pharisees, and were closely tied to Temple worship and Jewish Law. As previously indicated, the Ebionite sect probably represented the remnants of this movement, a group which did not die out until the fourth century. A second distinguishable group was the free-thinking Hellenistic party. The Hellenists had one foot planted in the turf of Judaism. But the other, more firmly set in Greek soil, caused this group to lean to the West. A third segment held to a middle or mainstream position. It reflected the thinking of the council and presumably also the majority of the Jerusalem church (see Acts 15:22). Some of its leading voices were James, Peter ("an apostle to the Jews"), and Paul ("an apostle to the Gentiles"; cf. Gal. 2:8). Through the guidance of the Holy Spirit (Acts 15:28), this influential group sought to be open to Gentiles and yet sensitive to Jews.

The above sketch reminds us that the Church at this stage was still part of the Jewish community, although its growth was more and more pluralistic due to the large gentile influx and the need for Jewish Christians to accommodate themselves to the new work God was performing in their midst. Nevertheless, several factors contributed to the unity of the Body despite its growing diversity. Both Jew and Gentile in the Church had in common Israel's sacred writings, the Old Testament Scriptures—whether in Hebrew or Greek. In addition, all in the Church believed in the messiahship of Jesus, held central his teachings, and proclaimed the same *kerygma* (proclamation or message) regarding his death and resurrection (1 Cor. 15:3-4). Furthermore, those in the Church had a common experience and life in the Holy Spirit (i.e., "It seemed good to the Holy Spirit and to us"—Acts 15:28). But the Church would not permanently remain within its Jewish cradle.

Before we begin to explore the various factors which brought the Church and Synagogue to the parting of the way, we must make several introductory observations. First, and perhaps most crucial, we are dealing with a process which took place over at least a century. Although our discussion in the next few chapters will highlight certain events and conditions which directly contributed to the split, the gradual nature of this separation —rather than a precise moment of cleavage—will be crucial to its understanding. Second, we are faced with a rather complex issue which shuns oversimplification.[1] Each question has a Jewish side and a Christian side. Third, we must recognize that our sources are sketchy for certain aspects of this problem. No transcript has survived giving abundant details; thus we are dependent on compiling a mosaic from a variety of ancient sources. Finally, it must not be forgotten that authors, whether ancient or modern, have a particular point of view. Presuppositions and personal loyalties do sometimes enter into the weighing of an argument or source. Particularly in the always volatile area of the history of Christian-Jewish relations, both perspectives must be considered whenever possible. In this chapter we shall discuss two of the major factors in the separation of Church and Synagogue: theological differences and the issue of persecution.

1. Douglas R. A. Hare expresses the following noteworthy caution: "In studying the early conflict between Jews and Christians one must constantly guard against a tendency to over-simplify the issues in dispute and the causes of hostility. The conflict was as many-sided as the two opposing groups" (*The Theme of Jewish Persecution of Christians in the Gospel According to St. Matthew* [Cambridge: Cambridge University Press, 1967], p. 1).

## Theological Differences

The key theological issue which has divided Christians and Jews for nearly two millennia is Jesus. How is this Galilean carpenter's son to be perceived? Do we understand him as Messiah and God in accord with the witness of New Testament writers, or as one who had messianic aspirations but who, as a mere mortal, failed in his cause? Was he a son of God—like all human beings—or was he the unique Son of God that the Fourth Gospel declares him to be? Was he the apocalyptic son of man, the suffering servant, and the righteous king spoken of by the prophets? Or did the early Church merely attribute such titles to him after his death?

## *Jesus: Man or God?*

As far as the Gospel record is concerned, Jesus spoke from within Judaism; he never abandoned his ancestral faith.[2] Much of his activity was spent around the Temple and synagogue. As previously noted, his teaching reflected at most points a close relation to the Judaism of his own day. In the words of Joachim Jeremias, Jesus was "a prophet who completely remained within the limits of Judaism."[3]

But for most Jewish interpreters of Jesus the issue is deeper and far more complex than this brief description indicates. One crucial point is Jesus' failure to recognize other teaching authorities; even more crucial is his claim to the right of giving his own authoritative interpretation as to what God wants. Furthermore, Jesus claimed divine sonship (John 10:30, 36, 38) and announced his return accompanied by angels at the end of the age (Matt. 24:27-31). The Jesus of history, it is therefore argued, must be kept distinct from the Christ of faith.[4]

The early Jewish followers of Jesus, however, saw him as both God and man. The eyewitnesses of Jesus saw his miracles—which even his op-

---

2. Peter Richardson points out rightly that "Jesus works almost entirely with Israel —its institutions and peoples. His synagogue ministry seems to have been extensive" (*Israel in the Apostolic Church* [Cambridge: Cambridge University Press, 1969], p. 53).

3. Joachim Jeremias, *The Central Message of the New Testament* (Philadelphia: Fortress Press, 1965), p. 30.

4. According to Geza Vermes, "His [Jesus'] adherents transformed this lover and worshipper of his Father in heaven into an object of worship himself, a god; and his own people, under the pressures of persecution at the hands of those adherents, mistakenly attributed to Jesus Christian beliefs and dogmas, many of which—I feel quite sure—would have filled this Galilean Hasid with stupefaction, anger and deepest grief" (*Jesus and the World of Judaism* [Philadelphia: Fortress Press, 1984], p. 13). Cf. also James Parkes, *The Conflict of the Church and the Synagogue* (New York: Hermon Press, 1974), pp. 34-42.

ponents conceded he performed—as attesting to his deity. From the perspective of the New Testament, Jesus is presented as the "one who was to come" (Luke 7:19-20), the one of whom the prophets wrote. Accordingly, Longenecker has observed: "The primary tension of Judaism, which dominates all Old Testament and Jewish thought, is that of promise and fulfillment. And this was what the earliest Christians found resolved in Christ."[5] In short, Jesus himself becomes a new and living Torah, the very center of the thought and life of the early Church.

## A Radical Reinterpretation of Jewish Symbols

The two Testaments exhibit a strong continuity, but also a discontinuity. Many Old Testament institutions and themes are radically reinterpreted in the New Testament, often in ways—despite their foreshadowing—that the majority in New Testament times was unable to discern.[6] In addition, the embodiment of the Torah in Jesus created a major tension. Jesus subordinated many of the central symbols of Judaism to himself,[7] and the New Testament writers continued that subordination. Thus, Jesus became the Temple (John 2:19-21) and the atoning sacrifice ("the Lamb of God, who takes away the sin of the world"—John 1:29). At Passover the *matzah*, "unleavened bread," represented his body (Mark 14:22); likewise, the lamb sacrificed at Passover symbolized Jesus' sacrificial death (1 Cor. 5:7). In addition, Jesus declared himself Lord of the Sabbath (Mark 2:27-28). He also distinguished the ritually clean from unclean (Mark 7:1-23). In sum, in early Jewish Christianity the "Sabbath, Temple, Law, sacrifices are christologically reinterpreted by the One who is greater than them all."[8] The overall effect was that the first-century Jewish community largely considered these teachings strange and antiritualistic, a threat to the established religious beliefs of the day.

## The Unusual Mission of Jesus

The association of Jesus with questionable segments of society also brought serious conflict. The attention he gave to women was unusual considering their comparatively low position during his time. In addition, he

5. Richard N. Longenecker, *Paul: Apostle of Liberty* (New York: Harper & Row, 1964), p. 84.
6. John Bright, *The Authority of the Old Testament* (Nashville: Abingdon Press, 1967; repr. Grand Rapids: Baker Book House, 1975), p. 201.
7. See Hare, *Theme of Jewish Persecution*, pp. 3-7.
8. Richardson, *Israel in the Apostolic Church*, pp. 52, 53.

interacted with tax collectors, one of the most hated classes of people. He also dealt with lepers, who were shunned by all. Jesus was criticized for being a "glutton and a drunkard, a friend of tax collectors and 'sinners'" (Matt. 11:19). Furthermore, he had contact with the scorned, mixed race of the Samaritans (John 4:4-5). And he broke through the traditional thinking of his day by reaching out to the Gentiles (Mark 7:24-30), thus paving the way for the later Jewish Christian mission to the non-Jewish world.[9]

In that the love and compassion of Jesus knew no bounds, his actions often proved radical or scandalous to the religious community of his day. Accordingly, we must emphasize that Jesus had different plans; he did not come merely to maintain and reinforce the religious traditions which he inherited. Rather, his mission was to rework those traditions. John Riches has effectively summed up Jesus' transformation of Judaism: "he [Jesus] sought a renewal of the tradition by giving it a new direction: cutting away attempts to multiply the detailed prescriptions of the Law and directing them instead to personal standards as a means of regulating conduct; rejecting the belief in God's punitive justice and emphasizing instead God's mercy, his will to heal, to forgive, to overcome enmity with love . . . and calling them [others] to follow him in his ministry of love to the lost, the poor and the enemy."[10]

## Abba and the Uniqueness of Jesus

Jesus' claim to a unique relationship with the Father is nowhere stated in clearer terms than in his own use of *Abba*. Joachim Jeremias's groundbreaking historical study has shed much light on this oft-disputed claim.[11] He has pointed out that in a relatively small number of references in the Old Testament God is spoken of as Father, especially in the sense of Creator and source of mercy to his children Israel. No one, however, addressed God as "my Father." In Palestinian Judaism's liturgical prayers God was addressed as *abinu*, "our Father." But when Jesus prayed in the presence of his disciples he would often use "my Father." What is more, he also used the Aramaic term *Abba* (Mark 14:36). In first-century Jewish society a little

---

9. For a discussion of the above see Helmut Merkel, "The Opposition Between Jesus and Judaism," in *Jesus and the Politics of His Day,* ed. Ernst Bammel and C. F. D. Moule (Cambridge: Cambridge University Press, 1984), pp. 134-38.

10. John Riches, *Jesus and the Transformation of Judaism* (San Francisco: Harper & Row, 1982), p. 185.

11. See Joachim Jeremias, *Abba,* Studien zur neutestamentlichen Theologie und Zeitgeschichte (Göttingen: Vandenhoeck & Ruprecht, 1966); idem, *Central Message of the New Testament,* pp. 9-30; idem, *New Testament Theology* (New York: Scribner's, 1971), pp. 61-68.

child would call his father *abba,* or "Daddy"; but the term was so intimate and familiar that a Jew would be considered irreverent if he used it of God. The fatherhood of God was not a commonplace on the lips of Jesus, but something personal. To call God *Abba* was a revelation God granted to him; it is thus important to understand his consciousness of divine Sonship.

The same childlike closeness is central to the sonship that is at the heart of the Christian gospel; for those who, by faith, have been adopted into the Father's family as children may also address him as *Abba* (Rom. 8:15; Gal. 4:6). Jeremias sums up the striking significance of this theologically pregnant term used by Jesus: "with Abba we are behind the Kerygma. We are confronted with something new and unheard of which breaks through the limits of Judaism. Here we see who the historical Jesus was: the man who had the power to address God as *Abba* and who included the sinners and the publicans in the kingdom by authorizing them to repeat this one word, '*Abba,* dear Father.'"[12]

## Messianic Expectations and Jesus

Opposition to Christianity first arose not against Jesus' followers, but against Jesus himself.[13] From various quarters Jesus experienced theological conflict over his claims and teachings. Especially the scribes and Pharisees entered into intense discussion with him on more than one occasion. Jesus was a controversialist: he condemned various groups of Jewish religious leaders and faulted these same people for keeping others from entering the kingdom (Matt. 23:13).

In first-century Jewish thought messianic expectation was mainly focused on a Davidic Redeemer endowed with the qualities of soldierly prowess (a warrior-king), righteousness, and holiness; but there was also speculation of a priestly and prophetic Messiah, and other views as well.[14] With this variety of messianic expectations among both his followers and his opponents, Jesus likely opted to keep his messiahship secret (most scholars agree that Jesus never directly asserted it) in order to avoid a revolution or other crisis that could hinder him from completing his ultimate mission. On several occasions, after performing a miracle, Jesus instructed

12. Jeremias, *Central Message of the New Testament,* p. 30.

13. Jacob Jocz, *The Jewish People and Jesus Christ* (repr. Grand Rapids: Baker Book House, 1979), pp. 34-43.

14. Geza Vermes, *Jesus the Jew* (Philadelphia: Fortress Press, 1981), pp. 130-40. See also David Flusser, *Jesus* (New York: Herder and Herder, 1969), pp. 14ff.; Hans-Joachim Schoeps, *The Jewish-Christian Argument,* trans. David E. Green (New York: Holt, Rinehart and Winston, 1963), pp. 20ff.

his audience not to tell anyone about it (see Matt. 8:4; Mark 5:43). Likewise, after Peter's confession, Jesus "warned his disciples not to tell anyone that he was the Christ" (Matt. 16:20; cf. Mark 8:30; Luke 9:21). Jesus had a unique ministry to perform and his own time frame for accomplishing it.

Jesus' call was one of commitment, radical obedience, and a new way of life; his was not a call to join the Zealot underground in order to overthrow Roman rule. His kingdom was not of this world. His road was not paved with glory, like that of a conquering king; rather, as suffering servant, his road was one of humility and meekness that led to a cross. For some, he represented dashed expectations; for others, a curious tragedy of history. For yet others, he represented a threat to the establishment, whether religious or political.

However, a small committed band of Jewish men and women—most were unknown or relatively obscure—believed Jesus' teachings and miracles in Galilee. They later followed him to his crucifixion and burial in Jerusalem and were convinced that his tomb was empty because he appeared to them before he ascended. These were the ones prepared to die, if need be, to bear witness to the reality of the things they had seen with their own eyes.

## Belief in the Resurrection of Jesus

The belief in Jesus' messiahship was deeply grounded in faith in his resurrection from the dead (Rom. 1:4). Some sneered at this notion (Acts 17:32), but it is undeniable that the early Church's belief in this singular teaching turned what appeared to be a temporary, ill-fated, sectarian movement into a not-to-be-extinguished flame of hope.

The messianic role of Jesus as Redeemer had left the general populace with mixed responses: confusion, bewilderment, agitation, or unfulfilled expectations ("but we had hoped that he was the one who was going to redeem Israel"—Luke 24:21). Jesus did not fulfill nationalistic hopes, apocalyptic dreams, or holy-commonwealth aspirations. But faith in his resurrection changed an about-to-be-disbanded, crestfallen group of followers into decisive heralds of the kerygma. And the heart of that message became: "if you confess with your mouth, 'Jesus is Lord,' and believe in your heart God raised him from the dead, you will be saved" (Rom. 10:9).

## Persecutions

Between the death of Jesus (ca. A.D. 30) and the outbreak of the First Jewish Revolt (A.D. 66), the Jewish authorities or the mob repeatedly persecuted believers in Jesus. The high priest had accused Jesus of being a political troublemaker by not rendering taxes to Caesar and by claiming to be King of the Jews (Luke 23:2; cf. Matt. 27:37). Jesus warned his followers that they too would be persecuted through arrest and be flogged in synagogues (Matt. 10:17-25).[15]

## Jews Persecuting Jews

Jewish persecution of Christians was originally viewed as a controversy between Jewish sects. Only later, when the Church had become separate from the Synagogue, did Roman opposition to Christianity play a major role.[16] Prior to the fall of Jerusalem (A.D. 70), the messianic movement was viewed as another type of Jewish heresy. After Rome had crushed the Jewish nation, however, the Jewish establishment was more threatened by Jewish Christianity, which had no strong interest in national politics and did not support the Zealot cause. Thus its existence constituted a menace. As the Jewish national position worsened, opposition to Jewish Christianity tended to grow proportionately more violent. The issue of the messiahship of Jesus created two diametrically opposed groups within Judaism, and the process of separation began immediately after the death of Jesus.[17] The Jewish community apparently tied the death of Jesus to the charge of blasphemy (John 10:36); hence persecution was inevitable for his followers, who vocalized the same beliefs as their Master.

## Acts of Mob Violence

It is evident from the book of Acts that Jews persecuted Christians prior to the First Jewish Revolt. But these incidents seem more often to have been acts of mob violence rather than official persecutions. Christian sources external to the New Testament show that from the time of Jesus' death until the First Jewish Revolt there is not one clear case of the Jewish religious leadership having a judicial execution of a Christian solely for religious purposes.[18] Though the book of Acts does record two martyrdoms, these appear to be relatively rare incidents during the tumultuous first few decades of the Church's growth. The first martyr was

15. See Bo Reicke, "Judaeo-Christianity and the Jewish Establishment, A.D. 33-66," in *Jesus and the Politics of His Day,* ed. Ernst Bammel and C. F. D. Moule (Cambridge: Cambridge University Press, 1984), pp. 145ff.

16. Richardson, *Israel in the Apostolic Church,* p. 47.

17. Jocz, *Jewish People and Jesus Christ,* pp. 44-45, 162-63.

18. Hare, *Theme of Jewish Persecution,* pp. 20, 35.

Stephen (Acts 6:9–8:2). His death was probably the result of an angry mob's violence rather than a formal decree of the Sanhedrin, for which evidence is lacking. The second martyr, James the son of Zebedee (12:2), was apparently put to death by Herod Agrippa for political rather than religious reasons.

Several other examples of opposition at the hands of Jewish authorities may also be cited from Acts. The Sadducees had the apostles arrested and put in jail for preaching the resurrection of Jesus (Acts 4:2-3; 5:17-18). The Sanhedrin warned Peter and John not to teach any longer in the name of Jesus (4:17-18). Though the Sanhedrin ordered the apostles flogged for their teaching (5:40), they refused to stop "proclaiming the good news that Jesus is the Christ" (5:42). Again Peter was seized and placed in prison (12:1ff.). This action, which was part of a larger persecution by Herod Agrippa, "pleased the Jews" (12:3). Furthermore, the Church had been scattered by a persecution that came in the wake of the stoning of Stephen (8:4; 11:19).

## Saul the Persecutor

Saul, a zealous young Pharisee at the time, was one of the chief opponents of the early Church. He helped bring on the scattering after Stephen's death and played a major role in a great persecution which broke out against the Jerusalem church (8:1). Saul went house to house and dragged off Jewish Christians to prison (8:3). But as a result of his experience on the Damascus road (ch. 9), Saul "underwent the revolutionary change which turned him from the most active persecutor of the new order into its most energetic champion,"[19] Paul the apostle.

The evidence of Acts (9:1-3; 22:5; 26:12) suggests that the high priest provided documents that authorized Saul to seek out Jewish Christians from the synagogues of Damascus and take them as prisoners to Jerusalem. Though early Jewish sources indicate that the Sanhedrin of Jerusalem at this time did not have civil jurisdiction beyond Judea proper, it is possible that in the enforcement of Jewish Law the Sanhedrin carried a de facto authority in more distant administrative divisions.[20] This authority would account for the sending of Saul to Damascus to arrest Jewish Christians. It is likely, however, that the political tinderbox created by Roman occupation in the land would have normally prompted the

19. F. F. Bruce, *The Defense of the Gospel in the New Testament,* rev. ed. (Grand Rapids: William B. Eerdmans Publishing Co., 1977), p. 28.

20. Emil Schürer, *The History of the Jewish People in the Age of Jesus Christ (175 B.C.–A.D. 135),* rev. ed., ed. G. Vermes, et al. (Edinburgh: T. & T. Clark, 1979), 2:197-98.

Sanhedrin to exercise some restraint and discretion in the application of its authority.

## Paul the Persecuted

Paul himself met with considerable opposition from Jews during his missionary journeys. The Jews of Thessalonica incited a riot which drove Paul out of that city (Acts 17:1-10). In Corinth, Jews brought Paul to court before Gallio, charging he had broken the Law (18:12-17). Later, at the Temple in Jerusalem, Paul was seized and thrown into the hands of an angry mob, who beat him before his formal arrest (21:27-36). Not long after this incident, forty Jewish men plotted to kill him (23:12-22). This threat eventually led to his trials before Felix (ch. 24) and Festus (ch. 25) and to his imprisonment in Rome (ch. 28).

In 2 Corinthians, Paul's most autobiographical letter, he states that on five occasions he received from the Jews thirty-nine lashes (11:24). No further explanation is given. The Mishnah allows for the administration of a flogging of thirty-nine stripes for violating a negative Mosaic commandment not joined with the performing of a positive one (Makkot 3:4). But, as far as we know from Paul's writings, he had no blatant disregard of Mosaic Law; rather, he upheld it (cf. Rom. 7:12; 1 Cor. 9:20). Therefore, corporal punishment may have been meted out to Paul for other reasons. Since he was a "troublemaker" and "ringleader" (Acts 24:5), he could have become the target of those responsible for maintaining public order.[21] Thus he may have received floggings for disturbing the public peace. At any rate, we must not assume that every instance of Jewish flogging implied a form of religious persecution directed specifically against Jewish Christians.

## Summary

The split between Church and Synagogue was a gradual phenomenon involving several major factors. In this chapter we have considered two of these. The first issue was that of theological differences, many of which centered on Jesus. Disagreements about the divinity of Jesus, his reinterpretation of Jewish symbols, his unusual mission to those suspect to the Jewish religious community, his claim to unique Sonship with the Father, his fulfilling popular messianic expectations, and the belief of his fol-

---

21. Hare, *Theme of Jewish Persecution*, pp. 43-46.

lowers that he had risen from the dead—these all proved scandalous, controversial, or unsettling.

Second, a further wedge was driven between both communities because of an outbreak of persecution within the early Church. Jewish Christianity became more and more a threat to the Jewish establishment. This development resulted in acts of mob violence, arrests, imprisonments, and even martyrdom, as in the case of Stephen. During this time, Saul of Tarsus was among the persecutors. But after his revolutionary about-face on the road to Damascus, he himself soon became one of the persecuted. In the next chapter we will consider a third, and related, major factor in the split, namely, the ostracism of Jewish Christians from the synagogue.

## UNDERSTANDING CHAPTER FOUR

1. Describe the three main groups within the Jerusalem church at the middle of the first century.

2. Despite the growing diversity of the expanding Church at this time, cite at least three factors which contributed to the unity of the body.

3. What observations and limitations must be kept in mind when seeking to gain an accurate understanding of how the Church and Synagogue split?

4. From New Testament times to the present the question of the divinity of Jesus has remained a watershed separating Jews and Christians. Historically, while the Synagogue has taught that the Jesus of history must be kept distinct from the Christ of faith, the Church has adhered to the Gospel record that presents Jesus as both God and man. With this in mind, give your personal response to the perspective on Jesus set forth by Jewish scholar Geza Vermes in the footnotes to this chapter.

5. A further division between Jesus and the religious authorities of his day came through his taking many central symbols of Judaism and subordinating these to himself by radical reinterpretation. Give several New Testament illustrations of this christological type of reinterpretation.

6. What was considered unusual about the mission of Jesus that often proved radical or scandalous to the religious establishment of his day?

7. Explain the significance of Jesus' use of the Aramaic term *Abba* in relation to the question of his divine Sonship. How does the same term relate to the New Testament concept of the sonship of believers?

8. Describe the not-so-clear subject of messianic expectation(s) in first-century Jewish thought. Why do you think Jesus was secretive about his messiahship? How did the ministry and mission of Jesus differ from the messianic expectations current in his day?

9. After the rejection and death of Jesus, what impact did belief in Jesus' resurrection have upon his Jewish followers?

10. On account of what two charges was Jesus accused of being a political troublemaker (Luke 23:2)?

11. Prior to the fall of Jerusalem, the messianic movement was viewed as another type of Jewish heresy. But after Rome crushed the Jewish nation the Jewish establishment was more threatened by this movement. Why the change of attitude?

12. The book of Acts records two martyrdoms. Who were they? Were the charges leading to death purely of a religious nature, or otherwise?

13. Describe some of the acts of mob violence directed against Jewish Christians recorded in the book of Acts.

14. Discuss Saul's (Paul's) early activity as a persecutor of the Church. How could Saul have been authorized by the religious leadership to seek out Jewish believers from as far away as the synagogues of Damascus when the Sanhedrin of Jerusalem at this time did not have jurisdiction beyond Judea proper?

15. Summarize some of the occasions when Paul experienced persecution in his various travels.

16. Paul relates that on five occasions he received thirty-nine lashes. What light does the Mishnah shed on this issue? For what possible reasons might these five floggings have been administered?

17. Summarize the two major factors dealt with in this chapter leading to the separation of Church and Synagogue: theological differences and the issue of persecution.

# Chapter Five

# "Heretics" and the Synagogue

*Anyone who acknowledged that Jesus was the Christ would be put out of the synagogue*

John 9:22

The Judaism of Jesus' day was far from monolithic. A variety of sects had sprung up, each espousing a remedy for the malady of national despair. The Sadducees had a religious program that drew inspiration primarily from the Temple. The Essenes had withdrawn to the wilderness near the Dead Sea to await a messianic intervention that would usher in the end of the age. And the sect of Nazarenes, "followers of the Way," who had Paul as their "ringleader" (Acts 24:5, 14), had agitated the Jewish establishment with their reputation for "causing trouble all over the world" (17:6). During the first century, these and other Jewish parties vied for a hearing among the people. But the Jewish religious leadership eyed warily the Nazarenes in particular, for the Nazarenes were aggressive in their outreach and remained within the synagogue. Indeed, it was said that Jewish Christians filled Jerusalem with their teaching (Acts 5:28).

In the previous chapter we indicated that as the gap gradually widened between Church and Synagogue hostility and persecution toward Jewish Christians also intensified. Hence, the Jewish authorities were increasingly concerned to warn people of the dangers that the Nazarenes—and all other Jewish dissidents, sectarians, or heretics—be eliminated from the mainstream of Jewish religious life. Accordingly, in this chapter we will consider the first-century malediction to exclude heretics from the synagogue, and what relation, if any, this malediction has to the Fourth Gospel.

## The *Birkat ha-Minim:* Definition

The so-called *Birkat ha-Minim* is the exclusionary benediction or blessing —but more properly understood as malediction or curse—directed against heretics. (The *Birkat ha-Minim* is often translated "the Heretic Benediction.") It is the Twelfth Benediction of the set daily prayer commonly referred to as the *Shemoneh Esreh* (the Eighteen Benedictions) or *Amidah.*[1] Along with the Shema, the Shemoneh Esreh is one of the most important rabbinic prayers. Thus the Mishnah refers to the Shemoneh Esreh as simply *ha-tephillah,* "the Prayer." It is to be recited three times a day by every Jew, including women, slaves, and children (Berakot 3:3; 4:1).

In discussion of the separation of Church and Synagogue, scholars have attached varying degrees of importance to the Twelfth Benediction. About the turn of the twentieth century, particular interest was generated through the publication of the Cairo Genizah version of the *Birkat ha-Minim,* now commonly referred to as the Palestinian recension.[2] Today, with scholarship focused on the history of Christian-Jewish relations, new light has been shed on the claim that the *Birkat ha-Minim* was originally composed as an anti-Christian Jewish prayer.

The Twelfth Benediction of the Genizah text (the Palestinian recension) reads: "For apostates *[meshumaddim]* let there be no hope, and the dominion of arrogance do Thou speedily root out in our days; and let Christians *[ve-ha-Notzrim]* and *minim* perish in a moment, let them be blotted out of the book of the living and let them not be written with the righteous."[3] The above text has often been discussed in connection with three passages in the Gospel of John (9:22; 12:42; 16:2) which deal with the ex-

---

1. For a text of the complete Prayer, see Emil Schürer, *The History of the Jewish People in the Age of Jesus Christ (175 B.C.–A.D. 135),* rev. ed., ed. G. Vermes, et al. (Edinburgh: T. & T. Clark, 1979), 2:456-59. It will be observed, however, that there are not eighteen but nineteen benedictions, since Schürer follows the later Babylonian recension (as does the modern Prayer Book). Furthermore, the Twelfth Benediction reflects both internal and external censorship (cf. Steven T. Katz, "Issues in the Separation of Judaism and Christianity after 70 C.E.: A Reconsideration," *Journal of Biblical Literature* 103 [1984]: 64). The Twelfth Benediction in the altered Babylonian recension reads: "And for informers let there be no hope; and let all who do wickedness quickly perish; and let them all be speedily destroyed; and uproot and crush and hurl down and humble the insolent, speedily in our days. Blessed art thou, Lord, who crushest enemies and humblest the insolent" (Schürer, p. 457). In the altered rendering above, commonly used in various versions of the liturgy today, there is no mention about sectarians or *minim.*

2. This material was first published by Solomon Schechter in *Jewish Quarterly Review* 10 (1898): 197-206, 654-59.

3. This translation is from Steven T. Katz, "Issues in the Separation of Judaism and Christianity After 70 C.E.: A Reconsideration," *Journal of Biblical Literature* 103 (1984): 64.

pulsion of Christians from the synagogue. Therefore, it is important that we comment on its original form, the identification of the *minim* ("heretics"), and its intended purpose.[4]

Earlier in this work we noted the widespread view that the separation of Church and Synagogue occurred rather abruptly, at a particular point in time. The proponents of this view have tended to place considerable emphasis upon the Twelfth Benediction, also known as the Heretic Benediction. This Benediction, it is argued, was added around A.D. 90, following the destruction of the Temple.[5] It was intended as a type of liturgical instrument to drive Jewish Christians out of the synagogue. The eminent Jewish historian Salo Baron gives typical expression to this view: "[The Twelfth Benediction] represented the formal recognition by official Judaism of the severance of all ties between the Christian and other schismatic bodies, and the national body of Judaism."[6]

However, a more careful recent assessment of the evidence by other scholars has led to a different, and far more plausible, understanding of the Benediction.[7] Representative is the analysis of Reuven Kimelman. He argues that the *Birkat ha-Minim* does not reflect a watershed in the early history of Jewish-Christian relations. Rather, he concludes, "Apparently, there never was a single edict which caused the so-called irreparable separation between Judaism and Christianity. The separation was rather the result of a long process."[8] We are in basic agreement with this contention. Thus it will be our next task to assess the evidence leading to this conclusion in the light of those who claim the *Birkat ha-Minim* represents an anti-Christian Jewish prayer.


## The Origin of the Benediction

The Talmud provides information about the origin of the Benediction. It states that the prayer was added to the Eighteen Benedictions by Rabbi

4. Here I am following the useful outline of Katz, "Issues," pp. 63-76.

5. See Jacob Jocz, *The Jewish People and Jesus Christ* (repr. Grand Rapids: Baker Book House, 1979), pp. 55-56.

6. Cited in *Encyclopedia Judaica* (Jerusalem: Keter Publishing House, 1971), 12:3.

7. Note especially the following: David Flusser, "The Jewish-Christian Schism (Part II)," *Immanuel* 17 (Winter, 1983/84): 32-38; Reuven Kimelman, "*Birkat Ha-Minim* and the Lack of Evidence for an Anti-Christian Jewish Prayer in Late Antiquity," in *Jewish and Christian Self-Definition,* ed. E. P. Sanders (Philadelphia: Fortress Press, 1981), 2:226-44; Ephraim Urbach, "Self-Isolation or Self-Affirmation in Judaism in the First Three Centuries," in *Jewish and Christian Self-Definition,* 2:288ff.; and Stephen T. Katz, "Issues," pp. 63-76.

8. Kimelman, in *Jewish and Christian Self-Definition,* 2:244.

Samuel the Small at Yavneh (Jamnia) (see Berakot 28b-29a); this would have been around A.D. 90. The rabbi's work was in reply to Rabbi Gamaliel II's query: "Is there no one who knows how to compose a benediction against the *minim*?" Thus, according to the talmudic tradition which has come through the Babylonian recension (see Berakot 28b-29a), there are a total of nineteen benedictions, including Rabbi Samuel the Small's *Birkat ha-Minim*. But this present-day Babylonian recension of "the Prayer" is still known as the Shemoneh Esreh (literally "eighteen"), though it consists of nineteen parts.[9]

David Flusser is doubtless correct, however, when he argues that at Yavneh Rabbi Samuel the Small did not insert the word *minim* ("heretics") into the text. Rather, the word was part of the original text of the *Birkat ha-Minim* and is pre-Christian (probably late Maccabean) in origin.[10] Flusser attributes this original benediction to the work of the Pharisees. Further, he argues that at Yavneh Rabbi Samuel the Small served as an editor, bringing together two previously unlinked benedictions: one benediction was against "heretics" *(minim)* and the other against the "dominion of arrogance" *(zedim)*—probably a reference to the gentile dominance of Rome. Thus, in its initial pre-Christian setting, the *Birkat ha-Minim* was not directed at Jewish Christians but rather "coined against dissidents, apostates and traitors—including those who delivered Jews to the Gentile government—and similar wicked men who separated themselves from the Jewish collectivity."[11] Specifically, this term would include Hellenizers, Sadducees, Essenes, and any other sectarians who departed from Pharisaic standards and beliefs.[12] Since the original Yavnean benediction cannot now be fully recovered, we can offer only a hypothetical reconstruction of that text.[13] But, as indicated, this term would seem to include a very broad range of Jewish heretical groups. Accordingly, Katz suggests that "in all probability, it addressed itself to 'outsiders' *(perushim)*, 'heretics' *(minim)*, and the 'arrogant of the nations' *(zedim)*."[14]

9. Schürer, *History*, p. 462.

10. David Flusser, "The Jewish-Christian Schism (Part II)," *Immanuel* 17 (Winter, 1983/84): 35-37. Note also idem, "The Jewish Religion in the Second Temple Period," in *The World History of the Jewish People, Society and Religion in the Second Temple Period*, ed. M. Avi-Yonah and A. Baras (Jerusalem: Massada, 1977), 8:23, 24. In addition, see the summary and evaluation of Flusser's argument by Katz, "Issues," pp. 67-68.

11. David Flusser, "Jewish-Christian Schism," p. 34. Ephraim Urbach essentially agrees with Flusser, stating that the original invocation was "intended to include all groups who separated themselves from the community" (*Jewish and Christian Self-Definition*, 2:288).

12. Flusser, "Jewish-Christian Schism," p. 33; see also Katz, "Issues," p. 69.

13. See Flusser's suggested reconstruction, "Jewish-Christian Schism," p. 36.

14. Katz, "Issues," p. 69.

## The *Minim* and *Notzrim*

Since the term *minim* was a general expression for many types of sectarian or deviant Jews, Jewish Christians would have been defined as *minim* well before the time of Yavneh (ca. A.D. 90). But to argue as Horbury has done that "Christians were prominently in view" during the formulation of the *Birkat ha-Minim* at Yavneh is probably to imply more than the evidence warrants.[15] For if Christians were prominently in view, the Yavnean benediction would not have needed to introduce the word *notzrim* (as found in the Genizah text of the *Birkat ha-Minim* cited toward the beginning of this discussion).

We must emphasize that only two texts of the *Birkat ha-Minim* (both found in the Cairo Genizah) explicitly mention Christians. Both texts refer to "the Christians [*notzrim*, i.e., the Nazarenes] and the heretics [*minim*]." Flusser has made several important observations about these texts.[16] First, *notzrim*, the word for "Christians," was added to an earlier text, which spoke only of heretics; this addition was likely made to emphasize that "heretics" *(minim)* refers chiefly to Christians. Furthermore, it is very significant that *notzrim* ("Christians") appears only in the two Genizah versions of the *Birkat ha-Minim*, for in all other versions—whether from Christian or non-Christian countries (which would not have any Christian censors)—only the word *minim* ("heretics") appears. If *notzrim* were added by a formal decision at Yavneh, why is it not found more widely in the liturgy?

Evidence is lacking as to the precise date that *notzrim* was added to the Yavnean benediction of Rabbi Samuel the Small. Justin Martyr (ca. A.D. 160) refers to Jews cursing Christians,[17] though he does not categorize them as "Nazaraei" (i.e., "Nazarenes"). But Jerome (ca. A.D. 400) and Epiphanius (ca. A.D. 375) do state that Jews curse "the Nazoraeans."[18]

---

15. William Horbury, "The Benediction of the *Minim* and early Jewish-Christian Controversy," *Journal of Theological Studies* 33 (1982): 60; cf. also Katz, "Issues," p. 71. But Gedaliah Alon presses this point even further than Horbury when he states that the main intention of the *Birkat ha-Minim* was to make all Jews aware they could *"no longer be called Jews. "* He concludes, "Whatever way we look at it, it will be seen that the Beth Din of Rabban Gamaliel at Yavneh took a fatal step, one that was to have far-reaching historical consequences. They declared in unequivocal terms that the Jewish Christians could no longer be considered part of the Jewish community nor of the Jewish people" (*The Jews in Their Land in the Talmudic Age* [Jerusalem: Magnes Press, 1980], 1:307).

16. Flusser, "Jewish-Christian Schism," pp. 33-34.

17. Justin Martyr, *Dialogue* 16.4.

18. For an extensive list of references see Kimelman, in *Jewish and Christian Self-Definition*, 2:237-39, 398-99.

Therefore, one could safely suggest that the term *notzrim* was added to the Yavnean benediction sometime after A.D. 150 but prior to A.D. 400.

To sum up, the *Birkat ha-Minim* was not composed at Yavneh to be a document specially aimed at Jewish Christians, though it included them. All Jews not living according to Pharisaic norms after A.D. 70 might be the object of the curse directed against *minim* ("heretics"). The word *notzrim*, "Christians," appears to have been added to the malediction long after Yavneh, when the breach between Synagogue and Church had widened considerably. The *Birkat ha-Minim,* therefore, did not mark any direct break between Synagogue and Church. In the succinct words of Katz: "there was no official anti-Christian policy at Yavneh or elsewhere before the Bar Kochba revolt [A.D. 132-135] and no total separation between Jews and Christians before (if immediately after?) the Bar Kochba revolt."[19]

## "Put out of the Synagogue"

The question next arises whether the *Birkat ha-Minim* relates to the three instances in the Gospel of John (9:22; 12:42; 16:2) which refer to Jewish Christians being "put out of the synagogue" (Greek *aposynágōgos*). Some scholars, such as J. Louis Martyn, have argued that these Johannine passages reflect the Yavnean formulation of the *Birkat ha-Minim* by Rabbi Samuel the Small.[20] This position, however, fails to convince. The Gospel of John may have been written around the time of Yavneh (ca. A.D. 90), a period when the Pharisees were diligently working to preserve ethnic purity and to uphold the Law.[21] But if one argues, as does Martyn, that the *Birkat ha-Minim* was directed against Jewish Christians by the inclusion of *notzrim* in the Yavnean text—a position we have above sought to show untenable—then he has exceeded the evidence available. Furthermore, the *Birkat ha-Minim* was not a tool of excommunication, but a recitation which proved to be a "test" involving self-exclusion.[22] Contrary to Martyn's contention, it simply cannot be demonstrated that these Johannine exclusion-

19. Katz, "Issues," p. 76.
20. See J. Louis Martyn, *History and Theology in the Fourth Gospel,* rev. ed. (Nashville: Abingdon Press, 1979), pp. 37-62. Cf. also Rodney A. Whitacre, *Johannine Polemic,* SBL Dissertation Series 67 (Chico, CA: Scholars Press, 1980), pp. 5-25.
21. See Barnabas Lindars, "The Persecution of Christians in John 15:18–16:4a," in *Suffering and Martyrdom in the New Testament,* ed. William Horbury and Brian McNeil (Cambridge: Cambridge University Press, 1981), p. 49.
22. Douglas R. A. Hare, *The Theme of Jewish Persecution of Christians in the Gospel According to St. Matthew* (Cambridge: Cambridge University Press, 1967), pp. 54-55.

ary texts point to the conclusion that "the Heretic Benediction is now employed in order formally and irretrievably to separate such Jews from the synagogue."[23]

It is difficult to conclude, however, what sort of ban John has in mind for those Jews "who acknowledged that Jesus was the Christ" (cf. John 9:22). Nowhere else in the New Testament (apart from the Gospel of John) or in the Apostolic Fathers is there any evidence that exclusion from the synagogue, *aposynágōgos,* was practiced for acknowledging Jesus as the Christ.[24] The failure to attest this practice in early Christian literature parallels a similar silence in rabbinic literature.[25] This lack of evidence has led Kimelman to suggest that "the whole charge was concocted" to keep Christians away from the synagogue out of fear of facing hostility there.[26] Carroll argues that the author of the Fourth Gospel was a Gentile with strong anti-Jewish sentiments.[27] Other scholars suggest that John is reading back into the Gospel narrative his antipathy to "the Jews." For example, Samuel Sandmel argues that the controversies in John "reflect not Jesus in his age but the ongoing bitterness between Jews and Christians that had accumulated in the intervening decades."[28]

But such explanations of *aposynágōgos,* while on the surface appearing viable, are in the end unsatisfactory. In the first place, the Old Testament clearly indicates that Jews were used to practicing excommunication (Ezra 10:8; Neh. 13:3; Isa. 66:5). Furthermore, the Qumran community had rules for punishing violators with either temporary or permanent exclusion (cf. 1QS 6:24–7:25).[29] Thus, to imply that exclusion from the synagogue during the first century A.D. would have been thought a strange practice is indeed unwarranted. To be sure, "the evidence for excommunication from the general Jewish body in the pre-rabbinic period is not plentiful, but it is enough to suggest the existence of a recognized custom."[30] For this reason, in regard to *aposynágōgos,* we concur

23. Martyn, *History and Theology in the Fourth Gospel,* p. 62.

24. Hare, *Theme of Jewish Persecution,* p. 55.

25. See W. Schrage, *Theological Dictionary of the New Testament* (Grand Rapids: William B. Eerdmans Publishing Co., 1971), 7:848.

26. Kimelman, in *Jewish and Christian Self-Definition,* 2:234-35.

27. Kenneth L. Carroll, "The Fourth Gospel and the Exclusion of Christians from the Synagogues," *Bulletin of John Rylands Library* 40 (1957-58): 19-20, 31-32.

28. Samuel Sandmel, *Anti-Semitism in the New Testament?* (Philadelphia: Fortress Press, 1978), p. 118.

29. William S. LaSor, *The Dead Sea Scrolls and the New Testament* (Grand Rapids: William B. Eerdmans Publishing Co., 1972), pp. 73-74.

30. William Horbury, "Extirpation and Excommunication," *Vetus Testamentum* 35 (1985): 38.

with the observation of Barnabas Lindars that some kind of exclusion from the synagogue is implied, and that "this must be taken seriously, however difficult it is to correlate with information derived from Jewish sources."[31]

## The *Nidduy* and *Ḥerem*

The solution doubtless lies in gaining a correct understanding of the nature of the exclusion. If one holds to the essential historical reliability of the Johannine account, then it is quite unlikely that full "exclusion from the national and religious fellowship of the Jews"[32] is what is meant. As we have previously pointed out, during the ministry of Jesus—despite the opposition he encountered from Jewish leadership—his followers were considered part of the Jewish community, albeit controversially so. The synagogue admitted a wide range of freedom, even in conceptions of messianism.

Rabbinic literature records two types of bans which may shed some light on the *aposynágōgos* of John's Gospel. The first-degree ban was know as *nidduy*. It normally involved a thirty-day period of isolation from the congregation. The Talmud lists twenty-four minor offenses for which *nidduy* was imposed, including violations such as profaning God's name, nonpayment of judgment debts, negligence in ritual slaughtering, disrespecting a teacher of the Torah, or testifying against a Jew in a non-Jewish court.[33] The *nidduy* was a corrective measure, not intended to banish the errant one forever from the congregation but to make him conscious of his sin and to aid in his return.

The more severe ban was the *ḥerem*, an unlimited exclusion from the congregation which could, however, be lifted. Although the concept of *ḥerem* is deeply rooted in the Hebrew Scriptures, until the third century A.D. rabbinic literature appears to lack references to *ḥerem* in the sense of "excommunicate." Raymond Brown, however, sees the references in the Fourth Gospel to the exclusion of Jewish Christians from the synagogue as being closest to the practice of *ḥerem*, although he confesses uncertainty about the matter.[34] But it is probably correct to state that neither the *nid-

---

31. Lindars, in *Suffering and Martyrdom in the New Testament*, p. 67.

32. Schrage, *Theological Dictionary of the New Testament*, 7:849.

33. For a complete listing of offenses, see Haim Cohn in *Encyclopedia Judaica*, 8:351-52.

34. Raymond E. Brown, *The Gospel According to John*, Anchor Bible (Garden City, NY: Doubleday & Co., 1966), 1:374.

*duy* nor the *ḥerem* was widely used against Jewish Christians in the first century. Hence, we must seek a solution elsewhere.

## Conclusion

It appears that the expression "to put out of the synagogue" must be taken in an informal rather than a formal sense. Perhaps Jesus alluded to this action when he warned that his disciples would be "beaten in synagogues" (Mark 13:9; cf. Acts 5:40). In any case, since there is little collaborative textual evidence that formal excommunication was practiced during this formative period of the Church, *aposynágōgos* may have reference to a kind of informal social ostracism. Hare may be correct in suggesting that this form of pressure by public censure was likely "directed not so much against faith in Christ *per se* as against those activities of Christians which were regarded as objectionable by the synagogue-community involved (cf. Acts 18:5-7, 13)."[35] Thus, we conclude tentatively that the Fourth Gospel may refer to a kind of ad hoc, spontaneous community disapproval to the preaching that "Jesus was the Christ." This action would amount to removing someone from the synagogue more by group outrage than by formal ban. It is probable that only later, when Synagogue and Church had come close to the brink of final separation, were any formal bans imposed.

## UNDERSTANDING CHAPTER FIVE

1. Three of the major Jewish sects in Jesus' day were the Sadducees, Essenes, and Nazarenes. Each had a different focus or philosophy from which its inspiration and program derived. In briefest terms, what main feature distinguished one group from the other?

2. Translate the Hebrew expression *Birkat ha-Minim* into English. Define what is meant by the expression. Why is it misleading to refer to this as a "blessing" or "benediction" without some further explanation?

3. Define the terms *Shemoneh Esreh* and *ha-tephillah*. In the present-day Babylonian recension of the Shemoneh Esreh, how many benedictions are found? In the Twelfth Benediction of the Babylonian recension used in synagogue liturgy today, what has been altered due to censorship (see the first footnote)? According to the Mishnah, how often is the Shemoneh Esreh to be recited?

---

35. Hare, *Theme of Jewish Persecution*, pp. 55-56.

4. In the Twelfth Benediction of the Cairo Genizah text (the Palestinian recension) a malediction is brought upon the *notzrim* and the *minim* (viz. "Let the *notzrim* and *minim* perish in a moment, let them be blotted out of the book of the living"). Define these two terms.

5. According to talmudic tradition, Rabbi Gamaliel II inquired, "Is there no one who knows how to compose a benediction against the *minim?*" (a) What rabbi is said to have composed the *Birkat ha-Minim?* (b) Where was this done and in what year?

6. David Flusser of the Hebrew University in Jerusalem argues that the word "heretics" *(minim)* was not composed at Yavneh for insertion into the text. (a) When and by whom, does Flusser argue, was the original benediction produced? (b) What function then did Rabbi Samuel the Small have? (c) Against whom was the original benediction directed?

7. Were Jewish Christians included in the *minim* prior to A.D. 90, the date when the benediction was taken and edited from a previous source?

8. Only two texts of the *Birkat ha-Minim* (both are the Palestinian recension from the Cairo Genizah) explicitly mention the Christians *(notzrim),* i.e., "Nazarenes," and the heretics *(minim).* Flusser points out that it is remarkable that in non-Christian countries, where no Christian censors would be present to eliminate *notzrim* from the benediction, only *minim* occurs in the text. In short, if *notzrim* was added at Yavneh, why is this term not found more universally in the liturgy? When does Flusser suggest *notzrim* was added to the benediction? What historical evidence is cited to support this conclusion?

9. Sum up the history of the formulation of the *Birkat ha-Minim* and what role—if any—it had in marking a formal split between Synagogue and Church.

10. Which Gospel refers three times to Jewish Christians being "put out of the synagogue"?

11. Was the *Birkat ha-Minim* a tool to ban or excommunicate formally someone from the synagogue? Explain.

12. In addition to the Gospel of John, is there any other evidence in early Christian literature that Jews were excluded from the synagogue *(aposynágōgos)* for acknowledging Jesus as the Christ?

13. What evidence is there that excommunication or banishment was practiced—for whatever reason—in the Jewish community prior to the writing of John's Gospel (i.e., before the rabbinic period)?

14. Rabbinic literature records two types of bans which may shed some light on the references to being "put out of the synagogue" in the Gospel of John. Name and describe these two bans. Do either of them clearly fit the context of John's Gospel? Explain.

15. Based on the evidence available, set forth a more likely explanation of what the Gospel of John means by being "put out of the synagogue."

## Chapter Six

# The Jewish Revolts and the Parting of the Way

*"Do you see all these great buildings?" replied Jesus. "Not one stone here will be left on another; every one will be thrown down"*

Mark 13:2

In 63 B.C., Pompey took the city of Jerusalem by storm and established Roman rule over the land. In the decades to follow, the Jewish community chafed under the yoke of ruthless procurators (governors) and other overlords. Rulers such as Pontius Pilate (A.D. 26-37) had military and civil jurisdiction over their Jewish subjects, including the collection of taxes for the Roman coffers. Idolatrous and pagan practices abounded everywhere, as Jews writhed under foreign domination within their ancestral homeland. Jesus' death at the hands of Roman soldiers dramatically displayed one of the most barbaric and torturous forms of execution known to the world of that day.

In A.D. 49, a dispute between Jews and Jewish Christians developed in Rome. In an effort to restore order, Emperor Claudius expelled both groups from Rome, apparently making no distinction between them.[1] By A.D. 64, however, during the reign of Nero, Christians were distinguished from Jews. Tradition asserts that the apostle Paul was imprisoned in Rome, where he later died a martyr in about A.D. 64, the time of the great fire. The Roman historian Tacitus states that Nero was suspected of setting the fire and then, to avert suspicion, blamed the Christians for it.[2]

---

1. This expulsion is described by the historian Suetonius. Cf. Peter Richardson, *Israel in the Apostolic Church* (Cambridge: Cambridge University Press, 1969), p. 42.
    2. Tacitus, *Annals* 15.38ff.

## The First Jewish Revolt (A.D. 66-73)

By the time of Paul's death, in the Jewish homeland the Zealots had gained considerable influence among the people. In their rejection of Rome and opposition to other segments of their Jewish community, the Zealots were eagerly awaiting an opportune moment to vindicate their cause. Through a fanatic nationalism and drive to power, the Zealots were committed to end Roman rule and bring the salvation of God's elect people. In A.D. 66, when Eleazar the priest, then apparently Captain of the Temple, stopped offering the daily sacrifice in behalf of the emperor's health, war became a reality. Though certain Jewish citizens sought to head off the revolt, it was too late. The Zealots had now moved into action. Their hope: victory and political power for Israel.

The war centered in Jerusalem and Judea and in other areas of heavy Jewish population—the provinces of Idumea on the south, Perea in the east, and Galilee in the north. Vespasian had begun the Roman conquest in the north. In Galilee he was met by Josephus, who had organized the Jewish revolt. After three years of conflict, in the year 69, Vespasian was recalled to Rome to become emperor. His son Titus took over.

Jerusalem, which had been largely unscathed until this time, braced for attack. In A.D. 70, after several months of intense fighting, the holy precinct was taken and the Temple destroyed. Soon the rest of the besieged city was in Roman hands. Tens of thousands of Jews were put to the sword, died of starvation, or were enslaved. Today in Rome, the famous Arch of Titus gives graphic witness to this event. It depicts the golden lampstand *(menorah)* from the Temple in Jerusalem being carried away as booty to Rome.

### The Fall of Masada

For three years after the fall of Jerusalem, Rome continued its mopping-up operations. Several Jewish strongholds yet remained, Masada being the last one to hold out. The isolated fortress of Masada, beautified decades earlier as a palace for the troubled Herod the Great, was located in the Judean wilderness overlooking the Dead Sea. On the top of Masada, 967 Jewish Zealots had valiantly taken refuge, determined to hold out to the bitter end. With the Tenth Roman Legion, General Silva besieged the fortress, finally storming it by means of a huge man-made ramp on the west. When the Roman soldiers reached the Zealots' camp at the top, only dead Jewish bodies were found—a most unusual instance of mass suicide. Josephus, who had defected from the Jewish side to that of Rome, records this remarkable story.[3] These Zealots, he points out, chose to take their own lives while free, rather than be enslaved or die at the hands of Rome. At Masada, in April of 73, the First Jewish Revolt was finally crushed.

## The Flight to Pella

Sometime before the fall of Jerusalem—probably between A.D. 66 and 68 —the Jewish Christian community fled to Pella in Perea. Located in the foothills east of the Jordan Valley about 60 miles northeast of Jerusalem, Pella became an important center for early Jewish Christianity. Perhaps at this time the Jerusalem church recalled the words of Jesus: "When you see Jerusalem being surrounded by armies, you will know that its desolation is near. Then let those who are in Judea flee to the mountains, let those in the city get out, and let those in the country not enter the city" (Luke 21:20-21).

The flight to Pella marks an important juncture in the gradual break between Synagogue and Church. The failure of Jewish Christians at this time to support the nationalist movement against Rome did not endear them to the general population. In the face of national crisis such aloofness and lack of patriotism branded Jewish Christians with a stigma of disloyalty and treason. Furthermore, the geographical removal of Jewish Christians from Jerusalem and its Temple area affected the growing schism by loosening their close religious connection to Judaism, the strongest potential unifying force the Jewish people had.

At the same time, however, the Jewish Christians used the fall of Jerusalem in their polemic against the Synagogue. They pointed to the ruins of Jerusalem as God's judgment upon Israel for rejecting the Messiah.[4] After the First Jewish Revolt, however, we know that some from the Jerusalem church returned there. According to Eusebius of Caesarea (ca. A.D. 325), later known as the father of church history, a succession of fif-

---

3. Josephus, *Jewish War* 7.8.1-9.2 (252-406).

4. It has been generally accepted that the sacrificial cult in Jerusalem ceased altogether in A.D. 70. But according to Kenneth W. Clark ("Worship in the Jerusalem Temple after A.D. 70," *New Testament Studies* 6 [1959-60]: 269-80), a diminished form of worship may still have been maintained between A.D. 70 and the Second Jewish Revolt of 132-135. Whatever the extent of the damage to the Temple area—and Clark cites some accounts which conflict to a certain degree—he is correct in stating that there is no evidence of any edict by the Romans forbidding Temple worship during this period. We do, however, find such an edict issued ca. A.D. 73 for the Temple of Onias in Leontopolis in the district of Heliopolis in Egypt. Jews had fled there from Palestine just prior to A.D. 70 to stir up the Jewish community against Rome. The temple in Leontopolis had stood for more than 200

teen Jewish Christian bishops served in Jerusalem until the start of the Second Jewish Revolt.[5]

The First Jewish Revolt marked a turning point in the history of Judaism. "The early Church up to 70 C.E. was a daughter of Judaism: only after that did it leave the nest."[6] As we have stressed, however, the leaving was a process. It would not become finalized until well into the second century. But the date of A.D. 70 basically marked the end of the Zealot, Sadducean, and Essene sects. Only the Pharisees and the struggling Nazarenes remained as parties in major contention.

## Between Revolts: The Academy at Yavneh

With the destruction of the Temple, the priests and Pharisees became entangled in disputes over questions of ritual. It now became the role of the Pharisees to begin an intensive restructuring of Judaism. Rituals of the temple were transferred to the home. Acts of kindness and charity began to replace atonement by sacrifice. Much of this comprehensive reformulation of Judaism by the Pharisees took place at an academy *(bet midrash)* at Yavneh (Jabne or Jamnia), west of Jerusalem. The Sanhedrin, composed of the leading scribes, was transferred to Yavneh. The first head of the academy was Rabbi Johanan (or Yohanan) ben Zakkai,[7] who served until around the year 80 or 85. A student of the famous Hillel, Johanan would be succeeded by Gamaliel II, mentioned earlier in regard to his request at Yavneh for the composition of the *Birkat ha-Minim.*

Johanan marked the start of a new era in the history of Judaism. "When the Jewish people lost the very ground under its feet, Rabban Johannan stepped into the breach and by reformulating Judaism on a new basis—a spiritual instead of a territorial one—assured the millennial survival of the people and its faith."[8] As founder of the academy, Johanan ini-

---

years, since Judean Jews first settled in this area during the outbreak of the Maccabean Revolt. If the date of A.D. 70 does not mark the final end of all sacrifices in the Jerusalem Temple, the date of 135 becomes of much greater importance in understanding the break between Synagogue and Church.

5. See Eusebius, *Ecclesiastical History* 4.5.1-4.

6. W. D. Davies, *Paul and Rabbinic Judaism,* 4th ed. (Philadelphia: Fortress Press, 1980), p. xxviii.

7. See Gedaliah Alon, "Rabban Johanan B. Zakkai's removal to Jabneh," in *Jews, Judaism and the Classical World* (Jerusalem: Magnes Press, 1977), pp. 269-343.

8. Gedaliah Alon, *The Jews in Their Land in the Talmudic Age* (Jerusalem: Magnes Press, 1980), 1:86.

tiated an ambitious agenda.[9] In the academy he sought to preserve Jewish tradition and to enhance unity among various divisions. At that time among the Pharisees, the schools of Hillel and Shammai had considerable differences to iron out. Thus Johanan sought to effect a greater unification in the interpretation of the Law. The pluralism within Jewry prior to the fall of Jerusalem was no longer possible. In addition, the need for codification of the Oral Law became apparent at Yavneh, though no tangible realization of this need would be finalized until the Mishnah was compiled under the direction of Rabbi Judah the Prince, more than a century later.

The sages at Yavneh were also responsible for reworking the Temple ritual so as to standardize it into the order and liturgy of the synagogue service. Furthermore, they discussed and settled questions concerning the canonicity of certain Old Testament books. The books of the Apocrypha were now apparently clearly distinguished from Holy Writ, and in the opinion of certain scholars, considerable work toward the finalizing of the official text of the Hebrew Bible—the *Massorah*—was carried on.[10] Also at Yavneh the division of the Old Testament into Law, Prophets, and Writings was first clearly attested.[11]

The importance of Yavneh in the history of the Jewish people can hardly be overestimated. The emergence of Rabbinic Judaism may be traced to Yavneh. Through ordination (*semikhah*, "laying on of hands") of the disciples of Johanan ben Zakkai, the title *rabbi* acquired new significance. Yavneh marks the setting in motion of a succession of sages or rabbis through formal ordination. Here the meaning of *rabbi* must be carefully contrasted with the use of the term in the New Testament, where it was an informal term of honor bestowed on a learned teacher and hence primarily an esteemed form of address.

As noted in chapter five above, at Yavneh the *Birkat ha-Minim*, "the Heretic Benediction," was composed. This composition underscores that the scholars of Yavneh were interested in protecting and preserving Judaism from all its foes—both inside and out. But this attitude did not mean that Yavneh established any official policy against Christians. Rather, the cursing of the *minim* ("heretics") was in essence a renewed call to vigilance about Jewish survival. It was to awaken the collective consciousness of Jewry not simply to the growth of Christians in its midst, but also to the existence of sectarians, detractors, and defectors of any stripe.

---

9. For a comprehensive summary of the significance of Yavneh see W. D. Davies, *The Setting of the Sermon on the Mount* (Cambridge: Cambridge University Press, 1964), pp. 256-315.

10. Alon, *Jews in Their Land*, 1:272.

11. Davies, *Setting of the Sermon on the Mount*, p. 273.

During the years between the First and Second Jewish Revolts, the Jewish Christians and traditional Jews continued to exchange bitter accusations. Gentiles who entered the Church, unlike proselytes who entered Judaism, did not have to deal with the barrier of adult circumcision and other regulations of Jewish Law. Hence many potential proselytes found it more attractive to join the Church rather than the Synagogue.[12] To compound the tension further, the growth of Gentiles within the Jewish church compromised the Jewish position in the mind of the rabbis. After the apostles died, the next generation of leaders was mostly gentile, especially in the great centers of Christian growth, which included Antioch and Rome. The Church had begun within Judaism as an all-Jewish sect, but by the early part of the second century its adherents—especially in the Diaspora—were predominantly non-Jews.

## From Sabbath to Lord's Day

Between the First and Second Jewish Revolts the widening breach between Synagogue and Church also manifested itself through changing attitudes regarding Sabbath worship.[13] The issue of the Sabbath provides a useful historical example of a point at which the Church became separated from its original place within the structure of Judaism. But in addition, by Christianity's rejection of the Sabbath and much of the rest of the Mosaic Law, it sent out a clear message that it had rejected Israel as well.

Though the early Church observed the Sabbath, in time it came to worship on Sunday, the day of Jesus' resurrection (cf. Matt. 28:1). But both Jew and Christian recognized that Sunday was also a Roman holy day tied to sun-worship. Ignatius, bishop of Antioch, indicates that this change had begun to take place as early as about A.D. 115. He wrote to the Magnesians, telling them to "no longer live for the Sabbath but for the Lord's Day, on which day our life arose."[14] *The Didache,* a manual of church instruction written around A.D. 120, also directs Christians to come together on the Lord's Day to worship.

On this issue of the Sabbath as well as other matters related to Jewish

12. This argument is made by Daniel Juster in *Jewish Roots* (Rockville, MD: Davar, 1986), pp. 138-39.

13. For thorough studies on this issue see D. A. Carson, ed., *From Sabbath to Lord's Day* (Grand Rapids: Zondervan Publishing House, 1982); and Paul K. Jewett, *The Lord's Day* (Grand Rapids: William B. Eerdmans Publishing Co., 1971).

14. Ignatius of Antioch, *Letter to the Magnesians* 9.1.

practice, the two communities—Church and Synagogue—took up opposing positions. Over the centuries the Jewish community has interpreted the Church's decision to worship on Sunday as a rejection of the very heart of Jewish experience—rejection of the Law. This move to Sunday worship made it exceedingly difficult, if not virtually impossible, for the Jew to give any serious consideration to the Christian message, or even to enter into Christian-Jewish dialogue without suspicion. The Jew saw the Church's move to Sunday worship as a call to abandon the Law and embrace a "new covenant" that had now replaced the "old covenant," which was thus declared ineffective and passé. In short, to become a Christian was considered as leaving behind the Jewishness of one's past, hardly a live option for any faithful Jew to consider. In the words of historian Jules Isaac, "The Jewish rejection of Christ was triggered by the Christian rejection of the Law. . . . The rejection of the Law was enough; to ask the Jewish people that they accept this rejection . . . was like asking them to tear out their heart. History records no example of such collective suicide."[15]

The point we are making here is not that the contemporary Church should adopt a view of strict Sabbatarianism. That would require that Old Testament Sabbath laws concerning ritual rest be carefully observed on Saturday, the seventh day of the week. The Council of Jerusalem made no such teaching binding on non-Jewish believers (see Acts 15:28-29). Indeed, the council took care that they "should not make it difficult for the Gentiles who are turning to God" (15:19). During the Reformation, both Luther and Calvin steered clear of the Sabbatarian position because it contained many legalistic pitfalls.

It is not known when the early Church began Sunday worship. Both Acts 20:7 and 1 Corinthians 16:2 may allude to Sunday as a day for meeting. But the New Testament writers provide us with no clear rationale for a shift from the seventh to the first day of the week. Perhaps the early Jewish followers of Jesus met in the synagogues on the Sabbath, and then met again as Christians (or *ma'aminim,* "believers"), following the *Habdalah* ceremony (a ritual which ended the Sabbath), on Saturday evening after sundown to begin the first day of the week. Some New Testament texts hint that Saturday was not consistently observed as the one day of worship and rest (Rom. 14:5-6; Gal. 4:8-11; Col. 2:16-17), perhaps largely due to the sudden influx of many non-Jews into the early Church. The Sabbath commandment seems to have been considered part of the ceremonial law of

15. Cited in Jacques Doukhan, *Drinking at the Sources* (Mountain View, California: Mountain Press Publishing Association, 1981), p. 25.

Israel, and as such not a sine qua non for Church unity. Rather, the Church was to be a body not divided over Sabbath regulations, but united as a people among whom there is "neither Jew nor Greek . . . but all one in Christ Jesus" (Gal. 3:28).

Apparently, the precise day of worship was not the key issue for the New Testament Church. Every day was to be holy unto the Lord. What is important for us to remember, however, is that behind the various reasons which eventually led to Sunday worship was the desire on the part of the early Church, which had become increasingly non-Jewish in its composition, to distinguish itself from Judaism and its special Sabbath laws. Thus the gap between Christianity and Judaism, between non-Jews and Jews, continued to widen.

## The Second Jewish Revolt (A.D. 132-135)

The First Jewish Revolt had been a decisive turning point in the relation of Judaism to Christianity. But the war of A.D. 132-135 was, for all essential purposes, the final major national blow that severed the two communities.[16] Exactly what triggered the war remains a debated issue. It may have been prompted by dissillusionment and the later resentment of the Jews following a rumor that Emperor Hadrian was rebuilding the Temple.[17] The severe rule of the Roman governor of Judea, Tinneius Rufus, may also have been a factor in provoking the revolt. But the immediate cause was more likely a prohibition against circumcision, and other acts of Hellenization enforced on the Jews.

### The Leadership of Bar Kokhba

Simon, popularly known as Bar Kokhba ("son of a star"), led the revolt. He laid claim to messiahship, and Rabbi Akiba (or Aqiba; ca. A.D. 50-135), perhaps the most respected scholar of the time, upheld this claim. He appealed to a text from the Torah that "A star will come out of Jacob; a scepter will rise out of Israel. He will crush the foreheads of Moab, the skulls of all the sons of Sheth" (Num. 24:17). Worship now resumed at the Temple altar, and Jews throughout the land followed Bar Kokhba in a valiant

---

16. Richardson, *Israel in the Apostolic Church,* pp. 36, 203.

17. So Werner Förster, *Palestinian Judaism in New Testament Times,* trans. Gordon E. Harris (London: Oliver & Boyd, 1964), p. 116. See also *Encyclopedia Judaica* (Jerusalem: Keter Publishing House, 1971), 4:231-39.

struggle for freedom. Letters bearing the signature of Bar Kokhba shed light on his vast territorial rule and his mobilization of men and supplies for the war.[18]

## A Defeated Jewish Nation

From A.D. 132 to 135 hundreds of Jewish villages joined in the bitter fighting. The Romans called Julius Severus from his governorship in Britain to come and crush the Jewish resistance. More than half a million Jews perished and nearly all of Judea lay in ruins. Hadrian destroyed Jerusalem completely; every wall was leveled and the city plowed. He then built a new city which he called "Aelia Capitolina" in honor of himself, the ruling Aelius Hadrianus. He constructed a temple to Jupiter on the site of the Temple.[19] Hadrian immediately began to populate this once Jewish Holy City with Greek-speaking pagans, and he forbade Jews to come near the city on pain of death.

Rome's crushing of two national revolts about sixty years apart had far-reaching consequences for the Jewish people. These defeats spelled the death of Israel's quest for national identity. The hopes and dreams of the Zealot movement now vanished. Instead of victors, the Jews were victims, vanquished by a pagan people more potent than they.

## Jewish Christians and the War

As they had in the First Jewish Revolt, the Jewish Christians refused to fight. Failure to assist their countrymen in this final ill-fated drive for national independence alienated them even further from the Jewish community. It also left them more vulnerable to persecution. A second factor which created a significant wedge between the two groups centered on Bar Kokhba. The Jewish Christians had but one Messiah, the risen Jesus of Nazareth, who could command their allegiance. Their loyalty could not be directed to both Yeshua (Jesus) and Simon. Thus commitment to the cause of Bar Kokhba may have "virtually meant a denial of the Messiahship of Jesus."[20]

18. See Keith Schoville, *Biblical Archaeology in Focus* (Grand Rapids: Baker Book House, 1978), pp. 303-13.

19. G. W. H. Lampe concurs with K. W. Clark in emphasizing that "the decisive catastrophe was not the destruction of the Temple by Titus but Hadrian's establishment of the cult of Jupiter on its site" ("A.D. 70 in Christian Reflection," in *Jesus and the Politics of His Day*, ed. Ernst Bammel and C. F. D. Moule [Cambridge: Cambridge University Press, 1984], p. 153).

20. Jacob Jocz, *The Jewish People and Jesus Christ* (repr. Grand Rapids: Baker Book House, 1979), p. 71.

But in a parallel vein, the Jewish community made its own state-ment to the Jewish Christians by supporting Bar Kokhba's cause. Its al-legiance to its own messianic movement, spawned by its own charismatic leader, signaled clearly its final rejection of Jesus as Messiah. Henceforth, this would result in a marked change in missionary activity. As Jewish historian Haim Hillel Ben-Sasson has observed, "The disasters of the Bar Kokhba War handicapped Jewish proselytism (although it was not quite extinct) while Christian missionaries flourished. The result was a bitter struggle, which has left its mark in the centuries in which the church was victorious."[21]

Until this point, the pressure for separation of the two communi-ties had come from the Jewish side. But those Jews who believed in Jesus sought to remain within the synagogue, or at the very least, under the re-ligious umbrella of Judaism. The *Birkat ha-Minim*—whatever its pur-pose and direction—had not been fully successful in rooting these believers out of the synagogue. They still had hope that their fellow Jews would believe in the messiahship and resurrection of Jesus as they did. But the Second Jewish Revolt forced Jewish Christians to separate them-selves from those associated with Bar Kokhba's cause. The impetus for dissociation and detachment came from them and no longer from the other side.

## The Parting of the Way

Although a few Jewish Christians apparently still attended synagogue in Jerome's day (ca. A.D. 400),[22] the parting of the way seems to have been largely finalized by around the middle of the second century. By the time of Justin Martyr (ca. A.D. 160) a new attitude prevailed in the Church, evi-denced by its appropriating the title "Israel" for itself.[23] Until this time the Church had defined itself more in terms of continuity with the Jewish people; that is, it was an extension of Israel. There was a growing aware-

---

21. Haim Hillel Ben-Sasson, "History," in *Encyclopedia Judaica*, 8:647.

22. Jerome and Epiphanius (both late fourth-century Christian writers) state that the "Nazoreans" are cursed by Jews in their synagogues; cf. David Flusser, "The Jewish-Christian Schism (Part II)," *Immanuel* 17 (Winter, 1983-84): 33; note also Gedaliah Alon, *Jews in Their Land*, 1:289.

23. Richardson, *Israel in the Apostolic Church*, p. 1. Richardson concludes further, "the war of A.D. 132-5 did what the Synagogue Ban did not: to all intents and purposes it severed the two groups, freeing later Christians from the need to assert close contact with Judaism and providing for them evidence of the full 'judgment' of God upon Israel. From this point, Christians polemize more consistently" (p. 203).

ness, however, that the Synagogue was firm in its stance that Jesus was not the Messiah of Israel, and that on this point the Synagogue was not going to change its mind. The realization of this impasse gradually drew the Church to define itself in terms of discontinuity with—indeed, as the replacement of—Israel. To this point not only had Jewish Christians considered themselves part of the national body of Israel, but so too had gentile believers. They saw themselves as grafted into Israel, as part of a believing remnant within Israel, not those who had usurped the place of Israel, not as a separate people independent of Israel. Therefore, as long as the Church had a reasonable balance of Jews and Gentiles in the same body, there was no tendency to take over the term *Israel*. But by Justin's time that balance had been lost.

Though the break between Synagogue and Church had now essentially been made, the struggle between the two was far from over. A triumphalistic and arrogant Church, largely gentile in makeup, would now become more and more de-Judaized—severed from its Jewish roots. This de-Judaizing developed into a history of anti-Judaism, a travesty which has extended from the second century to the present day. This disquieting story of the Church's negation of Judaism and the Jewish people will be the theme of our next chapter.

# UNDERSTANDING CHAPTER SIX

1. The city of Jerusalem was taken in 63 B.C. and Roman rule was established over the land. Who was the leader of this conquest?

2. What emperor expelled Jews and Christians from Rome in A.D. 49? Why?

3. According to tradition, what Roman emperor was responsible for the death of Paul?

4. When did the First Jewish Revolt against Rome take place? The Second?

5. What Roman leader began an attack on Galilee only to be confronted there by Jewish forces led by Josephus?

6. Who was Titus and what does the famous Arch of Titus commemorate?

7. Describe the fall of Masada. What action on the part of the Jewish resistance makes this one of the most remarkable events of Jewish history? Explain the importance of the following terms: (a) Tenth Roman Legion, (b) Zealots, (c) Herod the Great, (d) ramp, (e) Josephus.

8. Before Jerusalem fell, who fled from there to Pella? Locate Pella. Pella became an important center for early Jewish Christianity. Give two important reasons why the flight to Pella marks an important juncture in the growing breach between Synagogue and Church.

9. How did Jewish Christians use the fall of Jerusalem in their polemic against the Synagogue?

10. In the decades immediately after the fall of Jerusalem, is there any evidence that Jews continued to assume positions of leadership in the Jerusalem church?

11. How did the fall of Jerusalem influence the future of the various sects within the Jewish community? What two Jewish sects remained in major contention?

12. After the year 70, what group was responsible for an intensive restructuring of Judaism? Where did this take place? Following the destruction of the Temple, in what ways were the rituals of the Temple reformulated by transference?

13. Who was the founder and first head of the academy at Yavneh? Briefly summarize at least six specific areas in which the academy at Yavneh brought new direction, innovation, or revision as it sought to effect a reformulation to Judaism.

14. About a century after Yavneh, what rabbi was responsible for compiling the Mishnah?

15. How does the use of the term *rabbi* in the New Testament differ from its use in relation to the disciples of Johanan ben Zakkai in the period of Yavneh?

16. How did the death of the major apostles influence the growing separation between Synagogue and Church, especially in cities like Antioch and Rome?

17. Name two sources from the early second century that indicate that the Church had already begun to worship on the Lord's Day (Sunday).

18. Why did the eventual move to Sunday worship make it exceedingly difficult—if not virtually impossible—for the Jew to give any serious consideration to the Christian message, or even to enter into Christian-Jewish dialogue without suspicion?

19. What hints are there in the New Testament that the Sabbath commandment may have been considered part of the ceremonial law, and as such not a sine qua non for Church unity?

20. It is likely that early Christians may at first have met both on the Sabbath and on the first day of the week. According to the Jewish reckoning of time, when did the Sabbath end and when did Sunday begin? What is the function of the Habdalah ceremony?

21. Describe the Second Jewish Revolt. Be able to identify the significance of the following: (a) Bar Kokhba, (b) Rabbi Akiba, (c) "A star will come out of Jacob," (d) Julius Severus, (e) Hadrian, (f) Aelia Capitolina, (g) Temple to Jupiter, (h) archeological light shed on the revolt.

22. What two main factors related to the revolt created a significant wedge between Jewish Christians and other Jews?

23. Until this point (A.D. 132-135), pressure for separation of the two communities had come from the Jewish side. Now, however, the impetus for dissociation and detachment begins to come from Jewish Christians. Why had Jewish Christians been determined to maintain synagogue ties to this point? Why did the Second Jewish Revolt force them to rethink this issue?

24. By what date had the parting of the way between Synagogue and Church largely become finalized? What does the use of the term *Israel* in the writings of Justin Martyr and later Church Fathers indicate about the separation of the two bodies? Explain how this position regarding Israel differs from that of the earliest days of the Church (cf. Rom. 11).

25. Review the main developments between the middle of the first century and the middle of the second that had a major impact on the parting of the way between Christians and Jews.

# Chapter Seven

## A History of Contempt:
## Anti-Semitism and the Church

*I will make those who are of the synagogue of Satan, who claim
to be Jews though they are not, but are liars—I will make them
come and fall down at your feet*

Revelation 3:9

In the last four chapters we have traced the major historical, political, and religious factors that led to the separation of Church and Synagogue by the middle of the second century. We observed that Jesus and his followers and the believers of the earliest Church found their identity as *part of* Judaism. But by the time of Justin Martyr (ca. A.D. 160), the Church defined itself *apart from*, that is, in place of, Judaism. The present chapter will conclude our five-part diachronic study of the relation between Church and Synagogue. Its range will be broad: from the Church Fathers to modern times.

As a preface to our discussion of the consequences of the split, let us first briefly summarize some of the more important aspects of our findings to this point. We observed that a number of critical developments brought the tension that had been mounting for more than a century to a decisive breaking point. First there were theological differences centering on the teachings of Jesus, particularly on the question of his messiahship. Despite shouts of "Hosanna!" (Hebrew for "Save—please!") and "Blessed is the King of Israel" (John 12:13), sword had not become sickle, for the land yet writhed under Roman oppression. By presenting himself as a "new Torah," Jesus did not meet the expectation of the masses. For them he did not embody or represent the hope of Israel.

Second, the Church was successful in reaching out to Gentiles, and this success led to the landmark ruling of the Jerusalem Council. That decision, about A.D. 49, released gentile converts from the necessity of circumcision and adherence to the Law of Moses. By championing the cause of gentile freedom from Jewish rituals and regulations, Paul and the apostolic leaders had opened a door that allowed for a rapid transition to a reconstituted community. This change created a new challenge, for Jews and Gentiles immediately had difficulty learning to live harmoniously within the same body rather than forming separate communities. The move from worship on the Sabbath to the Lord's Day is but one important example of change which the Church faced at this time.

Third, as particularly chronicled in the book of Acts, the persecution of Jewish Christians was a factor in the split. The growing antagonism between both bodies also resulted in a specific effort to root out from the synagogue all *minim* ("heretics"). Thus all who deviated—both Jews and Jewish Christians—from Pharisaic norms were no longer welcome within the community. This action was an attempt to enforce a particular definition of Jewish purity with the thought of preservation and survival.

Fourth, in the two Jewish Revolts against Rome (A.D. 66-73 and 132-135) Jewish Christians refused to fight, thus compromising their allegiance to the Jewish community and their identity with the Jewish state. From the other side, the Jewish support of the messianic claimant, Bar Kokhba, nailed shut the door of lingering hope that Jewish Christians had for a change in the majority's convictions. Further, the destruction of Jerusalem and the disappearance of all major sects but the Pharisees forced a reformulation of Judaism. At Yavneh, through the work of the Pharisees, a new Judaism gradually emerged. Rabbinic Judaism, as it came to be called, was a separate religion from Christianity that considered all Jewish Christians personae non gratae in relation to the synagogue. Thus, what had begun as an inner-Jewish dispute, or an intrafamily debate, developed into a permanent breach. It was now "a rivalry between the religions of the synagogue and of the Church."[1]

## The "New" Israel Emerges

Paul's warning to gentile believers about pride (see Rom. 11:17-24) went unheeded. The Church had become overwhelmingly gentile, so it reasoned that there was no more need for the support of the root (Israel).

---

1. Otto A. Piper, "Church and Judaism in Holy History," *Theology Today* 18 (1961): 65.

What presumption! At first, the Gentiles were but a rejected wild olive branch allowed by God's mercy to be grafted into the believing family of Abraham. But in the second, third, and fourth centuries a new spirit of arrogance and supersessionism had arisen. Paul never anticipated that things would develop this far. He insisted that God did not reject his people, for "God's gifts and his call are irrevocable" (Rom. 11:29; cf. v. 1). Yet Gentiles claimed to have replaced Israel. As the "new" Israel, the gentile church spiritually expropriated what had belonged to Israel. Though some of this spiritualizing interpretation begins in certain passages of the New Testament, it becomes fully developed in the writings of early Church Fathers.

At first the Church was a remnant within Israel, participating in new-covenant life inside a renewed "Israel of God." Of this Jewish *haburah* (religious brotherhood), Gentiles had no part. For when the Church began, Gentiles were described as those "who do not know God" (1 Thess. 4:5). But now, those formerly outside the covenant had displaced those physical sons of Abraham who had given them spiritual birth. This displacement resulted in many institutions and concepts of Israel being de-Judaized or Hellenized by the gentile church. In his *Dialogue with Trypho, A Jew,* Justin Martyr emphasized that what was of old and had belonged to Israel was now the property of Christians. The Jewish Scriptures were a central part of this transference. They are "not yours but ours," Justin stated emphatically to Trypho.[2]

The tearing away from Jewish roots resulted in the Church defining itself largely in non-Jewish terminology. The word *Christianity,* derived from a Greek rendering *(Christós)* of the Hebrew *mashiah,* meaning "Messiah," is representative of this process. Dom Gregory Dix has called attention to some of the other significant changes: "'The Living God' became 'the God and Father of our Lord Jesus' and ultimately 'God the Father.' 'The Messiah Jeshua' became 'Jesus Christ the Son of God' and, ultimately, 'God the Son.' The 'New-Covenant-life' became 'the Spirit' and 'the Paraclete' and, ultimately, 'God the Holy Ghost.' The 'New Covenant' became 'the Atonement.' 'The Nazarenes' became 'the Christians.' The 'Scriptures' became 'the Old Testament.' The 'Israel of God' became 'the Holy Church.'"[3] In addition, the memorial feast of the Last Supper came to be known as the "Eucharist." Furthermore, the Church came to refer to the Scriptures with new terminology: "The Torah" became

---

2. Justin Martyr, *Dialogue with Trypho, A Jew* 29.2.
3. Dom Gregory Dix, *Jew And Greek: A Study in the Primitive Church* (London: Dacre Press, 1953), p. 109.

"the Pentateuch," "Tehillim" (Psalms) became "the Psalter," and Greek names such as Genesis and Exodus also gradually replaced their Hebrew counterparts. The origin and development of the word *Bible* is also Greek. The term derived from the port of Gebal (Greek *Byblos*) in Phoenicia where papyrus was imported as writing material.

Paul spent much of his life in the Hellenistic world where the majority of Jews were dispersed. But apparently he had considerable misgivings about those whose philosophy centered solely on the wisdom of the Greek world. Accordingly, he expounded to the Corinthians what he found as a new and better worldview. To know "Christ crucified," argued Paul to both Jews and Greeks, was to know "the wisdom of God" (see 1 Cor. 1:18-25). Yet, by the middle of the second century, "Christianity ultimately accepted and used Greek philosophy."[4] As the "new" Israel sought to gain a hearing for the gospel among Gentiles, the Church moved, as it were, further from Mount Sinai and closer to Mars Hill.

Justin Martyr had been influenced by Platonic thought before his conversion.[5] After he became a Christian, Justin brought many of Plato's ideas into his teaching. As the Hebrew Scriptures were used to bring Jews to Christ, Justin used Platonic thought to reach Greeks. In the following century, Clement and others from Alexandria would place even greater emphasis upon reading the Bible through Platonic eyes. One of the results was that third-century Christians began to view the physical world of flesh and matter as evil. The perpetuation of this view throughout the centuries would have dire consequences for the Church, especially in the understanding of such areas as salvation, spirituality, marriage, and the family. Since Platonism and Gnosticism have had such a profound effect upon the thinking of the Church, we will treat these and other related themes in more detail later in this volume.

## From De-Judaizing to Anti-Judaism

From the biblical period to the present day one would be hard-pressed to find a single century in which the Church has not in some significant way

4. See Samuel Sandmel, *Judaism and Christian Beginnings* (New York: Oxford University Press, 1978), p. 410. Thorleif Boman confirms Sandmel's observation by stating that "it is not accidental that during the first five foundation-laying centuries of the Christian Church, Plato was its philosophical authority" (*Hebrew Thought Compared with Greek,* trans. Jules L. Moreau [repr. New York: W. W. Norton & Co., 1970], p. 53).

5. For a discussion of the influence of Plato upon early Christian thought see Ranald Macauley and Jerram Barrs, *Being Human: The Nature of Spiritual Experience* (Downers Grove: InterVarsity Press, 1978), pp. 42ff.

contributed to the anguish of the Jewish people. Sadly, both anti-Judaism and anti-Semitism have occupied a major portion of Jewish history. In this connection, Stuart Rosenberg has perceptively observed, "Antisemitism and anti-Judaism, history teaches, feed upon each other; they are twin phenomena."[6] The point is that Christian hostility to Judaism has also usually brought in its wake hostility to Jews. The two are so intimately connected that they are often inseparable. The term *anti-Semitism,* however, was not introduced until 1879, by Wilhelm Marr, a German political agitator. At that time it designated anti-Jewish campaigns in Europe. But soon it came to be applied to the hostility and hatred directed toward Jews since before the Christian era. One must observe, however, that Jews of the ancient world did not experience anti-Semitism in exactly the same way in which the word has been often defined in the modern world. For example, as Shaye Cohen has pointed out, the Germans at the time of Marr considered Jews to be a different species or "race" than they, whereas the ancients held no similar racial theory. Also, the social and economic tensions in Europe during the nineteenth and twentieth centuries that produced waves of anti-Semitism find no parallels in antiquity. Indeed, no text from the ancient world states or implies that people hated Jews for their economic power.[7] Hence, "anti-Judaism" is sometimes considered a more accurate term to describe this hostility during the ancient period.[8]

The topic of anti-Semitism is never far from the collective conscience of world Jewry since this seemingly ubiquitous evil continues to exist. In today's Church, the often sordid and self-indicting story of animosity, enmity, and strife directed by Christians toward Jews remains generally untold. Perhaps this is the case because the history of the Church is about as long as the history of the evils directed toward Jews—if not in the overt acts of Christians, certainly in their guilty silence.[9]

Portions of the New Testament and other early Christian literature contain rather striking anti-Jewish rhetoric. It is crucial, however, to make an important distinction about these polemical outbursts against Jews and Judaism. In the New Testament the *adversus Judaeos* polemic was "an intra-family device used to win Jews to the Christian faith, in the second

---

6. Stuart E. Rosenberg, *The Christian Problem: A Jewish View* (New York: Hippocrene Books, 1986), p. 11.

7. Shaye J. D. Cohen, *From the Maccabees to the Mishnah* (Philadelphia: Westminster Press, 1987), pp. 47-48.

8. See ibid., pp. 48-49.

9. This point has been strikingly documented in the comprehensive study of Edward H. Flannery, *The Anguish of the Jews: Twenty-three Centuries of Antisemitism,* rev. ed. (Mahwah, NJ: Paulist Press, 1985).

century it became anti-Semitic and was used to win Gentiles."[10] In the first case it was directed mainly by Jews against Jews, and in the second mainly by Gentiles against Jews.

The attacks in the New Testament sound harsh, for these were Jews speaking to other Jews about very visceral and, to be sure, revolutionary issues. Traditional Jews did not believe that the Messiah had come. The followers of the Nazarene did believe it. Hence each group fired bitter accusations against the other. In Matthew 23 Jesus is roundly critical of the Pharisees; but he himself was likely representative of the same Jewish sect. He calls them "hypocrites" (v. 15), "blind guides" (v. 16), "blind fools" (v. 17), and "snakes" (v. 33), and he compares them to "whitewashed tombs" (v. 27). In another context Jesus rebukes his fleshly kinsmen by saying, "You belong to your father, the devil" (John 8:44). Paul writes to the Thessalonians about "the Jews" who "drove us out. They displease God and are hostile to all men" (1 Thess. 2:15). John writes to the church at Smyrna about Jews who are "a synagogue of Satan" (Rev. 2:9).

It is one thing to read the above inflammatory language in the context of the first-century intramural Jewish debate. It is another thing, however, to take this stinging rhetoric—as the Church has done tragically over the centuries—and use it to promote the condemnation of Jews and the negation of all that is Jewish. The latter type of anti-Judaism, very prevalent in the gentile Christian writings of the early Church Fathers, will be our next focus.

## The Early Fathers: Blaming the Victims

By the middle of the second century the writings of the Church Fathers reveal considerable antagonism between gentile Christians and Jews. The Letter of Barnabas and the works of Ignatius of Antioch and of Justin Martyr are particularly worthy of note.

The posture of the Church was decisively set *against* the Synagogue. Whereas one gentile nation after another had responded positively to the Christian missionary outreach, the Synagogue continued to cling stubbornly to its ancestral faith, leaving the Church increasingly frustrated and embittered. Sermons, dialogues, diatribes, and polemics became the order of the day. The Church sought to conquer its opponent by demonstrating with every possible evidence that Judaism was a dead and legalistic faith. Thereby the schism became greater as Jews increasingly became victims

---

10. Richard N. Longenecker, *New Testament Social Ethics for Today* (Grand Rapids: William B. Eerdmans Publishing Co., 1984), p. 40.

of discrimination and contempt at the hands of those whose faith was said to have superseded theirs. Adding a further wedge between the two communities was the fact that in many locations throughout the Mediterranean world Jews separated themselves from Christians by living in their own neighborhoods and also by adopting their own customs in matters such as eating, dressing, and burial.

The two thwarted Jewish Revolts against Rome provided the gentile Church with an ideological leverage that it applied immediately. The overthrow of the Jewish nation—especially the fall of Jerusalem and destruction of the Temple—by gentile armies was seen as chastisement, proof that God had rejected his once chosen people. The crushing defeat of the nation provided ammunition for apologists who now insisted that the Church was the authentic Israel of God. The death, exile, or slavery of thousands of Jews allowed for further arguments against Judaism. In the Roman empire Judaism lost its status as a *religio licita* ("legal religion"), a lawful exception to the cult of emperor-worship. No Jew was allowed to come near the city of Jerusalem. The *Pax Romana* would not be denied. Forever cast away, Jews were now condemned to wander among the so-called Christian nations, those new inheritors of the covenant promises.

The Church also viewed the sack of Jerusalem as punishment of Jews for the crime of crucifying Jesus. Jewish suffering and ostracism were attributed to the ignorance and apostasy of a reprobate people who had put to death the Christ. The theme of "Christ-killer" is accordingly now picked up in the writings of the Church Fathers. Let us note two examples, Justin Martyr and Origen.

Justin Martyr was a converted gentile philosopher who died a martyr in Rome. Justin's second-century *Dialogue with Trypho, A Jew* represents "the prototypical contrast of the Christian protagonist triumphant and the nervous Jew on the defensive."[11] Justin argues his case with Trypho by stating that Jews are separated from other nations and "justly suffer." Justin specifically hammers home his point by focusing on the fact that Jewish cities are "burned with fire" and Jews are "desolate," forbidden to go up to Jerusalem, "for you have slain the Just One, and His prophets before Him; and now you reject those who hope in Him."[12]

In the third century Origen wrote similarly, "And these calamities they [the Jews] have suffered, because they were a most wicked nation,

---

11. Pinchas E. Lapide, *Hebrew in the Church: The Foundations of Jewish-Christian Dialogue,* trans. Erroll F. Rhodes (Grand Rapids: William B. Eerdmans Publishing Co., 1984), p. 21.

12. Justin Martyr, *Dialogue with Trypho* 16.

which, although guilty of many other sins, yet has been punished so severely for none, as for those that were committed against our Jesus."[13] Again, in clear terms, the suffering of the Jewish people is directly related to their "sin" of rejecting Jesus.

Furthermore, the Church Fathers taught that the unfaithfulness of the Jewish people resulted in a collective guilt which made them subject to the permanent curse of God. Accordingly, Church Fathers from the time of Jerome and Augustine (late 4th century) applied the lesson of the barren fig tree (Matt. 21:18-22) to the Jewish people.[14] Jesus had said, "May you never bear fruit again" (v. 19). Thus the Church argued that Jews were a people eternally cursed by God. The Church now designated to itself all blessings in Scripture earlier ascribed to Israel. All curses, however, it left for the Jews.

From a non-Jewish perspective it has often been assumed that the catastrophic fall of Jerusalem and the miserable suffering of the Jewish people spoke in the most dramatic way not only about the identity of God's elect but especially about the vindication of Christian claims made for Jesus. As G. W. H. Lampe correctly observes, however, for Gentiles and Jewish Christians "the decisive event which vindicated Jesus as the Christ, the Lord, the Son of God, was not the destruction of his enemies but his resurrection from the dead."[15]

Most of the Christian literature throughout the second and third centuries reveals more of the same: a general ridicule and contempt for Jews and Judaism. For example, in the Epistle to Diognetus, an exposition of gentile Christianity to Gentiles, the writer calls attention to the Jews' "mutilation of the flesh as a proof of election, as if they were, for this reason, especially beloved of God." He also cites their "general silliness and deceit and fussiness and pride."[16] Other writers from this period reflect the same *adversus Judaeos* tradition.[17] The works of Cyprian *(Three Books of*

13. Origen, *Against Celsus* 2.8.
14. Lapide, *Hebrew in the Church,* p. 3.
15. G. W. H. Lampe, "A.D. 70 in Christian Reflection," in *Jesus and the Politics of His Day,* ed. Ernst Bammel and C. F. D. Moule (Cambridge: Cambridge University Press, 1984), p. 157. In this connection, the reader should note our mention of the significance of the resurrection found above in chapter four.
16. *Epistle to Diognetus* 4.4, 6.
17. For a sequential development of anti-Jewish teaching in the Church, see the outlined account of Terrance Callan, *Forgetting the Root: The Emergence of Christianity From Judaism* (New York: Paulist Press, 1986); and the more thorough work of John C. Gager, *The Origins of Anti-Semitism* (New York: Oxford University Press, 1985). For a useful, well-documented work on the history of anti-Semitism written from the viewpoint of a Christian historian, see David A. Rausch, *A Legacy of Hatred* (Chicago: Moody Press, 1984).

*Testimonies Against the Jews),* Hippolytus *(Expository Treatise Against the Jews),* Tertullian *(Against the Jews),* Irenaeus, and others are among those of special note.

In the fourth century, when Constantine made Christianity the official religion of the Roman empire, Jews experienced a further wave of discrimination and persecution. They lost many of their legal rights; they were not permitted to dwell in Jerusalem or to seek converts. In 339 it was considered a criminal offense to convert to Judaism. Several decades later the Synod of Laodicea ruled against Christians feasting with Jews, classifying those that did so as heretics. Around 380, Ambrose, bishop of Milan, praised the burning of a synagogue as an act pleasing to God.

Before the end of the century, in Antioch, John Chrysostom (ca. 347-407) unleashed a series of eight *Homilies against the Jews.* Because of his eloquence, John was dubbed *chrysostom,* the "golden-mouthed." The sermons of Chrysostom were primarily intended to keep Gentiles from being drawn to Jewish worship and Law. He attacked Jews vehemently and irrationally, excoriating them on every front. In his homilies Chrysostom, like many of the Fathers before him, emphasized that because "the Jews" killed Christ, God has rejected them, destroying Jerusalem to display his disfavor. But in his First Discourse, his choice of anti-Judaic rhetoric is utterly crude and thoroughly offensive—and all the more so coming from the lips of a presbyter from Antioch, where believers first bore the name "Christian" (Acts 11:26).[18] A selected sample from this most Judaeophobic Father reads:

> Many, I know, respect the Jews and think that their present way of life is a venerable one. This is why I hasten to uproot and tear out this deadly opinion . . . the synagogue is not only a brothel and a theatre; it also is a den of robbers and a lodging for wild beasts . . . when God forsakes a people, what hope of salvation is left? When God forsakes a place, that place becomes the dwelling of demons. . . . The Jews live for their bellies, they gape for the things of this world, their condition is no better than that of pigs or goats because of their wanton ways and excessive gluttony. They know but one thing: to fill their bellies and be drunk.[19]

Throughout the centuries such vilifying of the Jewish people has not been confined to sermons like that of Chrysostom. It has also been perpet-

---

18. See the superb study of D. S. Wallace-Hadrill, *Christian Antioch: A Study of Early Christian Thought in the East* (Cambridge: Cambridge University Press, 1982).

19. John Chrysostom, *Adversus Iudaeos* 1.3.1; 1.4.1. Translation from *The Fathers of the Church: Saint John Chrysostom,* vol. 68 (Washington, D.C.: The Catholic University of America Press, 1979).

uated through grievous acts of hatred and shame by confessing members of the Christian community—so much as to make the gospel all the more incredible to Jewish ears. Little wonder that the rabbis in the talmudic period sometimes used a pun to refer to the gospel. For Jews, the "gospel" (Greek *euangélion*) became the "wicked scroll" (Hebrew *aven gilyon*).[20]

## Allegory: An Attempt to Rescue the Jewish Scriptures

The early Church Fathers had to solve the problem of what to do with the Old Testament. Their anti-Judaic stance forced them to view the Jewish Scriptures with its many strange laws and customs as offensive at worst and little more than antiquated at best. In addition, the position of the Church was that it had replaced Israel. No longer a remnant within Israel, it had become a separate gentile body. Accordingly, it proudly bore a new role, that of adversary to the parent that had given it birth. For the Church, therefore, to admit any real connection with the Old Testament as a propaedeutic to the gospel would be to grant a measure of legitimacy and historical validity to the Jewish people.[21] Since the Church would not allow such a validation, it was caught in a bind.

Marcion offered one solution. He violently opposed anything Jewish and argued that the Old Testament should be done away with, removed from the canon of the Church. The position of Marcion will be discussed at greater length in our next chapter. It is sufficient for now, however, to state briefly that his position was unacceptable to the Church. Although his solution generally reflected the anti-Judaic attitude of the second-century Church, the Church could not totally cut itself off from the Jewish Scriptures. These Scriptures provided the Church with its raison d'être. The Church had superseded Israel, and the Old Testament was the descriptive document that defined the inheritance to which this "new" Israel laid claim. Furthermore, to eliminate the Old Testament would remove from the Church a major apologetic tool in its controversy with Judaism. In order to support the messianic claims of Jesus the Church adduced before its Jewish opponents hundreds of Old Testament prophetic texts. So the Church needed to save the Old Testament from total destruction and accordingly rejected Marcion's extreme position. Instead, it found an alternative solution—allegory.

20. See Sandmel, *Judaism and Christian Beginnings*, p. 397; Lapide, *Hebrew in the Church*, pp. 32, 51, 52, 185.
21. Longenecker, *New Testament Social Ethics*, p. 42.

In allegory, the Old Testament could be made a "Christian" document. Through their efforts to spiritualize, typologize, and christologize the text, the early Church Fathers were able to find abundant Christian meaning in the Old Testament. Christ, or New Testament thought, was read *into,* rather than *out of,* the biblical text in some of the most obscure places. Accordingly, Irenaeus, Origen, Augustine, and others developed a system of allegorical exegesis that had the disastrous effect of wrenching the biblical text from its plain historical meaning. During the Reformation, Luther denounced Origen's allegories and called allegory "the scum on Scripture," "a monkey-game," and a "nose of wax" (i.e., something which can be bent any way desired).[22]

The transferring of the Jewish Scriptures to the "new" Israel meant clothing them in Christian dress. For example, the sacrifices of the Old Testament became bread and wine; the twelve bells on the robe of the priest now signified the twelve disciples.[23] In the allegory of early Christian literature different levels of meaning may sometimes be distinguished, such as moral, spiritual, and eschatological. But the christological meaning is especially common. For instance, patristic hermeneutics widely interpreted the scarlet cord of Rahab (Josh. 2:17-21) as salvation through the blood of Christ; and in the account of the flood (Gen. 6–8), Noah symbolizes Christ and the ark the Church.[24]

As we shall point out in chapter eight below, the history of biblical interpretation proves that at best allegorical exegesis is both suspect and risky. The exegetical integrity of the text is surrendered to the wasteland of subjectivity. The authorial intent of the passage stands in jeopardy of being compromised or entirely lost if mystical, figurative, or hidden meanings are thought to burst forth from the text without some criteria of control. That control of a passage is normally achieved when attention is given to the plain meaning of words in context (the immediate context and that of the rest of Scripture) within the specific historical and cultural setting. Though the New Testament authors view all of the Old Testament Scriptures as having their deepest meaning in Christ, and these authors use these texts—to us sometimes in very puzzling and abstruse ways—in the New Testament to argue this point, they were divinely inspired to make these textual connections. But for us (including the Church Fathers) to assume

---

22. See John Bright, *The Authority of the Old Testament* (repr. Grand Rapids: Baker Book House, 1975), p. 82.

23. For these and other examples from the writings of Justin Martyr see Peter Richardson, *Israel in the Apostolic Church* (Cambridge: Cambridge University Press, 1969), pp. 10, 28, 30.

24. Bright, *Authority of the Old Testament,* p. 81.

that we can interpret the Old Testament in exactly the same way is presumptuous.

Vapidity of meaning may not be the only loss sustained by a hermeneutic which focuses primarily on spiritualizing the biblical text. There may be implications for the issue of anti-Semitism as well. In this connection Harold O. J. Brown has observed that "Christians have tended to be more hostile to the unconverted Jews of their day as they tended to spiritualize the biblical doctrine of the millennium and advocate an otherworldly, ascetic approach to discipleship."[25] Brown's point that the Church—especially since Augustine (ca. 400)—tends toward amillennialism, a tendency accompanied by an increasing disdain for Jewish people, is worthy of further reflection. We will address the question of otherworldliness versus this-worldliness at greater length in chapter ten.

## Anti-Semitism in the Middle Ages

In the Middle Ages, Christian culture largely excluded Jews. Jews sought to avoid social, economic, and ecclesiastical pressures by living in secluded quarters of cities. They were considered useful primarily for one purpose, money-lending. This isolation from the larger society led Christians to accuse Jews of being a pariah people. Stripped of many personal liberties and victimized by an elitist "Christian" culture, Jews were required to wear a distinctive hat or patch sewn on their clothing. The very idea of "Hebraic" was commonly equated with "satanic."[26]

Jews experienced a barrage of accusations. They were said to have had a peculiar smell, in contrast to the "odor of sanctity." Jews were also said to be sucklers of sows. They were held responsible for many evils, the "Christ-killer" charge still prominent. Jews were also called desecraters of the Host, allegedly entering churches secretly and piercing the holy wafer out of which the "real blood" of Jesus flowed. They were accused of murdering Christian infants in order to use their blood (instead of wine) at the Passover Seder. During the Black Plague, which killed one-third of Europe's population, Jews were blamed for causing the plague by poisoning wells.

The Church launched the First Crusade in 1096. Pope Urban II called for soldiers of Christ to liberate the Holy Land from the Muslim invaders. On the way, however, the "infidel" Jews suffered gravely at the hands of

---

25. Harold O. J. Brown, "Christians and Jews—Bound Together," *Christianity Today* (August 18, 1978): 18.
26. Lapide, *Hebrew in the Church*, p. 3.

the Crusaders. Thousands of Jews who had refused baptism were murdered in the streets. Numerous mass suicides also occurred. Synagogues were torched. But with all this persecution, most Jews steadfastly refused attempts at conversion.

During the twelfth and thirteenth centuries, especially in France, Germany, and England, Christian art and sculpture represents the Jews as humbled and downcast rather than proud and upright. Of particular note is the artwork depicting two female figures, Ecclesia and Synagoga, symbolizing the triumphant Church and the defeated Synagogue. Ecclesia is often portrayed as graceful and crowned, with staff in hand. Synagoga, however, is often represented as blindfolded, with broken staff, and sometimes decorated with broken tablets of the Law. Ecclesia and Synagoga are often located on the exterior of cathedrals as stone figures or statues, and elsewhere are depicted on such items as medieval manuscripts, missals, stained-glass windows, and baptismal fonts.[27]

As the Middle Ages drew to a close, Jews experienced many additional indignities and forms of persecution. During the thirteenth century, holy books were seized and burned by cartloads. In Spain, a church council ruled that if a Jew tried to convert a Christian he was to be killed and his property seized. Jews were forbidden to eat with or talk to Christians. They became homeless wanderers, expelled from England in 1290, from France in 1306, and subsequently from cities in Spain, Germany, and Austria.

The Inquisition and expulsion of 1492 resulted in thousands of torturings, burnings at the stake, and forced conversions. Jews were ordered to leave Spain or face death. Many Jews converted to Catholicism in public, but remained Jews in private. These Jews were known as Marranos. More than 150,000 others fled Spain, but they were not allowed to settle in western Europe. Eventually, however, these refugees made their way to North Africa, Morocco, and eastern Mediterranean lands.

## From Luther to the Present

Martin Luther made a decisive break with the Catholic Church. The issues most central to this German Reformer included faith and works, Scripture and tradition, and the priesthood of believers. But these issues did not constitute Luther's total theological agenda. Toward the start of his influen-

---

27. For illustrations and discussion of Ecclesia and Synagoga see Binyamin Eliav, "Anti-Semitism," in *Encyclopedia Judaica* (Jerusalem: Keter Publishing House, 1971), 3:91-94; also Helen Rosenau, "Ecclesia et Synagoga," *Encyclopedia Judaica*, 6:346-49.

tial career he expressed hope of reaching the Jewish community with the Christian gospel. In 1523 he issued a tract, *That Jesus Christ Was Born a Jew*, which affirmed the Jewish descent of Jesus. Luther pointed out that early missionary outreach to Jews failed not because of evil or obstinacy on the part of Jews but because of the "wicked and shameless" life of popes, priests, and scholars.

However well-meant or kindly intentioned Luther's attitude was at the start, he changed. When he saw that Jews failed to respond to the Christian message, he became hostile toward them. He issued a series of vitriolic pamphlets, including *On the Jews and Their Lies* (1543). In these bitter diatribes he labeled Jews as "venomous," "thieves," and "disgusting vermin." Furthermore, Luther called for Jews to be permanently driven out of the country. Appealing to this and other anti-Semitic doctrine, four centuries later the Nazis carried out Luther's desire with horrifying success. Fortunately, in recent years, the efforts of both Jewish and Lutheran leaders have considerably improved interfaith relations.

Toward the start of the modern age a bloody revolt against the Cossacks occurred in Poland (1648-58). Caught in the middle, several hundred thousand Jews were killed or enslaved. In other European countries at the time, Jews continued to be persecuted or, at best, viewed with suspicion or contempt. Many Jews chose baptism in these lands as an escape from persecution. In the nineteenth century, Heinrich Heine, who had followed this route, contemptuously observed that the act of his baptism was "an entrance-ticket to European Society."[28]

In the later part of the nineteenth century the largest Jewish population in the world (six million) was in czarist Russia. There Jews experienced a series of vicious pogroms which left thousands dead. Those who survived joined Jews from different European lands in fleeing to America. There they hoped to find a place, as George Washington earlier described, that offered "to bigotry no sanction, to persecution no assistance." Between 1880 and 1910 more than two million Jews immigrated to America through New York City. The year 1894 marked the celebrated Dreyfus trial in France. Alfred Dreyfus, a Jew serving in the French military, was falsely accused of giving secret documents to the Germans. Convicted of being a traitor, then imprisoned, Dreyfus was eventually exonerated. This sensational episode drew the problem of anti-Semitism to world attention.

Rooted in the soil of Germany, the Holocaust of the twentieth century stands as an unparalleled event. Nazi propaganda stated that the human race must be "purified" by ridding it of Jews. The "final solution"

28. Paul Johnson, *A History of the Jews* (New York: Harper & Row, 1987), p. 312.

to the Jewish "problem" was camps, gas chambers, and crematoria. Between 1933, when Hitler came to power, and 1945, the end of World War II, some six million Jewish lives were destroyed. It is to the shame of Christians everywhere that the established Church did so little to prevent or protest the slaughter.

Today in Jerusalem the Yad Vashem (literally "hand [i.e., monument] and name"; the name is taken from Isa. 56:5) stands as a memorial to Jewish people who died as victims of the Nazis and their collaborators. The Yad Vashem contains a museum, library, research center, synagogue, and a Hall of Remembrance which lists the names of those who perished. Room after room of this Holocaust memorial provides detailed documentation of the life and death of European Jewry under Nazism. Outside the Yad Vashem is a tree-lined walk called the "Avenue of the Just" (i.e., the righteous Gentiles) commemorating the few non-Jews who courageously risked their lives to save Jews. Here one will find trees planted in honor of Raoul Wallenberg, Corrie ten Boom, and others.

At present, anti-Semitism persists wherever Jews are found. Jews of Russia and France have been especially oppressed. In European countries and in the United States recent anti-Jewish incidents have included synagogue smearings and bombings, desecration of gravestones, vicious graffiti, Nazi pamphlets, and grotesque Jewish stereotypes in the press. At other times the so-called polite variety of anti-Semitism is found, namely, discrimination or antipathy displayed toward Jews in the social, educational, and economic realms.

In this chapter we have covered all too briefly nearly two millennia of the "history of contempt." We must emphasize in conclusion that the Holocaust did not happen in a vacuum. Though it was devised in a country with an enviable reputation for brilliant culture and intellectual sophistication, the seeds of anti-Semitism had been planted much earlier. The Holocaust represents the tragic culmination of anti-Jewish attitudes and practices which had been allowed to manifest themselves—largely unchecked —in or nearby the Church for nearly two thousand years. Perhaps the most important reason the Holocaust happened is that the Church had forgotten its Jewish roots.


## UNDERSTANDING CHAPTER SEVEN

1. From the previous four chapters, be able to summarize the critical developments that led to the breach between Synagogue and Church.

2. Define what is meant by the expression *new Israel*. Is this expression

found in the New Testament? In your opinion, has the teaching that the Church has replaced or superseded Israel (rather than being a remnant within Israel, i.e., "grafted" into Israel) contributed in any significant way to the history of contempt between Church and Synagogue?

3. *Christianity,* a word derived from a Greek term, is linked in meaning to what Hebrew term in Scripture?

4. What is the origin and development of the word *Bible*?

5. What ancient, nonbiblical source influenced Justin Martyr's teaching of the Bible and overall perspective on the Christian faith?

6. Explain the difference between anti-Judaism and anti-Semitism. Why are these terms so intimately connected that they are often inseparable? Identify Wilhelm Marr. Did Jews of the ancient world experience anti-Semitism? Explain.

7. In general, what important distinction may be made concerning the polemical outbursts against Jews and Judaism of the first century (New Testament times) as compared with the second century?

8. Cite at least five phrases from the New Testament that illustrate harsh or inflammatory language directed toward Jews. When heard and interpreted in their first-century Jewish milieu, is it proper to label these words "anti-Judaic" or "anti-Semitic"? In short, is the teaching of contempt for Jews and Judaism inextricably and unavoidably tied to the New Testament? Discuss.

9. How do the writings of the early Church Fathers theologically interpret the overthrow of the Jewish nation? In particular, how do they interpret the fall of Jerusalem, the destruction of the Temple, and the death, exile, or slavery of thousands of Jews?

10. What is the specific sin that Justin Martyr and Origen single out and attribute to the calamities and suffering of the Jewish people?

11. According to G. W. H. Lampe, the fall of Jerusalem and miserable suffering of Jews were important facts in the Church's polemic against the Jewish people. But what does Lampe say was the most decisive event that the early Church used to vindicate Christian claims made for Jesus?

12. In the fourth century, who made Christianity the official religion of the Roman empire? Name two prohibitions imposed on Jewish people at this time.

13. At the end of the fourth century, who was the "golden-mouthed" presbyter from Antioch famous for his series of eight *Homilies against the Jews*? What terms does he use to describe the synagogue? What place, if any, should exposure to vilifying rhetoric such as this have in the educational curriculum of today's Church?

14. Because of the disputations and hostility brought by Christians against Jews over the gospel, in the talmudic period the rabbis developed a Hebrew pun to refer to the Greek term for "gospel." What is the English meaning of the Hebrew pun?

15. Why did the early Church Fathers consider the Old Testament to be a problem? Describe both sides of this tension facing the Church. What solution did the early Fathers use to find abundant Christian meaning in the Old Testament?

16. Give several Old Testament examples of allegorical or christological interpretation found in early Christian literature.

17. Over the centuries, what weaknesses or limitations have demonstrated that allegorical exegesis of the Old Testament is indeed suspect and risky business?

18. During the Middle Ages, Jews experienced a barrage of accusations. Explain what was implied by or was thought to lie behind each of the following charges: (a) "Christ-killers," (b) desecraters of the Host, (c) murderers of Christian infants, (d) poisoners of wells.

19. In what year was the First Crusade launched? What was the aim of the Crusaders? What impact did the Crusaders have upon the Jews of Europe? Discuss the difference between a forced conversion and one brought about through sincere search and personal choice.

20. In the artwork of the Middle Ages, what is meant by Ecclesia and Synagoga? Describe how the artists depicted Ecclesia and Synagoga. How are these two figures important to any study of the history of anti-Semitism?

21. In 1492, in what European country were Jewish people faced with the Inquisition and expulsion? Who are the Marranos?

22. At the start of Martin Luther's life as a reformer, what was his attitude toward the Jewish community? Why did his attitude change? (Note the titles of two of his works which illustrate this shift.) Discuss Martin Luther as a useful example for study by those engaged in interfaith relations. Discuss specifically the importance of learning to accept those of another faith tradition for the reality of what they are rather than for the ideal that one may long for them to become.

23. What act did Heinrich Heine once contemptuously state was his "entrance-ticket to European society"?

24. Toward the end of the nineteenth century, which country had the largest Jewish population? Pogroms soon began to destroy this population. Check a dictionary for the definition of *pogrom*.

25. What was the period during which the largest wave of Jewish immigration came to America?

26. Which president of the United States proclaimed to the Jewish community of Newport, Rhode Island, that America is a place offering "to bigotry no sanction, to persecution no assistance"?

27. Who was Alfred Dreyfus? In what way did the episode surrounding his life become a "shot heard round the world"?

28. In relation to the Holocaust, what is meant by the term *final solution*? What is the Yad Vashem? What is the "Avenue of the Just"?

29. Describe some of the more commonly found present-day examples of anti-Semitic activity. Apart from the countries of the Middle East, where anti-Semitism has persisted, where else in the world have Jewish people been especially oppressed?

30. In the light of two millennia of the "history of contempt," what seems to be the most important reason that the Holocaust was allowed to happen? Discuss this and other reasons.

*Part III*

---

# Understanding Hebrew Thought

## Chapter Eight

# The Old Testament:
# Hebraic Foundation of the Church

*From infancy you have known the holy Scriptures, which are
able to make you wise for salvation through faith in Christ Jesus*

2 Timothy 3:15

The bedrock upon which New Testament faith rests securely is the Hebrew Bible. Christians more commonly refer to it as the "Old Testament,"
and Jews the *Tenakh* (also spelled *Tenach* and *Tanuk*).[1] It is the chief source
from which our common Judeo-Christian heritage derives.

It was certainly an unfortunate day for the Church when the Jewish
Scriptures began to be called the "Old Testament." Such a title implies
that this Testament is now passé. Indeed, the Church would have been
far better off if it had decided from the outset to use a name such as the
"First" or the "Original" Testament. As we shall soon emphasize, neither
Jesus nor the apostles ever declared the first thirty-nine books of Sacred
Scripture dead or abolished, and they must never become so for the
Church.

The value of the Old Testament for the disciplines of biblical stud-

1. The Jewish community usually refers to the Old Testament as the Hebrew Bible,
Jewish Scriptures, Bible, or *Tenakh*. The last term has reference to the threefold division of
the Hebrew Bible, with *T* standing for *Torah* ("Law"), *N* for *Nebi'im* ("Prophets"), and *K*
for *Ketubim* ("Writings"). Judaism has recognized only one covenant. Thus, Jewish people
have frequently considered Christians' reference to the "old" covenant as a misleading or
condescending way of describing the Jewish faith. Throughout this book we have used "Old
Testament" as an accommodation to popular reference, as a tool of convention to facilitate
communication, not in any way intending to demean that part of Holy Scripture.

ies and theology can scarcely be overestimated. "The Old Testament is the parent of the New Testament and the religion of the Old Testament is the cradle from which Christianity came."[2] As Emil Brunner observed, however, "the Church of Christ has to struggle against a rationalistic culture and a spirituality steeped completely in idealism and mysticism." He concluded wisely, therefore, that "the normal path to a genuine understanding of the New Testament is by way of the Old. For in the Old Testament we come upon a world completely unaffected by the whole Hellenic spirit."[3] Thorough knowledge of the Old Testament is thus imperative if one is to grasp the Hebraic foundation which underpins the theology and life of the earliest Church.

For nearly two thousand years Christianity has been debtor to the Jewish people for sharing this rich legacy. But it is tragic to realize that many Christians have avoided the Old Testament as a matter of "benign neglect." Typically, these Christians have received little emphasis on the Old Testament in sermons, church school teaching, and group Bible study; they have come to believe that the Old Testament is, for the most part, boring and irrelevant. Consequently, churches have conveyed the attitude that a thorough understanding of this Testament and its history concerning the Jewish people is, more or less, optional for today's Christian. This kind of warped thinking may be traced, at least in part, to the curricula of Christian colleges and theological seminaries. Many of these schools require more New Testament courses than Old Testament ones, and they often require study of Greek but make Hebrew optional. In actuality, however, the strains of a deeper dynamic are at work, an historical cancer that may be traced to Marcion in the second century. Accordingly, let us now turn to consider the teaching and impact of this influential Christian, whom we mentioned briefly in our last chapter.

## The Heresy of Marcion

Following the New Testament era, one of the first heresies that the Church faced was propounded by Marcion. He was a wealthy shipowner from Sinope (in what is now northern Turkey) who came to Rome. About A.D.

2. William Barclay, *Ethics in a Permissive Society* (New York: Harper & Row, 1971), pp. 13-14.
3. Emil Brunner, "The Significance of the Old Testament for Our Faith," in *The Old Testament and Christian Faith: A Theological Discussion,* ed. Bernhard W. Anderson (repr. New York: Herder and Herder, 1969), p. 249.

138, Marcion began to argue that the Old Testament was inferior to the New and hence had no part of authoritative revelation. He therefore fought to have it removed from the canon.

To some degree, Marcion appears to have been influenced by the dualistic teachings of Gnosticism. Thus he held that the world, with its appalling evils, was created by a Demiurge (a term Gnostics borrowed from Platonism). This cruel god of battles and bloody sacrifices, so Marcion contended, was revealed in the pages of the Old Testament. He insisted that since an evil world could not be created by a good God, the Old Testament was really the Demiurge's book and hence of lesser status than the New. The Old was the great antithesis of the New and thus was demeaned as being imperfect, offensive, and unedifying.

But the New Testament, Marcion insisted, revealed the true God in the coming of Christ from heaven. Unlike the Demiurge, this God was a God of love. Marcion argued that the New Testament, being Christ's book (not that of the Demiurge), was unquestionably superior to the Old Testament. Furthermore, in his quest to demote the Old Testament from its recognized position of authority, he began to extol the writings of Paul, which held that Christians were "free from the Law" (cf. Gal. 5:1). He contended firmly that the Church was wrong in attempting to combine the gospel with Judaism. Indeed, Marcion's principal goal was to rid Christianity of every trace of Judaism. Hence, Marcion became known as the archenemy of the "Jew God."

In A.D. 144 the issue finally came to a head, and the church in Rome excommunicated Marcion. But his heresy did not end. Justin Martyr informs us that Marcion's followers—later known as "Marcionites"—soon spread throughout the Roman empire. Despite his own anti-Judaic stance, Justin considered Marcionism to be the most dangerous heresy of his day.

## Neo-Marcionism

Though often cunningly concealed, in today's Church rather strong vestiges of Marcionism have survived. But we are polite. Hardly aware of its subtle presence, we do not call it "Neo-Marcionism," "heresy," or "anti-Judaism." Nevertheless, in our concerted effort to be "New Testament" believers, we have too often unconsciously minimized the place and importance of the Old Testament and the Church's Hebraic roots. At worst, many so-called Bible-believing Christians have become de facto "quarter-of-the-Bible" adherents (the New Testament has 260 chapters compared to the Old Testament's 929 chapters); at best, they rely on a "loose-leaf" edition of the Old Testament (i.e., they select only a few portions of the Old Testament), in addition to the New Testament. This selectivity has had the effect of neglecting the totality of written revelation, severing the Hebrew roots of the Christian faith, and thus eroding the full authority of the Holy Scriptures.

In addition to relegating the Old Testament to secondary importance in preaching and teaching, Neo-Marcionism continues to plague today's Church in other ways. For instance, it is often found in those theological circles where the displacement or supersession theory is taught concerning Israel. This teaching is tantamount to saying that Israel has been permanently cast aside and thus has had no theological relevance for the last nineteen hundred years. In our opinion, this position fails to give satisfactory explanation to Paul's argument that "a hardening has come upon part of Israel, until the full number of the Gentiles come in, and so all Israel will be saved" (Rom. 11:25-26).

Neo-Marcionism is also manifested in the Christian art which tends to downplay, whether consciously or unconsciously, the Jewishness of Jesus and the early Church. This tendency may be as subtle as an artist's depiction of the facial features of Jesus in a non-Jewish way. Or artwork may overtly display—either ignorantly or deliberately—non-Jewish or anti-Jewish subject matter, for example, the sculpturing of an uncircumcised infant Jesus, or the Last Supper scene with no common cup of wine or the disciples in a seated, rather than reclining, posture.

Neo-Marcionism also tends to be advanced when a church communicates to a nearby synagogue the impression, "We don't have anything to learn from you and your dead, legalistic religion, but you've got everything to learn from us." Such an attitude smacks of an exclusivism and elitism that can only further fortify the barrier which has divided Synagogue and Church since the first century. Finally, the phenomenon of anti-Zionism—denouncing Israel's national liberation movement and right to a homeland—may be nothing more than anti-Judaism or Neo-Marcionism in disguise.

## A Neglected Treasure

Several other factors have contributed to this general malaise that has brought apathy, de-emphasis, and even avoidance of the Old Testament. First, the size of the Old Testament has intimidated many Christians. Though shorter in English translation, the Hebrew text (Stuttgartensia edition) of the Old Testament contains over fifteen hundred pages. Furthermore, the Old Testament contains hundreds of different characters and place-names. It also has numerous lists of tribes and foreign nations, long genealogical tables, and a chronology that embraces thousands of years from the very dawn of history.

Second, the time and language of the Old Testament era seem remote and strange to modern Christians. They have been told that the Old Testament is a book for Jews and about Jews. As such, it is purportedly a document of the past which witnesses to a former age. Filled with poetry, metaphor, and unfamiliar Hebrew idioms, its ancient Near Eastern thought-forms are difficult to grasp.

Third, some Christians stumble over the so-called sub-Christian contents of the Old Testament. They question various accounts involving polygamy, slavery, and gross acts of violence. They ask, "Did a *good* God and loving Father actually approve the Canaanite bloodbath as a *holy* war, and bless the bashing of Babylonian babies against the rocks?" (cf. Deut. 7:1-5; 20:16-18; Ps. 137:9).

Finally, the Church has been guilty of overemphasizing the dissimilarities of the Testaments. It has stressed the antithetical relationship of the Testaments rather than their continuity. This problem is very old, for as the early Church became increasingly influenced by Greek culture and other non-Jewish thought, "contrast and contradiction, rather than acknowledgment of roots, relatedness and indebtedness, became the perspective."[4] Many examples of this phenomenon may be cited: the Old Covenant is contrasted to the New, the "book of wrath" to the "book of love," and "law" to "gospel." There is also Israel and the Church, promise and fulfillment, B.C. and A.D. Furthermore, we hear that the New Testament has "done away with," "abrogated," or "superseded" the Old Testament, that the New Testament is "better" than the Old, that the Old Testament "came *before* the cross," that we are now in "the age of grace." The unhappy result is that many Christians have been semantically preconditioned to view the New Testament as a separate Bible from (and superior to) the Old Testament.

What can be done to overcome the apathy and neglect of this great treasure of our Hebrew foundation? How can the Church become renourished from that Hebraic "root that supports it"? In short, what guidelines should the Church follow if the Old Testament is to be restored to its proper place of emphasis and authority? It is our next purpose in this discussion to point the way toward solving this problem.

4. Abraham J. Heschel, *The Insecurity of Freedom* (New York: Schocken Books, 1972), p. 169.

## The Bible of the Early Church

A first guideline to restore the Old Testament to its proper place is to follow the attitude of Jesus and the New Testament writers toward the Old Testament. Both Jesus and the apostles granted full authority and inspiration to the Old Testament writings (Matt. 5:17-18; John 10:35; 2 Tim. 3:14-17; 2 Pet. 1:20-21). Only one document was normative for them; they lived their lives "according to the Scripture." They knew no Bible but the Hebrew Scriptures, for the New Testament writings were not widely circulated until many years after the death of Jesus. The Old Testament was the primary source used for teaching and the settling of arguments with opponents (including Satan). And the book of Psalms was the "hymnbook" of the early Church (cf. 1 Cor. 14:26).

Of equal importance was the use of the Old Testament for the proclamation of the gospel. Jesus launched his public Galilean ministry "preaching good news to the poor," reading from the scroll of Isaiah in his hometown synagogue at Nazareth (Luke 4:16-19). Both Philip (Acts 8:28-35) and Apollos (Acts 18:24-28) led people to faith in Jesus as Messiah "by the [Old Testament] scriptures." Would not seminary courses in homiletics be doing students a favor to require that at least one "evangelistic" sermon be preached in class using an Old Testament text?

## Two Parts, Yet One Book

A second guideline is to remember that the Bible is an incomplete book, of limited value, without both Testaments. It is crucial for Christians to understand this point, for the New Testament Scriptures sound the note of fulfillment in looking back toward the Old. Thus, the entire Old Testament is pointing beyond itself. It anticipates a climax and ending. It leans toward the announcement that "the time had fully come" (Gal. 4:4). As John Bright suggests, it is like a single play with two acts. Without the second act, the first is "incomplete and unsatisfying; but without Act I, Act II is incomprehensible and impossible."[5]

The Testaments are inseparably linked. It should not surprise us, therefore, that scholars point to over sixteen hundred quotations, references, and allusions which connect the New Testament with the Old. As numerous small cables on a suspension bridge combine in a single cable

5. John Bright, *The Authority of the Old Testament* (repr. Grand Rapids: Baker Book House, 1975), p. 202.

to join both shores, so hundreds of texts combine to link the Testaments together inextricably.

The relationship between the Testaments is complex. On the one hand, we are not arguing that both Testaments are identical, for they differ significantly and have elements of discontinuity. On the other hand, we are not exalting the position of the Old Testament so that the New becomes reduced to little more than a glossary appended to the Old to interpret it. Indeed, each Testament is fully the Word of God; authority resides equally in both parts.

Perhaps no clearer analogy of the relationship between Testaments has been made than the following: "The Old is incomplete without the New, for in all its portions it is looking forward to its fulfillment, but the New is also incomplete without the Old. To use it alone is like taking the roofs and towers of a great cathedral in isolation and suggesting that the walls exist only that they may bear the roof."[6]

## The Theological Key

A third guideline for overcoming indifference and apathy is to remember that the Old Testament is the theological key for opening the door to the New Testament. The theology of the early Church was Hebraic to its very heart; it was Old Testament theology now raised to its ultimate spiritual significance in the coming of Jesus. Accordingly, today's Christian must be aware of what would be lost if this Old Testament theological background were suddenly discarded. What theological pillars would begin to shake and then start to crumble?

From the pages of the Old Testament comes the concept of monotheism, of the one true and living God. Also from the Old Testament derives our foundational understanding of creation, the fall of humanity, and the divine grace which brings salvation through a faith-love relationship between God and humanity. Throughout the Old Testament, mankind's sinfulness is set in contrast with the holiness and righteousness of God. In addition, here we begin to trace such great overarching theological themes as election-love, the covenant, and the kingdom of God. It is to the Old Testament that we look for the moral law of the Ten Commandments and the social and ethical teachings of the prophets. It is here that we also turn for our biblical background for understanding the claims of Jesus concerning his messiahship, priesthood, and atonement. The Old Testament teaches that

6. H. L. Ellison, *The Message of the Old Testament* (Grand Rapids: William B. Eerdmans Publishing Co., 1969), p. 11.

*113*

life is sacred, and though death is no respecter of persons, ultimately God's people await a brighter hope in the resurrection. Furthermore, the last book of the New Testament, the Apocalypse of John (or Revelation), is incomprehensible to the Christian without an understanding of its hundreds of Old Testament allusions. In sum, the Church can hardly afford to minimize its appreciation of the Old Testament. Far from being optional reading, these Scriptures constitute nearly eighty percent of the Bible.

## God-Breathed and Useful

Our fourth guideline is to examine carefully the issues of Old Testament authority and interpretation. Much like the early Church Fathers, some Christians have tried to preserve the place of the Old Testament in the Church by reading christological, allegorical, or spiritual meaning into various texts.[7] Looking for the so-called *sensus plenior* (fullest or deepest meaning), these interpreters often go far beyond the plain meaning of the text without clear biblical warrant. Bogged down in the quagmire of excessive spiritualization of the text, these interpreters often bypass the fundamental principle that a text must first be heard on its own terms, in its distinct literary genre, in its own Testament. For a case in point, the Song of Songs (also called the Song of Solomon or Canticles) has been interpreted as a picture of Christ's love for his bride, the Church.[8] However, the New Testament offers no clear-cut basis for this interpretation of Old Testament love poetry.

Other Christians have tried to save the authority of the Old Testament by separating those passages of "timeless" and "continuing" value from those which are "outdated" or "no longer useful." They accomplish this task by appealing to some normative principle of morality and ethics derived from the New Testament. Such an approach, unfortunately, turns

7. Under the guidance of the Holy Spirit the New Testament writers sometimes used typological exegesis and other nonliteral forms of interpretation in their establishing of Christian meaning in the Old Testament Scriptures (e.g., Matt. 2:15; 12:40; John 3:14; 1 Cor. 10:1-4). The Reformers, however, were in general disagreement with this approach; it tended to be highly subjective, uncontrolled, and had been widely abused centuries earlier by the Church Fathers (note our discussion of allegory in chapter seven above). If modern interpreters resort to typological, allegorical, or other related systems of exegesis, one must remember that in coming to their conclusions they have no claim for being inspired by the Holy Spirit in exactly the same way that the New Testament writers were inspired.

8. For a useful critique of this method of interpretation see the discussion in the commentary of my colleague, G. Lloyd Carr, *The Song of Solomon,* Tyndale Old Testament Commentaries (Downers Grove: InterVarsity Press, 1984), pp. 21ff.

out to be largely a whimsical matter of picking and choosing. Again, the modus operandi is highly subjective. It leaves many Old Testament texts with no authority whatsoever, if only for the reason that the New Testament fails to validate them in some way.

How, then, should one interpret the Old Testament, accepting its full and inspired authority? Our goal must be to uncover the rich, diverse theologies of the Old Testament, from which its authority and abiding value ultimately derive. In certain areas, Christianity has emphasized different teachings from those of Judaism; hence we are not to expect a leveling out or complete uniformity between the Testaments. The Bible did not come out of heaven on a parachute all at once, but revelation unfolded progressively over hundreds of years. Thus, within the structural unity of Scripture we encounter variations of theological emphasis. Every text of Scripture is there not simply to take up space, but because it is given by the Spirit of God and contains some theological concern which prompted it to be taken, by God's providence, into the canon.

Though some texts are more directly normative for theology than others (e.g., the Ten Commandments may hold greater relevance for Christians by way of application than the levitical laws concerning animal sacrifice), all of the Old Testament is "God-breathed and useful" (2 Tim. 3:16). We must carefully distinguish what the Bible reports from what it teaches. A careful contextual study of what each text says should lead to the theological teaching of the passage in keeping with the original author's intention. Since every Old Testament text is pregnant with theological significance, one should seek the ultimate value and authority of a text at the theological level.[9]

The above task is seldom easy, however; biblical interpretation is more an art than a science. Individual Christians have the assurance that the Holy Spirit will guide in this process (cf. John 16:13; 1 Cor. 2:10-16). But the Holy Spirit does not normally work in a vacuum; every interpreter has an obligation to engage in personal study, while at the same time to be sensitive to what the rest of the Church has taught and is teaching concerning the Old Testament text under consideration.

## Discovering the Jewish Jesus

A fifth consideration for restoring the Old Testament to its proper place in the Church centers on the need to recover the Jewishness of Jesus. If Jesus

---

9. For a more detailed study on the entire issue of Old Testament authority see John Bright, *Authority of the Old Testament*.

is the Christian's model, then one can learn much from this first-century teacher's relation to Judaism and the Hebrew Scriptures.

The question of the Jewishness of Jesus, however, is not something biblical scholarship has always taken for granted. Earlier this century Friedrich Delitzsch (son of the noted Old Testament scholar Franz Delitzsch) not only denied the Jewish origin of Christianity but went so far as to suggest that Jesus was a Gentile.[10] Recently, however, an almost uniform voice of both Christian and Jewish scholars strongly supports the Jewish background to the life and teachings of Jesus. Representative of this group is Rabbi Harvey Falk. He affirms that "Jesus of Nazareth . . . never wished to see his fellow Jews change one iota of their traditional faith. He himself remained an Orthodox Jew to his last moment."[11] Eugene Fisher, a Roman Catholic scholar, concurs: "He [Jesus] considered himself to be a faithful Jew. He was brought up to observe the Jewish Law, the Torah. . . . When he spoke, he spoke to his fellow Jews and presumed their knowledge of and love for the Hebrew Scriptures."[12] Indeed, Jesus and his first followers thought and spoke within a Jewish framework. Therefore, the only way for Christians to understand the life and words of Jesus is from a Jewish perspective.[13] The Synoptic Gospels contain no evidence that Jesus visualized a Church which would grow "separate from and at daggers drawn with God's chosen people of Israel."[14] Accordingly, it is most ironic that, despite all the hatred and persecution the Church directed toward the Jewish people for centuries, it would be the Jews—not the Christians—who would preserve the very same Hebrew Scriptures used by Jesus and his followers.[15]

It is significant that the New Testament writers stress that a Jew is to represent all of humanity. Jesus would not be chosen by vote or democratic process, but would be sent by God (John 3:17; Gal. 4:4; Rom. 8:3).[16] The New Testament introduces the human ancestry of Jesus in a very Jewish manner. Matthew opens his Gospel by apparently making a wordplay on the Davidic origin of Jesus. In ancient times letters had numerical values:

10. Ibid., pp. 65-66.

11. Harvey Falk, *Jesus the Pharisee: A New Look at the Jewishness of Jesus* (New York: Paulist Press, 1985), p. 158.

12. Eugene J. Fisher, *Faith Without Prejudice* (New York: Paulist Press, 1977), p. 33.

13. See Leonard Swidler, "The Jewishness of Jesus: Some Religious Implications for Christians," *Journal of Ecumenical Studies* 18 (Winter, 1981): 104-13.

14. G. A. F. Knight, *A Biblical Approach to the Doctrine of the Trinity* (Edinburgh: Oliver & Boyd, 1953), p. 2.

15. Ibid., p. 3.

16. See Markus Barth, *Jesus the Jew* (Atlanta: John Knox Press, 1978), p. 34.

the first letter of the alphabet was 1, the second letter 2, etc. The numerical value of the Hebrew letters for the name "David" equals fourteen. This number is used three times in summing up the generations: from Abraham to David, from David to the Exile, and from the Exile to Jesus (Matt. 1:17). Furthermore, this unique Jew is very bone and flesh of "a certain people ... whose customs are different from those of all other people" (Esth. 3:8). Thus, according to Matthew 5:17, the intent of Jesus was not to "abolish" or "destroy" the Law of Israel (i.e., to uproot or negate it through misinterpretation), but to "fulfill" it (i.e., to establish or support it through correct interpretation).[17]

Certainly the Christian is dependent upon Judaism for an understanding of Jesus' comment that the Pharisees "make their phylacteries wide and the tassels on their garments long" (Matt. 23:5). The Law of Moses mentions the *tephillin* (or *tefillin*, "phylacteries") when the Hebrews were instructed: "Tie them [God's words] as symbols on your hands and bind them on your foreheads" (Deut. 6:8). The phylacteries are two small boxes containing pieces of parchment with portions of the Torah written on them. During morning prayer, one is attached with straps to the left arm (opposite the heart) and the other to the head (on top of the brain). Through this exercise the Jew shows his dedication and love for God in both heart (emotions) and mind (intellect or thoughts). At Qumran, where the Dead Sea Scrolls were discovered, *tephillin* from the time of Jesus were found, providing archeological light on Matthew 23:5.

The *tzitzit* (or *zizith*, "tassels") are also to be worn in accord with biblical teaching: "The LORD said to Moses, 'Speak to the Israelites and say to them: "Throughout the generations to come you are to make tassels *[tzitzit]* on the corners of your garments, with a cord of blue on each tassel. You will have these tassels to look at and so you will remember all the commands of the LORD, that you may obey them"'" (Num. 15:37-39; cf. Matt. 9:20; Luke 8:44). Four fringes were to be attached to the garment of each Jew. Today, these are attached to the *tallit*, "prayer shawl," worn during morning prayer services. (An interesting numerological aside: each fringe consists of eight strands and five double knots, hence a total of 13. When taken with the numerical value of *tzitzit*, 600, the total is 613, the number of commandments in the Torah.) As a first-century Jew, faithful to the Law of Moses, Jesus wore *tephillin* and *tzitzit* (cf. Deut. 22:12).

The Jewishness of Jesus is further illustrated in the Lord's Prayer

---

17. Such is the meaning of this Hebrew idiom as found in early rabbinic discussion, cf. David Bivin and Roy B. Blizzard, *Understanding the Difficult Words of Jesus* (Austin, TX: Center for Judaic-Christian Studies, 1984), pp. 152-55.

(Matt. 6:9-13).[18] The prayer is thoroughly Jewish and "could readily have appeared without change in Rabbinic literature."[19] It reflects such ancient Jewish prayers as the mourner's *Kaddish,* a prayer which sanctifies God's name in the presence of death, and the Shemoneh Esreh, the "eighteen" (benedictions), discussed in chapter five above. Jesus was also faithful in keeping the Jewish festivals of his day. He observed such holidays as *Sukkot,* "Tabernacles" (John 7:1-39), and *Pesaḥ* (or *Pesach*), "Passover" (Mark 14:12-25).

The life of Hillel, the great sage of classical Judaism, overlapped with that of Jesus. Though Hillel still taught after the birth of Jesus, most of his teaching was apparently carried on in the century preceding the Christian era. When a Gentile once asked Hillel to teach him the whole of Judaism while standing on one foot, he replied, "What is hateful to yourself do not do to your fellowman. That is the whole Torah. All the rest is commentary. Now go and study" (Shabbat 31a). Lest one think that Hillel and Jesus were poles apart, it should be observed that this definition of Judaism was at the heart of Jesus' definition of what it means to have eternal life. Both Hillel and Jesus appealed to Leviticus 19:18, "Love your neighbor as yourself." Jesus taught several significant things about this commandment, and another like it, "Love the LORD your God with all your heart and with all your soul and with all your strength" (Deut. 6:5). Jesus said, "All the Law and the Prophets hang on these two commandments" (Matt. 22:40), and "There is no commandment greater than these" (Mark 12:31). Furthermore, pointing to obedience of these commandments as the evidence of true and living faith, Jesus told an expert in the Law, "Do this, and you will live" (Luke 10:28).

These and other passages in the Gospels clearly affirm the Jewishness of Jesus and his strong endorsement of the Old Testament by his close attachment to its teachings. Surely the attitude of the Church in these matters must be no different from its Lord's.

## Other Early Jewish Sources

A sixth guideline concerns the need to be familiar with other early Jewish sources which provide linguistic, theological, and historical insight into

18. For a scholarly exposition of this subject see Bradford H. Young, *The Jewish Background to the Lord's Prayer* (Austin, TX: Center for Judaic-Christian Studies, 1984).
19. Samuel Sandmel, *Judaism and Christian Beginnings* (New York: Oxford University Press, 1978), p. 358.

both Testaments. We have already seen that the Old Testament is the main source upon which New Testament thought and life are based. But we have also observed that it is not the only Jewish literature essential for understanding the Judaism of Jesus' day.

For nearly four thousand years the Jewish people have belonged to an evolving religious civilization. Accordingly, we would do well to remember that just as patriarchal religion differed somewhat from Mosaic, so also did the Temple religion of Solomon differ from that of the Exile. And just as the postexilic religion of Ezra was not identical to that of Jesus' day, so also the Rabbinic Judaism of the talmudic period is not the same as modern Judaism. Although a strong common thread runs throughout the history of Jewish religion, the Christian community must be especially cautious about seeking a complete equation of the Judaism of New Testament times with either earlier or later periods.

Perhaps the most important reason for this caution is the impact of the Oral Law upon the teaching of Jesus, Paul, and others. Various scribal and Pharisaic traditions significantly influenced the biblical Judaism practiced at the close of the Old Testament period. Though most of the sayings of the rabbis were not reduced to writing until after the New Testament era, numerous common links have been established between rabbinic literature and the New Testament text. Furthermore, the Qumran Scrolls, apocryphal writings, and apocalyptic literature also contribute to our understanding of Jewish religious thought during the period between the Testaments. We shall cite several brief examples from some of these Jewish sources. Then we will treat more extensively the Shema, probably the most important single Old Testament passage mentioned in both the New Testament and other early Jewish sources.

The Qumran writings or Dead Sea Scrolls illumine a number of obscure New Testament expressions. For example, in Matthew 5:43 Jesus refers to the command "hate your enemy."[20] As far as we know, however, this expression does not occur in the Old Testament or in Rabbinic Judaism. But the idea is found at Qumran. The people of Qumran had withdrawn to the wilderness to await the end of the age. They were the "sons of light," equipping themselves through intense discipline, rituals of purity, and scriptural study to overcome their enemy, the "sons of darkness." The Manual of Discipline (1:9-11) reads: "to love all the sons of light, each according to his lot in the Council of God, and to hate all the sons of dark-

20. For a useful discussion of this concept see William S. LaSor, *The Dead Sea Scrolls and the New Testament* (Grand Rapids: William B. Eerdmans Publishing Co., 1972), pp. 200-201, 240-41.

ness, each according to his guilt in the vengeance of God." In the Sermon on the Mount, Jesus thus refutes this concept of vengeance—which at the very least was a sectarian belief in his day—and emphasizes the need to pay back good for evil.

The Apocrypha also sheds light on various New Testament texts. To illustrate, let us note one passage from the Gospels, John 10:22-23: "Then came the Feast of Dedication at Jerusalem. It was winter, and Jesus was in the temple area walking in Solomon's Colonnade." The feast Jesus is then attending is the Jewish festival of Hanukkah. This holiday is not mentioned in the Old Testament; its origin is intertestamental. Hanukkah goes back to the 25th of the month Kislev, 165 B.C., when the Maccabees "rededicated" the Temple after Antiochus IV Epiphanes had desecrated it. Judas Maccabeus was responsible for inaugurating this festival (1 Macc. 4:53-59; cf. 2 Macc. 10:5). Thus the Apocrypha indicates why Jesus was in Jerusalem to celebrate Hanukkah: "Then Judas, his brothers, and the whole congregation of Israel decreed that the rededication of the altar should be observed with joy and gladness at the same season each year, for eight days, beginning on the twenty-fifth of Kislev" (1 Macc. 4:59). The above account from the life of Jesus indicates how dependent we are upon Jewish sources other than the Old Testament for understanding the Judaism of New Testament times.

Many of Jesus' parabolic stories have been clarified through a study of rabbinic literature. The parable was a favorite teaching tool of Jesus, especially the so-called king parable. Rabbinic literature has almost 5,000 parables, and more than 800 are king parables. Though Aramaic was widely used in the Jewish community, only a scant number of these parables are known in Aramaic; virtually all are written in Hebrew, a strong indication that Jesus' parabolic teachings were probably also originally delivered in Hebrew.[21] A detailed consideration of the parables falls outside the scope of this present study; the reader should refer to the work of organizations like the Jerusalem School for the Study of the Synoptic Gospels, where current research is taking place in this field.[22]

In the Sermon on the Mount, Jesus states, "With the measure you use, it will be measured to you" (Matt. 7:2). Here he is enunciating one of the most important rabbinic principles, the concept of *middah ke-neged middah* ("measure for measure"). Countless rabbinic passages stress this

---

21. See Bivin and Blizzard, *Understanding the Difficult Words of Jesus,* pp. 73ff.
22. An extensive work by one of the research scholars associated with the Jerusalem School is that of Bradford H. Young, *Jesus and His Jewish Parables* (Mahwah, NJ: Paulist Press, 1989).

principle of tit for tat, which was strongly believed to govern the divine rule of reward and punishment. The Talmud states, "all the measures [of punishment and reward] taken by the Holy One, blessed be He, are in accordance with the principle of measure for measure" (Sanhedrin 90a). The Apocrypha also clearly states this concept: "By what things a man sins, by these is he punished" (Wisdom of Solomon 1:16). When Jesus emphasizes this idea of "measure for measure," he is doing so in the context of judgment. In effect he is saying, "Do not judge other people, because you will be judged by the way you condemn them." In short, the measure you give (judgment) is the measure you get back.[23]

Elsewhere in the Sermon on the Mount Jesus uses the Hebrew idiom "if your eyes are good . . . if your eyes are bad" (Matt. 6:22-23). Most translations have failed to clarify that the meaning has nothing to do with the quality of the eyes or physical condition of eyesight. Rather, the concept is ethical. In rabbinic literature, if you have a "good eye" you are a generous person; but if you have an "evil eye" you are a stingy or greedy person.[24]

Later in the Gospel of Matthew we confront the teaching of Jesus concerning "binding" and "loosing" (18:18; cf. 16:19). Here Jesus says, "I tell you the truth, whatever you bind on earth will be bound in heaven, and whatever you loose on earth will be loosed in heaven." "To bind" was a common rabbinic expression meaning "to forbid" or "to prohibit" a certain activity, while "to loose" means "to permit" or "to allow."[25] In connection with this idiom of "binding" and "loosing," W. D. Davies observes about Jesus that "he could hold his own with scribal opponents, and must, therefore, have had a lively awareness of their method, if not an exact knowledge of it."[26]

Another expression in Matthew's Gospel deserving comment is "weightier [or 'more important'] matters of the law" (23:23). At first reading it might appear that Jesus considered the moral or ethical aspects of the Law (i.e., "justice and mercy and faithfulness") to be far more important than the ceremonial or civil teachings. However, a careful study of both Jesus' teachings and rabbinic literature does not support this conclu-

---

23. See C. G. Montefiore and H. Loewe, *A Rabbinic Anthology* (repr. Cleveland: Meridian Books; Philadelphia: Jewish Publication Society, 1963), pp. xxxv, 222-25.

24. Robert A. Guelich, *The Sermon on the Mount* (Waco, TX: Word Books, 1982), pp. 329-32. Cf. also Bivin and Blizzard, *Understanding the Difficult Words of Jesus,* pp. 144-45.

25. Bivin and Blizzard, *Understanding the Difficult Words of Jesus,* pp. 143-49.

26. W. D. Davies, *The Setting of the Sermon on the Mount* (Cambridge: Cambridge University Press, 1964), p. 424.

sion. Indeed, Jesus taught that the so-called lighter matters should not be neglected (23:23b).[27] Thus, as E. P. Sanders has rightly pointed out, in the "Rabbis' view of the matter . . . God had given all the commandments, and they were all to be obeyed alike. It would be presumptuous of man to determine that some should be neglected."[28] By stressing, then, the "weightier" matters, Jesus was hardly stating to his Jewish hearers that the non-ethical dimensions of the Law were no longer authoritative or binding. But, as was his custom, he emphasized again the need for an inner obedience and spiritual devotion which cultic conformity or externalistic religion alone could not produce.

We are vitally dependent upon sources other than the Old Testament for the background to many other concepts central to New Testament teaching. These subjects include the synagogue, the Sanhedrin, the sects of Judaism, and the itinerant rabbi. But in addition, this common substructure of early Christianity and Judaism is illustrated in smaller—yet no less important—details such as the use of wine at Passover (cf. Luke 22:17-20; 1 Cor. 11:25ff.). In the Old Testament, wine is not mentioned in connection with Passover. But, as we will point out later in this volume, wine is discussed in the Oral Law, a crucial source for understanding the precise function of wine at the Last Supper.

## The Shema: Core Affirmation of Israel's Faith

To round out this present discussion, we shall now turn to a more detailed illustration of our sixth guideline above, a study of Deuteronomy 6:4, "Hear, O Israel: The LORD our God, the LORD is one."[29] Known as the *Shema* (explained below), this is one of the most crucial Old Testament texts for the foundational teachings of both Jesus and Judaism. A careful

---

27. See Walter C. Kaiser, Jr., "The Place of Law and Good Works in Evangelical Christianity," in *A Time to Speak: The Evangelical-Jewish Encounter,* ed. A. James Rudin and Marvin R. Wilson (Grand Rapids: William B. Eerdmans Publishing Co., 1987), pp. 123-24. Cf. also Gordon Tucker, "Response to Walter C. Kaiser, Jr.," in *A Time to Speak,* pp. 134-37.

28. E. P. Sanders, *Paul and Palestinian Judaism* (Philadelphia: Fortress Press, 1977), p. 112.

29. For useful discussions of this passage, see the following: Morris Adler, "Judaism's Central Affirmation," in *Jewish Heritage Reader,* ed. Lily Edelman (New York: Taplinger Publishing Co., 1965), pp. 38-43; Louis Jacobs in *Encyclopedia Judaica,* 14:1370-74; Joseph H. Hertz, *The Authorized Daily Prayer Book,* rev. ed. (New York: Block Publishing Co., 1948), pp. 108-29, 263-69; Joachim Jeremias, *The Prayers of Jesus,* trans. John Bowden and John Reumann (repr. Philadelphia: Fortress Press, 1984), pp. 66-81.

investigation of early sources suggests that Deuteronomy 6:4 must have been the first portion from the Hebrew Bible that Jesus committed to memory. According to the Babylonian Talmud (Sukkah 42a), Jewish boys were taught this biblical passage as soon as they could speak. Since the Talmud specifies that "the father must teach him" (i.e., the son), we may confidently assume that Joseph, Jesus' earthly father, was responsible for fulfilling this task.

This text from the Law of Moses comprises only six Hebrew words: *Shema yisra'el adonai eloheynu adonai ehad.* It is important to note that it is located in the book of Deuteronomy, which in Jesus' day was the most widely circulated and popular book of the Pentateuch. We know that Deuteronomy carried this broad influence for two main reasons: (1) The New Testament has more quotations from Deuteronomy than from any other book of Moses. (2) Among the Dead Sea Scrolls at Qumran, more separate copies of the scroll of Deuteronomy were found than of any other Mosaic writing. But the importance of the book of Deuteronomy is not limited to the early childhood of Jesus and others from his period. As an adult, Jesus, at the beginning of his ministry, quotes three times from this book in mustering spiritual support in response to the three temptations of Satan (Matt. 4:1-11).

Today, Deuteronomy 6:4 is referred to as the *Shema* (literally "Hear!"), based on the verbal imperative at the start of the verse. The Shema is often called the watchword of Israel's faith because it declares the oneness and uniqueness of God. Since this verse held such great significance in the life and teachings of Jesus (see Mark 12:29) as well as in the history of the Jewish people, it is important that we explore its background and meaning in greater depth.

The Shema is not a prayer (rabbinic literature never refers to "praying" the Shema) but a confession of faith or a creed. The practice of reciting the Shema daily is firmly established in the Mishnah (ca. A.D. 200). The important place of the Shema in Jewish religious experience is underscored by the fact that the entire Mishnah begins, "From what time in the evening may the *Shema* be recited?" (Berakhot 1:1). But there is also evidence of the Shema's use during and even before the New Testament era, for the Letter of Aristeas (ca. 150 B.C.) alludes to it. In addition, the Mishnah states that the Shema was recited by the priests in the Temple—indication of its use prior to A.D. 70 (Tamid 4:3; 5:1).

As the Shema developed it came to include three passages from the Law of Moses. The first (Deut. 6:4-9) proclaims God's oneness (v. 4) and calls Israel to love him and obey his commandments (vv. 5-9). The second (Deut. 11:13-21) details the rewards promised for obeying these commandments and the punishments for disobeying them. The third (Num. 15:37-41) sets forth the law concerning tassels on the garments as a reminder to keep "all the commandments of the LORD" (v. 39).

In accordance with Deuteronomy 6:7 the Shema was recited twice a day, in the morning and evening: "when you lie down and when you rise" (cf. Mishnah, Berakhot 1:1-2). During the talmudic period much rabbinic debate focused on the question of precisely how long after dawn or sunset the Shema should be read (Babylonian Talmud, Berakhot 2a-3a, 9b). The School of Shammai also debated the School of Hillel about the proper posture for reciting it (Berakhot 10b-11a; cf. Deut. 6:7). Women, slaves, and children were exempt from the obligation to recite the Shema (Mishnah, Berakhot 3:3). The Shema was recited as the last utterance of martyrs being led to their death, and to this day it is recited at the conclusion to deathbed confessions. Thus, Jews are taught to have the name of God on their lips from early childhood to the moment of death.

The Mishnah teaches that the morning recitation of the Shema is to be preceded by two benedictions and concluded by one. In the evening it is preceded by two and followed by two (Berakhot 1:4; 2:2). The main theme of the morning benedictions is praise to God for creating the light of day, giving the Torah, and redeeming Israel. The evening blessings likewise give thanks for physical and spiritual light but also attest to the truths of God and plead for a peaceful rest.

Of the 5,845 verses in the Pentateuch, "Hear, O Israel: The LORD our God, the LORD is one" sounds the historic keynote of all Judaism. This fundamental truth and leitmotif of God's uniqueness prompts one to respond by fulfilling the fundamental obligation to love God (Deut. 6:5). Accordingly, when Jesus was asked about the "most important commandment," his reply did not contradict this central theme of Judaism (Mark 12:28-34; cf. Matt. 22:34-40). With 613 individual statutes of the Torah from which to choose, Jesus cited the Shema, including the command to love God; but he also extended the definition of the "first" and "great" commandment to include love for one's neighbor (Lev. 19:18).

Scholars have differed in their renderings of Deuteronomy 6:4 (the NIV and RSV give four possible translations, including those in the margin). Some translators have considered these six Hebrew words to be one nominative sentence, while others have taken them as two. Perhaps of greater importance, however, is the implication of the final word, *ehad* ("one"). Jewish interpreters have largely understood the phrase "the LORD is one" to carry either or both of the following emphases: (1) It is an affirmation of monotheism. In opposition to their polytheistic environment, the Hebrews were to know that there was only one God, not many. Yahweh is one in that there is no other God. Cyrus H. Gordon has suggested further that Deuteronomy 6:4 means not only that there is one God, but that "One" is his name (cf. Zech. 14:9).[30] (2) It declares the uniqueness of God. Yahweh is the Supreme Being, wholly unlike all other things in the universe, which have been created by him.

In the Old Testament *eḥad* usually refers to a single unit such as a person. Certain interpreters have insisted, however, that *eḥad* may also be used to designate a collective unit (e.g., Gen. 1:5; 2:24; Num. 13:23), a diversity within unity. Thus some Christian scholars have found room for trinitarian monotheism in the *eḥad* of Deuteronomy 6:4. So interpreted, God is seen as a complex unity, not simply as numerically one. It must be remembered, however, that the main focus of the Shema in its original setting—ancient Near Eastern polytheism—is clearly upon the fact that there is one God (cf. Deut. 4:39). Yahweh alone claims the unqualified love and obedience of all his creation.

## Christianity Is Jewish

A seventh guideline for rediscovering the Hebraic foundation of the Church is the need to remember that the core of Christianity—its life, structure, and practices—is Jewish. Throughout this book it is our purpose to illustrate many dimensions of this theme. For, to be sure, as Otto Piper reminds us: "Christianity and Judaism have a broad common basis. Even if they wished to do so, they could not completely dissociate themselves from each other."[31] As we have seen, the Old and New Testaments are two parts of the same book and are thus interrelated and interdependent. Perhaps no words capture the current significance of this point for the discipline of biblical studies better than these of Jürgen Moltmann: "We stand today in a remarkable period of transition. On the one side the hellenistically structured form of the Christian faith is ebbing. . . . On the other side the Christian faith is experiencing what I would like to call a 'hebraic wave.'" He then concludes by noting that "the New Testament cannot be read apart from the Old Testament, but that only when both are read together beside and with each other does the fullness of life in the faith unfold."[32]

30. Cyrus H. Gordon, "His Name is 'One,'" *Journal of Near Eastern Studies* 29 (1970): 198ff.

31. Otto A. Piper, "Church and Judaism in Holy History," *Theology Today* 18 (1961): 67.

32. Quoted in Pinchas E. Lapide, *Hebrew in the Church* (Grand Rapids: William B. Eerdmans Publishing Co., 1984), p. 202.

This interpenetration of Judaism and Christianity may be observed on many levels. Let us note briefly several pertinent examples. The Church is debtor to the Synagogue for the idea of a canon, the concept of a sacred, authoritative Scripture to rule and guide in all areas of one's life. In the early synagogue the Scripture was employed in four ways,[33] each of which has its counterpart in Christianity. The Scripture was (a) read (seder, haftarah), (b) preached (homilies as found in Midrashim), (c) translated and often paraphrased so as to be understandable (Targums), and (d) used in set prayers (liturgy). Furthermore, methods of biblical interpretation, the form and order of worship, the church altar, the use of a pulpit, the titles of church offices (e.g., "elder," "teacher," "shepherd"), and the vocabulary of prayer (e.g., "amen," "hallelujah") all have been taken over and adopted from Judaism. Likewise, the practice of baptism (by self-immersion) in the early Church,[34] and, as alluded to above, the observance of the Lord's Supper (a communal gathering, linked to Passover, commemorating redemption) have their roots in Judaism.

Furthermore, insight into the nature of Christian experience as taught in the New Testament may be gained from a study of Jewish heritage. For example, in the book of Romans, one of the earliest doctrinal church letters, Paul describes a significant spiritual concept drawn from his Pharisaic background. In Romans 7 and 8 he writes of his struggle between the old man (sinful nature) and the new man (spiritual nature). This concept may well reflect the teaching of Judaism concerning the human drive, impulse, or inclination toward evil (*yetzer ha-ra*) and the drive toward good (*yetzer ha-tob*).[35] In Romans 3:23 Paul writes, "All have sinned and fall short of the glory of God." Rabbinic Judaism teaches that Adam at the time of his fall lost the image of God. Paul's theology is not new; Paul's Bible, the Old Testament, states "there is no man who does not sin" (1 Kgs. 8:46). The idea of sin as "falling short" is a thoroughly Jewish idiom. One of the main Hebrew words used to describe sin is *het*, which is a term from the world of archery or marksmanship. It means to miss the mark or fall short of a target, in the same way an arrow or sling-

---

33. See Daniel Patte, *Early Jewish Hermeneutic in Palestine* (Missoula, MT: Scholars Press, 1975), pp. 35ff.

34. See David Daube, *The New Testament and Rabbinic Judaism* (London: Athlone Press, 1956), pp. 106-40; Bivin and Blizzard, *Understanding the Difficult Words of Jesus,* pp. 133-37; William S. LaSor, "Discovering What Jewish *Miqva'ot* Can Tell Us About Christian Baptism," *Biblical Archaeology Review* 13/1 (1987): 52-59.

35. W. D. Davies notes that in Romans 7 "we are justified in tracing a direct connection with the doctrine of the Two Impulses. Paul's description of his moral experience in that chapter is probably an account of his struggle against his evil *yetzer*" (*Paul and Rabbinic Judaism,* 4th ed. [Philadelphia: Fortress Press, 1980], pp. 23-24).

stone misses the bull's-eye.[36] Through the above and other concepts, we are reminded that a knowledge of the Old Testament and Judaism is absolutely essential for understanding the foundation upon which Christianity was established.

## The Hebrew Bible and American Beginnings

A discussion of the importance of the Jewish roots of the Christian faith would be incomplete without a more immediate historical perspective on this topic. Thus it is our aim in the remainder of this chapter to provide some insight into the specific role that Old Testament and Hebraic studies held during the formative years of American society and life.

As we pointed out in the opening chapters of this book, the early Christian centuries brought the de-Judaization of Church and society. During the period of the Protestant Reformation (16th century), however, some signs of the *re-Judaization* of the Christian faith began to surface, as certain Hebraic biblical categories were rediscovered. The Reformers put great stress on the principle of *sola scriptura* (Scripture as the sole and final authority for the Christian). The consequent de-emphasis on tradition brought with it a measure of return to biblical roots. Accordingly, during the two centuries following the Reformation, several groups recognized the importance of once again emphasizing the Hebraic heritage of the Church. Among these people were the Puritans who founded Pilgrim America, and the leaders who pioneered American education. We shall comment briefly on the first of these groups before concentrating on the second.

The Puritans came to America deeply rooted in the Hebraic tradition. Most bore Hebrew names. The Pilgrim fathers considered themselves as the children of Israel fleeing "Egypt" (England), crossing the "Red Sea" (the Atlantic Ocean), and emerging from this "Exodus" to their own "promised land" (New England). The Pilgrims thought of themselves as "all the children of Abraham" and thus under the covenant of Abraham.[37] Their influence on American society was not soon forgotten: more than a century and a half after the first Puritan settlers reached New England, the

---

36. Note the verb form of *ḥet* is *ḥata*. In addition to this Hebrew verb being translated "to sin" (see Deut. 1:41), it may be rendered "miss (the mark)" as in Judg. 20:16.

37. This was the teaching of Puritan thinker Joshua Moody. See Henry L. Feingold, "The Jewish Role in Shaping American Society," in *A Time to Speak: The Evangelical-Jewish Encounter,* ed. A. James Rudin and Marvin R. Wilson (Grand Rapids: William B. Eerdmans Publishing Co., 1987), p. 46.

American people were referred to in a State Assembly as "God's American Israel."[38]

Thus, the seeds of religious liberty for the American Church did not come from New England leaders like Roger Williams and Anne Hutchinson—as noble as they and others were. Rather, it came from the Hebrews themselves, whose sacred Writings inspired the Puritans.[39] Accordingly, many of the Puritans in seventeenth-century England were learned Hebraists. William Bradford (1590-1657), prominent early American and Governor of Plymouth Colony for more than three decades, reflected this intense interest in Hebrew. Bradford stated that he studied Hebrew so that when he died he might be able to speak in the "most ancient language, the Holy Tongue in which God and, the angels, spake."[40] Cotton Mather (1663-1728), a well-known Puritan minister and scholar from Massachusetts, had a similar deep respect for the Hebrew language. Concerning its importance Mather once observed, "I promise that those who spend as much time morning and evening in Hebrew studies as they do in smoking tobacco, would quickly make excellent progress in the language."[41]

Early American educators are another influential segment that placed a strong emphasis upon Old Testament and Hebrew studies. These people were closely connected to the "olive root" and insisted—in keeping with their Puritan heritage—that Hebrew be center stage in the realm of higher education. A study of the beginnings and curricula of many of the Ivy League colleges in the East is a case in point. Hebrew inscriptions, for example, are found on the insignias or seals of such schools as Columbia and Dartmouth. Of particular interest for our purposes are the early years of Harvard, Yale, and Dartmouth.

Harvard University has the distinction of being the oldest institution of higher learning in America. It was founded in 1636, just sixteen years after the Pilgrims landed the Mayflower at Plymouth. The school was named for John Harvard (1607-1638), a Puritan minister. According to the *Proceedings of the Massachusetts Historical Society,* Hebrew was an important component of a Harvard education from the day its doors

38. The President of Yale College used these words before the Governor and General Assembly of the State of Connecticut in 1783. See Abraham J. Feldman, *Contributions of Judaism to Modern Society* (New York: The Union of American Hebrew Congregations, n.d.), p. 5.

39. David de Sola Pool, *Why I Am A Jew* (Boston: Beacon Press, 1957), pp. 184-85.

40. Quoted in Nitza Rosovsky, *The Jewish Experience at Harvard and Radcliffe* (Cambridge: Harvard University Press, 1986), p. 2.

41. Quoted by Bea Stadtler in "Hebrew's Influence on English," *Jewish Advocate,* October 22, 1987, p. 19.

opened: "Hebrew had been an obligatory study from the foundation of the College. In the beginning it was taught by the presidents, some of whom, like Chauncy, had a great reputation as Hebraists."[42] Indeed, Hebrew was a favorite subject of Harvard president Henry Dunster, whose translation of the Psalms was printed in 1651 on the Harvard College press.[43] Little wonder, therefore, as Jewish historian Henry Feingold has noted, that in early America "Congregationalists were better Hebraists than Jews."[44]

An important figure in the development of Hebrew studies at Harvard was Rabbi Judah Monis (1683-1764). Born in Italy, Monis—it has been widely assumed—was the first Jew to receive a college degree in America. Around 1720 he received the Master of Arts degree from Harvard College.[45] In conjunction with his graduation requirements, he submitted a handwritten manuscript of a Hebrew grammar. During the spring of 1722, Monis publicly embraced Christianity and was baptized. In the summer of 1722, Harvard College appointed Monis instructor of Hebrew, a post he held for forty years. When Monis received his notice of appointment to the Harvard teaching faculty, he wrote a letter to the President of Harvard College. In this letter he affirmed the importance of Hebrew study, particularly for would-be clergymen, by stating, "I think the More acquainted the Ministers of the Gospel are with the Hebrew tongue, and so with the Old Testament, the Better able they will be to understand the New Testament and so to preach. . . ."[46] Today, over two and one-half centuries later, the wisdom of such a statement is vindicated more than ever.

The year 1735 marked an unprecedented event in the history of Hebrew studies in America: on this date Monis published his Hebrew grammar, the first Hebrew grammar to be printed in the New World. He did so

---

42. *Proceedings of the Massachusetts Historical Society* 52 (May, 1919): 285. Also see Arnold Zeitlin, "Boston's Jews: The Best of Times," *Boston Magazine,* September 1984, p. 136.

43. Rosovsky, *Jewish Experience at Harvard and Radcliffe,* p. 3.

44. Feingold, "The Jewish Role in Shaping American Society," in *A Time to Speak,* p. 46.

45. According to Rosovsky, Monis received a Master of Arts degree in either 1720, 1722, or 1723. The sources are not clear whether Monis took an M.A. at Harvard or was given an honorary degree. In any case, sources from this period indicate that in 1720 Jews were not yet permitted to enroll at Cambridge or Oxford. This may well explain why he was not appointed to the faculty until after his acceptance into the Church. In addition, the question of Monis's move from Judaism to Christianity may also affect how one interprets the statement that "Monis was the first Jew to receive a college degree in America." See Nitza Rosovsky, *Jewish Experience at Harvard and Radcliffe,* pp. 4-5.

46. *Proceedings,* p. 294.

with the aid of a loan from Harvard College. A font of Hebrew type had to be sent over from England for the purpose. Printed in Boston by Jonas Green, and sold by Monis at his house in Cambridge, Massachusetts, the book bears this curious and cumbersome title: *A Grammar of the Hebrew Tongue, Being An Essay To bring the Hebrew Grammar into English, to Facilitate the Instruction Of all those who are desirous of acquiring a clear Idea of this Primitive Tongue by their own Studies.* On the back of the title page Monis wrote this sage advice: "I advise Beginners not to perplex themselves about any Rule that at first view seems difficult, which will be of great Advantage to carry on their design in the knowledge of this *Primitive Tongue* with Success." This same pedagogic maxim, now reduced to simpler expression, has been gratefully taken to heart by many first-year Hebrew students in need of an encouraging word at the start of their language study.

On the tombstone of Judah Monis in Northboro, Massachusetts, is engraved this poetic epitaph:

> A native branch of Jacob see,
> Which once from off its olive broke,
> Regrafted from the living tree
> Of the reviving sap partook.
> From teeming Zion's fertile womb,
> As dewy drops in early morn,
> Or rising bodies from the tomb
> At once be Israel's nation born.

The influence of Judah Monis upon the early stages of Hebrew studies in America can hardly be overestimated. For many years the study of the Hebrew language held a central place in the core curriculum of Harvard. But, like many other schools of higher education, especially in the last hundred years, the composition and curriculum of Harvard has changed. No longer do today's students have the opportunity or feel the need to partake of that reviving sap of the olive tree in the same way as Monis and his learners did. But of this lost perspective, one solitary Northboro tombstone continues to speak.

The colleges of Yale and Dartmouth also demonstrated a strong tie to Hebraic studies in their early years. Several brief historical comments on this tie will suffice. In the year 1777, immediately after the establishment of this nation, Ezra Stiles, President of Yale, declared that study of the Hebrew language was "essential to a gentleman's education." In so doing, Stiles is said to have reasoned to himself, as did Governor Bradford, "Isn't it [Hebrew] the language I am sure to hear first in heaven?"[47] At Dartmouth, Hebrew was in the original curriculum of the College. In 1803 John Smith, a Dartmouth faculty member, published the nation's second Hebrew grammar. (This came sixty-eight years after Monis's ground-breaking work.) At the start of the twentieth century, however, Hebrew was dropped from course offerings. Only recently have efforts been made to restore Hebrew as an elective in the curriculum.

## Foundational, Not Optional

During the last century the Church has had little sustained success remaining attached to its Hebraic foundation. With the secularization of higher education, schools which originally had close ties to the Church now found themselves suddenly severed from their biblical Hebraic roots. Hebrew and Old Testament studies became optional or were entirely removed from the curriculum. As a result, few Hebrewphiles—whether professional clergy or laypeople—were being channeled into positions of influence within the American Church. Instead, the Church has struggled vainly to support itself by a variety of artificial roots. Consequently, its growth has been stunted, its fruitfulness impaired.

But today we stand on the threshold of a new era. More and more Christians are coming to realize that Old Testament and Hebrew studies are not optional matters; indeed, they are the very bedrock upon which the Christian faith rests. They are what Paul refers to as "the holy Scriptures, which are able to make you wise for salvation" (2 Tim. 3:15). We must, therefore, continue urging a return to the position of the early Church, where today's Christian can, as John Bright has forcefully written, "claim the Old Testament, as the New Testament did, for it belongs to him no less than it did—and does—to Israel. Indeed, the Christian has through Christ in the truest sense been made an Israelite, grafted onto Israel like a wild branch onto a tree (Romans 11:17-24). He must therefore see the Old Testament history as *his* history, the history of his own heritage of faith, its God as *his* God, its saints and sinners as men who had to do with that God. The Christian who refuses to see it so, flies in the face of the New Testament's witness and does no less than reject his own past."[48]

47. Quoted in Marcus Konick, "Jewish Influence on American Life and Culture," *The Principal* 20/10 (June, 1975): 25.
48. Bright, *Authority of the Old Testament*, pp. 199-200.

The Old Testament is foundational, not optional, for it is the history of our "own heritage of faith." It is God-breathed, fully authoritative, and "useful for teaching, rebuking, correcting and training in righteousness" (2 Tim. 3:16). Furthermore, the Old Testament was written to give the Church faith to face tomorrow. In Paul's words, "For everything that was written in the past was written to teach us, so that through endurance and the encouragement of the Scriptures we might have hope" (Rom. 15:4). Thus the Old Testament must hold a central place in the life of today's Church. Can we afford to view the Old Testament with any less esteem than did Jesus, Paul, and the early Church?

## UNDERSTANDING CHAPTER EIGHT

1. The Jewish community does not normally use the term *Old Testament*. Why? Instead of "Old Testament," what other terms are frequently used by Jewish people? Explain how the term *Tenakh* stands for the threefold division of the Hebrew Bible (see footnotes to this chapter).

2. Suggest two other possible adjectives different from the word *Old* as preferable terms by which Christians could make reference to that Testament.

3. Who was Marcion? What was his position concerning the Old Testament? Why did he hold this view? What teachings helped influence his thinking? What New Testament author did Marcion extol? Why? In the year 144, what did the church at Rome decide concerning Marcion?

4. Define "Neo-Marcionism." Point out several different areas or examples that illustrate how this teaching has adversely influenced today's Church.

5. Suggest at least four main factors which have contributed to Christian apathy, de-emphasis, or neglect of the Old Testament. Give several examples to substantiate each of these points.

6. What attitude did Jesus and the New Testament writers take toward the Old Testament? Cite several key New Testament passages to buttress your answer. Was the gospel of the early Church proclaimed from the Old Testament or was the gospel strictly a New Testament teaching? Explain. What Old Testament document served as the "hymnbook" of the early Church?

7. In what sense is it a useful analogy for Christians to view the Bible as a single play with two acts? How does the Jewish community of today differ when considering this analogy?

8. If the Old Testament were suddenly discarded, what key theological pillars undergirding New Testament thought would be lost?

9. Discuss three main approaches to interpretation that the Church has followed in an attempt to preserve the place and authority of the Old Testament. Evaluate each of these methods of interpretation.

10. Discuss the problem of interpreting the Song of Songs. What considerations should be observed in this task?

11. Discuss the following statement: "The Bible did not come out of heaven on a parachute all at once, but revelation unfolded progressively over hundreds of years."

12. Do you agree with the following statements: (a) "Biblical interpretation is more an art than a science." (b) "The Holy Spirit does not ordinarily work in a vacuum." Discuss the implications of each statement.

13. Describe the unusual position taken by Friedrich Delitzsch concerning the origin of Christianity and the ancestry of Jesus. Discuss the potential impact of such teaching upon biblical studies and anti-Semitic activity.

14. In presenting the Jewish ancestry of Jesus, the Gospel of Matthew opens with an apparent wordplay on the Davidic origin of Jesus. Explain.

15. Jesus states that his intent was not to "abolish" or "destroy" the Law of Israel, but to "fulfill" it (Matt. 5:17). What light does rabbinic literature shed on understanding what Jesus meant by these words?

16. What are *tephillin* and why are they worn?

17. What are *tzitzit*? What does the Law of Moses say about their use? How does the life of Jesus reflect his own adherence to this Jewish custom?

18. The Jewish background to the Lord's Prayer is clearly seen in its similarity to two other well-known Jewish prayers. What are they?

19. What Jewish holidays do we know Jesus observed?

20. When did Hillel live in relation to the birth of Jesus? What famous reply did Hillel give on one foot concerning what an individual needs to know about the whole of Judaism? In what way did the teaching of Jesus parallel that of Hillel? Explain.

21. After considering some of the New Testament evidence concerning the Jewishness of Jesus, respond to the following question: If Jesus were to visit New York City today and decide some weekend to attend a local "house of worship," would he choose to visit a local church or a synagogue? Why? Discuss.

22. How do the Dead Sea Scrolls shed light on the command alluded to by Jesus to "hate your enemy" (Matt. 5:43)?

23. Hanukkah is an intertestamental holiday. What does the Apocrypha say about the historical origin of Hanukkah? Why is it called the Feast of Dedication?

24. What type of parable frequently used by Jesus is widely found in early rabbinic literature?

25. One of the most important rabbinic principles was the concept of "measure for measure." Briefly explain what is meant by this principle. How does the "measure for measure" principle shed light on the warning of Jesus, "Do not judge" (Matt. 7:1)?

26. How does rabbinic literature help clarify the saying of Jesus about "if your eyes are good . . . if your eyes are bad" (Matt. 6:22-23)?

27. What did Jesus mean by the "weightier" or "more important matters of the law" (Matt. 23:23)?

28. Give careful attention to the following concerning the Shema: (a) Be able to quote Deuteronomy 6:4. (b) What evidence is there to support that the Shema was the first portion from the Hebrew Bible that Jesus committed to memory? (c) What two lines of evidence point to Deuteronomy being the most widely circulated and popular book of the Pentateuch in Jesus' time? (d) What indication is there from ancient sources that the Shema was recited regularly as early as the New Testament period? (e) How often each day is this creed to be recited? (f) On what other occasion is it customarily recited? (g) How important in the teachings of Jesus is the Shema (see Mark 12:28-34)? (h) What two main emphases do Jewish interpreters stress in the phrase "the Lord is one" (*ehad*)?

29. In what four ways did the early synagogue (as later did the Church) employ Scripture?

30. What practices or institutions of the Church have been taken over and adapted from Judaism?

31. Define *yetzer ha-ra* and *yetzer ha-tob*. How do these concepts likely provide the Jewish background to Paul's discussion in Romans 7 and 8? Is Paul's description of sin as "falling short" a Jewish idiom? Explain.

32. How did the Puritans who came to America show as a people their deep rootedness in the Hebraic tradition? Name two well-known Puritan leaders who had high respect for the Hebrew language.

33. Discuss the observation of Jewish historian Henry Feingold that in early America "Congregationalists were better Hebraists than Jews."

34. Summarize the important role that Harvard University's Judah Monis played in the early stages of the development of Hebrew studies in America.

35. How did the colleges of Yale and Dartmouth demonstrate a strong tie to Hebrew studies in their early years? From your knowledge of American history, what factors contributed to the gradual de-emphasis of Hebrew and biblical studies in higher education? How has archeology in the Middle East and the Holy Land during the twentieth century helped bring a new awareness and renewal of Hebraica and a search for Jewish biblical roots?

36. Discuss the implications of John Bright's statement that "the Old Testament . . . belongs to [today's Church] no less than it did—and does—to Israel. Indeed, the Christian has through Christ in the truest sense been made an Israelite."

## Chapter Nine

# The Contour of Hebrew Thought

*But his delight is in the law of the LORD, and on his law he meditates day and night*

Psalm 1:2

In the opening chapter of this book we established that the biblical writers reflect a Hebraic mind-set. These authors, in both Old and New Testaments, find their primary orientation in the Semitic culture of the East. Accordingly, we have argued that Christianity does not derive from pagan, Hellenistic sources, or from speculative worldviews. Neither is it a syncretistic religion deeply rooted in mystery cults, Gnostic sects, naturalistic philosophies, or polytheistic thought. Rather, the Christian faith is divinely revealed and is securely anchored in the Hebrew Bible —the Law, Prophets, and Writings. God breathed his word into the minds of the biblical authors within a Jewish cultural environment. Consequently, for us, in the most succinct terms, "to ignore Hebraic ways of thinking is to subvert Christian understanding."[1] We must, therefore, focus on the language and thought-patterns found in the Scriptures so that we are able to penetrate the mind of the Hebrew people. When we enter their civilization and view it through their eyes, we find that the contour of their thought is vibrant, rich, and colorful. It has its own nuances and features. Indeed, the Hebraic background to Christian thought is at the heart of the rich spiritual

---

1. John Dillenberger, "Revelational Discernment and the Problem of the Two Testaments," in *The Old Testament and Christian Faith,* ed. Bernhard W. Anderson (repr. New York: Herder and Herder, 1969), p. 160.

legacy that Jews have shared with Christians. Accordingly, in this chapter we will examine the Hebrew mentality and seek to discover how the Hebrews viewed their world.

## An Energetic People, a Descriptive Language

Through modern invention and outright apathy, our present Western world has grown more and more passive. We have developed a TV-obsessed, entertainment-prone, and spectator-minded generation which seems to be content to watch life rather than to live it. By contrast, the Hebrews were largely an energetic, robust, and, at times, even turbulent people. They were primarily outdoor folk—farmers, fishermen, tradesmen—who lived life to the full. For them, truth was not so much an idea to be contemplated as an experience to be lived, a deed to be done. The biblical writers often use vocabulary which is highly colorful, dynamic, and action-centered. They tell the story of a people on the move, a people who approached living with boldness, drive, and expectation. In a true sense, Israel's religion might be called a "pup-tent" religion. Israel followed a "God-on-the-move," and they were his "movable treasure" (cf. Exod. 19:5).[2]

A careful study of the Hebrew Bible will reveal what Martin Luther called a "special energy" in its vocabulary. In his struggle to translate the Hebrew Bible into German, Luther discovered in the sixteenth century what many Hebraists of the twentieth century have recently come to affirm with him: it is impossible to convey so much so briefly in any other language. Little wonder, then, that Luther wrote: "Even if this language [Hebrew] were useless otherwise, one should still learn it out of thankfulness." Furthermore, Luther states: "In it [the Hebrew language] we hear God speak . . . thus study directed toward learning this language might rightly be called a kind of Mass or divine service."[3] Indeed, Luther, who during his life had very mixed attitudes toward the Jewish people, concluded the following: "The Hebrew language is the best language of all, with the richest vocabulary. . . . If I were younger I would want to learn this language, because no one can really understand the Scriptures without it. For although the New Testament is written in Greek, it is full of hebraisms and Hebrew expressions. It has therefore been aptly said that the

---

2. Walter C. Kaiser, Jr., *The Old Testament in Contemporary Preaching* (Grand Rapids: Baker Book House, 1973), pp. 43-44.

3. *Luther's Works,* vol. 12: *Selected Psalms,* ed. Jaroslav Pelikan (St. Louis: Concordia Publishing House, 1955), 198-99.

Hebrews drink from the spring, the Greeks from the stream that flows from it, and the Latins from a downstream pool."[4] What Luther expressed at the time of the Reformation has been effectively rephrased in modern times through the words of Christian Hebraist Leslie Allen: "Hebrew enables one to see the Old Testament from inside instead of peering through the telescope of a version."[5]

The action-centered life-style of the Hebrews is often reflected in Hebrew sentence structure. The English language usually places the noun or subject first in the clause, then the verb or action-word; for example, "The king judged." In the narrative of biblical Hebrew, however, the order is normally the reverse. That is, the verb most often comes first in the clause, then the noun; thus, "He judged, (namely) the king." In Hebrew grammar, the position of emphasis is usually the beginning of the clause. Unfortunately, our English translation of the Hebrew text does not always reveal this emphasis. So it should not be forgotten that Hebrew—unlike English—usually confronts the listener or reader immediately with a verbal form (often a transitive verb, but sometimes an intransitive or "stative" form) even before the subject itself is designated.

Laziness, inertia, or passivity were hardly marks of the Hebrews' life-style. Rather, the Hebrews were mainly a doing and feeling people. Thus their language has few abstract terms. Rather, "Hebrew may be called primarily a language of the senses. The words originally expressed concrete or material things and movements or actions which struck the senses or started the emotions. Only secondarily and in metaphor could they be used to denote abstract or metaphysical ideas."[6] The Bible contains many Hebraisms in which abstract thoughts or immaterial conceptions are conveyed through material or physical terminology. We shall give a number of examples to illustrate this point: "look" is "lift up the eyes" (Gen. 22:4); "be angry" is "burn in one's nostrils" (Exod. 4:14); "disclose something to another" or "reveal" is "unstop someone's ears" (Ruth 4:4); "have no compassion" is "hard-heartedness" (1 Sam. 6:6); "stubborn" is "stiff-necked" (2 Chr. 30:8; cf. Acts 7:51); "get ready" or "brace oneself" is "gird up the loins" (Jer. 1:17); and "to be determined to go" is "set one's face to go" (Jer. 42:15, 17; cf. Luke 9:51). In addition, the Hebrews often refer to God by

4. This striking metaphor is from Luther's *Tischreden* (Table Talk), and is quoted here from Pinchas E. Lapide, *Hebrew in the Church*, trans. Erroll F. Rhodes (Grand Rapids: William B. Eerdmans Publishing Co., 1984), p. x.

5. Leslie C. Allen, "Why Not Learn Hebrew?" *TSF Bulletin* 30 (Summer, 1961): 3.

6. George Adam Smith, "The Hebrew Genius as Exhibited in the Old Testament," in *The Legacy of Israel*, ed. Edwyn R. Bevan and Charles Singer (Oxford: Clarendon Press, 1944), p. 10.

use of anthropomorphisms (i.e., representations of God with human attributes). The "living" and "active" God of the Hebrews is thus never reduced to mere impersonal abstraction. For instance, the Ten Commandments are said to be "inscribed by the finger of God" (Exod. 31:18). The prophet Isaiah states, "Surely the arm of the LORD is not too short to save, nor his ear too dull to hear" (Isa. 59:1). And again, a well-known proverb states, "The eyes of the LORD are everywhere" (Prov. 15:3).

Jewish anthropologist Raphael Patai has observed that because the Hebrews liked the concrete and tended to avoid the abstract, the idea of doctrinal formulation was alien to their mind.[7] In Hebrew thought the essence of true godliness is tied primarily to a relationship, not to a creed. The Lord is the God of Israel, and Israel is the people of God (Lev. 26:12; 2 Sam. 7:24; Jer. 31:33; cf. Heb. 8:8-12). Here is the leitmotif of biblical theology. The Torah gives direction to Israel on how to relate to the Creator, his people, and his world. Sin ruptures that relationship, but repentance brings forgiveness and restoration to fellowship. For the Hebrews, personal or individual relationship has always been far more expressive of the heart of religious faith than mere intellectual assent to abstract statements or religious ideas.

In the same vein, today's Church must not forget that the earliest theology in the New Testament is relational or existential rather than propositional or creedal. This is not to imply that doctrine plays an inconsequential role in the New Testament. But note that Jesus initially appoints the Twelve "that they might be with him" (Mark 3:14). Certainly the parable of the Gracious Father (often called the parable of the Prodigal Son) in Luke 15 and the adoption of believers into the divine family as "children of God" (John 1:12-13) are powerful New Testament examples of the importance of relationship. In sum, creedal formulation (as expressed in the book of Acts and especially in the Epistles) grows primarily out of the need in the early Church to explain—that is, make a theological statement about —its personal encounter with Jesus (as recorded in the Gospels).

The Hebrews have sometimes been described as a very visceral people. From a physiological and anthropological perspective, the seat of the will, emotions, mind, and spiritual powers is often found in the general area of the gastrointestinal tract. The Hebrews had little knowledge of anatomy and physiology; thus the functions that we normally ascribe to the mind the Hebrews considered to be taking place in an organ of their body. For example, the Old Testament indicates that in the heart (*leb* or *lebab*) a

7. Raphael Patai, *The Jewish Mind* (New York: Charles Scribner's Sons, 1977), p. 67.

person may love (Deut. 6:5), may fear (28:65), and may sin (Jer. 17:9). In the bowels or intestines *(me'eh)* one may feel anguish, as from the sound of a trumpet announcing war (Jer. 4:19). In the liver *(kabed,* literally "heavy," probably reflecting the fact that this organ weighs over three pounds and is the largest gland in the body) a person may experience the horror of Jerusalem's fall (Lam. 2:11). And in the kidneys *(kelayot)* one may rejoice (Prov. 23:16).

The New Testament reflects this same visceral Hebraic perspective on human nature. A person may believe with his heart (Rom. 10:10). One may refresh spiritually the bowels of other believers (Phlm. 7, 20). A person may come under the judgment of God when the Lord searches his kidneys (Rev. 2:23). These texts illustrate that for the New Testament authors passion was tied to their belief that human beings were "whole"; that is, they considered one's physical, psychological, and spiritual functions to be one indivisible entity. Both Testaments affirm this perspective, as seen in the above passages. They describe a person's various mental, spiritual, and emotional reactions to stress by locating these reactions in the organs of the body where a person actually feels the effects of that stress.

Modern man in the Western world thinks he has an image to defend. He is supposed to be macho and keep his cool. He is expected to be made of steel, always in control. He does not allow himself to become vulnerable by revealing much of his emotions. It is usually considered unmanly for him to cry. Yet Jesus, the exemplary man, wept (Luke 19:41; John 11:35). This display of emotion was in sharp contrast to the Greco-Roman world of the Stoics, who sought to be indifferent to pleasure or pain; they were determined never to submit or to yield; they were resolved to overcome their emotions and desires. The Hebrews, however, were a very passionate people; they did not hide or suppress their emotions.

The Hebrews—both men and women—were able to affirm their full humanity. They gave vent unashamedly to their feelings, for each emotion had "a time" appropriate for its expression: being angry, crying, laughing, singing, feasting, dancing, hand clapping, shouting, embracing, and loving (see Eccl. 3:1-8). The warrior-king David, a skillful musician and poet, provides a notable biblical example of one giving open expression to both extreme excitability and deep depression. David's emotions ran with the flow of his life. When the ark was brought to Jerusalem, he leaped and danced before the Lord "with all his might" (2 Sam. 6:14-16). But when his child borne by Bathsheba became sick and died, he wept and fasted for a week and spent the nights lying on the ground (12:15-23). The book of Psalms—particularly those penned by David—allows us to peer into some of the deepest emotional crevices of the human heart. And in our recitation of them, the Psalms provide a vehicle for us to express our own emotions before God.

Since Bible times, the various holidays and rites of passage throughout life have provided particular opportunities for Jewish people to rejoice and to celebrate.[8] The Song of Songs is an example of a passion-filled love poem that celebrates openly the sensual purity of marital love. Wine is a symbol of joy and often accompanies special celebrations (cf. Ps. 104:15; Eccl. 10:19; John 2:1-11). A brief summary of the holidays described in the Bible reveals a decisive emphasis on the release of emotion, especially joy. The weekly Sabbath is a time of rejoicing as God is celebrated as Creator (Isa. 58:13-14; cf. Exod. 20:8-11). *Rosh Hashanah,* "the New Year," celebrates the creation of the world. The harvest holiday of *Sukkot,* "Tabernacles," is called "the festival for rejoicing" (cf. Lev. 23:40; Neh. 8:17). *Hanukkah,* "the Feast of Dedication" (see John 10:22), commemorates religious freedom won by the Maccabean revolt. *Purim,* "the Feast of Lots," celebrates Esther's great bravery and the overthrow of Haman's plot to destroy the Jews of Persia (cf. Esth. 9:22). *Pesah,* "Passover," is the festival of redemption that celebrates freedom from enslavement in Egypt. The pilgrimage festival of *Shabuot,* "Weeks" (Pentecost), was celebrated in Bible times amidst singing and dancing, as *bikkurim,* "firstfruits," were brought to the Temple. Finally, to remember Jerusalem was considered to be one's "highest joy" (Ps. 137:6). In the midst of the summer, the 9th of Ab is a day of fasting and mourning over the destruction of Jerusalem. On this occasion the dirge of Lamentations is read. In sum, the entire annual calendar of festivals shows that the Hebrews were not afraid to release their emotions, in collective historical memory, before God and one another. The Hebrews were hardly halfhearted or reserved in their approach to life.

Is there a message in all of this for Christians today? How ought this Hebraic disposition of being a dynamic, feeling, and fully human people affect the modern Church? One Old Testament scholar, John Bright, addresses this issue in these apt words:

> We shall never hear the Old Testament's word rightly unless we are willing to hear it all. That is to say, we must hear it in its full humanity. There is a drive toward incarnation in the biblical revelation . . . it pleased God to reveal himself not through timeless teachings, or some heavenly *gnosis,* but through the events of a particular history, and to and through men who were caught up in history, and who were in every case men of like passions with

8. See Yechiel Eckstein, *What Christians Should Know About Jews and Judaism* (Waco, TX: Word Books, 1984), pp. 85ff.

ourselves and subject to all the limitations of our flesh. And God's final revelation of himself was given—so the New Testament declares—when "the Word became flesh and dwelt among us," in the form of a man who had a body like our own and feelings like our own, and whose mortal life, like ours, ended in death. It is incumbent upon us to take this aspect of the biblical revelation seriously.[9]

Here is one of the most crucial factors which makes the Bible so vital. It is a realistic, down-to-earth piece of literature. Its characters are not halo-bearing, otherworldly spirits, but men and women of flesh and blood whose total humanity is boldly displayed. Hence we meet ourselves in the Bible, for its characters are people just like us. Their struggles, problems, and weaknesses are the same as ours. Their feelings and needs, their sorrows and joys, their doubts and dreams are ours too. The incarnation shows how far down God was willing to come to share the full humanity of his people. Because Christians from every nationality, age in life, and period of history can identify with the people of the Bible, the message of the Bible is timeless. Thus it meets all of us where we are, and still speaks forcefully today.

## The Power of Poetry

About one-third of the Hebrew Bible is poetry. Poetry was a welcome aid to memory, for it employed parallel lines that had a certain rhythm of thought, though no set meter. Furthermore, an abundant use of various figures of speech enhanced its liveliness, creativity, and depth of meaning.

The poetry of the prophets reveals a wide range of effective word-plays: for example, *mishpat* ("justice") and *mispah* ("bloodshed"), *tzedaqah* ("righteousness") and *tze'aqah* ("a cry") in Isaiah 5:7; *shaqed* ("almond tree") and *shoqed* ("watching") in Jeremiah 1:11-12; *qayitz* ("ripe fruit") and *qetz* ("time is ripe" or "end") in Amos 8:1-2; *heletikhah* ("I have burdened you") and *he'eletikhah* ("I brought you up") in Micah 6:3-4. Additional illustrations could readily be cited.

Other figures of speech lend further variety and creative power to biblical poetry. For instance, Psalm 1:3 uses a simile to describe a righteous man: "He is like a tree planted by streams of water, which yields its fruit in season and whose leaf does not wither." Joy is expressed through metaphor: "All the trees of the field will clap their hands" (Isa. 55:12), and

9. John Bright, *The Authority of the Old Testament* (repr. Grand Rapids: Baker Book House, 1975), p. 236.

"the mountains sing" (Ps. 98:8). God's protective care is shown through zoomorphism (the attributing of animal-like features to God): "Hide me in the shadow of your wings" (Ps. 17:8). Nature is personified, but not deified. Stars fight (Judg. 5:20), mountains skip (Ps. 114:6), and the heavens declare God's glory (Ps. 19:1).

Sometimes the emotional excitement and rapid heartbeat of the poetry is conveyed by the quickness of the meter and the shortness of the vowels. At other times, the lengthening of lines and the use of long vowels may have the opposite effect. In addition, Hebrew poets sometimes repeated key words in order to achieve a climactic effect. Unfortunately, however, when read in translation, the full impact and immediacy of poetry is usually lost. Nevertheless, the following passages will give one a certain feel for the situation that the poet is describing.

The climax of the story of Jael, the brave Hebrew woman who killed the Canaanite military commander Sisera with tent peg and hammer, reads this way:

> Her hand reached for the tent peg,
>     her right hand for the workman's hammer.
> She struck Sisera, she crushed his head,
>     she shattered and pierced his temple.
> At her feet he sank,
>     he fell; there he lay.
> At her feet he sank, he fell;
>     where he sank, there he fell—dead.

Judges 5:26-27

The prophet Nahum describes the fall of the city of Nineveh to the invading army of Babylon, which happened in 612 B.C. As capital of Assyria, Nineveh was intensely hated by its enemies because of its cruelty and bloodthirstiness. A portion of the fast-moving poetical account of the city's destruction is as follows:

> Woe to the city of blood,
>     full of lies,
> full of plunder,
>     never without victims!
> The crack of whips,
>     the clatter of wheels,
> galloping horses
>     and jolting chariots!

Charging cavalry,
    flashing swords
    and glittering spears!
Many casualties,
    piles of dead,
bodies without number,
    people stumbling over the corpses.

*ASSONANCE*

Nahum 3:1-3

The writers and poets of Israel skillfully used opportunities for assonance and onomatopoeia. Assonance is the resemblance or imitation
of sound between two words or syllables, or the repetition of vowels
without the repetition of consonants in two words, for example, *peloni
almoni,* "a certain one" (Ruth 4:1) and *tohu va-bohu,* "formless and
empty" (Gen. 1:2). Onomatopoeia is the formation of words that re-
semble those associated with the object or action to be named: for example, *tzeltzel,* "cymbal" (Ps. 150:5), and *zebub,* "fly" (Isa. 7:18). In the
brief selections of Hebrew poetry which follow we shall illustrate these
rhetorical skills.

The theme of Isaiah 1–39 is primarily that of judgment and rebuke.
But in chapters 40–66, the last half of the prophecy, the mood changes suddenly to one of comfort, blessing, and hope. Thus the prophet introduces
this section[10] with these tender onomatopoetic words to the people of
Jerusalem.

> *Nahamu nahamu ammi*
> Comfort, comfort my people

Isaiah 40:1a

One of the earliest Israelite poems is the Song of Deborah (Judg. 5),
which also illustrates onomatopoeia. Notice Deborah's ear for the charge
of horses in battle. One can almost hear their hoofbeats.

> *Daharot daharot abbirayv*
> Galloping, galloping go his mighty steeds

Judges 5:22b

With vibrant assonance and onomatopoeia the prophet Isaiah cap-

---

10. Note the discussion by George Adam Smith on this Hebrew passage and the two
following (Judges and Isaiah) in "The Hebrew Genius as Exhibited in the Old Testament,"
in *Legacy of Israel,* pp. 12-13.

tures one of the sounds of nature. Using the sound of the rolling and surging waters, he predicts the overthrow of Assyria and its allied nations. This clashing of armies and turmoil of battle can be heard in the movement of the stormy seas. As a poet, the prophet is able to produce his desired effect through the skillful lengthening of vowels and doubling of consonants. Hence, the slow lift and roll of the waves is brought out by the long vowels, while the doubled consonants echo the boom, crash, and hissing sweep of the waves all along the shore.

> *hoy hamon ammim rabbim*
> *kahamot yammim yehemayun*
> *u-she'on le'ummim*
> *kishe'on mayim kabbirim yishsha'un*
> *le'ummim kishe'on mayim rabbim yishsha'un*
> Oh, the raging of many nations—
>     they rage like the raging sea!
> Oh, the uproar of the peoples—
>     they roar like the roaring of great waters!
> Although the peoples roar like the roar of surging waters. . . .
>
> Isaiah 17:12-13a

One further example from the Hebrew Bible is worthy of our attention. It, too, illustrates an imitation of sound, this time apparently that of a children's spelling lesson. In Isaiah 28:7-13 the prophet confronts the religious leaders of his day, who were in a state of drunken stupor. As he seeks to explain God's message to these "children" who reel and stagger in their vomit and filth (vv. 7-9), he finds them making a parody of his teaching. They seek to imitate his words by mocking and scoffing (v. 14). They mimic the prophet as if he were teaching a beginner's spelling lesson to a group of adults. This spelling lesson on the Hebrew alphabet sounds this way:

> *tzav latzav tzav latzav*
> *qav laqav qav laqav*
> *ze'er sham ze'er sham*
> Tzadhe (ṣ) tzadhe (ṣ), tzadhe (ṣ) tzadhe (ṣ)
> Qoph (q) qoph (q), qoph (q) qoph (q)
> a little (boy) here (and) a little (boy) there
>
> Isaiah 28:10a, repeated in v. 13b

The letters *tzadhe (ṣ)* and *qoph (q)* occur together in this order in the Hebrew alphabet. The point of this taunt appears to be that the prophet is like a teacher who takes it upon himself to instruct adults in their ABCs.

The common translations, "Precept upon precept, line upon line," or "do and do, rule on rule," seem to obscure the point of the passage.[11]

## Painting Verbal Pictures

As one may deduce from our discussion thus far, Hebrew is a very colorful language, and the biblical writers knew how to use it to great advantage. But Hebrew is not a precise analytical language, prone to conveying subtle nuances of meaning. For example, Hebrew has but two verbal tenses. It normally uses the imperfect tense for incomplete action and the perfect tense for completed action. In general, the syntax and grammar of Hebrew are far less complex than the inflectional languages of Latin and Greek.

The nature of Hebrew is to paint verbal pictures with broad strokes of the brush. The Hebrew authors of Scripture were not so much interested in the fine details and harmonious pattern of what is painted as they were in the picture as a whole. Theirs was primarily a description of what the eye sees rather than what the mind speculates. In brief, the whole world is a mystery which the Hebrew neither comprehends nor thoroughly investigates. "He takes things as they are, as he himself sees them. He accepts them, and marvels."[12]

To gain additional perspective on the nature of Hebrew thought, the analogy of an orchestra might be helpful. When viewed collectively, the Hebrew authors of Scripture are not primarily concerned to function like an orchestra which has each instrument finely tuned, each fully audible, and each playing in precise harmony and coordination with every other instrument. Rather, the inspired Hebrew sages are like the full impact and rich blended sound of an orchestra as a whole, though—and it is nothing to cause any great concern—some instruments sometimes may appear to be playing out of tune.

11. See E. W. Heaton, *Everyday Life in Old Testament Times* (New York: Charles Scribner's Sons, 1956), p. 179. It should be pointed out in passing that all alphabets used in the world today—about fifty in number—are derived from the Phoenician or Canaanite alphabet, which was invented ca. 1500 B.C. The Hebrews borrowed their alphabet of twenty-two letters directly from the Phoenicians. The word *alphabet* is derived from a Latin word *alphabetum*, which received its components from the Greek words for *a (alpha)* and *b (beta)*, which in turn represent the Phoenician (Canaanite) and Hebrew words *aleph* and *bet*. See Keith Schoville, *Biblical Archaeology in Focus* (Grand Rapids: Baker Book House, 1978), pp. 127-52.

12. Ludwig Köhler, *Hebrew Man*, trans. Peter R. Ackroyd (Nashville: Abingdon Press, 1957), p. 132.

Having drawn the broad picture of Hebrew thought, let us now consider briefly how the Hebrews viewed God. The biblical authors never argue the existence of God; they only assume it. God is not understood philosophically, but functionally. He acts. The Hebrews primarily thought of him pictorially, in terms of personality and activity, not in terms of pure being or in any static sense. That is, to express the divine attribute of love, the Hebrews would normally think in terms of a "loving God" (i.e., a God who loves), rather than "God is love." Certainly, therefore, the Hebrew mind-set of Bible times would find little or no interest in many of the issues the Church has debated over the centuries. These issues include theoretical arguments for the existence of God, the nature of the Godhead, free will and predestination, the specifics of the life to come, the word-for-word accuracy and use of quotations, and the precise way in which the divine and human mesh in the inspiration of Scripture.

The verbal pictures painted by the Hebrew writers in the Bible are at times earthy, pungent, and direct. Leslie Allen reminds us: "From the sophistication and highbrow intellectualism of this age one can travel back to thought-forms refreshing in their moving simplicity, naive but dignified, to solid sense, to air laden with earthy tang."[13] Indeed, the word *earth* (Hebrew *eretz*) is used in the Old Testament five times more frequently than *heaven* (Hebrew *shamayim*). For the Hebrews, the daily events in the lives of people are second only to God in significance. In the Hebrew Bible one encounters a down-to-earth humanness and openness—at times even bluntness and sensuousness—in some of the verbal pictures. Western tastes may be offended at this earthiness. Nevertheless, much of the theology in the Bible comes from terminology rooted in the experiences of everyday life. This was the world of the Hebrews, and underscores again how much God cared to bring the divine word of Scripture fully down to our human level, where we can grasp it.

Let us consider several examples of this earthiness. The prophecy of Isaiah describes graphically the intended fate of the people of Jerusalem. Trapped in the year 701 B.C. by the powerful Assyrian army of Sennacherib, they are described as those who have to "eat their own filth and drink their own urine" (Isa. 36:12). Though Jerusalem was miraculously spared this Assyrian attack (see Isa. 37; cf. 2 Kgs. 19), more than a century later (586 B.C.) Babylon destroyed Jerusalem. Jeremiah was one of the leading prophets of the Southern Kingdom at the time. With the same candor as Isaiah, Jeremiah depicts sorrowfully the acts of cannibalism performed by his own people as Jerusalem was brought to the very brink of starvation: "With their

13. Leslie C. Allen, "Why Not Learn Hebrew?" *TSF Bulletin* 30 (Summer, 1961): 4.

own hands compassionate women have cooked their own children, who became their food when my people were destroyed" (Lam. 4:10; cf. Deut. 28:53-57). Against the background of their Babylonian exile God's people are described as sinful and unclean, whose "righteous acts are like filthy rags" (Isa. 64:6). However, the Hebrew for "filthy rags" is far more explicit, reflecting the Hebrews' vivid, earthy style of expression. It is *beged iddim*, literally "garment of menstruation." In similarly graphic words, Jeremiah likens Israel's sexual excesses at Canaanite shrines to that of a female wild donkey in heat: "[You are] a wild donkey accustomed to the desert, sniffing the wind in her craving—in her heat who can restrain her? Any males that pursue her need not tire themselves; at mating time they will find her" (Jer. 2:24). William Holladay explains this striking verbal picture: "When her season comes, she is frantic by the scent of the urine which he has deposited. When she picks up the scent, she goes frantic with joy and races off to find a mate."[14] These powerful descriptions of Israel's spiritual condition point to the reason why the prophets were often personae non gratae among their own people: not so much because of their predictions of judgment—which were few but severe—but because the prophets were revealers of God's words.

Such vivid biblical imagery reminds us that the Hebrew people lived close to nature; they were not afraid to face head-on those areas of life that people in the Western world normally either mention euphemistically or avoid discussing altogether. It should not seem strange, therefore, that circumcision is still performed in the Jewish community today in the presence of a group of people, sometimes before the entire synagogue. In this vein, we may well ask how Western Christians today would respond if a circumcision were held before the church body—not even to suggest mentioning from the pulpit the above themes of menstruation, animals in heat, or simply reading selections from the Song of Songs. Likely, many Christians would be somewhat ill at ease. Such a response may again underline the fact that the cultural perspective of the modern Church in the Western world is different from the Eastern, Semitic world of the Hebrews that gave the Church birth. But more importantly, it is also a fitting reminder of the ongoing need for Christian study of Hebrew thought.

The Hebrew creation story (Gen. 1 and 2) is unrivaled in the ancient world from a literary point of view. In a number of ways it illustrates beautifully the Hebrews' adeptness with words; they were "word-smiths." Through use of the recurring formula "And there was evening, and there

14. William L. Holladay, *Jeremiah: Spokesman Out of Time* (Philadelphia: United Church Press, 1974), p. 41.

was morning," the writer builds gradually from "the first day" of creation to his climax, "the seventh day." Figures of speech and plays on words also punctuate the narrative. The earth is *tohu* and *bohu,* "formless, and empty" (Gen. 1:2). God said to the man and woman, *peru* and *rebu,* "be fruitful and increase in number" (1:28). The "Spirit of God was hovering over the waters" (1:2). The Hebrew term translated "hovering" *(meraḥephet)* is an ornithological term, used in Scripture of an eagle who hovers with loving care over the nest of its young (see Deut. 32:11). In Genesis 2, this creation hymn goes on to say that God "formed" man from the dust of the ground (v. 7). The verb translated "formed" *(yatzar)* is taken from the world of pottery; the prophets used it of one who forms or shapes vessels from clay (Jer. 18:4, 6). In a magnificent play on words the writer further states that God formed "man" *(adam)* from the dust of the "ground" *(adamah),* and he named him "Adam" (Gen. 2:7, 20).

The prophecy of Isaiah provides a further example of the colorful verbal imagery characteristic of the Hebrews. The prophecy opens with a description of Israel's spiritual sickness. The rebellious nation has become like a totally wounded and diseased body. Accordingly, the prophet says,

> Why should you be beaten anymore?
>> Why do you persist in rebellion?
> Your whole head is injured,
>> your whole heart afflicted.
> From the sole of your foot to the top of your head
>> there is no soundness—
> only wounds and welts
>> and open sores,
> not cleansed or bandaged
>> or soothed with oil.

Isaiah 1:5-6

But God still holds out hope which can radically transform his sinful people. Thus Isaiah pleads God's message with his countrymen, "Come now, let us reason together, says the LORD: Though your sins are like scarlet, they shall be as white as snow; though they are red as crimson, they shall be like wool" (1:18). The word translated "crimson" is *tola,* which provides a vivid picture for understanding the nature of forgiveness. The term *tola* refers primarily to a "worm" and secondarily to the color crimson. This secondary meaning developed because this worm (the technical name today is *coccus ilicis*), when crushed and placed in hot water, produced a brilliant crimson color that was colorfast and indelible. Thus it was a valuable commodity in the ancient dyeing industry (cf. Lam. 4:5).

The dye-stuff of this crimson-producing worm was used for the curtains of the tabernacle (Exod. 26:1).

What, then, is the lesson of the prophet and its application for today? It is the life-changing message of God's good news for the sinner, told in Hebraic imagery. The power of God's forgiveness to remove mankind's sin is like the whiteness and purity of new-fallen snow on Mount Hermon's peak, or like the naturally white, undyed wool of sheep washed in the Jordan, before shearing. That which to human beings appears to be a permanent stain of sin upon their lives, incapable of being removed, can, by God's cleansing power, be made clean. One may feel ineradicable guilt, much like Lady MacBeth, who cried, "All the perfumes of Arabia cannot sweeten this little hand." Yet, a person can be purified, changed, and forgiven by God's power. In New Testament terms, some from every nation, tribe, people, and language will one day stand before the throne of God, dressed in white robes, and shout, "Salvation belongs to our God" (Rev. 7:9-10). This is God's joyous announcement to us today as it was to ancient Israel: "Even though your sins are red, indelible as the crimson dye of the *tola*, I am able to forgive your sin, renew your life, and allow you to stand totally in the clear."

One of the methods by which verbal pictures are painted in biblical literature is through the art of storytelling. The Hebrew narrator made his story come alive by usually letting the characters speak for themselves. In addition, he could enhance the vividness of his story by using the Hebrew participle, which normally conveyed the idea of an action in progress, much like our use of the historic present tense today. Thus a whole series of actions could be dramatically portrayed, like the moving of the frames of a film, as they passed before the eyes of the storyteller.[15]

Jesus provides a striking example of one skilled in the art of storytelling. Like most of his Jewish forebears and contemporaries, when Jesus was asked questions he did not respond by reasoning from a starting point to a conclusion. Rather, he usually replied by telling a story, often in the form of a parable. By this method he engaged his audience, that is, he got them involved in arriving at the answer in a vivid and personal way. At the same time, this was how he made his point. The point, however, was usually made subtly, imaginatively, and indirectly. Jesus does not always spell out the truth he is communicating. He allows the one listening to the story to draw his own conclusions. The truth thus comes across in an allusive

---

15. See Leslie McFall, "Hebrew Language," in *The International Standard Bible Encyclopedia,* rev. ed., ed. Geoffrey W. Bromiley, et al. (Grand Rapids: William B. Eerdmans Publishing Co., 1982), 2:663.

rather than a direct way; it is implicit rather than explicit. By means of this creative approach, the listener usually ends up convicting himself. This common rabbinical teaching technique was effective, for it veiled the truth from frontal view. Central to the teachings of Jesus, it is found also in the writings of Paul, who stated of Jesus, "though he was rich, yet for your sakes he became poor, so that you through his poverty might become rich" (2 Cor. 8:9).

## Block Logic

The use of what may be termed *block logic* is another important contour of Hebrew thought. Greek logic, which has to a large extent influenced the Western world, was different. The Greeks often used a tightly contained step logic whereby one would argue from premises to a conclusion, each step linked tightly to the next in coherent, rational, logical fashion. The conclusion, however, was usually limited to one point of view—the human being's perception of reality.

By contrast, the Hebrews often made use of block logic. That is, concepts were expressed in self-contained units or blocks of thought. These blocks did not necessarily fit together in any obviously rational or harmonious pattern, particularly when one block represented the human perspective on truth and the other represented the divine. This way of thinking created a propensity for paradox, antinomy, or apparent contradiction, as one block stood in tension—and often illogical relation—to the other. Hence, polarity of thought or dialectic often characterized block logic.

It is particularly difficult for Westerners—those whose thought-patterns have been influenced more by the Greeks and Romans than by the Hebrews—to piece together the block logic of Scripture. When we open the Bible, therefore, since we are not Orientals, we are invited, as Robert Martin-Achard states, to "undergo a kind of intellectual conversion" to the Hebraic world of the East.[16]

Let us turn, then, to some of the many examples of block logic found throughout Scripture. The book of Exodus says that Pharaoh hardened his heart, but it also says that God hardened it (Exod. 8:15; cf. 7:3). The prophets teach that God is both wrathful and merciful (Isa. 45:7; Hab. 3:2). The New Testament refers to Jesus as the "Lamb of God" and the "Lion of the

16. Robert Martin-Achard, *An Approach to the Old Testament*, trans. J. C. G. Greig (Edinburgh: Oliver & Boyd, 1965), p. 46.

tribe of Judah" (John 1:29, 36; Rev. 5:5). Hell is described as both "blackest darkness" and the "fiery lake" (Jude 13; Rev. 19:20). In terms of salvation, Jesus said, "whoever comes to me I will never drive away," yet no one can come "unless the Father draws him" (John 6:37, 44). To find life you must lose it (Matt. 10:39). When you are weak, then you are strong (2 Cor. 12:10). The way up (exaltation) is the way down (humility) (Luke 14:11). "Jacob have I loved and Esau have I hated" (Rom. 9:13; cf. Mal. 1:3). More illustrations could easily be added.

Consideration of certain forms of block logic may give one the impression that divine sovereignty and human responsibility were incompatible. The Hebrews, however, sense no violation of their freedom as they accomplish God's purposes. Upon a more careful reading of the biblical text one can often observe that the Bible views one block from the perspective of divine transcendence—God says, "I will harden Pharaoh's heart"—and the other from a human point of view—"Pharaoh hardened his heart" (Exod. 4:21; 7:3, 13; 8:15). The same is often true of scriptures which deal with themes of predestination/election and free will/human freedom. Samuel Sandmel's discussion is particularly helpful in comparing Greek and Jewish perspectives on this point. He states:

> The view that the destiny of each man is predetermined by God is only superficially similar to the Greek view of fate. Fate was a blind force which dictated what was to happen to men and gods alike, and what was fated could not be altered. It is different too from the view known as predestination, which, in a sense, is kindred to fate except that it is God who fixes the unalterable fate. The Jewish view—we might call it providence—never concluded that a totally unalterable future lay ahead, for such a view contradicted God's omnipotence and mercy. Nor did the view that God fixed a man's destiny eliminate either man's free will or his moral responsibility; if, philosophically, a doctrine of providence and a doctrine of free will and moral responsibility seem contradictory (as, when carried to extremes, they are), Jewish thought never so extended either doctrine so as to preclude the other. The dictum of Rabbi Akiba is in effect an affirmation of the two contradictory sentiments: "All is subject to providence [i.e., everything is foreseen], yet man possesses free will" [Mishnah, Abot 3:16]. Unless God's proposed destiny for a man is subject to alteration, prayer to God to institute such alternation [sic] is nonsensical.[17]

In sum, the Hebrew mind could handle this dynamic tension of the language of paradox, confident that "all is in the hands of Heaven except the

17. Samuel Sandmel, *Judaism and Christian Beginnings* (New York: Oxford University Press, 1978), p. 226. See also Josephus, *Antiquities* 18.1.3 (12-15).

fear of Heaven" (Babylonian Talmud, Berakhot 33b). Divine sovereignty and human responsibility were not incompatible.

The Hebrew knew he did not know all the answers. His position was "under the sun" (Eccl. 8:17), so his words were few (5:2). He refused to oversystematize or force harmonization on the enigmas of God's truth or the puzzles of the universe. He realized that no one could straighten what God has made crooked (7:13). All things, therefore, did not need to be fully rational. The Hebrew mind was willing to accept the truths taught on both sides of the paradox; it recognized that mystery and apparent contradictions are often signs of the divine. Stated succinctly, the Hebrews knew the wisdom of learning to trust in matters that they could not fully understand.

While philosophical and structural divisions of learning obviously have an important role to play in contemporary education, our Western culture—especially on most levels of secular and Christian instruction—has provided little understanding concerning the nature of Hebrew thought. Thus we have the natural tendency to impose more rational and systematic categories of thought on the Bible. The Bible, however, tends to reject most carefully worked-out charts and thoroughgoing attempts at schematization. Neither God nor his Word may be easily contained in a box for logical or scientific analysis. Both God and his Word have a sovereign unpredictability that defies rational, human explanation. The Christian dogmatic tradition has much to learn from the Jewish community at this point, particularly in its attempt to understand Jesus and Paul. In this connection, Jewish biblical scholar Pinchas Lapide writes this provocative word for Christians to ponder:

> Jesus was certainly no theologian in any Western sense of the word, because he was a Jew. Like the prophets before him he gave concrete biblical answers to the pressing questions of daily life—poverty, payment of taxes, feuding between relatives or colleagues, and daily subsistence. He would certainly have detested as arrogant blasphemy any attempt to unravel and neatly systematize the mysteries of God. The same holds true for Paul . . . whose letters addressed very concrete, contemporary, and local problems and whose style reveals unmistakably rabbinic thought forms and lets Pharisaic dialogue patterns shimmer through. All of his responses, even the most well-reasoned, seem curiously fragmentary, and remain, in truly Jewish manner, open-ended both vertically as well as horizontally.[18]

In a similar context, Lapide reinforces the above point by commenting on

18. Pinchas Lapide and Peter Stuhlmacher, *Paul: Rabbi and Apostle,* trans. Lawrence W. Denef (Minneapolis: Augsburg Publishing House, 1984), pp. 34-35.

gentile Christians who try to squeeze Jesus and his paradoxes into a "logical straitjacket." Says Lapide, "He [Jesus] is still protesting, 'I am no cleverly-thought-out book; I am a human being, with all the inherent contradictions.'"[19] Lapide's point is well taken. It drives the Christian back to the Gospels to consider anew such sayings as Matthew 10:34, in which the "Prince of Peace" (Matt. 5:9; cf. Isa. 9:6-7) says, "Do not suppose that I have come to bring peace to the earth. I did not come to bring peace, but a sword."

The Semites of Bible times did not simply *think* truth—they *experienced* truth. As we have previously emphasized, truth is as much encounter as it is propositions. This experiential perspective on reality explains, in part, why Judaism never really developed vast systems of thought. It also allows us to understand how Judaism could live with the tensions and paradoxes surrounding block logic. To the Jew, the deed was always more important than the creed. He was not stymied by language that appeared contradictory from a human point of view. Neither did he feel compelled to reconcile what seemed irreconcilable. He believed that God ultimately was greater than any human attempt at systematizing truth. "Walking in the truth" (2 John 4) and "living the truth" (1 John 1:6) were a higher priority than rationally analyzing the truth. In the words of the renowned biblical scholar Rabbi Joseph Soloveitchik, "We [Jews] are practical. We are more interested in discovering what God wants man to do than we are in describing God's essence. . . . As a teacher, I never try to solve questions because most questions are unsolvable." He concludes, "Judaism is never afraid of contradictions . . . it acknowledges that full reconciliation of the two is possible only in God. He is the coincidence of opposites."[20]

It is our conclusion that the Church's propensity for categorizing or methodologically organizing great theological systems of thought is at best risky business. Not that the Bible is a dumping ground or random repository for eclectic jottings about God and life—far from it! It is God's inspired Word. If that divinely breathed message has cohesiveness and an overarching structure—and it does—this coherence and structure are not to be imposed upon the Bible. Rather, one must discover inductively this interrelatedness within Scripture, while at the same time giving free play to the loose ends and paradoxical language found therein.

19. Pinchas Lapide and Ulrich Luz, *Jesus in Two Perspectives* (Minneapolis: Augsburg Publishing House, 1985), pp. 18-19.
20. Quoted in Paul R. Carlson, *O Christian! O Jew!* (Elgin, IL: David C. Cook, 1974), pp. 142-43.

## A Time for Meditation

The world of the Hebrews was such that they had long periods of time for uninterrupted meditation. The rhythm of their lives was not ordered by alarm clocks or factory whistles but by the sun. Living outside as shepherds, farmers, and fishermen, the Hebrews were close to both soil and sea. In addition to the weekly Sabbath rest, each day, when the sun was high, the Hebrews took a break from work. When the sun set, their evenings were free. They also had periodic times for fasting. When we recognize these realities of ancient life, as well as the fact that both day and night they did not have to deal with the competition of telephones, TVs, and other modern sappers of time, we realize that they had considerable opportunity for meditation.

The subject of meditation is crucial for understanding the precise organization of the Hebrew Bible's threefold division into Law, Prophets, and Writings. Joshua is the first book in the Prophets, the second major division of the Hebrew Bible.[21] It opens with God commanding the Israelites to meditate on the Law of Moses (the first major division of the Bible) "day and night" (Josh. 1:8). The book of Psalms is the first book in the Writings, the third major division, and it opens with the same motif—that of meditating on God's Law "day and night" (Ps. 1:2). Elsewhere, the psalmist says, "I will meditate on all your works" (Ps. 77:12). Viewed contextually, these passages indicate that meditation is the key theme which binds the three divisions of the Hebrew Bible together.

In each of the three texts cited above, the Hebrew word for "meditate" is *hagah*. The word properly means "emit a sound," "murmur," "mutter," "speak in an undertone." For the Hebrews, meditation was not like a Quaker meeting; it was not silent. Several texts clearly support this contention that meditation was normally verbal, that is, expressed in spoken words. In Psalm 49:3 (RSV) we read, "My mouth shall speak wisdom; the meditation *[hagut]* of my heart shall be understanding." The Hebrew parallelism indicates that what is spoken with the mouth is the same as "meditation." Hence, the NIV renders *hagut* not "meditation" but "utterance." Again, in the well-known Psalm 19:14, the expression "words of my mouth" parallels "meditation *[hegyon]* of my heart." Furthermore, Joshua 1:8 states, "Do not let this Book of the Law depart from your mouth; med-

---

21. The *Nebi'im*, "Prophets," comprise two sections, the Former and the Latter Prophets. The Former Prophets include the books of Joshua, Judges, Samuel, and Kings. The Latter (or "Writing") Prophets include Isaiah, Jeremiah, Ezekiel, and the Twelve (or "Minor Prophets").

itate *[ve-hagita]* on it day and night." In this context, "meditate" is defined by the command not to let the Law ever be out of one's mouth. "This negative way of speaking implies a strong positive. . . . The mouth is here the organ of speech."[22] Furthermore, *hagah* is used in the Hebrew Bible to indicate such varied sounds as the "growl" of a lion (Isa. 31:4) and the "moaning" of a dove (Isa. 38:14).

Such passages give graphic insight into what meditation involves. Meditation is the outward verbalizing of one's thoughts before God, of the poring over his teachings and works. It means to articulate, in a low tone, thoughts of worship, wonder, and praise. But in addition, the use of *hagah* in texts such as Joshua 1:8 and Psalm 1:2 implies that the Scriptures were not primarily written to be read silently. Indeed, in the words of Otto Kaiser, the Law itself was to be "read aloud" by day and by night.[23]

This biblical style of meditation may be observed today in many Orthodox synagogues and at the Western (Wailing) Wall in Jerusalem. A Jew will *daven* ("pray"), *siddur* ("prayer book") in hand, expressing his thoughts audibly. This verbalization enables him to pray with a greater sense of intensity and *kavanah*, that is, purpose, attentiveness, direction. If the din about him increases so he has trouble concentrating—and it can —he wraps his prayer shawl more tightly around his head.

Another contemporary example of Hebraic meditation is found in the ultra-Orthodox community of the Hasidim, who practice *hitboddadut*. This Hebrew term means "to be alone," "to seclude oneself" (for purposes of meditation). Each day it is customary for an observant Hasid to make time to be alone for awhile so he can meditate by talking aloud with God. This meditation is a private pouring out of personal prayers, doubts, or problems. To recover a childlike quality of faith (cf. Matt. 18:3-4) the rabbis recommended *hitboddadut* at night in an open field. A familiar illustration of this personal articulation of thoughts to God is beautifully portrayed by Tevye, the dairyman of *Fiddler on the Roof,* in a number of scenes from that popular musical.

Some contemporary forms of church worship may appear to be a bit boisterous or too extemporaneous for those of us with more subdued and orderly Western tastes. But we should not forget that Hebrew worship— including prayer and the study of the holy books—was no sedate or dreary event. It included dancing with tambourine (Ps. 149:3; 150:4), all kinds of

22. Marten H. Woudstra, *The Book of Joshua,* New International Commentary on the Old Testament (Grand Rapids: William B. Eerdmans Publishing Co., 1981), p. 63.

23. From a lecture by Otto Kaiser of Marburg University entitled "The Law as Center of the Hebrew Bible," at Cambridge University, Faculty of Oriental Studies, May 13, 1987.

instruments—including trumpets and cymbals (Ps. 150)—singing (33:3), hand clapping (47:1), and even shouting (95:1). For the Hebrews, praise was the basic token of being alive; it was the way to observe the command, "You shall meditate on it day and night."

## Everything Is Theological

To the Hebrew mind, everything is theological. That is, the Hebrews make no distinction between the sacred and the secular areas of life.[24] They see all of life as a unity. It is all God's domain. He has a stake in all that comes to pass—whether trials or joys. And human beings have an awareness of God in all that they do. The psalmist states clearly this aspect of Hebrew thought: "I have set the LORD always before me" (Ps. 16:8). It is also taught in the proverb, "In all your ways acknowledge him, and he will make your paths straight" (Prov. 3:6). Thus God is seen to control both fertility (Gen. 30:22) and barrenness (1 Sam. 1:5-6). The book of Ruth gives concrete examples of this teaching. Ruth 1:6 states that "the LORD came to the aid of his people by providing food for them," a reference to relief from a famine that had ravaged the city of Bethlehem and the territory of Judah. Later on in this chapter, Naomi says, "the Almighty has brought misfortune upon me" (1:21), a reference to the recent loss of her husband and two sons in Moab. Thus, to the Hebrew mind, all the circumstances of life —the good times and the hard times—come not by chance but under the sovereign control of Almighty God.

Both Testaments emphasize this teaching concerning the sacredness of all of life. In Old Testament times the Hebrew farmer recited a special

---

24. At an early time the Church unfortunately emphasized this distinction through the monastic movement of the cloister and nunnery. W. D. Davies has effectively summarized the historical implications of this loss in the context of the Church's separation from the Synagogue: "A double morality arose: a higher morality for life out of the world and a lower one for life in it. The affirmation of all life as sacred, which has generally characterized the Synagogue, was ignored—and the Christian world became divided into clerical and lay people, secular and sacred institutions, holy persons and holy things being set over against unholy things. The wholeness of life that Judaism has stressed was lost. Nor has Protestantism escaped the sacred-secular dualism. The divorce of religion from life is part of the price paid for our neglect of the Synagogue. This is true despite the separation of things clean and unclean in Judaism, and the separation from the world involved in keeping the Law; throughout all this 'separation' Judaism was attempting to take seriously the application of the Law, that is, God's will, to all life" (*The Gospel and the Land* [Berkeley: University of California Press, 1974], pp. 387-88). For a useful Christian critique of this theme, see Ranald Macauley and Jerram Barrs, *Being Human: The Nature of Spiritual Experience* (Downers Grove: InterVarsity Press, 1978).

prayer (Deut. 26:5-10a) in order to remind him that the occupation of till-ing the soil is sacred.[25] Reflecting his strong Hebrew background (see Phil. 3:4-6), Paul writes, "So, whether you eat or drink, or whatever you do, do it all for the glory of God" (1 Cor. 10:31; see also Col. 3:17). Likewise, Peter exhorts that in speech as in action, "in all things God may be praised" (1 Pet. 4:11).

Prayer is the means by which Jews—both ancient and modern—have stayed attuned to the concept that all of life is sacred. Jewish prayers tend to be short because the entire working day of an observant Jew is punctuated with sentence prayers. More than one hundred of these *bera-khot,* "blessings," are recited throughout the day (cf. Mishnah, Berakhot 9:1-5). They customarily begin, *Barukh attah adonai,* "Blessed are you, O LORD." As King and Creator of the universe, God's presence is acknowl-edged at all times and in every sphere of activity within his world. Moses commanded the Israelites to bless the Lord for his goodness (Deut. 8:10). Building on this and other texts, the rabbis taught, "It is forbidden to a man to enjoy anything of this world without a benediction, and if anyone en-joys anything of this world without a benediction, he commits sacrilege" (Babylonian Talmud, Berakhot 35a). Hence a Jew recites a prayer upon hearing bad news and good news, when smelling fragrant plants, and when eating food or drinking wine. A Jew offers a prayer in the presence of thunder, lightning, rainbows, and comets. There is a prayer on seeing strangely formed persons, such as giants or dwarfs. A Jew is even in-structed to offer a prayer (several times each day) to bless God that one is able to urinate. The prayer reads: "Blessed is He who has formed man in wisdom and created in him many orifices and many cavities. It is fully known before the throne of Thy glory that if one of them should be [im-properly] opened or one of them closed it would be impossible for a man to stand before Thee" (Babylonian Talmud, Berakhot 60b).

It is, therefore, not pure facetiousness when, in *Fiddler on the Roof,* the rabbi is asked, "Is there a blessing for the Tsar?", and again, "Is there a blessing [i.e., to God] for a sewing machine?" These Jews, in their Russian village, are reflecting the ancient Hebraic belief that everything is theological. This is the way one stays in touch with the Almighty and keeps a divine perspective on life. It means constantly praising God for all things, with sentence prayers, throughout the day. Abraham Heschel poi-gnantly describes this Jewish mind-set as follows: "Saintliness was not thought to consist in specific acts, such as excessive prayer . . . but was an

---

25. See Walther Zimmerli, *The Old Testament and the World,* trans. John J. Scul-lion (Atlanta: John Knox Press, 1976), p. 10.

attitude bound up with all actions, concomitant with all doings, accompanying and shaping all life's activities."[26] Indeed, today's Christians will fail to grasp Paul's admonition to "Pray without ceasing," that is, "Pray continually" (1 Thess. 5:17), unless they understand that a main feature of Jewish prayer is its pervasiveness.

There is an authentic biblical humanism. It is to find the divine in the commonplace, even in the mysterious reversals of life. It is to be able, like Job, to bless the name of the Lord—whether he gives or takes away (Job 1:21). It is to have the confidence that Joseph expressed at the end of his life to his brothers who had double-crossed him, "You intended to harm me; but God intended it for good" (Gen. 50:20). It is to believe that "in all things God works for the good of those who love him" (Rom. 8:28). It is the challenge for human beings to elevate all of life so that at each place, each hour, in each act, and each speech, the holy can blossom forth.

To this day, the world of Hasidic Jewry has especially emphasized that no aspect of life is devoid of God's presence. One of the ways in which the Hasidim stress this point is through the singing of *A Dudule,* a song with a mixed Hebrew-Yiddish text. In the *A Dudule,* the Hasid addresses God using the German *du,* "you." (*A Dudule* refers to the "tootling" made on a simple shepherd's instrument; here, however, the word *du-du-le* is a play on words meaning "You, You!" with the German diminutive of endearment *-le.*)[27] In the English translation of *A Dudule* below, the words illustrate beautifully that God's involvement with his people is total.

> Lord of the universe,
> I would sing You a song *[du-du-le].*
> Where can I find You,
> And where can I not find You?
> Wherever I go there are You,
> Wherever I stay there are You,
> Only You, You, You, You.
>     If good comes, there are You,
> And if, Heaven forfend, trouble comes,
> There are You, You, You, You, You
>     You are, You were, You will be,
> You, You, You.
> In heaven and on earth, there are You,

26. Abraham J. Heschel, *The Earth is the Lord's* (New York: Henry Schuman, 1950), p. 20.

27. A. Z. Idelsohn, *Jewish Music in Its Historical Development* (New York: Schocken Books, 1956), pp. 420ff.

On high, below, there are You,
You, You, You, You, You.
  Wherever I may go,
There are You.[28]


# Religion as a Way of Life

Some would define religion as a system of ethics, a code of conduct, an ideology, or a creed. To a Hebrew it is none of these; such definitions are misleading, deficient, or inaccurate. Rather, a Hebrew understood his daily life of faith in terms of a journey or pilgrimage. His religion was tantamount to the way in which he chose to walk. Even before the Flood, people such as Enoch and Noah "walked with God" (Gen. 5:24; 6:9). If a person knows God, he is daily at God's disposal and walks in close fellowship with him, along the road of life. Ceremonialism and ritualism alone do not meet God's requirement for the good life (Isa. 1:11-14; Amos 5:21-23). But those who act justly and love mercy and *walk humbly* with God do please him (Mic. 6:8). Thus, we return to the fact that the essence of religion is relationship; it is walking with God in his path of wisdom and righteousness and in his way of service to others.

Everyone who walks through this life chooses a road or way for his journey. There is the "way of the wicked" (Prov. 15:9) and the "way of the righteous" (Ps. 1:6), and God knows the way a person takes (Job 23:10). God enjoins us "to walk in all his ways" (Deut. 11:22), so that we may say before him, "My steps have held to your paths; my feet have not slipped" (Ps. 17:5). There is the path of God's commands (Ps. 119:35), the course of the just (Prov. 2:8); there is a counterfeit way which "seems right to a man, but in the end it leads to death" (Prov. 14:12; 16:25); but "the path of life leads upward for the wise" (Prov. 15:24). One is instructed to "ask for the ancient paths, ask where the good way is, and walk in it" (Jer. 6:16). The prophetic vision of the last days is that of many peoples coming to Zion, where the Lord will teach them his ways so that they may walk in his paths (Isa. 2:3). When a person commits his way to the Lord (Ps. 37:5), then he is considered blessed (Ps. 128:1). God's word is a light for our path (Ps. 119:105). As we walk the road of life, we may become weary and faint; the Lord, however, renews our strength (Isa. 40:31). If we stumble on our way, we will not fall, for the Lord upholds us with his hand (Ps.

28. Quoted in David de Sola Pool, *Why I Am A Jew* (Boston: Beacon Press, 1957), p. 73.

37:23-24). When we acknowledge God in all our ways, God makes straight our paths (Prov. 3:6). God's ways, however, are not always clear to us; they are higher than our ways (Isa. 55:9) and sometimes inscrutable (Rom. 11:33).

In the Sermon on the Mount, Jesus uses this familiar Hebraic imagery to teach about the two ways. The broad one leads to destruction, and the narrow one to life (Matt. 7:13-14). In one of the eight Johannine "I am" pronouncements, Jesus clarifies this concept even further. He states, "I am the way" (John 14:6). In the book of Acts, the early Christians designate their movement as "the Way" (Acts 9:2; 19:9, 23; 22:4; 24:14, 22). These uses in Acts are likely connected to Jesus' identification of himself as "the way"; that is, the early Church saw itself as having the supreme truth about the way to salvation and life.

The concept of "the way" is also found in other religious literature outside the Bible. For example, the Dead Sea Scrolls indicate that the Qumran community called itself and its life "the Way." In addition, the Didache, a short anonymous book of Christian instruction from the second century, discusses extensively the "Two Ways," the Way of Life and the Way of Death. The former is described as loving both God and one's neighbor, vigilantly protecting oneself from sin in its various forms, and being faithful to perform Christian obligations at home and church. The Way of Death is indicated by a list of particular sins. Readers are admonished to follow the Way of Life.

During the period of Rabbinic Judaism, the Hebrew term *halakhah* (literally "walking, proceeding, going") took on special significance. It designated the religious laws and regulations to follow so one might keep straight on the road of life. It provided a map from the start to the end of one's journey. When one errs from God's path into crooked and perverse ways, one violates God's Torah and must "return." The Hebrew word for repentance is *teshubah,* suggesting the idea "turn around," "go back." The way back is the way of Torah; it gives the direction and guidance needed to remain on the way.

## A Different View of Time and History

The Bible is, first and foremost, God's revelation in history, and it is precisely this point that sets the Bible apart from other religious literature. The majority of the chapters in the Old Testament are either from the "historical books" or are placed in concrete historical settings. The Old Testament is concerned with a theological interpretation of history. "Jewish history is the record of a god-intoxicated, god-thirsty people"[29] (cf. Ps. 143:6). History is the arena where the track of the Almighty may be followed through specific revelatory events. The collective memory of the Jewish community has given it purpose and kept it alive. Knowledge of being summoned as a covenant people in the past gave the Jews both a sense of identity and mission for the present and a hope for the future. It is against this Jewish background of historical memory that the early Church saw the Lord's Supper (1 Cor. 11:25) and baptism (Rom. 6:3-5). Through these awe-inspiring ceremonies the Church is called to rehearse the meaning of the central salvific events in the life of its Lord.

Martin Buber once wrote, "divest the Bible of the acting character of God, and it loses its significance."[30] Indeed, the history of God's people involves a recital of the *magnalia* (a Latin term used by the Church Fathers for "great things," "mighty works" [of God]). Joshua (Josh. 24:1-15), Samuel (1 Sam. 12:6-12), and Stephen (Acts 7:1-53) are examples of biblical characters who recited the great redemptive acts of God. In the Old Testament, the greatest act by which God made himself known is the Exodus (Exod. 6:6-7). The acts of God reveal both his love and his judgment, his mercy and his wrath. Since God is invisible, he chose to reveal his nature through tangible events. We are reminded of this fact by the Hebrew title of the books of Chronicles, *dibre ha-yamin*, literally "the events of the days." The Chronicles were thought by the Hebrews to be much like a book of daily records outlining the events of the times. The same idea is generally reflected in the title of Luke's second scroll, the Acts of the Apostles *(práxeis apostólōn)*.

Unlike some of their neighbors, the Hebrews did not hold to a circular concept of history tied closely to the cycles of nature. Hebrew history was not a monotonous, purposeless, and eternal cycle of happenings. Nor did the Hebrews view life as a race toward death in which one desperately seeks to escape from the clutches of time. The Hebrew concept of history did not embrace any "blind, meaningless outcome of a fortuitous conglomeration of atoms, or the ever-recurring expression of uncontrolled and uncontrollable cosmic force, of fate and dearth."[31] Rather, in sharp distinction, the Hebrew view of time and history was essentially linear, durative, and progressive. In short, it was going somewhere; it was en route to a goal, a glorious climax at the end of this age. The consummation of history in the

---

29. S. Umen, *Jewish Concepts and Reflections* (New York: Philosophical Library, 1962), p. 32.

30. Martin Buber, *Israel and the World,* 2nd ed. (New York: Schocken Books, 1963), p. 99.

31. Davies, *The Gospel and the Land,* p. 385.

age to come will see nature transformed through the removal of evil from the earth. "On that day" God will judge the wicked and redeem the righteous, and "The LORD will be king over the whole earth" (Zech. 14:9).

Hebrew history is holy or sacred history *(Heilsgeschichte)*. God is the Lord of history, which is thus the account of Yahweh, "he who is actively present," at work in his world among his people. It is the story of divine redemption. Through his deeds and words (events and their interpretation) God brings meaning to Israel's earthly pilgrimage. He is above history (transcendent), sovereign, and responsible for bringing events to pass. Yet he is also immanent, present in and among his people, though they are responsible for their actions since they are free to choose.

Other ancient civilizations produced histories intended primarily to glorify a ruler among his subjects or to exalt that nation in the eyes of the world. Hebrew history, however, was written to glorify the Lord of the universe. It was written to inspire faith and trust in the living God. Whereas other peoples in the ancient Mediterranean world asked if there was anything worth living for (suicide or sudden death was always an option), the Hebrews taught the world to sanctify time. They believed that something sacred was at stake in each event and each life. Hence one must not kill time but redeem time (cf. Eph. 5:16).

Ours is a secular age. It is characterized by change, uncertainty, pessimism, and rootlessness. Many are asking today if there is anything to hold on to which is both stable and permanent and that can give hope and encouragement for tomorrow. When the hurricanes of life batter us so that we bend to the point of breaking, we are not rootless. There is a firm and secure root to support us. The "root that supports" (Rom. 11:18) and "nourishes" (11:17) is the godly, living faith of Israel. This is our foundation: to know the God of history, Israel's history (cf. Heb. 11). This concept of history brings ultimate meaning and purpose to both personal and global events. We are not alone.[32] The future is secure. God is alive, at work, and in control.

## UNDERSTANDING CHAPTER NINE

1. Some scholars have argued that Christianity is a syncretistic religion deeply rooted in mystery cults, Gnostic sects, naturalistic philosophies, or poly-

---

32. This biblical theme has been developed in Abraham J. Heschel's volume on philosophy of religion, *Man Is Not Alone* (New York: Farrar, Straus & Giroux, 1951; repr. New York: Harper & Row, 1966).

theistic thought. Discuss the implications of this view in regard to biblical authority and truth claims which are directly related to Jewish origins.

2. Discuss what you think Martin Luther meant when he said, "the Hebrews drink from the spring, the Greeks from the stream that flows from it, and the Latins from a downstream pool."

3. The Bible contains many Hebraisms in which abstract thoughts or immaterial conceptions are conveyed through material or physical terminology. Give several examples to illustrate this point. What is an anthropomorphism? Give an example from Scripture.

4. In Hebrew thought the essence of true godliness is not tied primarily to doctrine, creed, or theological proposition. Rather, the heart of religious faith is mainly focused in another area. What is this area? Do you agree? Discuss.

5. From a physiological and anthropological perspective, in what general area did the Hebrews normally place the seat of the will, emotions, mind, and spiritual powers? What specific bodily organs were included?

6. How did the ancient Stoics differ from the Hebrews in their approach to pleasure or pain?

7. True to his Semitic world of the ancient Near East, David's emotions ran with the flow of his life. Give examples.

8. Point out how the entire annual calendar of festivals demonstrates that the Hebrews were not afraid to release their emotions, in collective historic memory, before God and one another.

9. Discuss the implications of the following observation: "We shall never hear the Old Testament's word rightly unless we are willing to hear it all. That is to say, we must hear it in its full humanity."

10. How much of the Hebrew Bible is poetry?

11. From the poetical literature of the Old Testament, give at least one example of the following: (a) paranomasia (play on words), (b) simile, (c) personification of nature, (d) zoomorphism.

12. Define and illustrate assonance and onomatopoeia.

13. What is the origin of the Hebrew alphabet? To what Hebrew words do the Greek terms *alpha* and *beta* directly correspond? (See footnotes to this chapter.)

14. The Hebrews primarily thought of God pictorially, in terms of personality and activity, not in terms of pure being or any static sense. In this regard, how might the Hebrews express the divine attribute of love?

15. The pictorial vividness of the Eastern mind of the Hebrews often stands in sharp contrast to contemporary Western religious thought. Give several illustrations of the earthiness, openness, and candor with which the authors of the Hebrew Bible, through graphic imagery, drive home their points.

16. In what specific ways does the creation story in Genesis 1 and 2 illustrate the literary skill of the Hebrew authors of the Bible?

17. Discuss the meaning and application of Isaiah 1:18 as seen against the background of the dyeing industry of the ancient Near East.

18. What are some of the features that characterize the art of storytelling among the Hebrews? What is meant by the statement, "Jesus does not always spell out the truth he is communicating"?

19. What is meant by "block logic"? Give several biblical examples.

20. Discuss the implications of the observation that since we are not Orientals, we are invited to "undergo a kind of intellectual conversion" when we come to the Bible."

21. The issue of predestination/election and free will/human freedom has perplexed the most brilliant of minds since antiquity. How does Samuel Sandmel compare Greek and Jewish perspectives on this point?

22. Many Christians have a natural tendency to impose more rational, systematic, or schematic categories of thought on the Bible. In this regard, discuss some of the potential pitfalls and dangers to which the Christian dogmatic tradition has been prone over the centuries.

23. For the Semite of Bible times truth was far more than an array of static propositions; rather, truth was something living; it could be experienced. Discuss the relevance of this point for today's Church.

24. The Hebrew Bible is divided into the Law, the Prophets, and the Writings. Name the first book in each of these divisions. What is the key theme which binds the three divisions of the Hebrew Bible together?

25. What does the Hebrew word *hagah*, "to meditate," properly mean? Cite several passages to support this conclusion. Describe the biblical view of meditation.

26. Define the terms (a) *daven*, (b) *siddur*, and (c) *kavanah*.

27. What is the meaning of *hitboddadut*? How, where, and by whom is it customarily practiced today? Why did the rabbis recommend *hitboddadut*?

28. Compare ancient Hebrew worship with contemporary forms of Christian worship. Which Christian denominations tend to be closer to the Hebraic emphasis? Which least reflect it? Discuss.

29. Build a case from Scripture that "everything is theological" to the Hebrew mind.

30. How did the monastic movement highlight the fallacious distinction between the sacred and secular? What has been the position of the Synagogue in this sacred-secular dualism? (See the footnotes to this chapter.)

31. Define the term *berakhot*. Why do Jewish prayers tend to be short? According to Deuteronomy 8:10 and Babylonian Talmud, Berakhot 35a, why is it necessary to recite blessings? On what types of occasions are prayers to be offered? What do you think Paul means when he admonishes people to "pray without ceasing" (1 Thess. 5:17)?

32. What is the *A Dudule*? Explain the play on words in this title. What basic theological truth does the *A Dudule* illustrate?

33. Give some of the Old Testament texts that support the teaching that religion is in essence the way in which a person chooses to walk.

34. How is the term *the way* used in: (a) John 14:6, (b) the book of Acts, (c) the Dead Sea Scrolls, (d) the Didache?

35. What is *halakhah*? How does this word relate to the idea of Judaism being a "way of life"?

36. Define the term *magnalia*. Give several examples of biblical characters who recited the *magnalia*.

37. How does the Hebrew view of time and history differ from that of other ancient peoples? What is the literal translation of the Hebrew title for the book of Chronicles?

38. Go back and review the main points of this chapter. Be able to outline the basic contour of Hebrew thought.

*Chapter Ten*

# Where the Church Went Wrong

*He must hold firmly to the trustworthy message as it has been taught, so that he can encourage others by sound doctrine and refute those who oppose it*

Titus 1:9

In one of his letters to the young pastor Timothy, Paul wrote, "But as for you, continue in what you have learned and have become convinced of, because you know those from whom you learned it" (2 Tim. 3:14). Though Timothy's father was Greek, Timothy was reared by his godly Jewish mother, Eunice (cf. Acts 16:1; 2 Tim. 1:5).[1] Thus, the Old Testament was his heritage, and from infancy he was reared on its teachings (2 Tim. 3:15). Later, Paul instructed Timothy from the same Hebrew Scriptures and urged him to hand down this heritage to future generations, without dilution or compromise (see 2 Tim. 2:2). Accordingly, Timothy was a living link in preserving this legacy.

A study of the last nineteen hundred years reveals how the Church left its original Jewish nest and considerably distanced itself from the Semitic culture that gave it birth. The Church paid little heed to the exhortation of Paul to continue in what it had learned and believed in the context of its Hebrew beginnings. Rather, as it became more and more Hellenized by moving westward through the Mediterranean world, it began to be led away into strange teachings (cf. Heb. 13:9). Indeed, as Ralph Stob, a Chris-

---

1. See I. Howard Marshall, *The Acts of the Apostles,* Tyndale New Testament Commentaries (Grand Rapids: William B. Eerdmans Publishing Co., 1980), p. 259.

*166*

tian philosopher, has put it, "This element of the Greek spirit had great influence on . . . the Christian movement in the first three centuries. At the same time it was the factor which was operative at the bottom of some of the heresies which arose."[2] The Church became vulnerable to these heresies by cutting itself off from the very root that nourished its beginnings. John Spong has pointedly and succinctly explained the effect: "When Christianity severed itself from Judaism the Christian faith itself became distorted."[3]

We are still reaping the results of this severance today. Westerners have often found themselves in the confusing situation of trying to understand a Jewish Book through the eyes of Greek culture. This situation has led, in Dom Gregory Dix's view, to a "spiritual schizophrenia in the process."[4] What is more, over the centuries, it has had detrimental and ofttimes dire consequences for the life and teachings of the Church. Accordingly, the purpose of this chapter is to discuss three main areas where today's Church stands in need of correction and redirection by returning to its Hebraic biblical roots. The areas we have chosen to address have profound implications for the quality of life each believer intends to live within his own Christian community. But these matters are also significant for understanding the life of service that Scripture calls one to render to the larger outside community.

## Dynamic Unity versus Dualism

We turn then to a discussion of our first corrective, one taught by the Jewish writers of Scripture: *We must view ourselves and our world not dualistically but in terms of dynamic unity and oneness.* As students of Western civilization and the history of ideas, we stand in awe of Plato and other Greek philosophers. Their impact has been great not only upon the thought of the ancient world but also upon our world today. We owe much to Plato and his later disciples for what they have taught us through their penetrating insights about reason, truth, wisdom, beauty, and the good life. Nevertheless, another side of Plato and other Greek thinkers has manifested itself through a dualistic kind of thinking that has had largely negative consequences for the Church. We must, therefore, briefly note

2. Ralph Stob, *Christianity and Classical Civilization* (Grand Rapids: William B. Eerdmans Publishing Co., 1950), p. 49.

3. John Shelby Spong, "The Continuing Christian Need for Judaism," *Christian Century* (September 26, 1979): 918.

4. Dom Gregory Dix, *Jew and Greek* (London: Dacre Press, 1953), p. 14.

what this Greek dualism was and how the Hebrew view of mankind and the world differed from it.

Platonism holds that there are two worlds: the visible, material world and the invisible, spiritual world. The visible or phenomenal world is in tension with the invisible or conceptual world. Because it is imperfect and a source of evil, the material world is inferior to that of the spiritual. In this view, the human soul originates in the heavenly realm, from which it fell into the realm of matter. Though human beings find themselves related to both these worlds, they long for release from their physical bodies so that their true selves (their souls) might take flight back to the permanent world of the celestial and divine.

Related to Plato's dualistic view of the cosmos, then, is a dualistic view of man. Plato likens the body to a prison for the soul. The immortal soul—pure spirit—is incarcerated in a defective body of crumbling clay. Salvation comes at death, when the soul escapes the body and soars heavenward to the invisible realm of the pure and eternal spirit. The widespread influence of Plato upon the history of Christian thought can hardly be overestimated. Accordingly, Werner Jaeger states that "the most important fact in the history of Christian doctrine was that the father of Christian theology, Origen, was a Platonic philosopher at the school of Alexandria." Furthermore, he points out that "he [Origen] built into Christian doctrine the whole cosmic drama of the soul, which he took from Plato, and although later Christian fathers decided that he took over too much, that which they kept was still the essence of Plato's philosophy of the soul."[5]

Unlike the ancient Greek, the Hebrew viewed the world as good. Though fallen and unredeemed, it was created by a God who designed it with humanity's best interests at heart. So instead of fleeing from the world, human beings experienced God's fellowship, love, and saving activity in the historical order within the world. According to Hebrew thought there was neither cosmological dualism (the belief that the created world was evil, set apart from and opposed to the spiritual world) nor anthropological dualism (soul versus body). To the Hebrew mind a human being was a dynamic body-soul unity, called to serve God his Creator passionately, with his whole being, within the physical world. Certainly, the godly of the Old Testament could never have brought themselves to sing such patently foreign and heterodox words as the following, which may be heard in certain

---

5. Werner Jaeger, "The Greek Ideas of Immortality," *Harvard Theological Review* 52 (July, 1959): 146. For an argument in support of a case for biblical dualism, see John Cooper, "Dualism and the Biblical View of Human Beings," *Reformed Journal* 32/9 (September, 1982): 13-16.

churches today: "This world is not my home, I'm just a-passin' through," or "Some glad morning when this life is o'er, I'll fly away," or "When all my labors and trials are o'er, and I am safe on the beautiful shore." To any Hebrew of Bible times this kind of language would be unrealistic and irresponsible, a cop-out—seeking to abandon the present, material world, while focusing on the joys of the "truly" spiritual world to come.

## To Enjoy or Not to Enjoy?

Dualism brought in its wake an emphasis upon asceticism. This life-style, a stark departure from the Jewish norm of Scripture, is still present in varying degrees in the Church today. Asceticism results in a debasement of life. The enjoyment of the physical is rejected in favor of the general mortification of the flesh. Physical appetites and pleasures are considered unworthy indulgences which foster entrapment, so the body must be policed by rules. Thus one must seek to restrict or restrain oneself from, to deny or give up, anything enjoyable which may prove a hindrance to the cultivation of one's "spiritual" life. The abstention from various physical and material pleasures through dietary limitations, self-imposed silence, forfeiting possessions, social seclusion, glorification of hardships, and other austere observances are thought to bring mastery over one's body.

Gnosticism (a widespread sectarian heresy against which certain New Testament writings such as Colossians and 1 John seem to have been written) viewed matter itself as being evil. Much of Gnosticism was influenced by Platonic dualism and was ascetic in nature. Gnostics taught that salvation is the escaping of the body by esoteric knowledge (the Greek term *gnôsis* means knowledge) rather than something presently to be enjoyed in this world. Gnostics tended to treat their bodies austerely. For example, Edwin Yamauchi points out that the Mandeans (a Gnostic sect that has survived in Iraq and Iran) have taught that if a woman died during her menstrual period she was consigned to punishment in purgatory.[6]

Though rejected by Paul, the ascetic attitude of "Do not taste! Do not touch!" (Col. 2:21) remains deeply embedded in the history of Christian thought. At the time of the Reformation, the Dutch scholar Erasmus noted that Christianity in his day had come to be defined not in loving one's neighbor but in abstaining from cheese and butter for Lent.[7] Even the great

6. Edwin Yamauchi, *Pre-Christian Gnosticism* (Grand Rapids: William B. Eerdmans Publishing Co., 1973), pp. 23, 138.
7. See Walter M. Abbott, et al., eds., *The Bible Reader* (New York: Bruce Publishing Co., 1969), p. 742.

churchman John Wesley carried in his "theology of perfection" a strain of asceticism: "Beware of desiring anything but God. . . . Admit no desire of pleasing food, or any other pleasures of sense; no desire of pleasing the eye or the imagination by anything grand, or new or beautiful . . . [no desire] of happiness in any creature."[8]

The overall thrust of Scripture, however, reflects a different emphasis. Though physical pleasure is not the highest good or the solitary goal of life, one should receive and affirm it with an attitude of grateful acceptance. Anyone may become mastered by material possessions, physical passions, or the like. Many good things may be abused—indeed, become idols—if they come between a person and God (cf. 1 Tim. 6:9-10). But the biblical solution is not ascetic denial of such pleasures; rather, it is for one humbly to dedicate these to God, as a responsible steward of the Creator's good gifts.

The Hebrew Bible is clearly a "worldly book." Genesis 1 gives humanity a cultural mandate; it is a directive not to escape but to establish civilization (v. 28). Indeed, all things in heaven and earth come from the hand of the Lord alone (Isa. 44:24). Furthermore, the psalmist praises God for the crops and animals on this earth which he is privileged to enjoy (Ps. 65:9-13).[9] God is concerned with every aspect of human life, having given human beings pleasures in which to revel and take delight—with a sense of accountability. Kohelet (or Qohelet) admonishes that "A man can do nothing better than to eat and drink and find satisfaction in his work. This too, I see, is from the hand of God" (Eccl. 2:24). Even David's friend Barzillai, "a very old man, eighty years of age" (2 Sam. 19:32) and very near death (v. 37), still reflected his concern about being able to enjoy eating, drinking, and singing (v. 35).

In this same rich Hebraic tradition, Jesus says a full yes to creation and the material world. In the Gospels we read of farmers and fishermen, birds and flowers, weddings and holidays, eating, drinking, and celebrating. Jesus affirmed God as Creator of not only the heavenly, invisible world but also of the earthly and tangible.[10] Jesus called men and women not to escape from this earthly order but to act responsibly as thankful servants, those privileged to share in the temporal blessings that the Father had bestowed. In Paul's words, "all things are yours" (1 Cor. 3:21), implying that as God's own children we are to participate fully and responsibly in this

8. John Wesley, *The Works of John Wesley* (Grand Rapids: Zondervan Publishing House, 1958-59), 11:432.

9. Cf. Walther Zimmerli, *The Old Testament and the World,* trans. John J. Scullion (Atlanta: John Knox Press, 1971), pp. 18, 30.

10. See Markus Barth, *Jesus the Jew* (Atlanta: John Knox Press, 1978), p. 32.

present world of "flesh and blood." If we find enjoyment in the here and now (see Eccl. 3:12-13) we should not be surprised. We know this enjoyment comes from the hands of a loving Creator who brought us into being with our best interests at heart. Hence, the Jerusalem Talmud states that in the life to come a person must give an account of every good thing he might have enjoyed in this life but did not (Kiddushin 4:12). In the rabbis' view, not to enjoy every legitimate pleasure was in essence to be an ingrate before the Master of the Universe.

Often when Christians become too focused on enjoying the never-ending pleasures of the spiritual world to come, they also minimize the importance of the present, short-lived opportunity to glorify God in their bodies right now (cf. 1 Cor. 6:20). In the acute words of J. Stafford Wright, "We dwell upon the immortality of the soul, and forget that the vehicle for the service of God now is the body, and, if we fail to serve God in the body now, we shall never be able to make up in the future for what we have failed to do now."[11] One's body (i.e., entire being) is to be offered daily in joyful obedience as a "living sacrifice" to God (Rom. 12:1). On the one hand, pleasure and satisfaction are not ends to be pursued in themselves; on the other hand, enjoyment of the physical and material aspects of this life is far more than mere preparation for higher things. To enjoy is an opportunity to bring blessing to one's Creator, "So whether you eat or drink or whatever you do, do it all for the glory of God" (1 Cor. 10:31).

## To Marry or Not to Marry?

A second area where dualism has affected the Church is that of marriage and the family. In chapter eleven below we will explore in depth the Jewish concept of marriage and those family values and traditions that are central to this heritage.[12] But at this point our chief purpose is to show briefly how this legacy became distorted throughout the history of the Church.

As stated above, Greek thought commonly viewed the body as inferior to the soul. They were constantly at war with each other. The body was abhorrent, corruptible, and the source of sin. Hence, once Gentiles replaced the original Jewish leadership of the Church, marriage and the

11. J. Stafford Wright, "The Interpretation of Ecclesiastes," in *Classical Evangelical Essays in Old Testament Interpretation,* ed. Walter C. Kaiser, Jr. (Grand Rapids: Baker Book House, 1972), p. 146.

12. The purpose of chapter eleven below, "Marriage and the Family through Hebrew Eyes," is to complement this brief section. It is intended to provide a biblically based antidote to the unwholesome viewpoints which have plagued the Church from the early Christian centuries.

family soon began to be viewed negatively or with suspicion. Marriage came to be seen as an inferior way of life, for it was a concession to the physical impulses. By its failure to uphold the concept of a person as a dynamic unity or body-soul oneness, the Church went wrong. Through the subtle influence of dualism, marriage was demoted from being one of God's good gifts (see Gen. 1:31) to being a relationship of questionable status.

The Bible affirms clearly that marriage is an institution which is holy, honorable, and undefiled (1 Tim. 4:3-4; Heb. 13:4). Accordingly, the Hebrews did not treat the human body and its functions as evil, shameful, or indecent. The Song of Songs celebrates sexuality and human love in bold terms. The Hebrews were far from those who displayed an indifference or blandness about life. Though not hedonistic, their life-style was physical and robust. Hence the Hebrews, unlike other Mediterranean peoples, did not teach that celibacy was the ideal state or that the highest kind of human existence lay in the transcendence of the physical and in living simply on the spiritual level.[13]

The pages of Church history reveal how the Christian community twisted the Jewish concept of marriage. Let us note a variety of examples to document this point. Monks, living under the vow of chastity, were thought to live closer to God because they denied this world with its fleshly temptations. Certain monks considered it a snare to take a bath, for fear of seeing themselves naked! Priests, having embarked on a life of celibacy, were put on a spiritual pedestal for denying the sinful desires of the flesh. Some Gnostics, also influenced by dualistic thought, even went so far as to teach that marriage was "a foul and polluted way of life," and that eternal life could not be obtained if one remained in this relationship.

Jerome (5th century) wrote: "He who loves his own wife too ardently is an adulterer."[14] Augustine (also 5th century) said that the Hebrew patriarchs would have preferred to fulfill God's command to "be fruitful and multiply" without indulging in intercourse. But since this was obviously impossible, Augustine suggested that they must have had sexual union with their wives only reluctantly and out of duty.

In a similar vein, Thomas Aquinas (13th century) taught that "every carnal act done in such a way that generation cannot follow is a vice against nature and a sin ranking in gravity to homicide."[15] Martin Luther (16th

13. Robert Gordis, *Sex and the Family in the Jewish Tradition* (New York: Burning Bush Press, 1967), p. 17.
14. Quoted in Roland B. Gittelsohn, *My Beloved is Mine: Judaism and Marriage* (New York: Union of American Hebrew Congregations, 1969), p. 176.
15. Also quoted in ibid., p. 177.

century) viewed marriage as a "remedy for concupiscence" or a cure for the unrestrained sexual desire disturbing every human being. He wrote, "No matter what praise is given to marriage, I will not concede to nature that it is no sin."[16]

In modern times, it is reported that Pope Pius XII "severely censured those who, despite the Church's warnings and in contrast to her opinion, give marriage a preference in principle above virginity."[17] Such a statement indicates that sexual abstinence (celibacy) is still very much a revered value among some Christians.

Out of this long negative history of the physical and sexual side of humanity, certain teachings emerged regarding the Virgin Mary. These include her immaculate conception, her perpetual virginity, and her bodily assumption. In a dualistic worldview, where the human body and its functions were associated with evil, Mary could not have sexual relations or bear children. She had to be preserved from that evil, since the womb that carried the Christ to full term could not suffer defilement. The Church thus declared the immaculate conception of Mary. It taught that, at the instant she was conceived, by an act of God's grace, she was "kept free from all stain of original sin."[18] The Church also proclaimed the perpetual virginity of Mary, stating that the brothers and sisters of Jesus (Matt. 13:55-56; cf. 12:46-50 and parallels in Mark and Luke) were cousins or were children by a previous marriage of Joseph, not blood relatives.[19] Furthermore, the Church declared the bodily assumption of Mary into heaven. Since the human body was thought to be corruptible because of sin, the Church deemed it essential that Mary be preserved from bodily death and decay. To this day, these theological teachings remain as salient differences between Catholicism and Protestantism.

In sum, we have pointed out in this section that the Scriptures view both humanity and the world in terms of dynamic unity, not dualistically. But gradually unwholesome and unbiblical attitudes became embedded in Christian thought. Consequently, the Church's perspective on the enjoying of material and physical pleasures, and on the affirming of the goodness of marriage and the family, became distorted, and the Church went

16. Quoted in David M. Feldman, *Marital Relations, Birth Control and Abortion in Jewish Law* (New York: Schocken Books, 1968), p. 24.

17. *The New York Times,* September 21, 1952.

18. This dogma was proclaimed in 1854 by Pope Pius IX in the bull *Ineffabilis Deus.* See *The Oxford Dictionary of the Christian Church,* 2nd ed., ed. F. L. Cross and E. A. Livingstone (New York: Oxford University Press, 1983), pp. 692-93.

19. See the discussion by John Shelby Spong, *This Hebrew Lord* (New York: Seabury Press, 1974), p. 40.

wrong. But this state of affairs did not emerge from a vacuum. The Church left itself open to these strange teachings once it had cut itself off from the Jewish root which had supported it.

## Otherworldliness versus This-Worldliness

A second corrective from the biblical world of Hebraic thought is: *The fixation upon otherworldliness, so much a part of the Church's history, must be brought back into biblical balance by a return to this-worldly concerns.* Under this second main point we have selected three theological concepts. Each of these illustrates a particular area where the Church has gone wrong, due to the influence of a worldview which dichotomized the cosmos and thus considered otherworldly emphases superior to this-worldly ones. In the discussion to follow, the corrective of Hebraic thought will be brought to bear on these concepts: spirituality, salvation, and faith.

### *Spirituality: Heavenly or Earthly?*

From the start of the Christian movement to the present day, various segments within the Christian community have given expression to a pallid kind of ascetic, otherworldly spirituality.[20] In popular religious terminology, to be "spiritual" has usually connoted the idea of otherworldly piety. We have been taught that a "spiritual" person is one whose inner eyes are cast heavenward in prayer and contemplation, focusing on the joys of the life to come. To be "spiritual" implies that one is life-denying; it suggests communing with one's heavenly Creator by focusing upon the invisible realities and eternal mysteries of God's holiness. To live "spiritually" is often thought of in terms of passive detachment from this world, a transcending of the self to a higher, sublime, more exalted world. A "spiritual" person is really consumed with one agenda: to win souls for the kingdom of heaven. All other activity, such as that which seeks to address the physical, material, and social needs of this world, is inferior and lacking in priority.

The above teaching about spirituality derives largely from the Greek understanding of the *psychē*, the "soul" or "spirit." The Greeks taught that the *psychē* is the nonphysical, immortal part of a person. At death it escapes

20. In the discussion of the concepts of spirituality, salvation, and faith within this section, I am especially indebted to John Spong for his insightful treatment of these themes in ibid., pp. 15-30.

the burden of the body and makes its way back to the world of eternal reality. Though Paul was a Jew of the Diaspora and hence doubtless familiar with the Greek perspective concerning the *psyche*, he "never conceives of the salvation of the soul apart from the body. Salvation means the redemption of the body and of the whole created order as well (Rom. 8:21-23)."[21]

In Hebrew thought, a person is a body-soul. He is viewed as a unity, a single entity, an indivisible whole. To the Hebrews, a person is not a soul or spirit which now inhabits and will at death desert a body. None of the Hebrew terms translated "soul" or "spirit" refers to the nonphysical part of a human being; this is dualistic Greek thinking, which, unfortunately, has influenced our understanding of these English terms. In Hebraic thought, "soul" or "spirit" refers to the whole person or individual as a living being. It stands for the person himself. "The Old Testament view of man is that he is an animated body rather than an incarnated soul."[22] In short, human beings live as souls; they do not "have" souls.[23]

A study of the meaning of the Hebrew words *nephesh* ("soul") and *ruah* ("spirit") will provide additional insight. The creation narrative states that God formed man from the dust of the ground and "breathed into his nostrils the breath of life, and the man became a living being" (Gen. 2:7). The Hebrew for "living being" in this passage is *nephesh hayyah*. Man becomes a "living being" by God's breathing. "Man's 'soul' *(nephesh)* is primarily his vitality, his life—never a separate 'part' of man."[24] The term *ruah* means "wind" or "breath" (i.e., "air in motion") and is often equivalent to *nephesh*. "'Spirit' is first of all God's spirit *(ruah)*, his breath, his power (Isa. 31:3; 40:7) which created and sustains all living things (Ps. 33:6; 104:29-30)."[25] Both these words carry the idea of "animation,"

---

21. George E. Ladd, *I Believe in the Resurrection of Jesus* (Grand Rapids: William B. Eerdmans Publishing Co., 1975), p. 45.

22. Ibid.

23. William Dyrness, *Themes in Old Testament Theology* (Downers Grove, IL: InterVarsity Press, 1979), p. 85.

24. Ladd, *I Believe in the Resurrection of Jesus*, p. 45. In the Hebrews' holistic view of anthropology, it is essential to point out that the Old Testament does not teach that the human soul or spirit is immortal. Only the immortal One can grant immortality (cf. Ps. 16:10). According to the Old Testament, the soul does not survive death, for when a person dies, so does his soul. But the New Testament views the soul (Greek *psyche*) as something that continues to exist after death. Paul's teaching regarding the resurrection thus went beyond the Old Testament. The Old Testament does affirm a resurrection of the body (Isa. 26:19; Dan. 12:2), but it is Paul who affirms the immortality of the body-soul. Greeks denied the resurrection of the body. They believed that only the soul survived death. In the New Testament, Paul brings both of these together, seeing the person as a unified whole—body and soul.

25. Ibid.

"vivaciousness," and "vigor." The function of wind and breath is to invigorate, to bring alive—to energize the total person, body and soul. Certainly such was the result of the Spirit's coming on Shabuot, described "like the blowing of a violent wind" (Acts 2:2). Spiritually, the Church came fully alive.

A poignant Old Testament image involving God's *ruah* is found in Ezekiel 37, the prophet's vision of a valley of dry bones. They rattle as they are brought together with sinews, flesh, and skin on them (vv. 7-8). God then causes his breath *(ruah)* to enter these dry bones, and they come alive and stand up (v. 10). God's *ruah* is his life-giving wind which dynamically revives his people and energizes them for service. The house of Israel is brought back to life and restored to its land that they might know the Lord (v. 13). To "know the Lord" (an expression which the prophet Ezekiel uses in various combinations about 70 times) was not to intellectualize about him. Rather, it was to experience his power existentially through his creative acts of grace and love.

With the above biblical background to the terms *soul* and *spirit,* it is now possible to define the nature of spirituality more precisely. For the Hebrews, spirituality did not mean turning inward; true piety was not simply the private nourishing of the virtues of one's soul. Rather, it meant to be fully human, every fiber of one's being alive, empowered in passionate and inspired service to God and humanity.

Westerners often define spirituality as denying oneself, being detached from earthly concerns, and being intent on otherworldly values. By contrast, the Hebrews experienced the world of the spirit as robust, life-affirming, and this-worldly in character. Such was the "spiritual" orientation of the Hebrews. So-called spirituality did not come by negating the richness of life's experiences or withdrawing from the world. Instead, they affirmed creation by finding a sense of holiness in the here and now. There was no division between the sacred and the secular areas of life. It was all God's world, and it was to be enjoyed without a sense of shame or guilt. In Paul's words, "to the pure, all things are pure" (Tit. 1:15). As trustees and stewards of God's world, human beings were to live within it and use it in accord with divine directives. Again, in Paul's familiar Hebraic idiom, "Whatever you do, work at it with all your heart, as working for the Lord, not for men" (Col. 3:23; cf. Eccl. 9:10).

Unfortunately, the history of the Church reveals that when Christians have become fixated upon finding the God of that other world to come, they have often missed finding the God of earth and history, the Creator of this world, in the here and now. Unlike the Hebrews of Bible times, who looked up to heaven but kept both feet squarely on the ground,

Christians have not always learned so to balance themselves. It is the age-old problem of how we can keep the invisible from consuming the visible, the spiritual from negating the material, the theoretical from eliminating the practical, and belief from making us blind to behavior.

Unlike the practice of most Western Christians today, in Bible times the Hebrew people did not see the need to bless food, drink, or other material things. In prayer they focused only on blessing God, the Creator and Giver. The Gospels indicate that Jesus followed this same custom (e.g., note the NIV translation of Matt. 26:26 and Luke 24:30), one commanded in the Torah: "When you have eaten and are satisfied, praise the LORD your God for the good land he has given you" (Deut. 8:10).[26] The Lord alone was worthy of receiving the blessing and praise as divine Provider. As we pointed out in the previous chapter, the Hebrew term *berakhot* (singular *berakhah*) means blessings. Yechiel Eckstein comments: "The berakhah does not transfer holiness to the object itself, but rather entitles us to partake of the world's pleasure. . . . We give thanks to the Lord and testify thereby that the earth is his and we are but its caretakers."[27] The following ancient blessing used in Judaism as grace before meals reflects the above point. *Barukh attah adonai elohenu melekh ha-olam ha-motzi lehem min ha-aretz*, "Blessed are you, LORD our God, King of the universe, who brings forth bread from the earth."[28] The ancient Hebrews would never have thought of blessing what they ate. The idea would have been totally foreign to them; it would also have been an insult, of sorts, to God. If everything God created was "very good" (Gen. 1:31), why should one imply that it is really unholy and profane? The postbiblical notion that one needed to sanctify, cleanse, or purify what God had already created and declared to be good would be strange theology to the biblical writers. It suggests that food and drink, in and of themselves, are unacceptable gifts until suddenly made holy through prayer.

How did this practice originate? Again, the Church went wrong because it severed its Hebrew roots. Grecianization was the consequence of de-Judaization. The influence of dualistic Greek thought created the need to "make holy" things related to the physical and material world. Hence, bread and wine, the elements of the Eucharist, were not only consecrated

---

26. See David Bivin, "Blessing: Jesus and the Oral Torah," *Jerusalem Perspective* 4 (January, 1988): 1-2.

27. Yechiel Eckstein, *What Christians Should Know About Jews and Judaism* (Waco, TX: Word Books, 1984), p. 163.

28. See J. H. Hertz, ed., *Daily Prayer Book*, rev. ed (New York: Bloch, 1948), pp. 962-63. See also Arthur Hertzberg, ed., *Judaism* (New York: Washington Square, 1961), pp. 240-47.

but changed into another substance (transubstantiation). The Church also sought to "sanctify" or "make holy" other physical things such as water, burial ground, crosses, and other religious objects.

It should be of more than passing interest to Christians that the first thing in Scripture God sanctifies is not a place or thing but time. "And God blessed the seventh day and made it holy" (Gen. 2:3). "Spiritual life begins to decay when we fail to sense the grandeur of what is eternal in time."[29] Biblical history is not the story of celebrating space, but the revelation of how a people learned to sanctify moments, events—time. Thus the essence of spirituality is for God's people to know the dynamic presence and quickening power of the heavenly Lord at work on earth in their daily lives and activities.

## Salvation: Escape or Involvement?

In the Middle Ages the concept of salvation revolved around the idea of being lifted out of life. Salvation came when one was delivered from the world. A glimpse of this salvation was often called the "beatific vision," which was a vision of God in which the visionary was taken beyond the world to realms sublime. The good life was the life of contemplation by which one could escape the pressures of this mortal life and achieve a quality of peace that was akin to a little taste of heaven.[30] Because many victims of violence, immorality, poverty, hunger, and disease have a deep desire to escape from a corrupt world, a kind of otherworldly theology proved attractive in medieval times, and still remains a compelling option today. Seemingly, people from all ages have found it relatively easy to focus on the future joys of the heavenly kingdom to come. Still today, church hymnals seem filled with words focusing on the present desire to be removed quickly from this "vale of tears." For example, the lines from one hymn are: "When my spirit, clothed immortal, Wings its flight to realms of day." Another hymn reads, "Soon, soon to faithful warriors cometh rest; and sweet the calm of Paradise, the blest."

By contrast, the Hebrews did not primarily view salvation as deliverance from this world. Their commitment was not to escape this life but to know God's power and presence, which could transform both their lives and their society. Accordingly, historian Timothy Smith acutely draws attention to this point: "The Hebrew sensibility, as contrasted with that of

29. Abraham J. Heschel, *The Sabbath: Its Meaning for Modern Man* (New York: Harper & Row, 1952), p. 6.
30. Spong, *This Hebrew Lord*, p. 24.

Hellenic Platonism, stressed the wholeness of human beings, the unity of their psychic and physical existence, and the bonds that link social experience to inward spirituality."[31] As a socially involved people, the Hebrews sought to live life to the hilt, entering into the fullness of the human experience. They knew that to seek flight from this life by death was no permanent solution to the ills of this world. The action of the Greek jailer at Philippi who thought of ending his life the moment Paul and Silas escaped from prison would have been strange to the Hebrew mind-set of the former Pharisee Paul (see Acts 16:27). Though numerous biblical characters among the Jewish people struggled with their humanity and failed God time and again, many experiencing far more agony than victory, they knew ultimately—no matter how desperate or bleak their circumstances—that they could not run from time. Rather, as people of God, they must affirm his presence in every experience of life, trusting themselves to his mercy and grace.

The Hebrews boldly affirmed their God-given humanity. Again and again in Scripture we see that their identity was found in society, not in isolation from others. They did not view the earth as an alien place but as a part of creation. It was on earth and on earth alone that human beings' highest duty and calling could be perfomed—namely, that of bringing glory to their Maker through the praise of their lips and the work of their hands.

The Hebrew verb *yasha* means "to save" or "to deliver," and the noun *yeshu'ah*, "salvation," derives from it. In the Hebrew Bible, this verb is not used in the sense of "escape to heaven." Rather, a careful study of its many occurrences reveals that the main idea is "to liberate," "to deliver from evil," or "to free from oppression." Hence the terms *safety, welfare, prosperity,* and *victory* all are used to define this saving activity. God is frequently pictured saving his people from external evils (Deut. 20:4; Josh. 22:22; Judg. 3:9), but often this rescue is effected by human agency (1 Sam. 11:9; 1 Chr. 19:12). The same Hebraic concept of salvation—one that embraces an earthly deliverance—is also found in the New Testament. Zechariah, father of John the Baptizer, prophesies that the salvation Jesus will bring includes the rescue of Israel from the hand of its enemies (Luke 1:71, 74), much like Yahweh brought salvation to Israel from its Egyptian foes (Ps. 106:9-11). The Exodus from Egypt reminds us that "God's salvation involves a concern for physical as well as spiritual well-being. Ex-

---

31. Timothy L. Smith, "Evangelical Christianity and American Culture," in *A Time to Speak: The Evangelical-Jewish Encounter,* ed. A. James Rudin and Marvin R. Wilson (Grand Rapids: William B. Eerdmans Publishing Co., 1987), p. 71.

odus is not just a spiritual metaphor. Indeed, it is out of Israel's experience of God's concrete, physical deliverance that a new relationship to God is possible."[32]

Sometimes the Old Testament concept of salvation carries the idea of spiritual rather than physical deliverance, as in Psalm 119:41, where God's "unfailing love" or mercy (ḥesed) parallels his "salvation." But in such passages, the emphasis is decisively not on removal from this life. Instead, salvation conveys the idea of God's liberating power that breaks the bonds of earthly oppression and sets his people free. In a word, the Hebraic concept of salvation is highly ethical in scope.

A vivid illustration of this definition of salvation is found in Matthew, a strongly Jewish Gospel with frequent quotations from the Old Testament. In the final hour of salvation the King will come to "separate the sheep from the goats" (Matt. 25:31-46). One must not forget, however, the criteria that the Judge uses for his decision. To those of "all the nations" selected to "inherit the kingdom" and enter "eternal life" the Judge says, "For I was hungry and you gave me something to eat, I was thirsty and you gave me something to drink, I was a stranger and you invited me in, I needed clothes and you clothed me, I was sick and you looked after me, I was in prison and you came to visit me" (vv. 35-36). The basis of the Savior's judgment is involvement in the lives of the needy so that they are delivered from the weaknesses, evils, and oppressions of this earthly pilgrimage. Jesus says, "Whatever you did for one of the least of these brothers of mine, you did for me" (v. 40). So to do the work of salvation is to bring healing, relief, and victory to those weighed down by the debilitating cares and concerns of the here and now.

Though salvation involves the ministry of deliverance and liberation in this present life, the full work of salvation awaits the resurrection, when humanity and the world are totally and perfectly transformed. As theologian Clark Pinnock has aptly put it, "The meaning of resurrection in the [Jewish] apocalyptic expectation . . . hopes for the complete redemption of man, body and soul. . . . It [salvation] speaks of the total transformation of the whole person in the new creation that God has promised."[33] Only then will salvation be consummated.

Another perspective on the nature of salvation concerns the name *Jesus.* In Hebrew thought, the name of an individual was considered to be

---

32. Bruce C. Birch, *What Does the Lord Require? The Old Testament Call to Social Witness* (Philadelphia: Westminster Press, 1985), p. 47.

33. Clark H. Pinnock, "The Incredible Resurrection: A Mandate for Faith," *Christianity Today* (April 6, 1979): 16-17.

more than a title or a label for identification. Rather, a name was believed to reveal the essence, character, reputation, or destiny of the one to whom it was given. This is why the moral law of Moses forbids defamation of another's name by false witness (Exod. 20:16). Indeed, "a good name [i.e., reputation] is more desirable than great riches" (Prov. 22:1). Thus the name of every Hebrew sent out some sort of message with it. This was particularly so in the case of Jesus, as we shall now demonstrate.

The fact that Jesus was a Jew by birth is crucial for understanding the nature and person of Jesus as presented in the Gospels. Jesus was given the Hebrew name *Yeshu'a*. ("Jesus" is the Latin form of *Iēsoús,* the Greek transliteration of *Yeshu'a*.) The name Yeshu'a, derived from the Hebrew verb *yasha* (discussed above), revealed the destiny he was to fulfill in his life and ministry on this earth. The angel of the Lord said, "You are to give him the name Jesus, because he will save his people from their sins" (Matt. 1:21).

In his teaching, preaching, and healing ministry, especially among the outcasts of society, Jesus demonstrated that God's salvation had come. He proclaimed that the kingdom of God had, in some real sense, arrived in his person (cf. Luke 17:21). As the reign of God broke into human lives, the power of the kingdom was unleashed (Luke 11:20). In Hebrew thought the kingdom is wherever God sovereignly takes charge and rules in human affairs. For example, in the Old Testament God's "reign" is associated with the crossing of the Red Sea (Exod. 15:18). In the case of Jesus, as the power of God penetrated lives through him by snapping the fetters that bound and the chains that oppressed, God's salvation had come.

At his hometown synagogue in Nazareth, Jesus launched his public ministry by announcing the program of God's salvation with these words: "He has anointed me to preach good news to the poor. He has sent me to proclaim freedom for the prisoners and recovery of sight for the blind, to release the oppressed" (Luke 4:18). This "kingly" announcement by God's Anointed bears a striking resemblance to the concept of kingship in the ancient Near East, where the "king is *ipso facto* a saviour."[34] It was customary for the monarch to bring salvation to his people (cf. "Hosanna!," meaning "Save!," in Matt. 21:9, 15 and parallels)[35] by meeting their practical needs of relief, care, and protection. More particularly, however, this concept is deeply rooted in the description of kingly rule in

34. See Roland de Vaux, *Ancient Israel,* trans. J. McHugh (repr. New York: McGraw-Hill, 1965), 1:110.
35. See Marvin H. Pope, "Hosanna—What It Really Means," *Bible Review* 4/2 (April, 1988): 16-25.

the Old Testament. Psalm 72 is a prayer which sets forth the virtues of the Davidic king in Jerusalem, who reigns in justice and righteousness over his people. Later Jewish tradition interpreted this psalm as referring to the Messiah, as did early Christianity. As savior, Israel's king "will deliver the needy who cry out, the afflicted who have no one to help. He will take pity on the weak and the needy and save the needy from death. He will rescue them from oppression and violence, for precious is their blood in his sight" (Ps. 72:12-14). This role of king as savior clarifies Jesus' announcement in Nazareth (Luke 4:18).

The entire ministry of Jesus was thus a commentary on his name. He came to this earth on a rescue mission, but not to help people escape this world. Instead, he came to free them from the clutches of sin, self, sickness, and oppression that they might be prepared for the *olam ha-ba,* the "age to come." Jesus came to serve, not to be served; to reconcile human beings to God and to each other (Matt. 22:34-40). By his example, he taught his followers how to be involved in the lives of people in order to make them whole. Jesus' concern with social justice and human need falls precisely within the historic Jewish tradition. Likewise, "it serves to Christianity as a corrective against the temptation to be carried away by dreams of an apocalyptic glory, and it reminds us that we are to live the life of faith under the conditions of this world."[36] This was the work of Yeshua, and this is the work of his people—to bring salvation down to earth.

## Faith: Thinking or Acting?

A third theological concept where an imbalance between otherworldliness and this-worldliness is often found is the biblical view of faith. What does it mean for today's Christian to have faith? Many Christians, particularly those ignorant of the Hebraic background of this word, understand faith mainly as an activity of the mind. For these Christians, to "believe" or "have faith" is largely a matter of intellectual assent to some proposition. The Hebrews, however, looked at faith differently.

The verb *aman* is one of the terms used in the Hebrew Bible for "believe," "trust," or "have faith." The term is sometimes translated "support," "nourish," "confirm," "make firm," or "make lasting." The word *omenet,* "nurse" (Ruth 4:16) and the word *omenot,* "pillars," "supports of the door" (2 Kgs. 18:16), also derive from the verb *aman.*

A more frequent cognate term is *emunah,* often translated "faithful-

36. Otto A. Piper, "Church and Judaism in Holy History," *Theology Today* 18 (1961): 68.

ness" or "trust." In various contexts this word conveys the idea of "firmness" or "steadfastness," or it may indicate constancy, stability, steadiness, reliability, and support. This meaning is clearly borne out in Exodus 17:12, where we read about God bringing victory to Israel against the Amalekites —as long as Moses holds up his hands. But the hands of Moses grew tired, so Aaron and Hur held his hands up, and "his hands remained *emunah* until sundown." In this passage, *emunah* carries the idea of steadiness or firmness, and accordingly, this meaning set the tone for succeeding occurrences of the term.[37]

When *emunah* is used of God, it usually points to his utter dependability and unwavering faithfulness; the term is often associated with God's words (Ps. 119:86) or attributes such as mercy (*hesed;* cf. Ps. 89:24). *Emunah* indicates one who endures, stands firm, and can be trusted.

*Emunah* is also used of human beings. In these contexts it often refers to those who have the capacity to remain stable (i.e., faithful) amid the unsettling circumstances of life, realizing God's truth has established them (Ps. 119:30). One of the most pivotal passages in the Hebrew Bible where *emunah* is used is Habakkuk 2:4: "the righteous will live by his faith *[emunah]*." This text was later quoted by Paul (Rom. 1:17; Gal. 3:11) and eventually became the battle cry of the Reformation. But we must first consider the original context. Habakkuk's people were about to fall on hard times, for God would be using one nation to punish another. This situation would require a deeply rooted reliance on God, especially his justice and his wisdom in running the universe. Stability and support were needed if God's people were to outlast and survive the impending "day of calamity" (3:16-17). We observe then that *emunah,* as Leo Baeck has stated, is the "inner firmness and peace, the strength and constancy of man's soul."[38] Many places in Scripture, however, indicate that the biblical ideal of faithfulness was not always practiced by God's people. Yet when their sin caused them to face circumstances as grim as the destruction of Jerusalem and exile, even then Jeremiah, weeping, affirmed to the Lord, "Great is your faithfulness *[emunah]*" (Lam. 3:23).

Also derived from *aman* is *emet,* "truth." Like *emunah, emet* may suggest the idea of firmness, sureness, and reliability. One of the attributes of God's nature is *emet* (Ps. 71:22). The Lord is described as *rab hesed ve-emet,* "abounding in love and faithfulness" (Exod. 34:6; cf. Num. 14:18;

---

37. See David R. Blumenthal, "The Place of Faith and Grace in Judaism," in *A Time to Speak: The Evangelical-Jewish Encounter,* ed. A. James Rudin and Marvin R. Wilson (Grand Rapids: William B. Eerdmans Publishing Co., 1987), p. 108.

38. Leo Baeck, *The Essence of Judaism* (New York: Schocken Books, 1961), p. 119.

Neh. 9:17; Ps. 86:15; 103:8; 145:8; Jon. 4:2). Those who know God "walk in *emet*" (i.e., "walk faithfully"; 1 Kgs. 2:4; Isa. 38:3), and, like God, are expected to administer *mishpat emet*, "true justice," to others (Zech. 7:9).

The rabbis attributed special significance to *emet*. The Talmud states that "the seal of the Holy One, blessed be He, is *emet*, 'truth'" (Sanhedrin 64a). The rabbis formulated various explanations for this divine seal. For example, George Foot Moore describes what he terms an "ingenious explanation" of Rabbi Simeon ben Lakish: "*Alef* is the first letter of the alphabet, *Mem* is the middle letter, and *Tav* the last, as much as to say, 'I the Lord am first,' for I did not take over the rule from another; 'and beside me there is no god,' for I have no partner; 'and with the last I am He,' for I shall not hand it over to another."[39] (*Aleph, mem,* and *tav,* three consonants of the Hebrew alphabet, spell *emet,* "truth.")

The word *amen,* used frequently in Jewish and Christian worship,[40] is also derived from the verb *aman.* "Amen" has come into the English language by direct translation from the Hebrew. When worshipers say "Amen," they are affirming, endorsing, or supporting the matter. They are saying, as it were, "this is worthy of trust; it is reliable, solid, stable, permanent, lasting; I affirm it as true; may God bring it to pass."

To the Hebrew mind, therefore, faith meant confidence. It was the capacity to "enter life with courageous expectation."[41] The person of faith did more than believe in his heart or develop an attitude of trust. He stepped out into life to act on that belief. His mental assurances and convictions were transformed into action. For the Hebrew, faith was more than a theory; it was wed to a life of service. Indeed, the Hebrew could serve God through work. He knew that God was always met in history, in the context of events, in the world of activity and doing. The person of faith was one who was so committed to God that, like Abraham, he ventured into the unknown with the full expectation that God would meet him there. Thus, in the biblical sense, to have faith was to move out in life and know God would be there waiting. It was "the call to step boldly into tomorrow, to embrace the new—with confidence that every new day would prove to be a meeting place with the holy and eternal God. The opposite of faith was to cling desperately to yesterday, fearing that if one ever left it, one would leave God."[42]

39. George Foot Moore, *Judaism in the First Centuries of the Christian Era* (Cambridge: Harvard University Press, 1927), 2:195.

40. *Amen* is found 30 times in the Massoretic text of the Old Testament, and 119 times in the New Testament.

41. Spong, *This Hebrew Lord,* p. 23.

42. John Shelby Spong, "The Continuing Christian Need for Judaism," *Christian Century* (September 26, 1979): 919.

This is the Hebraic and biblical model of faith. As Abraham Heschel has pithily stated, it requires "a *leap of action* rather than a *leap of thought*."[43] Again, in the polarity of expression that often characterizes Heschel, "Faith is not a state of passivity. . . . It is an enterprise, not inertia."[44] We must stress that this emphasis is clearly in accord with the New Testament teaching that "faith, by itself, if it is not accompanied by action, is dead" (Jas. 2:17). Biblical faith, though conscious of heaven, operates in, and is only at home in, the realm of flesh and blood. Removed from the sphere of the angels, such faith confronts idols and addresses the inhumanities and injustices of a sin-plagued world. This biblical quality of faith has the possibility of transforming this life so that those thereby changed may attain, by God's grace, of the life to come.

## The Individual versus the Community

We now point to a third, and final, area where the Church has gone wrong, and for which the Hebrew writers of Scripture offer a corrective: *The current display of rugged individualism and private Christianity seen within the Church must give way to a greater emphasis on the corporate life of the community of faith.* The makeup or sociological structure of the Church has been a subject of debate for centuries. One of the earliest movements in Christianity was monasticism, a term that comes from the Greek verb *monázein,* meaning "to be alone," "to live in solitude." Monasticism stressed seclusion from the world and society by withdrawal to a private life of faith. There have been and there still are many different expressions of independent, separatistic Christianity. At the same time, the Roman Catholic Church has for years held before the world the concept of the Church as an indispensable community of which each individual Christian must be a member. Historical testimony to this fact is borne out by the teaching of the Catholic Church that *extra ecclesiam nulla salus,* "outside the church there is no salvation."

From this brief introduction, several questions surface immediately. What is the Church? How are we to understand the relation between the individual and the community? Is there a model which emerges from our Hebraic heritage that may be useful as a pattern for correcting the imbalance evident in ecclesiastical circles today?

43. Abraham J. Heschel, *God in Search of Man* (New York: Farrar, Straus & Giroux, 1955), p. 283.

44. Abraham J. Heschel, *A Passion for Truth* (New York: Farrar, Straus and Giroux, 1973), p. 192.

## *Independent Christians*

Unhappily, one of the characteristics of contemporary Protestant Christianity is the emphasis on what might be called "Lone Ranger" Christianity. That is, people seem to be losing their biblical sense of accountability to each other and think that they can, for the most part, operate on their own. This dominant and sometimes rather blatant Protestant emphasis on individualism in piety and life has rightly been described as callousness.[45] At the present time we may observe an assorted array of dominating and independent church leaders who, through pious language and intimidation, impose their will upon the group. These authority figures frequently punctuate their conversation with such phrases as "the Lord told me" or "God revealed to me" or "the Lord spoke to me and said. . . ." And we need not limit our examples to cultic situations like Jonestown.

The community-centered focus of the Church as described in Scripture is now in danger of being replaced by the rugged individualism of a private kind of faith. The Church is responsible for bringing this danger upon itself. Let us think for a moment: Could it be that we have so stressed the freedom of conscience before God, the individual priesthood of the believer, the importance of personal devotions, the right of each person to interpret the Bible privately, the priority of private confession of sin directly to God, and the encouragement of independent churches and separatistic, autonomous parachurch agencies—could it be we have so stressed these things that we have come to believe that we can function, not only in these but also in other areas, as self-sufficient believers?

This issue was put in clear perspective by the Catholic priest who once was asked by a reporter of religious news if he could briefly delineate the major difference between Protestantism and Catholicism. "That's easy," the priest replied. "The Protestant Church says to people, 'The church needs you,' but the Catholic Church says, 'You need the church.'" Though such a reply obviously paints an overly simplistic picture of both Catholicism and Protestantism, what this priest said is in large measure true—namely, that the Church must be more than an ad hoc scramble of independent individualists, each going his own way. The individual can never survive apart from the group. Human beings were created to be social, and God has constituted his people to function within a body. A person's true meaning derives from relationships with God and with other human beings (Mark 12:28-34).

45. W. D. Davies, *The Gospel and the Land* (Berkeley: University of California Press, 1974), p. 388.

## A Corporate Body

Since Bible times Jews have generally embodied this concept in an exemplary way. God chose a people (Deut. 7:7), and, accordingly, the Jewish religion is characterized by peoplehood. Whereas Christians often define their faith primarily as a system of beliefs, Jews see doctrine or belief as only one—and not the most important—of several elements constituting the essence of Judaism. In the words of the Jewish scholar Nicholas De Lange, "To be a Jew means first and foremost to belong to a group, the Jewish people, and the religious beliefs are secondary, in a sense, to this corporate allegiance."[46] This deeply rooted biblical emphasis upon folk— that is, the group—is underscored by the fact that most Jewish prayer employs the plural "we," not the singular "I." Prayer expresses the "cry of the whole community."[47] One of the best-known biblical prayers expresses this communal factor in its opening words: "Our Father in heaven" (Matt. 6:9). In the words of an old Hasidic saying, "A prayer which is not spoken in the name of all Israel is no prayer at all."[48]

Central to the Hebraic concept of community is the idea of corporate personality.[49] This concept means that the individual was always thought of in the collective (family, tribe, nation) and the collective in the individual. This corporate solidarity[50] was reinforced by the fact that the entire community (past ancestors and future members) was viewed as one personality, "a living whole, a single animated mass of blood, flesh and bones."[51] God's covenant was made not only with those physically present in the wilderness but also with future generations, "those who are not here today" (Deut. 29:15).

That the Hebrew language is full of what we refer to in English as "collectives" gives additional undergirding to this concept of organic

46. Nicholas De Lange, *Judaism* (New York: Oxford University Press, 1986), p. 4.

47. David de Sola Pool, *Why I Am A Jew* (Boston: Beacon Press, 1957), p. 93.

48. Martin Buber, ed., *Ten Rungs: Hasidic Sayings* (New York: Schocken Books, 1947), p. 31.

49. See H. Wheeler Robinson, *Corporate Personality in Ancient Israel,* rev. ed. (Philadelphia: Fortress Press, 1980), pp. 25-44.

50. For a more recent discussion of corporeality in Judaism, see Michael Wyschogrod, *The Body of Faith* (New York: Seabury Press, 1983). Wyschogrod holds that the Jewish people is the dwelling place of God in the world. He stresses that while the Christian idea of God incarnate in the Jew Jesus concentrates all incarnation in one Jew, Judaism holds to a far more diffuse indwelling of God in the whole people of Israel.

51. Robinson, *Corporate Personality in Ancient Israel,* p. 28. The quotation is from W. Robertson Smith, *Lectures on the Religion of the Semites,* 2nd ed. (London: A. & C. Black, 1894), pp. 273-74.

solidarity.[52] For instance, in the Hebrew Bible the word *adam* may refer to man as an individual or to mankind in the collective sense. All Israelites are mutually accountable for one another, and they participate mutually in the life of one another. A striking example of this interrelatedness is the ancient biblical practice of blood revenge.[53]

In the modern Jewish community, each Jew at Passover is obligated to regard himself as if he personally—not simply his ancestors—had come out of Egypt (see chapter twelve below). In addition, each Jew is taught to think of himself as personally standing at Mount Sinai in order to receive the Torah. Thus the Law is given to every Jew, not simply to one Jew, Moses.[54] In a similar way, the concept of the sacredness of human life is basic to the idea of corporate personality. In the Mishnah we read, "He who destroys a single life is considered as if he had destroyed the whole world, and he who saves a single life is considered as having saved the whole world" (Sanhedrin 4:5).

World Jewry has long been a model of community. The Hebrew word *mishpaḥah* means "family." But *mishpaḥah* refers not only to parents and children; it is a whole social unit that includes uncles, aunts, and even remote cousins. Furthermore, each *mishpaḥah* sees itself as part of a single worldwide Jewish family. Thus it is clear why the concept of family solidarity has been one of the chief reasons behind the stability and survival of the Jewish community over the centuries.

Jewish people also customarily refer to themselves as *am* ("a people"), *ḥaburah* ("community"), and *qehillah*, ("congregation, assembly"). These terms emphasize togetherness and accountability. Synagogue membership is never figured on an individual basis but rather according to the number of family units. Furthermore, even the poorest Jew in a community is not exempt from giving to charity; he still has communal accountability.

From time immemorial Jews have also taken seriously the biblical teaching that everyone is his brother's keeper (cf. Gen. 4:9). Thus each senses a responsibility for his neighbor's shortcomings and needs. Indeed, no one lives in total isolation from his neighbor. A dramatic story illustrative of this point has been passed down from talmudic times. The tale is about three men in a boat. Suddenly one of the men begins to drill a hole

52. See Thorleif Boman, *Hebrew Thought Compared with Greek*, trans. Jules L. Moreau (repr. W. W. Norton & Co., 1970), p. 70.

53. See Albert Gelin, *The Key Concepts of the Old Testament*, trans. George Lamb (New York: Paulist Press, 1963), p. 64.

54. Samuel Umen, *Jewish Concepts and Reflections* (New York: Philosophical Library, 1962), p. 39.

beneath his seat. When his friends immediately plead with him to stop, he replies, "What are you worrying about? I'm only drilling under *my* seat." The moral drawn by the rabbis has been repeated again and again: "We're *all* in the same boat."[55]

## The Church as Community

How does the above concept of corporate personality in Hebrew thought apply to the life of the Church? First, the New Testament teaches that when one comes to saving faith one is incorporated into Christ so as to eat his flesh (John 6:35, 54), to be baptized into him (Rom. 6:3), and to exist in him as a "new creation" (2 Cor. 5:17).[56] Furthermore, as a visible body of believers, the Church is spiritually grafted into the family of Abraham (Rom. 4:11, 16; Gal. 3:26-29). "There is no mere individualistic experience for Christians, but a corporate one."[57] In Paul's words, "We were all baptized by one Spirit into one body—whether Jews or Greeks, slave or free" (1 Cor. 12:13). Thus the Pauline idea of the Church as a body is firmly rooted in the Old Testament concept of corporate personality. Accordingly, for Paul, as in the Israelite community of old, the individual incorporates in himself the group and illustrates in his person and life the ideals that the group professes, making its identity his own. But at the same time, the group derives its life and its distinct identity from the individual.[58]

In effect, the Church is a community of faith, learning, and living, just as the Synagogue serves as a house of worship, study, and assembly. Thus a Christian's actions within that fellowship are not solely a private matter. When one member suffers, the whole body shares the grief. When one rejoices, all share in that joy (cf. 1 Cor. 12:26). A body of Christian believers is only as strong as the sum of its individual members, for the Church, like Israel, functions as a corporate personality. The lives of its members are intertwined and find their truest meaning in a network of relationships within this body. As a Jewish sage once observed, "There is no room for God in him who is full of himself."[59] In the Bible, piety

---

55. See Morris N. Kertzer, *What is A Jew?* (New York: Collier Books, 1961), p. 39.

56. E. Earle Ellis, *Prophecy and Hermeneutic in Early Christianity* (Grand Rapids: William B. Eerdmans Publishing Co., 1978), p. 66.

57. Joseph A. Fitzmyer, *Pauline Theology* (Englewood Cliffs, NJ: Prentice-Hall, 1967), p. 66.

58. John McKenzie, "The Significance of the Old Testament for Christian Faith in Roman Catholicism," in *The Old Testament and the Christian Faith,* ed. Bernhard W. Anderson (repr. New York: Herder and Herder, 1969), p. 113.

59. Quoted in Buber, *Ten Rungs,* p. 102.

is always oriented toward community. Like Israel of old, the Church is called "the people of God" (1 Pet. 2:10) and is expected to function with communal self-awareness. Whenever the Church has forsaken this aspect of its Jewish roots—the so-called democracy of the synagogue—and become authoritarian or hierarchically centered, rather than lay- or people-centered, its social consciousness has been greatly blunted.[60] In Christianity, God and one's neighbor belong inseparably together. The Church must never become so self-centered and self-sufficient that it fails to grasp this fact, for the concept of the priesthood of the believer means that each Christian functions as a priest not only unto God but also unto his neighbor.

In ancient as well as modern synagogues, when the congregation completed the reading of one of the books of Moses the entire congregation exclaimed loudly, *ḥazaq, ḥazaq, ve-nithazeq!* ("Be strong, be strong, and let us strengthen one another!"). It is with this same sense of mutual dependence that today's Church must learn to stand in the full strength of its Hebrew heritage.

# UNDERSTANDING CHAPTER TEN

1. Timothy was a child of a mixed marriage. What was the background of his parents? From which parent did he find his religious identity? Why?

2. According to Dom Gregory Dix, what situation has led Western man to a type of "spiritual schizophrenia"?

3. Platonism holds to a dualistic view of the cosmos and a dualistic view of man. What is meant by this dualism? How does the Hebrew view of the world and man differ?

4. What great thinker influenced the Christian theology of Origen? Where in Egypt did Origen hold an influential teaching position?

5. What is asceticism? How is the teaching of asceticism related to dualism? Where are ascetic tendencies found in today's Church? What type of teaching and preaching feeds this point of view?

6. Who were the Gnostics and what did they believe? What New Testament books may have been written in part to counter this heresy?

7. If the overall thrust of Scripture does not support an ascetic life-style, what is the attitude and teaching of Scripture concerning physical pleasure and material possessions? Cite evidence from both the Old and New Testaments.

8. Building upon the foundation of the Hebrew Scriptures, what does the Talmud teach about the importance of enjoying the good things of this life?

60. Davies, *The Gospel and the Land,* pp. 384-87.

9. Why did the Church begin to view marriage negatively or as an inferior way of life?

10. What famous Christian thinkers from Church history reveal twisted views of marriage and sexuality? Give several examples of this type of thinking. Discuss the inherent dangers that any Christian faces when he places upon a pedestal the teachings of a theologian or church leader.

11. What three teachings within the Church concerning the Virgin Mary seem to reflect a dualistic worldview? Explain what is meant by each of these views. What alternative interpretation has Protestantism offered?

12. In the popular religious terminology of our day, what does it mean to be "spiritual"?

13. How did the Greek understanding of the soul differ from the Hebrew?

14. Compare the teaching of the Old Testament to the New on the immortality of the soul and the resurrection of the body. (See the footnotes to this chapter.)

15. How are the Hebrew words *nephesh* and *ruah* normally rendered in English? How does a study of these words in the Hebrew Bible help us define the nature of spirituality more precisely?

16. To the Hebrews, was spirituality primarily heavenly or earthly? Explain.

17. Unlike the practice of most Western Christians today, the ancient Hebrews would never have thought of blessing food, drink, or other material things. Why? What is a *berakhah?* From where did the notion arise that man can transfer holiness to things related to the material world?

18. In Scripture, what did God sanctify first?

19. Explain the popular concept of salvation present at the time of the Middle Ages. Why has this view proved especially attractive? By contrast, how did the Hebrews primarily view salvation?

20. Based on its many occurrences in the Hebrew Bible, define what is meant by *yeshu'ah,* "salvation."

21. How does the teaching of Jesus in Matthew 25:31-46 reflect the Old Testament Hebraic concept of salvation?

22. What final act does the full work of salvation await?

23. Among the Hebrews, in what way was the name of an individual considered to be more than a title or label for identification?

24. Explain the derivation of the Latin form *Jesus.*

25. When Jesus launched his public ministry in Nazareth, how did his announcement of the program of God's salvation parallel the Old Testament concept of salvation?

26. Explain how kingship in the ancient Near East is tied to the idea of the king being a savior. What were the king's responsibilities as savior of his people? What light does Psalm 72 shed on this theme? Against this background, explain what the crowd's cry of "Hosanna!" likely implied at the Triumphal Entry (Matt. 21:9, 15).

27. In what sense was the entire ministry of Jesus a commentary on his name?

28. What basic idea is behind the term *emunah?* What light does Exodus 17:12 shed on the meaning of this term?

29. According to rabbinic teaching, what Hebrew term is considered the seal of God? What unusual grouping of Hebrew consonants did the rabbis discover in this word? Discuss mystical tradition in both Judaism and Christianity.

30. Explain the context and meaning of *emunah* in Habakkuk 2:4, where the prophet says, "the righteous will live by his faith *[emunah]*." How does Paul's use of this verse in Romans 1:17 and Galatians 3:11 seem to differ in meaning from that of Habakkuk?

31. What is the origin and meaning of the word *Amen?*

32. For the Hebrews, is faith primarily a matter of thinking or of acting? Explain. In what way is Abraham an example of one who had faith?

33. How does the Roman Catholic teaching that *extra ecclesiam nulla salus* relate to the question of Christians who operate independently from the Church? Discuss Catholic and Protestant perspectives on this question.

34. Certain emphases that stress the growth of Christians as independent individuals with a private type of faith have threatened the community-centeredness of today's Church. What are some of these emphases? Discuss and evaluate.

35. What is your response to the perception of one religious leader who distinguishes the major difference between Protestantism and Catholicism in these words: "The Protestant Church says to people, 'The church needs you,' but the Catholic Church says, 'You need the church'"? Is this a stereotype or does it reflect a basically correct perspective? Discuss.

36. What aspect of most Jewish prayer underscores its corporateness and community-centeredness?

37. Central to the Hebraic concept of community is the idea of "corporate personality." Explain what this term means. Give at least three examples of this teaching from Jewish history or literature.

38. Give the meaning of the following Hebrew terms stressing group unity: (a) *mishpahah,* (b) *am,* (c) *haburah,* (d) *qehillah.*

39. Rabbinic literature tells the story of a boat in which a man drills a hole under his seat. What moral concerning community accountability did the rabbis draw from this story?

40. What specific New Testament concepts or passages illustrate how the New Testament authors utilize the Hebraic idea of corporate personality?

41. In the Jewish community, when the congregation has completed the reading of one of the books of Moses, what does the congregation exclaim? (Give English translation.)

42. Review the three main areas (discussed in this chapter) where the Church went wrong.

*Part IV*

---

# Jewish Heritage and the Church:
# Selected Studies

## Chapter Eleven

# Marriage and the Family
# through Hebrew Eyes

*He who finds a wife finds what is good and receives favor from
the LORD*

Proverbs 18:22

In part four of this volume we will focus our study on some of the main traditions, ideals, and institutions that have sustained the Jewish people and given them meaning from Bible times to the present day. As we shall seek to demonstrate in the next four chapters, these studies are also crucial for understanding the Jewish roots of the Christian faith.

Before we turn to the study of our first topic, marriage and the family, it is essential that readers bring to the topics under consideration a realistic perspective on the relation between Jewish tradition and life. Throughout this volume we uphold the view that the Christian community has much to learn from the Jewish people in regard to spiritual origins and heritage. We hasten to point out, however, that though Jews have collectively preserved their traditions and values from generation to generation, history reveals that there is often a gap between how individuals live and the ideals of their faith. That is, a Jewish person may not always correlate his life-style with what his religious tradition teaches (the same holds true for a Christian). It must be emphasized that we live in a fallen and imperfect world. A study of marriage and the family particularly reveals that all people are a mix of strength and weakness, good and evil, faithfulness and failure. In short, whether in Bible times or today, individuals do not always live by the ideals of the group with which they are most closely identified. But even the failure to attain or adhere to ideals does not necessarily negate the centrality and value of these ideals to the religious community as a whole.

For centuries Jewish tradition and secular culture have confronted each other head-on. A cursory look at modern Jewry reveals that the Jewish people respond to this confrontation in a variety of ways. First, some Jews are very observant; their aim is to preserve Jewish tradition and teaching at all cost. Their life-style is often deeply wed to *halakhah,* and their commitment strong to the Jewish people. Minimizing their contact with the secular culture around them, these Jews seek to practice the ideals of Judaism as handed down for centuries before them—without dilution or compromise.

Second, others may be ignorant of their traditions. Sometimes there is just cause for this lack of knowledge. For example, throughout most of the twentieth century, millions of Soviet Jews have not known full freedom of religion. As a consequence, most have not had the opportunity to be informed about their traditions. Rather, they have been often deprived of learning what Judaism teaches and of practicing their faith freely. Often such Jews are labeled "secular."

Third, another segment of Jewry may affirm a background or upbringing in the Jewish faith but choose to assimilate to modern culture. For personal reasons they may not wish to maintain any formal ties to the Jewish community or to identify themselves with an outwardly recognizable Jewish life-style. Many of these people may not consider themselves "practicing" Jews. But one should remember that, according to *halakhah,* birth, not personal beliefs or life-style, determines who is a Jew.

Fourth, Jewish people may interpret their collective traditions differently from one another. Judaism embraces a vast and rich tradition, and that tradition is not static. Jewish civilization is dynamic; it is evolving, expanding, changing. Like a great patchwork quilt, Judaism is polychromatic; one will find varying shades of opinion among the Jewish people in defining what is a "good" or a "faithful" Jew. In brief, since Judaism is not monolithic, wide differences often exist between what the tradition states and how individual Jews respond to it.

How does the above discussion relate to the Christian community? First, as we will argue in the pages that follow, it is important that Christians become informed about Jewish ideals and traditions. It is equally important, however, that Christians maintain a realistic understanding of the great diversity with which the Jewish community has understood and responded to these teachings. Let me illustrate further. It is not unusual to observe a Jew (or a Christian) presenting to a church group some of the basic traditions and teachings of Judaism and to hear someone from the audience respond to the speaker with, "But I know a Jew who. . . ." We can often cite from our personal experience examples of people who do not live up to some ideal. But we may not always understand a religion correctly, or judge a people fairly, when we form much of our opinion on the basis of limited contact with one of another faith community, one we have deemed precipitately to be a poor representative or questionable example. Think how many Jews or people of other faiths could say, when presented with Christian traditions and teachings, "But I know a Christian who. . . ." In sum, Christian understanding of the teachings and heritage of Judaism must be balanced by an acceptance and appreciation of individual Jewish differences.

Let us now turn to the principal subject of this chapter, marriage and the family. In the last chapter we showed how dualistic and ascetic thinking has made a negative impact upon the history of Christianity. We pointed out that the Church has often viewed marriage and the family as an inferior way of life relegated to the spiritually weak or those ensnared by this-worldly temptations. Clearly, the Church went wrong by espousing such distorted teaching. In this chapter we shall first briefly note some additional ways in which contemporary Christians continue to struggle with negative viewpoints or ambivalent attitudes about this matter. Our main focus, however, will be to develop a positive alternative and corrective, an understanding of marriage and the family through Hebrew eyes.

## Current Attitudes

Today's Christian is often caught in the web of working overtime or taking a second job, due both to spiraling inflation and a desire for material betterment. This additional work time has led to the fragmentation of family life. The majority of American wives now work outside the home. In the resulting quest for economic security, *things* seem to have suddenly become more valuable than *people*. For many Americans, to acquire a particular model of car seems more important than children. This materialism has had the insidious effect of depreciating marriage and the family through neglect. Moreover, it has sometimes led to postponing the thought of marriage or the starting of a family—many people value financial security above marriage and family.

Changing attitudes toward marriage are also reflected in those Christians who have succumbed to a way of thinking that has been called "the

Doomsday Syndrome." Victims of apocalyptic fever, these troubled saints read the so-called signs of the time and inform us that the world is going to pot: the Middle East is a tinderbox; civilization is at the brink of destruction; time is rapidly running out. If the Messiah does not present himself in our lifetime, so it is argued, the world will most certainly be brought to its knees by nuclear radiation, global warfare, economic collapse, or worldwide hunger.

Unfortunately, such thinking frequently leads to this paralyzing conclusion: "We're living in a death trap, so why bother to get married? And even if we do get married, why bother to have children?" When this thinking is carried to its logical conclusion, the God-pronounced goodness of the institution of marriage is undermined. To be specific, a marriage without children, or a life of singleness or celibacy, becomes a more viable option or even an attractive alternative. Such a choice may easily lead to the conclusion that this is not only a preferable but a superior way of life.

Now, I have nothing against the single life, except to say that it is not the normal and expected biblical pattern.[1] Its place within the Christian community should be upheld only as the exception rather than the rule. From God's point of view, there are valid and invalid reasons for being single. This is an individual matter between a person and the Lord. One must recognize that security is ultimately found only in God, not in a mate. For instance, Jeremiah had valid reasons for remaining single; his decision not to marry was specifically directed by the Lord (Jer. 16:1-4). But we must be careful not to conclude from this example that celibacy is, ipso facto, a higher or more God-honoring way of life.

In the present day, those who are unattached have often felt a need to compensate by substituting any number of platonic relationships with the opposite sex. In popular parlance, platonic love is a kind of deep spiritual comradeship between a man and a woman, free from sensual desire and the pursuit of sexual ends. With the right motivation, such friendships naturally have their place. But they are not to be thought of as a permanent substitute for the God-intended normality of marriage. Thus, it will now

---

1. Scripture indicates that celibacy is a special gift or vocation from God. Though some Jewish sects like the Essenes lived an ascetic life of voluntary celibacy (cf. Matt. 19:10-12), marriage was certainly the norm (cf. Eph. 5:22-33; Col. 3:18-19), central to the creation ordinance (Gen. 2:18). One of the signs of apostasy in the "later times," states Paul, is teaching which forbids people to marry (1 Tim. 4:3). Certainly Paul's caution to the Corinthians about getting married (1 Cor. 7:1) must not be taken as applying to every situation. But in the light of the "impending distress" or "present crisis" (NIV) mentioned in 1 Cor. 7:26, and the troubles associated with serving the Lord in a pagan environment while also trying to care for a family (v. 28), Paul recommends that one consider remaining single.

be our task to consider this positive and central position that marriage and the family have held in the history of Hebrew thought.

## Biblical Foundations: Genesis and Marriage

We have seen that much of the distorted teaching about marriage and the family within the Church reveals little knowledge of biblical foundations. A genuinely Christian understanding of this topic, however, must be securely anchored upon the bedrock of the Hebrew Scriptures. Thus, we shall begin our study with the book of Genesis. This introductory book of the Torah affirms the dignity and purity of the marriage relationship in several distinctive ways.

### The Goodness of Marriage and Sex

First, marriage and sex are from God and are therefore good. Our ability to establish a relationship with one of the opposite sex is directly tied to our creation in the image of God: "So God created man in his own image . . . male and female he created them" (Gen. 1:27). Everything that God made was "very good" (1:31; cf. 1 Tim. 4:4). Hebrew wisdom literature builds on this foundation of Moses by teaching that "He who finds a wife finds what is good and receives favor from the LORD" (Prov. 18:22). But human beings distorted marriage, this gracious gift given by the Creator and pronounced "good," by sin. Maleness and femaleness are at the heart of human relationships; they are good gifts from a loving God. Building upon the Hebrew Scriptures, the rabbis affirmed the goodness of marriage by insisting that a man should first take a wife for himself and then apply himself to the study of Torah. Furthermore, the rabbis decreed that if wedding and funeral processions happened to meet at an intersection simultaneously, the wedding party was to proceed first.[2] In the light of the goodness of marriage in the history of Jewish tradition, it is not surprising that biblical Hebrew has no word for "bachelor."

### The Blessing of Children

Second, children are a gift from God and are an expression of his blessing. Of the 613 commandments found in the Law of Moses, the first is to

---

2. For the above rabbinic material see Roland B. Gittelsohn, *My Beloved is Mine: Judaism and Marriage* (New York: Union of American Hebrew Congregations, 1969), p. 178.

"be fruitful and increase in number" (Gen. 1:28). The psalmist celebrates the goodness of a man's family by singing, "Sons are a heritage from the LORD" (Ps. 127:3), and again, "Your sons will be like olive shoots around your table. Thus is the man blessed who fears the LORD" (Ps. 128:3b-4). By contrast, childless marriages brought hardship and discouragement (Gen. 30:1-2; 1 Sam. 1:1-20).

Contrary to a certain teaching within the Church, the first sin was not sexual intercourse. As David Hubbard has pointed out, "The Fall did not create passion; it only perverted it. In the Creation story, the man is drawn to the woman from the minute he sees her. They are naked and not ashamed."[3] In God's eyes, sex is neither sin nor salvation. But in the context of marriage, God pronounces it a blessed gift because it is tied to the birth of children, an occasion for rejoicing (see 1 Sam. 2:1-10 and Luke 1).

## Companionship: "Leaving and Cleaving"

Third, the need for companionship is fulfilled by the God-ordained relationship of marriage. Genesis 2:18 states, "It is not good for the man to be alone." God created man and woman as social beings. He never intended for a person to be independent, cut off from the fulfilling relationship of being a companion to one of the opposite sex. Thus, "a man will leave his father and mother and be united to his wife, and they will become one flesh" (Gen. 2:24). Adam and Eve had become partners for life. Commenting on companionship, the great medieval Jewish scholar Maimonides observes that the marriage partnership grows from that of companions for help to companions for burdens, and is brought to its crowning height when the partners become companions for destiny.[4]

In a real sense, the Song of Songs is a dramatic commentary on what Moses taught about marriage. Throughout the Song, the mutuality, reciprocity, and partnership of the relationship between the lovers is emphasized as the dialogue is initiated first by one and then the other. Symbolic of this relationship is the Hebrew expression *Dodi li va-ani lo,* or, "My lover is mine and I am his" (Song of Songs 2:16). This verse is frequently inscribed inside wedding rings of Jewish couples to show their togetherness and commitment to make marriage work.

Thus, according to the Bible, the essence of marriage is together-

3. David Hubbard, "Old Testament Light on the Meaning of Marriage," *Theology News and Notes* (Pasadena, CA: Fuller Theological Seminary, March, 1969), p. 6.

4. See Maurice Lamm, *The Jewish Way in Love and Marriage* (New York: Harper & Row, 1980), p. 163.

ness; the reversal of marriage is separation (divorce). Marriage is symbolically described as being "glued" or "yoked" together (like two oxen; Matt. 19:5-6). For the person who is still single, however, this need for companionship must be satisfied through other fulfilling and creative relationships by which God's grace can be manifested. These may include building friendships or working closely with youth, adults, or the elderly. Our point is that through community one finds fulfillment.

## Matched to One Another

Fourth, through marriage one learns the uniqueness of maleness and femaleness by the one being matched to the other. Shakespeare, whose writings contain hundreds of biblical allusions, once wrote, "God, the best maker of all marriages, combine your hearts in one" (*Henry V*, act 5, scene 2). Jewish tradition teaches that marriage is a union whereby two people are matched by their Creator so as to form a unique oneness.[5] Accordingly, one of the vital functions of marriage is to complement (not to compete with) one's spouse. Genesis 2:18, 20 state that the woman is created to be *ezer kenegdo*. R. David Freedman has pointed out that the word *ezer*, often translated "helper," actually means "power" (or "strength"), as demonstrated by its use elsewhere in the Hebrew Bible. Furthermore, he takes *kenegdo*, an expression rendered "suitable for him" (NIV), as meaning one "equal to him," a rendering based on later Mishnaic Hebrew. Thus, when God says he will make a "helper suitable for him [i.e., the man]," he likely means that woman is a power equal to a man; she is his match; she corresponds to him in every way.[6] Indeed, "woman was not intended to be merely man's helper. She was to be instead his partner."[7] Man and woman are symbolically matched to one another in a mutually dependent relationship—hence the expression "one flesh" (Gen. 2:24).

Rabbinic literature describes God as the supreme Matchmaker, for whom the making of a successful match is as hard as the parting of the Red Sea (Babylonian Talmud, Sotah 2a). Similarly, in Peter Shaffer's remarkable play *Amadeus*, Mozart observes to Salieri, "Making music is easy; marriage is hard." If marriage is one of the richest experiences, it is

---

5. See I. Abrahams, "Marriages Are Made in Heaven," *Jewish Quarterly Review* 2 (1890): 172-77.

6. R. David Freedman, "Woman, a Power Equal to Man," *Biblical Archaeology Review* 9 (1983): 56-58. See also Walter C. Kaiser, Jr., *Hard Sayings of the Old Testament* (Downers Grove, IL: InterVarsity Press, 1988), pp. 23-26.

7. R. David Freedman, "Woman, a Power Equal to Man," p. 56.

likewise one of the riskiest. It takes hard work and the encouragement of the community to maintain a successful match.

## *Love after Marriage*

Finally, love comes after marriage, not simply before. Today, people living in the Western world are supposed to marry for love. Considerable emphasis is placed on romance and human emotion. The challenge each new couple always faces is how to mold this premarital feeling of romance into mature love.

For Hebrew men and women of Bible times, living in an Eastern society gave them a different perspective on love. To begin with, love was more a commitment than a feeling. It was seen foremost as a pledge rather than an emotional high. It was a person's good word to stick with someone, to make that relationship work; it was not merely a warm sensation inside.

For centuries, Jewish people have pointed to one particular verse to illustrate the need for love to develop and deepen *after* marriage. The passage is Genesis 24:67: "Isaac brought her [Rebekah] into the tent of his mother Sarah, and he married Rebekah. So she became his wife, and he loved her." In a world of arranged marriages, it was not uncommon for each partner to see each other for the first time on their wedding day. This was the case of Rebekah and Isaac. The text above says that after she became his wife, "he loved her." In short, for the Hebrew patriarchs, love came after marriage; it was not a matter of falling in love and then marrying.

Thus, in the biblical world of the ancient Near East, couples were expected to grow to love each other after marriage. In the modern West, however, the emphasis has been more on marrying the person that you love rather than learning to love the one that you marry. Though both dimensions of love are important for modern Christian marriage, there remains a decisive lack of emphasis in Christian preaching, teaching, and literature about the need for love to blossom after the marriage ceremony.

Psychologist and pastor Walter Trobisch has effectively summed up the difference between Eastern and Western marriage in his best-selling work, *I Loved a Girl.* In stressing the need for love to come after marriage, not simply before, he cites an Easterner who once said to a European, "We put cold soup on the fire, and it becomes slowly warm. You put hot soup into a cold plate, and it becomes slowly cold."[8] It is this very emphasis on

8. Walter Trobisch, *I Loved a Girl* (New York: Harper & Row, 1963), p. 93.

the need for love to grow warmer and to mature after the couple are joined that undergirds the biblical Hebraic concept of marriage.

## Marriage and Sinai: Two Covenants Compared

The essence of marriage—the content, the bond, and the relationship which results—is covenant.[9] God chides Israel directly for not being faithful to "the wife of your marriage covenant" (Mal. 2:14). In the allegory of God's covenant bonding to his chosen people, he states, "I passed by, and . . . saw that you were old enough for love. . . . I gave you my solemn oath and entered into a covenant with you . . . and you became mine" (Ezek. 16:8). Likewise, the book of Proverbs warns of a woman "who has left the partner of her youth and ignored the covenant she made before God" (Prov. 2:17).

The rabbis regarded the Jewish marriage service as reflecting the main features of God's covenant with Israel at Mount Sinai. The covenant ceremony of marriage was seen as a replica or reenactment of what happened at Sinai. It was designed to be a reminder of that basic covenant obligation which binds God to his people. We shall next examine some of the parallels that the Jewish sages drew from the Hebrew Scriptures.[10]

### The Bridegroom and His Bride

The Bible likens God to a bridegroom and the Hebrew people to his bride (Isa. 54:5, 6; 62:5). The Lord says through Jeremiah that when his new covenant is established someday, "It will not be like the covenant I made with their forefathers when I took them by the hand to lead them out of Egypt, because they broke my covenant, though I was a husband to them" (Jer. 31:32). The Lord also says to his people Israel that "you will call me 'my husband'" (Hos. 2:16). Furthermore, Hellenistic Judaism sought to interpret the biblical Song of Songs as an allegory illustrative of the love relation between God and Israel, his bride.[11] Hints of this method of interpretation of the Song of Songs are also found in the Mishnah (see Taanit 4:8).

9. See Maurice Lamm, *Jewish Way in Love and Marriage,* p. 163.

10. For this emphasis I am primarily indebted to the stimulating discussion of Theodor Gaster, *Customs and Folkways of Jewish Life* (New York: William Sloane Associates Publishers, 1955), pp. 109, 110, 126-28.

11. Brevard S. Childs, *Introduction to the Old Testament as Scripture* (Philadelphia: Fortress Press, 1979), p. 571.

## Marriage as Contract

The *ketubah*, "marriage contract," a document detailing the obligations and terms of the union, is read to the bride before she is asked to make her final commitment to the bridegroom. The rabbis point out that this act is biblically depicted when God, on Sinai, declared to Israel, "Now if you obey me fully and keep my covenant, then out of all nations you will be my treasured possession" (Exod. 19:5). The Scripture then says, "So Moses went back and summoned the elders of the people and set before them all the words the LORD had commanded him to speak. The people all responded together, 'We will do everything the LORD has said'" (Exod. 19:7-8). Just as the *ketubah* stipulated the fundamental expectations and conditions for the marriage, so the binding on Sinai detailed the divine stipulations in covenant formula. Though the Bible does not specifically mention the marriage contract in connection with Jewish weddings, evidence of its existence as early as the fifth century B.C. may be found in contracts of this type coming from Elephantine in Egypt (cf. also Tob. 7:12-15).

## The Groom Comes and Waits

In the Jewish marriage service the bridegroom comes first to the *huppah* (canopy) where the couple stands throughout the ceremony, and waits there for the coming of the bride. The rabbis indicate that the divine parallel of this action occurred when "The LORD came from Sinai and dawned over them from Seir; he shone forth from Mount Paran. He came . . ." (Deut. 33:2). He is the "God who comes." In the divine covenant formulas of the Old Testament, God initiates but Israel completes. He establishes and Israel responds. Accordingly, Abraham Heschel has stated, "There is no concept of a chosen God but there is the idea of a chosen people."[12]

## A Procession with Fire

In the ancient world, people carrying torches or candles usually escorted wedding processions. This practice is attested as early as the fourteenth century B.C. in Canaan and later became standard in ancient Greek and Roman weddings. In the Jewish community it has long been the practice for the bride and bridegroom to make their way to the wedding canopy ac-

12. Abraham J. Heschel, *God in Search of Man* (New York: Harper & Row, 1955), p. 425.

companied by attendants carrying candles. The modern play *Fiddler on the Roof* (discussed in more detail later in this chapter) provides a powerful visual example of such a wedding. A biblical wedding account which employs the use of lamps (or possibly torches on long poles with oil-drenched rags at the end) is the parable of the ten virgins (Matt. 25:1-13): "The kingdom of heaven will be like ten virgins who took their lamps and went out to meet the bridegroom" (v. 1).

Again, the rabbis point to a parallel from the ancient covenant ceremony on Sinai. There, on the day of revelation, the Scripture says the people of Israel saw thunder, lightning, and smoke (Exod. 20:18). In this passage the Hebrew term for lightning *(lappidim)* is the same word often rendered "torches." For example, elsewhere *lappidim* is used for the torches held by the three hundred men of Gideon who routed the Midianites (Judg. 7:16). It is possible that this same rich Old Testament imagery of light is behind the description of Jesus, the Bridegroom, coming to take the Church, his bride: "For as lightning that comes from the east is visible even in the west, so will be the coming of the Son of Man" (Matt. 24:27). Compare also Paul's description of the Second Coming: "when the Lord Jesus is revealed from heaven in blazing fire" (2 Thess. 1:7).

## Set apart unto the Other

In early rabbinic literature, the first part of the marriage ceremony which contractually sets the couple aside in betrothal is known as *kiddushin* (or *qiddushin*), properly an act of "sanctification" or "consecration." The basic meaning behind the term *kiddushin* is "be set apart," "be holy." Thus, from the Hebraic perspective, marriage is a "sacred bond," "a holy relationship," "an act of being set apart unto God and each other." The rabbis have long pointed to this concept of sanctification as central to the covenant at Sinai. Before the Law was even given, the Lord said to Moses, "Go to the people and consecrate them *[qiddashtam]*" (Exod. 19:10). Thus Israel is to be separated or consecrated to God in order to prepare for entering his holy presence and for being committed to his service. Israel's calling was to be a *goy qadosh*, "holy nation" (Exod. 19:6).

So, as we have seen above, Jewish tradition teaches in a striking way that the joining of a man and woman in the covenant of marriage is a reenactment or replica of God's eternal covenant relation to his chosen. We have emphasized, as did the rabbis of old, that to understand biblical marriage is to understand the biblical concept of covenant. In this light, we will now point to a number of broadly based practical observations which emerge from this study.

## A Time for Preparation

One must prepare for marriage by giving it a serious commitment of time and forethought. Marriage is no spur-of-the-moment, serendipitous encounter. A betrothal period was set aside as a time of preparation (cf. Deut. 20:7; 22:23ff.). Only later was the relationship fully consummated. Israel made specific preparations in order to ready herself to receive the covenant (Exod. 19:10-11). Scripture designates the Church as Christ's bride (Eph. 5:25-32). She is now preparing herself for her wedding. This event, anticipated in the book of Revelation, is described as a time of rejoicing: "For the wedding of the Lamb has come, and his bride has made herself ready" (Rev. 19:7). Today's Church must do more than deal with marriage in a remedial way. Its ministry must also be preventative by making a strong time commitment to education and counseling as sound preparation for marriage.

## A Permanent Covenant

We must always keep before us—despite discouraging trends—that marriage is a permanent covenant. It has an eternal quality, regardless of the circumstances. God's covenant with Israel is everlasting (Gen. 17:7); to Israel he said, "I will betroth you to me forever" (Hos. 2:19). God engraves Israel on the palms of his hands (Isa. 49:16) and pledges that his covenant loyalty will be as constant as the shining of the sun, moon, and stars (Jer. 31:35-36).

In Hebrew, "to make a covenant" is literally "to cut a covenant" *(karat berit)*. Biblical covenants were sometimes solemnized by cutting animals in two. The shedding of blood dramatically ratified and sealed the covenant (see Gen. 15:9ff.; Jer. 34:18-20). If one attempted to break the covenant, the blood served as a powerful visual lesson that one's own blood would be shed. In brief, it was a solemn oath to be kept on pain of death. It was thus inviolable and irrevocable.

Our present age is one of shattered promises and broken relationships. An age sick with sentimentality has lost sight of the pledge "till death do us part." Love is often defined in all kinds of terms except commitment. We must return to Sinai, for there we are reminded through Hebrew eyes that marriage is just as serious and binding as that spectacular covenant ceremony on the day of revelation.

## An Exclusive Commitment

We must further emphasize that marriage requires an exclusive commitment. This commitment rules out all potential rivals who might compete for the attention of a marriage partner. At Sinai, God said to Israel, "out of all nations you will be my treasured possession" (Exod. 19:5). Here is particularity. The sovereign of the whole earth chooses only Israel out of all nations to be his very own covenant people. Though today some argue that monogamy breeds monotony, marriage can only thrive when its unity is preserved. Competition for loyalty destroys the potential oneness of a covenant relationship. Is this not why the Lord said to his beloved at Sinai, "You shall have no other gods besides me"?[13]

## Word as Promise

The concept of covenant also teaches us that in marriage one must be a person of one's word. The covenant of marriage requires a response to a question. Just as Israel at Sinai pledged publicly their full agreement to the terms of the covenant (Exod. 19:7-8), so marriage requires no less a response. When Israel replied, "We will do everything . . ." (v. 8), they made a promise to uphold their end of the covenant stipulations; they vowed to keep their word.

In this modern world it is relatively easy to get in and out of promises by saying such things as, "I've changed my mind," or "I just don't feel that way about you any more." Words are often cheap. Among the Israelites, however, one's word was considered equal to one's promise (cf. Ps. 15:4). This identification is powerfully brought out in the Hebrew language. Biblical Hebrew has no special term for "promise." Rather, the term *dabar*, often translated "word," "speech," "commandment," is also used for "promise" (see Josh. 21:45). In Scripture *dabar* carries a broad range of meaning and is certainly not limited to mere verbiage. For example, *dabar* may refer to a concrete "act" or "event" (see 1 Kgs. 11:41; 1 Chr. 29:29). Thus, when *dabar* is rendered "promise," it implies something of substance—it was a pledge of one's good faith or promise to keep that word by pragmatic action. So today, only when the vows verbalized at marriage altars reflect this deeper understanding of "word" conveyed by *dabar* will the marriages survive.

## Periodic Renewal

The covenant of marriage also must be renewed. God's covenant with Abraham did not end with Abraham. It was reiterated to Isaac and Jacob. The covenant at Sinai was a renewal and extension of the earlier

13. For the translation "besides" in Exod. 20:3, see NIV and RSV notes.

Abrahamic covenant. The book of Deuteronomy doubtless reflects a covenant renewal ceremony. The Davidic Covenant (2 Sam. 7) was a restating and progressive enrichment of the Sinaitic Covenant. Christians see the New Covenant established through the blood of Jesus as the final and fullest expression of God's covenant love (Luke 22:20; 1 Cor. 11:25).

Because people forget, covenants had to be periodically renewed. Today, the emotion of the moment at a marriage altar may easily cause a couple later to forget what each pledged to the other. All spouses, from time to time, need to be reminded of their marriage vows. Just as Israel at Sinai was called to covenant obedience (Exod. 19:5), so the covenant of marriage requires a full acceptance of the terms and willingness to work honestly and conscientiously at keeping them. Israel's covenant had conditions. Disobedience meant forfeiting the personal benefits and blessings that would accrue only through faithfulness. In large measure, people get out of marriage what they invest in it. Renewal of marriage vows at regular intervals is an appropriate reminder of how that investment is doing.

## Jewish Insights into Marriage and the Family

In our discussion thus far we have sought to establish that the biblical concept of the family is the Hebraic concept. With the possible exception of Luke, all the authors of Scripture, both the Old and New Testaments, are Jews. They write from the heritage of their own Jewish family background. Accordingly, they remind us that to understand the Christian family correctly one must understand the Jewish family. To gain Jewish insight into marriage and the family, therefore, is not an optional matter for today's Christian—it is essential, for it concerns the very foundation of the Christian home. From the teachings of Judaism the Church can learn many vital lessons and thereby renew its perspective on the family. Consequently, we have chosen to discuss briefly some of the more significant Jewish family values and traditions. We believe that these insights, when rightly understood and applied, will lead to stronger Christian marriages and families.

### *Respect for Family Background*

Modern American marriages are often largely based on emotionalism, feeling, or simply being "in love with love." But traditional Jewish marriages seek to be based on *yihus,* that is, "family background," "stock," or "pedigree." For centuries the Jewish matchmaker *(shadkhan)* has been an important figure in the community. The matchmaker sought to arrange marriages on the basis of objective factors. One's reputation in the community, virtue as a person, and type of family background are all essential qualities of *yiḥus*. Though learning to love after marriage is not always easy, a couple matched on the basis of *yiḥus* normally had a firm point from which to begin.

As a rule, the more learning one has, the more one's *yiḥus* is enhanced. Learning becomes the door to self-respect as well as community respect. The Talmud thus teaches that the best guarantee for a successful home is in a mother whose father is known to be a "disciple of the wise" (Yoma 71a); such a woman has experienced the spirit of Torah and is able to pass it on to her children.

Contemporary Christians must take to heart this time-tested Jewish family value. They must seek to build friendships which can eventually lead to solid marriages because they are based on objective criteria. A piece of paper in the form of a marriage certificate can hardly be expected to hold a marriage together. Prayer alone is also not enough. Flaws, weaknesses, or insufficiencies—even when prayed over—may still remain problems. A reformed alcoholic is still an alcoholic. A high school dropout who suddenly becomes a deeply committed Christian is still a dropout. Prayer cannot erase the scars, gaps, and cultural, sociological, and psychological differences with which one enters marriage. If loving commitment is to blossom and thrive as a solid match, it must be supported from the beginning by the sound foundation of *yiḥus*.

## The Centrality of Prayer

In preparation for marriage, as well as during and after the ceremony, prayer has an important place in Jewish tradition. As the heavenly Matchmaker, God is vitally concerned about the right people being matched to each other. Rabbinic literature relates that since God completed his work of creation he has been spending his time making marriages. The Talmud states that forty days before a boy is to be born a heavenly voice declares that the daughter of such and such a man will be destined to become his wife.[14] Judaism places such importance upon the need of prayer for a mate that it begins at birth. Over the head of every newborn Jewish child a prayer is offered that the child might grow in body and mind, might demonstrate a life of good deeds, and might reach the marriage canopy.

Jewish tradition teaches that a bride and groom must fast on their

14. See David de Sola Pool, *Why I Am A Jew* (Boston: Beacon Press, 1957), p. 133; I. Abrahams, "Marriages Are Made in Heaven," *Jewish Quarterly Review* 2 (1890): 175-76.

wedding day until after the ceremony, focusing during this time on spiritual evaluation. Before the ceremony they make a prayer of confession directly to God. Furthermore, during the ceremony seven prayers of blessing are invoked upon the couple. There is also a prayer immediately before the marriage is consummated. The seven blessings are repeated at the festive banquet during the reception.

Often the Church has responded to the challenge of marriage in a restorative way rather than in a constructive and preventative manner. Proper preparation for marriage must first involve prayer on the part of parents. Their concern should be that God will guide their child in the selection of a mate over the years which lie ahead, and that after marriage the couple will learn to love more deeply with every passing day. At the same time, parents should rejoice in knowing that God, from the beginning, has been at work in bringing this union to pass, just as he did in Bible days (see Gen. 24:44).

## Support of the Community

From the biblical era to present times, Judaism has emphasized that marriage is not simply an individual or private matter. Rather, it is an institution in which the whole community has a stake. Just as most Jewish prayer is offered in the plural "we," that is, in the name of the whole community, so in marriage Jews recognize publicly the need for the love, support, nourishment, and blessing of all those within the body.

European Jews did not customarily send out invitations to a select list of guests. Instead, it was considered a *mitzvah,* or holy obligation, for everyone in the village to attend the wedding. Indeed, every person was expected to comment on the radiant beauty of the bride! If the bride happened to be from a poor family and unable to acquire a trousseau, the community had the responsibility of supplying her with one.

This support of the group is further underscored by the Hebrew word for "family," *mishpaḥah.* As we pointed out in the last chapter, *mishpaḥah* does not include only the nuclear family of mother, father, and children, but implies an extended family or clan. It often refers to a whole social unit including parents, children, grandparents, aunts, uncles, and cousins. Family solidarity has remained one of the hallmarks of Jewish survival. Thus *mishpaḥah* is a group concept implying togetherness, not fragmentation or isolation. The strength and encouragement provided by the *mishpaḥah* and larger community is an important concept for the Church to consider today. Some couples on the verge of marriage come into conflict with their families or churches. They reach an impasse, feel alienated and discouraged, and then run away in frustration to marry elsewhere, determined to handle life independently. At such a time, they give little thought to needing a body of caring friends and loved ones to help sustain and uphold them in marriage. When serious sickness, financial failure, adjustment problems, or unexpected trouble comes, the need for support—material, emotional, and spiritual— is hardly optional if the marriage is to survive. Where then can a couple turn if they have previously chosen to strike out on their own, often precipitately burning bridges between themselves and their own families and church communities?

No one is strong enough to make it through life alone. Everyone needs support. The Jewish concept of the family reminds us of this scriptural value so pertinent for the health and strength of today's Church and home.

## *Sharing a Common Destiny*

In the Jewish marriage ceremony the bride and groom twice share a cup of wine. The use of wine at a Jewish wedding, as on the weekly Sabbath, symbolizes the sanctifying and separating of these institutions to God.

For the Jewish community since Bible times, wine has represented happiness, festivity, and song. Hence its use has been customary at such joyous celebrations as the Sabbath and weddings (see Eccl. 10:19 and John 2:1-11). In that both Sabbaths and weddings involve feasts, it is significant to note that the Hebrew term for "feast" or "banquet" *(mishteh)* derives from the verb *shatah,* "to drink" (see Esth. 2:18). Though Scripture emphasizes the peril of drunkenness and the ugliness of the abuse of wine (Prov. 20:1; Isa. 28:7; Eph. 5:18), its special use in the life of God's covenant people must not be quickly or emotionally brushed aside.

The joint partaking of the common cup in the modern Jewish marriage ceremony is a symbolic act on the part of the couple. It is a reminder that two individual lives have now, in some new way, become one. It betokens an indivisible union of commitment and friendship. In the words of Jewish scholar T. H. Gaster, drinking from the same cup is a standard way of "signifying and cementing an alliance, as witness the very word 'companion,' which means properly 'one who shares bread with another.'"[15]

This idea of identification and oneness through joint participation is rooted in Scripture. For example, the concept of a shared cup is found in the teachings of Jesus. He asked James and John, "Can you drink the cup I am going to drink?" (Matt. 20:22). In this question, Jesus was probing to see if these disciples were prepared to share in his destiny, to experience his lot. James and John replied, "We can." The fate they would undergo

15. Theodor Gaster, *Customs and Folkways of Jewish Life,* p. 118.

*211*

involved suffering with their Lord. Their sharing the common cup in the Upper Room was a further affirmation of this fact. Jesus could not turn back; he had set his face toward Calvary to take upon himself God's judgment for human sin. Thus the disciples were choosing a road that would also eventually lead to their deaths: according to Church tradition, eleven of the twelve disciples were martyred.

Like the cup of Jesus described above, the two cups of wine shared by Jewish marriage partners also dramatize the concept of common destiny. The first cup is called the "cup of joy." It reminds the couple that when joys in life are shared, they are doubled. The second cup is the "cup of sacrifice." In the midst of their celebration, the bride and groom are sobered by recognizing that burdens and problems will someday come into their marriage. But if these troubles are shared, they are halved.

Contemporary Christian marriage can learn much from the symbolism of the Jewish marriage cup. In Christian marriage, a couple shares in the joys and challenges of a common destiny; each partner is bound to the other by love and mutual commitment. The cup of joy reminds the Christian of the need for celebration of life in a world daily marked by pain, tragedy, sickness, and death. Although marriage holds the potential of being one of the happiest experiences to be shared in life, it is also one of the most vulnerable; many enemies seek to destroy its unity and oneness. Thus, the cup of sacrifice sends a message to today's Church: hard times of testing and discouragement may work at tearing a marriage apart. So, by God's grace, marriage partners must band together through personal sacrifice and mutual submission to sustain each other (cf. Eph. 5:21). Here is the support needed to insure the outcome of the relationship.

## Lifting Each Other up

Psychologists and other professionals working in human relations have sometimes described our society as a "put-down" society. Children are put down at schools by being called failures; and at home they are often criticized far more than affirmed. Such negative influences decrease and even shatter self-esteem and the sense of personal worth.

The same is also true of adults within the home. Mothers-in-law are often put down by ridicule; they are objects of contemptuous laughter and humiliating insults. Elderly grandparents are frequently downgraded and pushed aside. No longer honored, they are made to wonder whether they have any reason for living.

Likewise, in their insecurity and thoughtlessness, husbands and wives often tear each other down. Though marriage is a high and holy calling, when a spouse fails to fulfill the responsibility to edify and support his or her partner, marriage can easily degenerate to one of the lowest levels of existence. But a marriage partner can be debased and suffer indignity only so long. When one spouse constantly denigrates the other, the reality of that broken relationship is often formalized by divorce.

There is, however, a more exalted way. In early rabbinic literature the second part of the marriage ceremony—that which consummated the event personally and privately rather than legally—was known as *nissu'in*. In modern Hebrew, *nissu'in* is one of several words translated "marriage." *Nissu'in* and the related form *nasu*, "married," derive from the verb *nasa*, "to lift up," "to bear," "to carry." *Nissu'in* suggests exactly the opposite of putting someone down. Indeed, marriage is graphically portrayed as lifting the other up. This concept is beautifully dramatized at traditional Jewish weddings. After the wedding ceremony, the bride and groom are lifted up on chairs by their guests, to the accompaniment of exuberant singing and dancing. Furthermore, *nissu'in* recalls a period in Jewish history when the people of a town would carry *(nasa)* the bride on a carriage from the home of her parents to her new home with her groom.[16] In short, "*Kiddushin* connects two equals, man and woman, in a relationship as husband and wife. *Nissu'in*, which also means elevation, connects husband, wife, and God in a permanent commitment."[17] This concept of marriage being an elevating experience thus underscores the calling of husband and wife to support, bear, and lift up each other. It also implies mutual dependence, as each partner carries the other along.

## Values within the Home

Sociologists and family counselors have long made the Jewish home an object of study and emulation. Like every modern family, today's Jewish home is undergoing pressures and challenges never before experienced. No family, Jewish or Christian, is immune to stress. Indeed, over the centuries Jewish people have probably experienced more hardship and adversity than any other ethnic group. More than two millennia of anti-Semitism—including the Holocaust years—give painful witness to this fact. But over the hundreds of years which stretch back to Bible times, the Jewish home has remained a bastion of strength. Throughout the ups and downs of life the Jewish home has stood firm with meaning and purpose. Jews have always viewed the

16. Maurice Lamm, *Jewish Way in Love and Marriage*, p. 161.
17. Ibid.

home as far more than "the place when you go there they have to take you in," as the poet Robert Frost once described it.

At the beginning of this chapter we emphasized that both Judaism and Christianity always have a gap between the ideal and the real, between the stated tradition and the actual practice. Those looking for perfect homes, by whatever measure, will never find them. Though hardly exempt from problems, the Jewish home has good reason for its survival. The home has had stability and permanency because the traditions and values of the home have brought self-understanding and direction to its members. When the Church discovers the Jewish home from the inside, it will find many useful lessons and values that can be incorporated into a Christian concept of the home. In this section we will discuss three of the most important and practical ones: the home as a small temple, peace in the home, and bringing guests home.

## The Home as a Small Temple

At the start of this chapter, we showed that the biblical view of marriage and the family is firmly rooted in Genesis, the book of beginnings. This teaching starts in the Creation account and continues throughout the patriarchal narratives. Hebraic teaching on this topic, however, is not limited to the book of Genesis; the rabbis also drew extensively from the remainder of the Pentateuch, the Prophets, and the Writings in order to develop the Jewish model of the home.

The Hebrew Bible refers to the Tabernacle of Moses (and, later, the Temple of Solomon) as a *miqdash*, "sanctuary" (Lev. 12:4; 19:30; Num. 3:38; cf. Ezek. 5:11; 9:6). The term *miqdash* comes from the Hebrew verb *qadash*. As we have previously observed, the verb *qadash* means to be "set apart," "consecrated," or "holy." Hence the structure or sanctuary *(miqdash)* at which the Israelites assembled and worshiped was viewed as a "place of holiness."

After the destruction of the Temple in Jerusalem and the scattering of the Jewish nation into *galut*, "exile," the rabbis began to refer to the home as a *miqdash me'at*,[18] that is, a "small sanctuary" or "miniature temple."

---

18. The expression *miqdash me'at* occurs in Ezek. 11:16. Unfortunately, most versions have not rendered it "small sanctuary." The AV, however, accurately reflects a literal rendering of the Hebrew: "Therefore say, Thus saith the Lord GOD: Although I have cast them far off among the heathen, and although I have scattered them among the countries, yet will I be to them as a little sanctuary *[miqdash me'at]* in the countries where they have come." The glory of God was not confined to one geographical territory. The Lord would be present among his people in exile, as they knew his presence in the sanctuary *(miqdash)* on the Temple Mount in the holy city of Jerusalem. In support of the rendering of *miqdash me'at* as "small sanctuary" in Ezek. 11:16, see Moshe Greenberg, *Ezekiel 1–20*, Anchor Bible, Vol. 22 (Garden City, NY: Doubleday & Co., 1983), pp. 186, 190.

Accordingly, it has been well observed that "The Jew's home has rarely been his 'castle.' Throughout the ages it has been something far higher—his sanctuary."[19] It is through the high calling of marriage, *qiddushin*—a term that we previously noted is derived from *qadash* —that a relationship of "holiness," a "sacred" bond, is established in the *miqdash me'at.*

As a small sanctuary, the rabbis taught that the home, like the Temple, was to be set aside for special purposes. These included the worship of God (a "house of prayer"), the learning of Torah (a "house of study"), and the serving of community needs (a "house of assembly"). Just as the *shekhinah* (the abiding presence of God) filled the Temple, and as light, a symbol of the Divine, brightened the holy place through the *menorah* (the seven-branched lampstand), so each home was to reflect God's glory through prayer and praise. In addition, just as the golden table for the bread of the Presence in the Tabernacle contained loaves of bread set in two rows (Exod. 25:23-30; Lev. 24:5-9), so on Sabbath eve in the home two loaves of *ḥallah* are set on the table to symbolize God's sustaining presence among his people.

The dinner table of the home became, as it were, the altar of the Temple.[20] Here is the origin of the family altar. Eating was to be more than a physical function; it was to be a spiritual instrument of religious service. Seen as an altar, the table was to be consecrated. It was to be a place where more than food was to be passed; it was also to be set apart, that words of Torah might be exchanged. For one "does not live on bread alone" (Deut. 8:3; cf. Matt. 4:4; Luke 4:4).

Around the table, the family sang *zimrot* ("songs") in praise of the Holy One, as the choirs used to sing in Solomon's Temple. At the table, the father served as priest of his own sanctuary, instructing his family in the words of Torah as one of the priests of old. As the Israelites came to the Temple to celebrate festivals such as Passover, so the later Jews viewed the home as the center of religious life. It was a place in which to celebrate holidays and festivals with joy and dedication. But it was more: the festivals at home provided an opportunity to inculcate religious values such as freedom and love for Torah.

By studying the Jewish concept of *miqdash me'at,* today's Christian family will gain greater insight into the holiness of the marriage relationship,

19. Joseph H. Hertz, ed., *A Book of Jewish Thoughts* (New York: Oxford University Press, 1920), p. 11.

20. Rabbi David de Sola Pool points out that "When the Jerusalem Temple was destroyed by the Romans, two leading rabbis of the day helped comfort their people by declaring that henceforth the table in the home could and should take the place of the altar in the Temple" (*Why I Am A Jew* [Boston: Beacon Press, 1957], p. 135).

and how each Christian home can become its own temple in miniature.[21] In this regard, three points of application for today's Church are in order.

Foundational to all theory on the biblical concept of family is the Jewish teaching that the home is more important than the synagogue. In Jewish tradition, the center of religious life has always been the home. The Church has yet to grapple seriously with this crucial concept. Unfortunately, many Christians believe it is God's purpose that the Church function as the main formative influence in the spiritual development of the family. For various reasons—ignorance, convenience, or default of responsibility—the Church has often taken the place of the family. But the Church was never intended to be a substitute for the home. Nothing in God's plan has ever replaced the home as bearing primary responsibility for imparting Christian values and insuring godly nourishment and growth for each family member. In the words of Moses, "*you* shall teach them [God's commandments] diligently to your children" (Deut. 6:7a, RSV, my emphasis), *not* somebody else.

The Hebrew word for "parent," *horeh,* is worthy of special note in regard to the role of teacher. The noun *horeh,* like *torah,* appears to be derived from the verb *yarah,* which means "cast," "shoot," "throw," "direct." (*Torah* thus properly means what is "cast forth," hence the idea of "instruction," "teaching," "direction" for life.) Accordingly, as priest in his family, the *horeh* ("parent") is to provide *torah* ("instruction") just as the priest expounded the Torah of Moses within the holy Temple.

Our second observation is that Judaism is a religion of laypeople. The Jewish faith has long taught that it is not to be viewed or to function merely as a religion with paid professionals called by congregations to perform religious duties and services. Indeed, even the rabbi is considered a layperson. Any member of the congregation may be called upon to read from the Torah, lead the congregational prayers, or preach from the pulpit. In this connection, a rabbi once commented to me, "If every synagogue were to close around the world, Judaism would survive; it would not be destroyed." The rabbi explained that every Jew is expected to be knowledgeable about his faith as a layperson. Hence, because of the way it is structured, Judaism will always survive in the home. And this is where the

---

21. Clearly the New Testament makes symbolic use of the word *temple.* Paul, a Jewish scholar from the city of Tarsus, teaches the Corinthian Church that they (plural) are God's temple (1 Cor. 3:16) and that "God's temple is sacred" (v. 17). Paul also teaches that each Christian is a temple: "Your body is a temple of the Holy Spirit" (6:19). This collective-individual notion is in keeping with the concept of *miqdash me'at,* in which the function and characteristics of the holy temple in Jerusalem are applied to a smaller, yet no less "sacred," entity.

*miqdash me'at* comes in. As a layperson, the parent is responsible to be familiar with the teachings of Judaism in order to serve as teacher within the sanctuary of the home. Christianity, too, must grasp that its function is to be that of a religion of laypeople. For too long it has largely contented itself with a passive, spectator-type mentality in which clergy are chosen, paid, and told to perform for the people.

One final practical teaching follows: the New Testament teaches the priesthood of all believers. Peter instructs the Church that "you also, like living stones, are being built into a spiritual house to be a holy priesthood, offering spiritual sacrifices acceptable to God through Jesus Christ" (1 Pet. 2:5). Clearly, the entire worldwide body of Christian believers is a holy priesthood. The image in the above passage is derived from the Old Testament Temple. There the Holy Scriptures were expounded, worship and sacrifice were carried on, and offerings of material goods and deeds of charity were extended to others. Christians must cease viewing the Church and home primarily as edifices. Only when the Church and home are seen as people—a community of priests ministering to God and to one another —will they fulfill their God-intended function.

## Peace in the Home

Many homes today are marked by internal strife, conflict, and tension. Too often they have become battlegrounds where quarrels and disputes break forth daily. The ancient rabbis warned about the danger of bickering and controversy within the home: "Anger in the home is like worms in grain" (Babylonian Talmud, Sotah 3b); "A home where there is dissension will not stand" (Derekh Eretz Zuta 9:12 [a section of one of the minor tractates in the Talmud]). The apostle Paul likewise cautioned about how lack of harmony brings sure destruction: "The entire law is summed up in a single command: 'Love your neighbor as yourself.' If you keep on biting and devouring each other, watch out or you will be destroyed by each other" (Gal. 5:14-15).

The Hebrew Scriptures command, however, that the people of God must "seek peace and pursue it" (Ps. 34:14b). In Judaism, therefore, one of the most important family values is that of *shalom bayit,* "a peaceful home." In the presence of strangers or among casual acquaintances in the community, it is usually not too difficult to pass the test of *shalom.* But *shalom* is difficult to maintain in the home. There the true mettle of one's character is tested on a day-by-day basis. It is in the home that tempers can flare up at the smallest provocation. Accordingly, the Talmud insists that conversation with people be "gentle" (Yoma 86a). Derogatory speech *(le-*

*shon ha-ra)* is forbidden. To insure a positive and peaceful spirit, good deeds are often acknowledged with the blessing, "more strength to you" *(yasher kohakhah)*.

Paul warns fathers, "do not exasperate your children" (Eph. 6:4). Rather than provoking their offspring to anger, fathers are to be a sensitive model of maturity and stability and peace before their children. Indeed, Paul exhorts all believers to "live in harmony with one another" (Rom. 12:16). Harmony is destroyed by the acts of the sinful nature, which include hatred, discord, jealousy, fits of rage, selfish ambition, dissensions, factions, and envy, and "those who live like this will not inherit the kingdom of God" (see Gal. 5:19-21).

A *shalom bayit* is a home marked by the absence of strife. But *shalom bayit* is far more than a negative concept; it is decisively positive. The Hebrew word *shalom* is filled with strong and rich imagery. *Shalom* comes from a verb meaning "to be whole, sound, entire, well, complete, perfect." The rabbis often used *shalom* as a name for God, in that he is the sum of perfection, and accordingly his Messiah is described as *sar shalom,* "Prince of Peace" (see Isa. 9:6). Furthermore, the Hebrew Bible often employs the word *shalom* in the sense of "be in friendship, in right relations, in harmony" with others. It may also convey the idea of tranquillity, the freedom from strife both externally and internally.

A beautiful practice is often followed in traditional Jewish homes on the eve of Sabbath. *Shabbat shalom* ("Sabbath peace") is the appropriate Sabbath greeting among members of the family. When the father arrives home from praying in synagogue he customarily blesses his sons and daughters. Putting his hands on the heads of his children, he recites this blessing for his sons: "May God make you like Ephraim and Manasseh." For his daughters he prays: "May God make you like Sarah, Rebekah, Rachel, and Leah. May the Lord bless you and keep you. May the Lord make his face to shine upon you, and be gracious to you. May the Lord lift up his countenance upon you, and give you peace *[shalom]*." The children reply, "Amen." Thus the Sabbath begins with a prayer for peace.[22]

A home of *shalom,* therefore, is a healthy home. Strife brings sickness, but *shalom* is wellness and wholeness. Strife divides, but *shalom* unites. Jesus taught, "Blessed are the peacemakers" (Matt. 5:9). Paul said that peace is the fruit of the Spirit within (Gal. 5:22). Here lies the Christian's key to *shalom bayit,* "a peaceful home." *Shalom* is supernaturally

---

22. See A. E. Kitov, *The Jew and His Home,* 5th ed. (New York: Shengold Publishers, 1963), pp. 50-51.

produced in the life of each believer. The unity of the home, and of all God's people, is the unity of the Spirit (cf. Eph. 4:3).

## Bringing Guests Home

Hospitality is a fundamental function of the Jewish home. This practice is also central in the Hebraic heritage of the Church. Schooled in a rich rabbinic background, Paul inculcates this teaching in his readers. He instructs the church at Rome to "practice hospitality" (Rom. 12:13). Here Paul reflects a sacred duty that was present from the earliest Old Testament times. Biblical law specified that it was an obligation to extend hospitality and love to the *ger,* "alien" or "stranger," for the Hebrew people themselves once were "aliens *[gerim]* in Egypt" (Lev. 19:34). Isaiah states that a genuinely righteous person will heed the obligation to "share your food with the hungry and to provide the poor wanderer with shelter" (Isa. 58:7). In his personal statement of ethical vindication, Job claims, "no stranger had to spend the night in the street, for my door was always open to the traveler" (Job 31:32).

The term used in rabbinic literature for hospitality is *hakhnasat orhim,* literally "bringing in of guests" or "gathering in of travelers."[23] Rabbinic literature provides considerable insight into the practice of *hakhnasat orhim,* the very term used in Franz Delitzsch's classic Hebrew New Testament translation for Paul's teaching on hospitality in Romans 12:13.

First, the rabbis considered hospitality one of the most important functions of the home. "Great is hospitality; greater even than early attendance at the house of study or than receiving the Shekhinah" (Babylonian Talmud, Shabbat 127a). Indeed, hospitality is listed first among six virtues, "the fruit of which man eats in this world" (Shabbat 127a).

Second, one was not to discriminate in the showing of hospitality. Whereas some people entertain only the rich, or people from a certain social or racial status, the rabbis taught that the home was to be open to all classes and kinds of people. There was a custom in Jerusalem to place a napkin over the doorway. "All the time the napkin was spread, guests (travelers) could enter" (Tosefta, Berakhot 4:9 [*Tosefta* is Aramaic for "addition" and refers to a collection of material that expands or comments upon the Mishnah]). Another practice in Jerusalem was to display a flag to show that a meal was in progress (Babylonian Talmud, Baba Batra 93b). The rab-

---

23. Note the useful treatment of this theme by R. Siegel, M. Strassfeld, and S. Strassfeld, *The First Jewish Catalog* (Philadelphia: Jewish Publication Society, 1973), pp. 275-77. See also A. E. Kitov, *The Jew and His Home,* pp. 90-94.

bis also stated, "Let your house be open wide, and let the poor be members of your household" (Mishnah, Abot 1:5). It was said of Rabbi Huna that "when he used to sit down to a meal, he opened the doors and exclaimed, 'Let whoever is in need enter and eat'" (Babylonian Talmud, Taanit 20b).

Third, children were taught to be hospitable. They were instructed when answering the door to invite guests to enter and to dine with the family. "Teach your household humility—so that if a poor man stands at the door and asks: 'Is father in?' they will respond: 'Yes, come in.' As soon as the poor man enters, let the table be set for him" (Abot of Rabbi Nathan 7 [this source, sometimes abbreviated ARN, is a commentary on the Mishnaic tractate Abot, and is often termed an "extracanonical" minor tractate of the Talmud]).

Fourth, guests were to be received graciously and cheerfully. Whereas many Westerners today avoid hospitality altogether, begrudgingly endure it, or tolerate it as a necessary evil, Middle Easterners have always considered hospitality to be a sacred obligation to be done with cheer. Rabbinic literature particularly emphasizes this obligation. "Let your house be wide open to guests. Receive people graciously. Lavish hospitality accompanied by a sour disposition means far less than modest hospitality which is extended cheerfully" (Abot of Rabbi Nathan 1).

Finally, guests had a responsibility to the host. Some food was expected to be left on the plate (Babylonian Talmud, Erubin 53b). They were not to take advantage of the host's kindness, but to be grateful (Berakhot 58a) and offer a special prayer for the host at the conclusion of the meal (Berakhot 46a). In addition, guests were not to ruffle the host or cause him anxiety: "A guest who unduly troubles his host is considered unworthy" (Derekh Eretz Zuta 8:9).

The Christian community must never consider the concept of hospitality to be optional. It is at the heart of the social consciousness of the Christian faith. The book of Hebrews reminds New Testament believers, recipients of the Jewish heritage of *hakhnasat orhim*, "Do not forget to entertain strangers, for by so doing some people have entertained angels without knowing it" (Heb. 13:2; cf. Jas. 2:14-17; 1 John 3:17).

## Learning about the Family through *Fiddler*

Almost everyone has heard of *Fiddler on the Roof*.[24] This musical first came to the Broadway stage in the early 1960s, and rapidly became a phe-

---

24. The quotations to follow in this chapter are from *Fiddler on the Roof*, ed. Joseph Stein (New York: Pocket Books, 1966).

nomenal box-office hit. Its popularity continued, and it became one of the longest-running musicals of all time. Since its U.S. debut, *Fiddler* has played around the world to tens of millions. In the early 1970s the film version appeared, starring Topol, an Israeli actor. Audience response was again remarkable. Writing in the *Saturday Review,* film critic Hollis Alpert stated, "If this is not the most satisfying musical film ever, it is awfully close to it."[25]

*Fiddler on the Roof* provides a delightfully entertaining story, illustrative of many traditional values of the Jewish family. I strongly urge all Christians to see *Fiddler* and then to discuss it. This artistic drama will enable Christians of all backgrounds to become aware of many Jewish values and customs, rooted in Scripture and rabbinic tradition, which have brought stability and meaning to the family. Some of the more important lessons for the family from *Fiddler* are discussed below. First, however, we shall provide a brief introduction to the story.

## The Plot of Fiddler

*Fiddler* takes place in Anatevka, a little town in czarist Russia, prior to World War I. Tevye, a dairyman, is seeking to rear his five daughters according to what the "Good Book" says. (The "Good Book" from which Tevye quotes, however, is made up mostly of verses invented by himself.) Trying to maintain Jewish tradition within his own home is not an easy task for Tevye. In fact, it is a losing battle, for, as the story unfolds, he sees his world of tradition gradually crumble around him. As each daughter comes to the marriage canopy, a larger chink is made in the armor of Jewish tradition. Though at first committed irreversibly to "Tradition" ("Without our traditions, our lives would be as shaky as . . . a fiddler on the roof!"), Tevye, in the final scene, stands stunned in icy silence before his daughter Chava, who has married outside the Jewish faith.

Thus Tevye's world of "Tradition" cracks, but in a sense Tevye's plight is that of every person—the struggle to remain true to the cherished family traditions of one's past in a changing and sometimes revolutionary world. It is precisely here that we find the timeless quality of this musical masterpiece: the indomitable ability to face difficult days with both humor and heart. Faced with a hostile environment and the day-by-day drudgery of scratching out a living, Tevye maintains his sanity in part by his ethnic wit—even amid his regular talks with God.

25. Hollis Alpert, "Big Fiddler," *Saturday Review* (November 13, 1974), p. 30.

## A Love That Grows after Marriage

To begin our discussion of the Jewish family values illustrated by *Fiddler,* we must immediately return to a point made earlier in this chapter. There we discussed how the Hebrews stressed the importance of love coming *after* marriage, not simply before. *Fiddler* provides a striking dramatic commentary on this principle. In the story, Tevye wants to arrange marriages for his daughters, as his own marriage to Golde had been arranged. His daughters, however, see things differently; it is for *love* that they wish to marry. Now forced to come to grips with a new concept, Tevye states, "It's a new world—love." He then asks his wife Golde (after twenty-five years of married life), "Do you love me?" The words which follow are beautiful and tender, reflecting the traditional Jewish concept of love after marriage. Tevye says to Golde, "The first time I met you was on our wedding day." Golde says, "I was shy." Tevye replies, "I was nervous." Golde: "So was I." Then Tevye counters, "But my father and my mother said we'd *learn to love* each other" (my italics). Once again, we are poignantly reminded that Hebrew tradition has taught, from the time of Abraham until today, that love is more than romance. It must grow and be nurtured *after* marriage in more than the romantic dimension, if marriage is to last.

## Respect for Manual Labor

Another lesson for the family illustrated by *Fiddler* has to do with dignity of and respect for manual labor. The Talmud states, "He who does not teach his son a trade is considered as having taught him thievery" (Kiddushin 29a). Such a view is reflected in the prologue of *Fiddler,* when the boys sing in unison, "At three I started Hebrew school; at ten I learned a trade." Though Tevye has no sons, each of his daughters has certain chores to do at home, such as milking, washing, and cleaning. Pulling his own milk cart among the villagers of Anatevka (his horse has become lame), Tevye meets a tailor (Motel), a butcher (Lazar Wolf), a hatter (Yussel), and others. Industriousness and manual skill have long characterized Jews. It is interesting to note that Jewish law prohibits anyone from earning a living through religion: "Do not make the Torah a spade to dig with" (Mishnah, Abot 4:5). Paul did not take money for his services among the Corinthians; rather, he preached the gospel "free of charge" (2 Cor. 11:7; cf. 2:17). For many centuries, most rabbis had secular occupations in addition to their duties as scholar-teachers of the tradition. The Mishnah also says, "An excellent thing is the study of the Torah combined with some secular occupation, for the labor demanded by them both puts sin out of one's mind" (Abot 2:2). This principle is undoubtedly reflected in Paul's skills as a leather-worker or tentmaker (Acts 18:3).

The Jew of Bible times saw his God-given vocation—whether that of herdsman, fisherman, tax collector, teacher, or scribe—as a means of bringing glory to God by the very privilege of work itself. A person was considered fortunate if he could eat the fruit of the labor of his own hands (Ps. 128:2). As we will again stress in chapter fourteen below, the Hebrew verb *abad*, "to work," "to labor," "to serve," is also translated "to worship" (see Isa. 19:21). The ancient Hebrews made no dichotomy between sacred and nonsacred occupations. Every domain of life belonged under the lordship of the King of the universe.

But the Western world today is different. Ours is largely a college-bound, profession-oriented society. Because the occupational status symbol tends to be cerebral rather than manual, we would do well to remind ourselves of the sanctity of hard physical work. Was not Jesus of Nazareth a carpenter (or stonemason; Mark 6:3; cf. Matt. 13:55)? We are in no way advocating that clergy go out and get a second job in the secular world. Few rabbis even do that anymore. But perhaps the village of Anatevka stands as a silent reminder, especially for those of us who sit at desks most of the day, that there remains from the time of creation a dignity to manual labor.

## Sabbath Observance

A third important principle concerning the stability of the Jewish family is seen in the description of the Sabbath observance that is given in *Fiddler.* In Anatevka there is a sense of joyous anticipation as the Sabbath draws near (see Isa. 58:13). The seventh day of the week is a dramatic symbol of community. It may be summed up in the word *holiness.* For Tevye and his family, holiness means an act of separation from many of the routine and mundane affairs of life. From the moment Golde lights the Sabbath Eve candles until the first star appears in the sky some twenty-four hours later, there is a sense of well-being and spiritual satisfaction in the midst of their seething society. The Jewish community of Anatevka is in constant threat of another Russian pogrom. Yet we catch a snatch of this spiritual serenity as, around the Sabbath table, Tevye and Golde sing "A Sabbath Prayer" to all five daughters. The song concludes, "May the Lord protect and defend, may the Lord preserve you from pain. Favor them, O Lord, with happiness and peace. O hear our Sabbath prayer. Amen."

Today, as we look at the oft-fragmented Christian family that rarely seems to anticipate joyously its day of worship, the Lord's Day, we must ponder again the Jewish saying, "More than Israel kept the Sabbath, the

Sabbath kept Israel."[26] In Abraham Heschel's words, "Judaism tries to foster the vision of life as a pilgrimage to the seventh day; the longing for the Sabbath all days of the week."[27] Judaism treats the Sabbath as a queen or bride; its holiness is a reminder of the world to come.[28] As the above imagery and teaching have helped the observant Jew to refocus, sustain serenity, and regain divine perspective in the midst of the weekly pressures of life, so the Lord's Day for the Christian ought—among other spiritual purposes—to provide renewal in similar ways.

## Parental Respect

*Fiddler* also raises the issue of honor and reverence for parents. Yente, the village *shadkhan* ("matchmaker"), tells Golde, "Ah, children, children! They are your blessing in your old age." Though, as the story turns out, this was somewhat wishful thinking on Yente's part, nevertheless the importance of honoring father and mother is as old as Moses and the Moral Law itself (Exod. 20:12). An inspired Hebrew sage once wrote, "Children's children are a crown to the aged, and parents are the pride of their children" (Prov. 17:6). Building on this theme, the rabbis of old taught, "Whoever hears a section of the Torah from his grandson is considered as hearing it at Mount Sinai on the day of Revelation" (Jerusalem Talmud, Shabbat 1:2).

The modern Jewish humorist, Sam Levenson, once recalled that his own childhood had a particular stress on parental respect: "Mama and Papa hoped to derive joy from their children. Honor brought to parents by their children was the accepted standard for measuring success. It also became an incentive for us. Our personal success was to a great extent predicated upon the happiness we could bring to our parents. It would not be long before this idea would be completely reversed. To make our children happy was to become the summum bonum of family life."[29] Lest we dismiss Levenson's point as relevant only for Jewish people, one may recall these familiar New Testament words, incumbent upon the Church: "Children, obey your parents in the Lord, for this is right. 'Honor your father and mother'—which is the first commandment with a promise—'that it may go well with you and that you may enjoy long life on the earth'" (Eph. 6:1-3).

---

26. See Morris N. Kertzer, *What Is A Jew?*, rev. ed. (New York: Macmillan Co., 1965), p. 136.

27. Abraham J. Heschel, *The Sabbath: Its Meaning for Modern Man* (New York: Farrar, Straus & Giroux, 1951), p. 90.

28. Ibid., pp. 59, 73.

29. Sam Levenson, *Everything But Money* (New York: Simon and Schuster, 1966), p. 17.

## We Are All Tevyes

If Tevye has an Achilles' heel, it centers around the truth of Levenson's last remark. When we first meet Tevye singing "Tradition," there is no mistake about his parental role in the family: "Who has the right, as master of the house, to have the final word at home? The papa, the papa —tradition!" As each of his daughters falls in love, however, Tevye finds that the firm grip he once held on tradition has somehow loosened. The tradition he insisted on at first, "to marry whomever Papa picks," has been set aside.

Here is the crucial question that *Fiddler* raises for both the Jewish and the Christian family today: Realizing that the world is changing and is morally in a state of flux, what values of the past are worth preserving at all cost? As Tevye asked observantly before the marriage of his first daughter Tzeitel, "One little time you pull out a prop, and where does it stop? Where does it stop?" When Hodel, Tevye's second daughter, plans to be married without even asking her father's permission, he erupts, "What's happening to the tradition? One little time I pulled out a thread, and where has it led? Where has it led?" Finally, Tevye realizes painfully the domino effect of "pulling out a prop." His third daughter, Chava, is about to marry a non-Jew. She says, "The world is changing, Papa." Tevye replies, "No. Some things do not change for us. Some things will never change."

But they do change. Chava soon gets married. Tevye then says to Golde his wife, "Chava is dead to us! We will forget her." This statement is more than a mere figure of speech. In the Jewish *shtetl* (East European ghetto), when a child married outside the faith, his parents referred to him as "dead." They would observe a week of formal mourning and sometimes would even conduct a burial with an empty casket.

In this short excursus on the family from *Fiddler*, we have not dealt with all the lessons raised by this delightful musical. But all of us can identify in one way or another with Tevye, whether or not we agree with the outcome of his situation. *Fiddler* poignantly poses the question of whether we do things simply because "we have always done them that way," or whether we do them because they are right to do and in accord with the pattern of eternal truth.

*Fiddler,* then, will cause Christians to reevaluate their traditions. Christians will see anew the need to sort out those values which may be only hand-me-down, dust-covered relics of the past, having already served their usefulness, from those with timeless and eternal value. This sorting is a complex and never-ending process, requiring the Scriptures, the wisdom of the Spirit, and a lot of common sense.

And so the plight of Tevye lives on. It continues in all of us, for we are all Tevyes.


## Older and Better: Aging through Hebrew Eyes

Our society places a decisive accent on youth and evokes a corresponding fear of old age. The increase in the number of elderly has paralleled a decrease in their role and status. We have so overemphasized the desirability of youth and its features that, as Jewish anthropologist Raphael Patai points out, "Youth is placed on so high a pedestal as to amount to idolization." He observes further that in our "child-dominated" society "extreme permissiveness on the part of the parents often makes the child or the teenager the dominant personality in the family, whose wishes and whims must be fulfilled."[30] As proved by the current direction and target of advertising in the Western world, youthfulness has indeed become one of the great desiderata.

This preoccupation with youthfulness has resulted in the great modern American obsession to eliminate, delay, or escape the fate of physical deterioration from growing old. Americans spend an enormous amount of money yearly on cosmetic surgery, hair-dyeing, and new wardrobes in an effort to support the cult of youthful attractiveness in the hope of staving off the horrors of aging. We Americans also euphemize about our age. People in their forties are still referred to as "young men" or "young women." People in their sixties or seventies may be "mature," "getting along in years," "senior citizens," or "golden-agers," but they are not "aged" or "old." We never seem to get "old"—not even in our "sunset years."


### The Pinnacle of Life

Our modern society says that people reach their most desired or peak phase in life either in their late teens or at that coveted milestone, age twenty-one. After that, they are thought to begin their downward journey, to be "over the hill." By contrast, the Hebrew Scriptures assert that the pinnacle of a person's life is in old age. Because one's inherent worth and prestige increase steadily with the years, the Bible never makes a secret of a person's age. Note, for example, these Hebrew characters whose age is care-

---

30. Raphael Patai, "Aging—The Biblical View," in *Jewish Heritage Reader*, ed. Lily Edelman (New York: Taplinger Publishing Co., 1965), p. 142.

fully given at death: Isaac, 180; Abraham, 175; Jacob, 147; Ishmael, 137; Sarah, 127; Moses, 120; Joseph and Joshua, 110; and Eli, 98.

The biblical emphasis, however, is not on one reaching his prime *physically* in old age, but rather spiritually, psychologically, and mentally. Therefore, one did not fear advancing years but welcomed them optimistically. "Old age was not a defeat but a victory, not a punishment but a privilege."[31] Such was the teaching of the ancient sages: "How welcome is old age! The aged are beloved by God" (Exodus Rabbah 5:12 [this source is an exegetical midrash to the book of Exodus and part of a larger collection known as *Midrash Rabbah*]). Thus, in the Hebrew community of Bible times, the elderly were not thought of as people who had outlived their usefulness. They were not made to feel that they ought to apologize for being alive. Thus aging was a cause for celebration; indeed, to be older was better.

A vital challenge now faces the Synagogue and the Church, the community and the home: understanding the aging and elderly and knowing how to minister effectively to them. The Scriptures are very practical and have much to teach on this theme. If our theology is incorrect, our sociology can hardly be right. If we are to build a viable theology of aging, we must actively attend to several important biblical concerns about those who are advanced in years.

## *Physical Decline*

First, we must help the elderly face physical decline (and learn to face it ourselves). Though the Bible views old age as a blessing of God (sometimes it is linked with personal piety and faithfulness to the covenant—Deut. 5:16; Job 5:26), increased physical decline and feebleness are to be expected. As the psalmist cries, "Do not cast me away when I am old; do not forsake me when my strength is gone. . . . Even when I am old and gray, do not forsake me, O God" (Ps. 71:9, 18), so every person must come to accept the physical limitations of a body which cannot perform at age 68 the way it did fifty years earlier at 18.

In a realistic way, adjustment must be made to such inevitable health problems linked to old age as difficulty in hearing (2 Sam. 19:35), poor eyesight (Gen. 48:10), being overweight (1 Sam. 4:18), and the inability to get warm (1 Kgs. 1:1). Ecclesiastes 12 is a striking figurative description of bodily decay, where old age affects the hands, legs, teeth, eyes, ears,

---

31. Abraham J. Heschel, *The Insecurity of Freedom* (New York: Schocken Books, 1972), pp. 71-72.

and the ability to sleep. Indeed, Scripture everywhere reminds us that this treasure of life is contained in "jars of clay" (2 Cor. 4:7).

No one lives forever—that is, in this battered bag of bones. Thus, the Church must help the elderly to face death honestly and to make provision for it. Unlike many people today, the Hebrews did not avoid the subject of death.[32] Both Jacob and Joseph (Gen. 50:5, 24-25) made arrangements for their funerals in advance, and Joseph of Arimathea already had his tomb prepared (Matt. 27:60).

## Honoring Those Worthy of Honor

A second biblical concern is that we are to honor those who are older than we. The fifth commandment, "Honor your father and mother," is repeated eight times throughout the Bible. We must observe that, in its original setting, it was primarily addressed to adult Hebrews, not exclusively to children. Later, both Jesus (Mark 7:9-13) and Paul (Eph. 6:2) singled out and emphasized the importance of this commandment, which heads the second main section of the Ten Commandments (the Moral Law), commandments five through ten. Heschel has observed that "God did not proclaim, 'Honor Me,' 'Revere Me.' He proclaimed instead: 'Revere your father and your mother.' There is no reverence for God without reverence for father and mother."[33]

The Talmud links honor of parents to honor of God in one more way: father, mother, and God are partners in the creation of the child. "There are three partners to [the creation of] a man: God, his father, and mother. When a man honors his father and his mother, God says, 'It is as if I dwelled among them and they honored Me'" (Kiddushin 30b).

One way of judging the overall character of a people is how they behave toward the old. When certain youths of Bethel mocked an elder (the prophet Elisha, calling him "baldhead"), they were severely punished by ravaging bears (2 Kgs. 2:23-24). Failure to honor the elderly eventually brought judgment on all God's people (Isa. 3:5; Lam. 5:12). Respect for the elderly was to begin at home: "Listen to your father, who gave you life, and do not despise your mother when she is old" (Prov. 23:22).

Although the Bible teaches that children are to be a blessing to parents in their old age, the attitude today is quite different. Traditional family values are now being threatened by change. A rabbi once bemoaned to me what he had been observing among his congregants: "When I was growing up, every-

---

32. See Ernest Becker, *The Denial of Death* (repr. New York: The Free Press, 1975).
33. Heschel, *Insecurity of Freedom*, p. 70.

thing had to be 'Yes, Father,' or 'Yes, Mother.' No one ever sat in my father's chair when father was absent from home." Then he added, "If we were ever slightly disrespectful, father would sternly demand, '*Kibbud ob* [Honor (your) father]!' Then he often reinforced his point by using a long switch."

## Need for Care and Support

A third emphasis found in Scripture deals with care for the elderly. The Hebrew word for family, *mishpaḥah,* implied in Bible times a societal unit that was (1) patriarchal (the father was the spiritual leader or tribal head of his family), (2) patrilocal (at marriage, a son would bring his bride into his father's household), and (3) extended (the family unit included grandparents, children, grandchildren, aunts, uncles, and cousins). Each family functioned as an economic group. Living under the same roof, family members were bound by great loyalty. Such an arrangement had its obvious advantages for the elderly: the family met their housing, economic, and health needs. The aged experienced the support of their extended family to life's end, including death, burial, and mourning thereafter.

Today, few celebrate the summit of their lives. Instead, many ask, "Am I really needed?" Often shunted away from the security of family and friends, and with death seemingly a heartbeat away, the elderly now pose for us a great challenge. What remedy is there for those who often feel rejected and have little self-worth, for those who suffer boredom and loneliness?

In Jesus, the Church has a striking example of one who cared for his parents. It appears that Joseph died young (he is not mentioned at the wedding in John 2, and the Gospels are silent about him after Jesus reaches his teen years). So Mary must have leaned heavily on Jesus, her eldest son. Jesus' care for his mother extended even to the moment of his own death on the cross: he told John to take Mary "into his own household" (John 19:27).

Although the health needs of many elderly people cannot be met adequately at home due to lack of proper facilities, equipment, and professional expertise, the sick and needy everywhere long for friends and visitors. The Church must not forget that at the judgment of the nations—the time of separating the sheep from the goats—the distinguishing criterion will not be creedal but practical: serving one's Lord by showing care and concern for others (Matt. 25:34-40).

## The Wisdom of Experience

A fourth biblical observation is that we are to seek out our elders for the wisdom of their years. The Hebrews equated age with wisdom and experience (Job 12:12, 20; 32:7). Because of the wisdom of their years, elders (a word which occurs about 175 times throughout Scripture) served as judges, counselors, military officials, and other kinds of leaders. The office of "elder" (Greek *presbýteros,* "old man") was a key position in the early Church (Acts 20:17; 1 Tim. 4:14; Jas. 5:14).

Rabbinic literature also stresses the importance of old people as a source of wisdom. "He who learns from the young is like one who eats unripe grapes and drinks wine from the winepress. But he who learns from the old is like one who eats ripe grapes and drinks old wine" (Mishnah, Abot 4:20). A midrash states, "One who takes advice from elders never stumbles" (Exodus Rabbah 3:8). The rabbis made it clear that every age group—from five years of age to one hundred—has its special function within the community: "At five years old [one is ready] for the study of Scripture, at ten for the Mishnah, at thirteen for [the fulfilling of] the commandments, at fifteen for the Talmud, at eighteen for marriage, at twenty for the pursuit [of a livelihood], at thirty [man reaches] full strength, at forty full understanding, at fifty able to give counsel, at sixty for old age [i.e., for to be an elder], at seventy for gray hairs, at eighty [his survival reflects] special strength, at ninety for a bent body, and at one hundred he is as good as dead and passed away and ceased from the world" (Abot 5:21).

In our day, gray hair may ruin one's chance for promotion or cost a worker his job. In the Hebrew community of Bible times, however, it was considered beautiful (Prov. 20:29), and greatly desired as a "crown of splendor" (Prov. 16:31). With gray hair came respect and honor: "Rise in the presence of the aged, show respect for the elderly and revere your God. I am the LORD" (Lev. 19:32). In the presence of gray hair, people of all ages stood silent, ready to be counseled in the way of wisdom. John (probably "the elder") fell as though dead before the man with hair as "white as snow" (Rev. 1:14), an obvious pictorial allusion to the wisdom of his Lord.

Here lies a great, untapped reservoir of knowledge for the Church, a deep sea of wisdom that should be sought out. Youthfulness is often characterized by inexperience and impetuousness. Those who have maturity of years, however, can bring a needed historical perspective to problems—a perspective too often lost in the rashness of today's world. Furthermore, if the Church draws upon the sagacity of those who are the seniors within the body, it will help to stabilize and bring to spiritual maturity those "infants" who are being "blown here and there by every wind of teaching" (Eph. 4:14).

## Active to the End

Yet another concern and challenge posed by Scripture is that we should seek to keep elderly people active to the end. After forty years in the wilderness, Caleb, then in his eighty-fifth year but still ready to conquer the Canaanites, declared, "I am still as strong today as the day Moses sent me out; I'm just as vigorous to go out to battle now as I was then" (Josh. 14:11). This Hebrew leader chose to keep actively exerting his energy rather than retiring out of sight. It was said of Moses, when he died at 120 years of age, that "his eyes were not weak nor his strength [i.e., virility] gone" (Deut. 34:7).

In the New Testament, two elderly Jews, Simeon and Anna, remained active in God's service at the Temple. Of Anna, a "very old" widow and prophetess from the tribe of Asher, the Gospel of Luke says, "She never left the Temple but worshiped night and day, fasting and praying" (2:37). Throughout Scripture, the Hebrew people—whatever their age—exhibited a life-style that was not passive, withdrawn, or relaxed. Rather, their style of life was active, vigorous, and hard-working. They understood that "faith without deeds is dead" (Jas. 2:26). In realistic terms, the rabbis encouraged all people to a similar persistency of labor: "It is not your obligation to complete the work, yet neither are you free to desist from it" (Mishnah, Abot 2:16).

## Hope of the Resurrection

Last, and perhaps most important of all, the elderly need to be reassured of the hope they possess beyond this life. During Bible times, those who faithfully walked with God in "this age" *(olam ha-zeh)* were also confident they would be with him in "the age to come" *(olam ha-ba)*. As we observed in the last chapter, in contrast to the ancient Greeks, the Hebrews did not teach salvation of a person's soul apart from the body. Rather, "salvation means the redemption of the body and of the whole created order as well (Rom. 8:21-23)."[34] The Hebrew Scriptures teach that neither death nor Sheol could terminate a person's relationship with his Creator (Ps. 49:15; 139:8). Indeed, at the end of the present age, God will act in behalf of his own and "he will swallow up death forever" (Isa. 25:8). Associated with this act is the assurance of the resurrection of the dead: "But your dead will live; their bodies will rise. You who dwell in the dust, wake up

34. George E. Ladd, *I Believe in the Resurrection of Jesus* (Grand Rapids: William B. Eerdmans Publishing Co., 1975), p. 45.

and shout for joy" (Isa. 26:19). And again, "Multitudes who sleep in the dust of the earth will awake: some to everlasting life, others to shame and everlasting contempt" (Dan. 12:2).

The ancient rabbis built with great conviction upon this Old Testament foundation. They considered belief in the resurrection to be a cardinal teaching.[35] They taught that if a person "repudiated belief in the resurrection of the dead, he will have no share in the resurrection" (Babylonian Talmud, Sanhedrin 90a).

By reflecting upon this rich Hebraic background and upon additional New Testament texts, today's Church must bring assurance and hope to its elderly who are nearing the end of life's journey. In this regard, the book of Revelation is especially pertinent. As the last book of the Bible, it contains the concluding account of a long and dynamic story. Its theme is redemption, the culmination of the story of God's search for man. If Genesis recounts "Paradise Lost," Revelation points to "Paradise Regained." Revelation is intimately tied to Israel's past, not mere dreams and visions of her future. In fact, the Hebrew Scriptures provide the key for interpreting Revelation, since John, its author, makes use of hundreds of allusions and references from them. John's Bible, like that of the other apostles, was the Old Testament. Writing in this strongly Hebraic context of thought, John alludes to the ultimate satisfaction of an active life span awaiting those who "age in the Lord." They will joyfully hear a voice from heaven saying, "Blessed are the dead who die in the Lord from now on . . . they will rest from their labor, for their deeds will follow them" (Rev. 14:13).

# UNDERSTANDING CHAPTER ELEVEN

1. For centuries Jewish tradition and secular culture have confronted one another head-on. Describe some of the Jewish responses to this confrontation in the modern world. Why is it important for Christians to have a realistic (rather than an idealistic) view of Jews and Judaism?

2. What areas of pressure and stress faced today by Christians in the home and in society have frequently led to changing attitudes toward marriage and the family?

3. It has often been argued that singleness or celibacy is a higher or more "God-honoring" way of life. Discuss the pros and cons of this issue in the light

---

35. A. Cohen goes so far as to say, "No aspect of the subject of the Hereafter has so important a place in the religious teaching of the Rabbis as the doctrine of the Resurrection" (*Everyman's Talmud* [New York: E. P. Dutton, 1949], p. 357).

of Scripture. If there is a biblical norm, how shall we explain the biblical exceptions (e.g., Jeremiah, Jesus, and Paul)? (See the footnotes to this chapter.)

4. Define platonic love. How does the very nature of a platonic relationship mirror the dualistic view of man discussed in the previous chapter?

5. Summarize some of the biblical and extrabiblical evidence in support of the goodness of marriage and sex in the Jewish tradition.

6. Of the 613 commandments in the Law of Moses, which is the first?

7. Discuss the implications of David Hubbard's comment that "the Fall did not create passion; it only perverted it."

8. Show how the wording of various passages in Genesis, the Song of Songs, and Matthew support the teaching that marriage is built on companionship and togetherness.

9. What phrase from Song of Song 2:16 is commonly inscribed inside wedding rings?

10. Explain the meaning of Genesis 2:18, which states the woman is created to be a "helper suitable for" the man. How does R. David Freedman suggest one should translate the expression *ezer kenegdo*?

11. Rabbinic literature describes God as the supreme matchmaker; however, his task is difficult to accomplish. To which miracle in Israelite history do the rabbis compare this hard chore of making a successful match? Discuss any additional lesson(s) to which you think the rabbis may here be alluding.

12. Compare the place of love in relation to marriage in the biblical world of the East with that of the West. What is there about the story of Isaac and Rebekah that Jewish people have long pointed to in illustrating the traditional role of love in relation to arranged marriages? Cite the illustration involving "soup" that Walter Trobisch has effectively used to show how Easterners and Westerners differ in their approach to marriage.

13. To the Hebrews, what one word sums up the essence of marriage according to the Bible?

14. What great event in the history of the Israelites did the rabbis see in replica or in reenactment through the marriage ceremony?

15. In the Hebrew Bible, to whom is the bridegroom likened, and to whom is his bride likened?

16. Define *ketubah*. How early, and to what place, are we able to trace the existence of the *ketubah*?

17. What is a *huppah*? Who comes to the *huppah* first in the Jewish marriage ceremony? In the divine covenant formulas of the Old Testament, who initiates the relationship? What is Israel's role?

18. Compare the presence of fire at the covenant ceremony on Sinai with the use of fire in traditional Jewish wedding ceremonies. What New Testament passages possibly give further insight to the theme of the Bridegroom coming amidst fire?

19. What term describes the first part of the marriage ceremony which con-

tractually sets the couple aside in betrothal? What is the basic meaning behind this Hebrew term? Discuss what can be done in today's Church to recover the sense of holiness in the marriage relationship.

20. Drawing upon Old Testament imagery, the New Testament uses the term *bride.* In Ephesians 5:25-32 and Revelation 19:7, who is the bride?

21. The permanent nature of God's covenant with Israel is taught in Isaiah 49:16 and Jeremiah 31:35-36. Give the gist of each of these passages.

22. What is the word picture that lies behind the Hebrew expression *karat berit,* "to make a covenant"? Why was the shedding of blood important to the parties involved?

23. Among the Israelites, a person's "word" was equal to his "promise." What light does biblical Hebrew shed on this point?

24. Starting with God's covenant with Abraham, outline the key stages of covenant renewal throughout Scripture. How do Christians and Jews differ in their understanding of the term *New Covenant*? Discuss.

25. What is *yihus*? What is the most desirable way to enhance one's *yihus*?

26. In brief, what was the function of the community *shadkhan*?

27. According to rabbinic tradition, since God completed his work of creation, how has he been spending his time?

28. What place does prayer have in conjunction with a Jewish wedding? What threefold prayer is traditionally offered over the head of a newborn Jewish child?

29. In European Jewry, why was it not customary to send out wedding invitations to a select list of guests?

30. What substance associated with joy and festivity is used at Jewish weddings and on the Sabbath to symbolize the sanctifying of these institutions to God?

31. In the ancient world, what was signified when two individuals drank from the same cup? Indicate two situations in the Gospels where we read of a shared cup. What specifically was Jesus probing to find out when he gave his disciples opportunity to share in a common cup? As events would turn out, what practically did this sharing mean?

32. In a contemporary Jewish marriage ceremony, what terms are used for the two cups of wine shared by the marriage partners? What common destiny is symbolically dramatized by each cup? Discuss some of the practical implications of this symbolism that can contribute to a more realistic approach to Christian marriage.

33. The first part of the marriage ceremony that legally (contractually) sets the couple aside in betrothal *(kiddushin)* is followed by the second part *(nissu'in).* As to actual status, what does this second stage of the relationship imply?

34. What is the root meaning of *nissu'in*? In conjunction with traditional Jewish weddings, how has this root meaning been dramatized publicly?

35. How is the term *miqdash* usually translated in the Hebrew Bible? Of what two structures is the term *miqdash* used in the Hebrew Bible? How is the

expression *miqdash me'at* translated? In postbiblical Judaism, to what structure does *miqdash me'at* refer?

36. Like the Temple, the rabbis taught that the home, as a "small sanctuary," had three main purposes or functions. What are these?

37. Explain how various aspects of the Temple and its worship are now reflected (i.e., find their modern equivalents) in the home or *miqdash me'at.*

38. Point out two different ways in which Paul makes symbolic use of the word *temple* in 1 Corinthians. (See footnotes to this chapter.)

39. In Jewish tradition, what institution is considered to be the center of religious life?

40. From what root does the Hebrew word for "parent," *horeh,* appear to derive? How might this further our understanding of the responsibility of the parent within the *miqdash me'at*?

41. Judaism is a religion of laypeople. Practically speaking, what does this mean? Is Christianity different from Judaism in this regard? Discuss.

42. Explain the meaning of *shalom bayit.* What are some of the things the rabbis warned about that could destroy *shalom bayit*? Does Paul have anything to contribute on this theme?

43. What basic idea stands behind the word *shalom*? In the Hebrew Bible, in what sense is *shalom* sometimes used that illuminates the concept of *shalom bayit*? Why did the rabbis employ *shalom* as a name for God?

44. Describe what a father often does with his children in a traditional Jewish home on the eve of the Sabbath. What is the appropriate Sabbath greeting among members of the family?

45. What is the biblical basis for the practice of hospitality?

46. Outline some of the main emphases and teachings regarding hospitality found in rabbinic literature.

47. *Fiddler on the Roof* illustrates many traditional values of the Jewish family. Be able to answer the following: (a) What is the plot of *Fiddler,* and in what sense is the plight of Tevye that of every person? (b) How do the Bible and early Jewish literature teach or illustrate the dignity of and respect for manual labor? (c) Discuss what you think the following saying means: "More than Israel kept the Sabbath, the Sabbath kept Israel." (d) What is the crucial question that *Fiddler* raises for both the Jewish and the Christian family?

48. Discuss the various ways our modern society places a decisive accent on youth and evokes a corresponding fear of old age.

49. From the viewpoint of the Hebrew Scriptures, in what sense may it be argued the pinnacle of a person's life is in old age and that aging is a cause for celebration?

50. What Old Testament passage presents a striking figurative description of bodily decay? What two people in the book of Genesis prearranged their funerals? Do people in the West today avoid the subject of death? Discuss.

51. One way of judging the overall character of a people is how they be-

have toward the old. Discuss this statement. What is entailed in honoring those older than we are?

52. What three main features characterized the *mishpaḥah* of Bible times?

53. With what traits did the Hebrews equate age? Name three important capacities of leadership served by the "elders" of Old Testament times.

54. The Mishnah (Abot 5:21) states that at various ages throughout life one is qualified for different functions. Indicate the significance of the following ages: (a) five, (b) ten, (c) thirteen, (d) fifteen, (e) eighteen, (f) twenty, (g) fifty, (h) sixty.

55. Discuss the difference of attitude concerning gray hair in our day as over against Bible times.

56. What does the Bible say about the later years of Moses, Caleb, and Anna? Discuss the modern concept of retirement in relation to the role of the older generation in biblical society.

57. The Jewish people of the biblical world distinguished time in relation to two different ages. What are these ages?

58. Is the concept of the resurrection found anywhere in the Hebrew Scriptures? Explain.

59. According to the Talmud, what was the consequence for any person who "repudiated belief in the resurrection of the dead"?

60. From the section titled "Older and Better," review the main biblical concerns which are essential in building a relevant theology of aging.

# Chapter Twelve

# Passover and Last Supper

*When I see the blood, I will pass over you*

Exodus 12:13

Passover is an event of central importance to both Jews and Christians. For the Jew, the Exodus and the revelation at Mount Sinai are great historical focal points of redemption and covenant. The Last Supper in the Upper Room and the crucifixion at Calvary are of similar importance to the Christian, recalling propitious historical occasions which also focus on the themes of redemption and covenant.

A straightforward reading of the Synoptic Gospels indicates that the Last Supper in the Upper Room in Jerusalem was a traditional Jewish Passover meal commemorating the Exodus (see Matt. 26:17-30; Mark 14:12-26; Luke 22:7-23). Jesus, however, went beyond the commonly held Jewish understanding of this celebration. He indicated to his disciples how this meal depicted his imminent suffering and death. It is of more than passing interest that both Judaism and Christianity exist today as two separate religious communities, each revolving around the mandate to remember perpetually the theme of redemption. At the first Passover, the Lord said to Israel, "This is a day you are to commemorate; for the generations to come you shall celebrate it as a festival to the LORD — a lasting ordinance" (Exod. 12:14; cf. v. 17). At the Last Supper, Jesus said, "Do this in remembrance of me" (Luke 22:19). Concerning the celebration of the Lord's Supper, Paul instructed, "Whenever you eat this bread and drink this cup, you proclaim the Lord's death until he comes" (1 Cor. 11:26).

For the Christian community, the Lord's Supper—also called the Eucharist or Holy Communion—is one of the pivotal New Testament institutions illustrating the impact that Hebrew thought has had upon the Church. The Lord's Supper was established by Jesus, in the presence of his Jewish disciples, in connection with the Passover meal that symbolically dramatized Israel's release from Egyptian slavery. Without a careful exegetical, theological, and historical study of this event, the rich Hebraic background of the Christian concept of redemption would be lost. This chapter addresses this task.[1]

## The Origin of Passover

The Hebrew term *pesah* (Passover) is derived from the verb *pasah*.[2] The Hebrew Bible uses this term in several different ways. In its broadest usage it refers to a major festival, held in the spring, commemorating Israel's deliverance from Egypt. The term is most often used of the entire festival

---

1. For further study on the themes of Passover and Last Supper, see the following: Markus Barth, *Rediscovering the Lord's Supper* (Atlanta: John Knox Press, 1988); Baruch M. Bokser, "Was the Last Supper a Passover Seder?" *Bible Review* 3/2 (Summer, 1987): 24-33; Roland de Vaux, *Ancient Israel: Its Life and Institutions,* trans. J. McHugh (repr. New York: McGraw-Hill, 1965), 2:484-93; Werner Elert, *Eucharist and Church Fellowship in the First Four Centuries,* trans. N. E. Nagel (St. Louis: Concordia Publishing House, 1966); Gillian Feeley-Harnik, *The Lord's Table: Eucharist and Passover in Early Christianity* (Philadelphia: University of Pennsylvania Press, 1981); Ruth G. Fredman, *The Passover Seder* (Philadelphia: University of Pennsylvania Press, 1981); Theodor Gaster, *Passover* (New York: H. Schuman, 1949); Joachim Jeremias, *The Eucharistic Words of Jesus,* trans. Norman Perrin, 3rd ed. (Philadelphia: Fortress Press, 1966); Abram Kanof, "Passover," in *Encyclopedia Judaica,* ed. Geoffrey Wigoder (Jerusalem: Keter Publishing House, 1971), 13:163-73; Mordell Klein, ed., *Passover* (Jerusalem: Keter Books, 1973); Isaac Levy, *A Guide to Passover* (London: Jewish Chronicle Publications, 1958); I. Howard Marshall, *Last Supper and Lord's Supper* (Grand Rapids: William B. Eerdmans Publishing Co., 1981); Willy Rordorf, et al., *The Eucharist of the Early Christians,* trans. Matthew J. O'Connell (New York: Pueblo Publishing Company, 1978); Anthony J. Saldarini, *Jesus and Passover* (New York: Paulist Press, 1984); Hayyim Schauss, *Guide to Jewish Holy Days* (New York: Schocken Books, 1938); Judah B. Segal, *The Hebrew Passover* (New York: Oxford University Press, 1963).

2. The origin of *pasah* is unknown. For Exod. 12:13ff. scholars have suggested a variety of meanings, including: (a) "to pass over" or "to leap over" (NIV, RSV); (b) "to limp," i.e., "to skip by, spare" (cf. 1 Kgs. 18:21, 26—RSV); (c) "to defend, protect, stand guard over" (cf. Exod. 12:13—NEB alternate reading; Exod. 12:23—Jewish Publication Society [1962] alternate reading; see also Isa. 31:5). Ultimately, however, the meaning of a term such as *pasah* must be established by context and a thorough study of its use in Hebrew and other cognate languages; cf. James Barr, *The Semantics of Biblical Language* (New York: Oxford University Press, 1961), pp. 100-157.

celebration (Exod. 12:48; 2 Kgs. 23:21). But it may more narrowly designate the Passover sacrifice to be eaten (Exod. 12:11; 2 Chr. 30:18) and the animal victim, that is, the "Passover lamb" (Exod. 12:21; 2 Chr. 30:15). Passover is the oldest of Jewish festivals; it originated over three thousand years ago. It appears originally to have combined two separate spring festivals. One rite involved unleavened bread, the other a sacrificial lamb. The Old Testament (Exod. 34:18, 25) distinguishes the festivals by using the terms "Feast of Unleavened Bread" (*hag ha-matzot*) and "Passover Feast" (*hag ha-pasah*).

The New Testament (Matt. 26:17; Mark 14:1; Luke 22:1) refers to both of these festivals as "the Passover," *tó páscha* (the Greek term *páscha* is closely related to the Hebrew), and "the Feast of Unleavened Bread," *tá ázyma* or *hē heortè tōn azýmōn*. These festivals were held in immediate sequence. Passover was celebrated at twilight of the 14th day of the month (Exod. 12:6) and the Feast of Unleavened Bread for the seven days following, namely, the 15th to the 21st (Exod. 12:15; Lev. 23:5-6; Num. 28:16-17; 2 Chr. 35:1, 17). Toward the end of the New Testament era, however, the one term *Passover* was generally used to designate the integrated celebration of what had begun as two festivals. Though by that time the title "Feast of Unleavened Bread" had not disappeared, Josephus indicates that "Passover" was commonly used to refer to both festivals.[3] In the Mishnah, the tractate Pesahim (the plural form of *pesah*), which deals with the laws concerning Passover, reveals a similar popular combining of the feasts.

Some scholars have postulated a prehistory to the Passover from references in Exodus, for example, "Let my people go, so that they may hold a festival to me in the desert" (5:1; cf. 10:9). This reference may be to a shepherd's festival kept by Semitic nomads in the spring as they would head for new pastures before the start of the dry season. The Feast of Unleavened Bread perhaps had its origin in an agricultural festival related to the spring barley harvest. After entering Canaan, the Hebrews may have adopted aspects of this feast from the Canaanites.[4]

Some scholars hold the more critical view that these separate festivals were not combined or historicized (connected to the actual Exodus) until about the time of the Exile or later. Of course, this line of reasoning is conjecture. Whatever the exact prehistory of the Passover, the festival cannot be separated from that historic moment in Israel's past which brought miraculous deliverance from Egypt.

3. Josephus, *Antiquities* 14.2.1 (21); 17.9.3 (213-14).
4. See Roland de Vaux, *Ancient Israel,* 2:490-93.

## Passover in Old Testament Times

The Exodus was the redemptive event par excellence in the life of God's covenant people. The Passover reenacted annually the greatest miracle the Lord performed out of grace for his chosen; it was to hold central importance in the history of world Jewry. The Passover celebration retold the story of freedom after more than four hundred years of Egyptian bondage. The pages of the Old Testament reverberate with references to the Exodus theme. These allusions to deliverance from the tyrant's hand awakened within each Israelite a hope for the nation's future redemption.

### Mosaic Teaching on the Passover

Instructions regarding the observance of Passover are found mainly in the Pentateuch. The account in Exodus 12:1–13:16 outlines the historical setting and ordinances governing the last meal in Egypt:

(1) Celebration was to be at the full moon (Exod. 12:6) on "the first month" (v. 2) of spring. The month was called Abib (cf. 13:4; Deut. 16:1), meaning "ears" (of grain), later called Nisan. It marked the start of the barley harvest.

(2) On the 10th of the month a year-old male lamb or kid, without defect, was to be selected according to the size of the household (Exod. 12:3-5).

(3) On the 14th of the month at twilight (literally "between the two evenings") the lamb was to be killed (12:6).

(4) Blood from the lamb, in a basin, must be applied by hyssop (a leafy plant) to the doorframes and lintels of the houses where the people gathered to eat the lambs (vv. 7, 22).

(5) The lamb must be roasted over the fire—head, legs, and inner parts, no bones broken (vv. 9, 46).

(6) Bitter herbs *(merorim)* and bread made without yeast *(matzot)* must also be eaten (v. 8).

(7) Any part of the meal not consumed was to be burned (v. 10).

(8) The meal was to be eaten in haste with cloak tucked into belt, sandals on feet, and staff in hand (v. 11).

(9) All future generations of Israelites were to celebrate Passover as a lasting ordinance (vv. 14, 24, 42, 47).

(10) Slaves and resident aliens were permitted to join the meal, provided they had been circumcised (vv. 44, 48).

On the next day, the 15th of Abib (Nisan), the Feast of Unleavened Bread began. This observance, distinct from the Passover proper, was to last seven days. During this time all bread made with yeast was to be destroyed and only unleavened bread eaten (Exod. 12:15, 17-20; 13:6-7). The first and seventh days of this feast were for holding sacred assemblies; no work was to be done, except to prepare food (12:16).

The Passover was to be an opportunity for the father to teach his children. He (not a substitute) was obliged to explain the meaning of the ceremony when his children asked (Exod. 12:26-27; 13:8, 14). From this practice of ritual questioning the term *haggadah* (literally "explaining," "telling") took on increased importance in the life of the community. (Today *Haggadah* is the name of the liturgical book that explains the meaning of the celebration at the Passover meal.) In the early period of Hebrew education, like today, the father held a key role in the transmission of the heritage (see Deut. 6:20-25). The importance played by recital of the *magnalia* (the great redemptive events of biblical faith) throughout Israelite history (see Deut. 26:5-9; see also chapter nine above) was vital in preserving memory of the Exodus "for the generations to come" (Exod. 12:42).

Other major pentateuchal references to the Passover (Lev. 23:5-8; Num. 28:16-25; Deut. 16:1-8) indicate that the Feast of Unleavened Bread was closely integrated with it. During this week, while the community ate bread without yeast (the *matzot,* Num. 28:16, 17) or "bread of affliction" as it is also called (Deut. 16:3), various offerings were prescribed (Num. 28:18-25). Though Passover began as a family festival in the home (Exod. 12:21-23, 46), Deuteronomy anticipates the time when wilderness wanderings would lead to permanent residence in Canaan, with worship at a central sanctuary (Deut. 16:2, 6-7). The changed circumstances would transmute the Passover into a pilgrimage festival at which all adult males were to appear (see Exod. 23:14-17; 34:23). The Law of Moses also makes provision for a second Passover, or "minor Passover" as it was called in the rabbinic period. This additional event was celebrated a month later (14th day of the second month) for any who were ceremonially unclean or away on a journey at the regular time (Num. 9:1-14; cf. 2 Chr. 30:2).

## Celebrations Throughout the Old Testament

Various Passover celebrations are recorded throughout the Old Testament, beginning from the moment Israel entered Canaan. On the plains of Jericho, prior to the Conquest, Passover was conducted under the leadership of Joshua (Josh. 5:10-12). Solomon celebrated the three pilgrimage festivals that now centered in Jerusalem (2 Chr. 8:13). From this point on, Passover focused upon a permanent central sanctuary, the blood of the paschal lamb now sprinkled by priests on the altar of burnt offering. Being more of a public ceremony, Passover was sometimes given strong support by religiously sensitive national leaders.

The Chronicler records two great Passover celebrations at the Temple in Jerusalem (2 Chr. 30:1-27; 35:1-19; cf. 2 Kgs. 23:21-23). These followed revivals during the reigns of King Hezekiah (716-687 B.C.) and King Josiah (640-609 B.C.). The magnitude of these observances was unparalleled in Israel for centuries (2 Chr. 30:26; 35:18). One other historical text to mention the Passover festival is Ezra. After rebuilding the Temple upon return from exile, the people celebrated Passover with considerable joy (Ezra 6:19-22). The Old Testament prophets have no specific references to Passover feasts apart from one projected by Ezekiel in his description of the new Temple (Ezek. 45:21-24).

During the intertestamental period, despite Seleucid and Roman control of Jerusalem, Passover was apparently still celebrated with some regularity. Two noncanonical writings from the second century B.C. emphasize the Passover theme. 1 Esdras, listed first in the Apocrypha, opens with an account of Josiah's Passover (1:1-22; cf. 2 Chr. 35:1-19). This account is in general agreement with the Chronicler's story, but the author of 1 Esdras has certain emphases (including omissions) that are distinctive. For example, the Chronicler describes the Levites as the "instructors" of all Israel (see 2 Chr. 35:3), whereas 1 Esdras states that the Levites were "temple servants" (1:3).[5] Jubilees, an important pseudepigraphical work, gives detailed procedures about the Passover festival (49:1-23). The author of Jubilees states that Passover is an ordinance "engraven on the heavenly tablets" and that all Israel must faithfully observe it forever (49:8). Jubilees also contains the first mention of the drinking of wine in conjunction with Passover (49:6).[6]

## Passover in New Testament Times

Our understanding of the Passover during the New Testament era comes largely from the writings of Josephus, the mishnaic tractate Pesahim, and the New Testament itself. Pilgrimages were made annually to Jerusalem for the Passover sacrifice until the Temple was destroyed in A.D. 70. Fol-

5. See Jacob M. Myers, *I and II Esdras*, Anchor Bible, Vol. 42 (Garden City, NY: Doubleday & Co., 1974), pp. 26-27.

6. See R. H. Charles, ed., *The Apocrypha and Pseudepigrapha of the Old Testament* (London: Oxford University Press, 1913), 2:12.

lowing this time, many Jews found themselves in *galut* ("exile"), scattered in communities among the nations of the world. Passover ceased being a pilgrimage festival at a central sanctuary. Once again, as in pharaonic Egypt, the Passover feast began to center upon the family in the home, a place where it has remained for more than nineteen centuries.

## A Spectacle of Excitement

Passover in New Testament days was a great spectacle of excitement and devotion. Pilgrims near and far ascended to the Holy City in large numbers (see John 11:55). Considering the area of Jerusalem at this time, scholars look on Josephus's figure of about three million Jews present for Passover as greatly exaggerated.[7] Many historians have suggested a more realistic figure would be under 200,000. Accommodations for both sleeping and feasting were sought out in every available space (see Mark 14:15). In lieu of rent, pilgrims gave their hosts the hides of the animals they slaughtered and consumed for the feast (Babylonian Talmud, Yoma 12a). Perhaps to help defuse the smoldering Jewish resentment of their presence, local Roman authorities released a prisoner at Passover time (Mark 15:6-15; cf. Mishnah, Pesahim 9:6).

Days before Passover began, Jerusalem was a hubbub of commercial activity. Many pilgrims who were also merchants arrived early to sell or barter their wares (cf. Matt. 21:12-13; John 2:13-16). Beggars stationed themselves strategically near bustling gates of the city. Jerusalem became an emporium not only for such domestic goods as clothing, jewelry, and exotic ointments, but also for spices, herbs, condiments, wheat, fish, and wine used throughout the week-long festivities. Of utmost importance to pilgrims, however, was the purchasing of sheep and goats for sacrifice at the temple. The animal (preferably a lamb) was selected on the 10th of Nisan (Mishnah, Pesahim 9:5). The size of the lamb varied, since a single individual was forbidden to eat an entire animal. Family groups, or companies of at least ten people (e.g., the disciples with their Master), were required to eat the entire lamb at one sitting (Babylonian Talmud, Pesahim 64b). No part of the animal was to remain until the next day.

## Passover Eve

Before the common meal on Passover eve, the day was filled with preparation for the event. A full contingent of priests—twenty-four divisions

7. Josephus, *Jewish War* 2.14.3 (280); 6.9.3 (420-25).

instead of the usual one—came early to the Temple. Their first task was the burning of the *ḥametz,* "leaven," which had been searched for by candlelight in each home the night before and then removed for burning the next morning (Mishnah, Pesahim 1–3). By midday all work stopped.

The afternoon was set aside for the ritual slaughtering of the lamb. The offering of the Passover sacrifice at the Temple began about 3:00 P.M. (Pesahim 5:1) and was conducted in three massive shifts. When the Temple court was filled with the first group of offerers, the gates of the court were closed. The ram's horn was sounded and the sacrifice began (Pesahim 5:5). Each Jew slaughtered his own lamb. The priests stood in two rows, one holding gold basins and the other silver. After the blood was drained into a basin, it was tossed against the base of the altar (Pesahim 5:6). While the offerings were going on, the Levites sang the *Hallel* (Pss. 113–118). Each lamb was then skinned and its fat with kidneys removed for burning on the altar (Pesahim 5:9-10; cf. Lev. 3:3-5). Before leaving the temple, each offerer slung his lamb—wrapped in its own hide—over his shoulder (Babylonian Talmud, Pesahim 65b). He then departed with his company to prepare the Passover meal. Immediately, the next division of offerers filed into the Temple court and the ritual was repeated.

## The Seder

The Passover evening meal was held at home or in a room within the city reserved for the occasion (cf. Matt. 26:17-19). In the courtyard of the home the carcass of the lamb, with legs unbroken, was roasted. It was placed in a clay oven on a skewer of pomegranate wood (Mishnah, Pesahim 7:1). Inside, the company gathered, dressed festively in white. The room was prepared with floor cushions for reclining and small tables for serving. At the head of the room sat the one leading the ritual meal.

By New Testament times, the Passover observance had features added to those already specified in the Old Testament. A *seder,* meaning a set "order of service," was now followed (cf. Pesahim 10:1-9). It was a festival that celebrated freedom; the celebrants reclined while they ate, a posture symbolic of leisure and ease (cf. Exod. 12:11). Each had to "regard himself as if he [personally] came forth out of Egypt" (Pesahim 10:5). The meal included various symbolic elements, each consumed at specified points throughout the evening: roasted lamb, bitter herbs, unleavened bread, *haroset* (a pasty mixture of nuts, fruit, and wine), and a raw vegetable dipped into tart liquid. At various intervals, four cups of wine, a symbol of joy, were consumed. The wine was probably mixed with water and heated (cf.

Pesahim 7:13). Ritual hand-washings, prayers, and portions of the *Hallel* (Pss. 113–118) also punctuated the observance. A key point of instruction in Israelite tradition came when the son asked his father the ceremonial question, *mah nishtannah ha-laylah ha-zeh mikkol ha-leylot?* "Why is this night different from all other nights?" (Pesahim 10:4). The father responded by giving an historical synopsis of God's redemptive dealings with Israel that led to deliverance from Egypt.

The ceremony concluded late, but many feasters then returned to the streets of Jerusalem to continue their celebration. Others returned to the Temple mount to await the reopening of the Temple gates at midnight so that they might spend the rest of the night in worship and prayer.[8]

## Jesus' Last Supper

Scholars have debated whether the Last Supper was a Passover meal. The Synoptic Gospels state that the day before Jesus' death (Thursday evening), the disciples joined their Master for the Passover meal (Matt. 26:17; Mark 14:12; Luke 22:15). Several passages in the Gospel of John, however, have cast some doubt on this identification. These texts seem to imply that the Jews were not scheduled to partake of their Passover meal until Friday evening (after Jesus had died). We shall briefly consider several of these passages.

John 18:28 states that the Jews who brought Jesus early in the morning to the Roman governor's palace did not want to defile themselves ceremonially (i.e., by going into the dwelling of a Gentile), but "they wanted to be able to eat the Passover." The phrase "eat the Passover," however, does not need to be understood as a reference to the "Passover supper." Rather, it could refer to the general Passover celebration, which lasted a week.[9]

In addition, John 19:14 equates the day on which Jesus was crucified (Friday) with the phrase "Now it was (the day of) Preparation of the Passover" *(én dè paraskeuè toú páscha)*. Again, this seems to conflict with the Synoptic tradition by suggesting that the Jews had not yet celebrated Passover (i.e., the lambs had not yet been slain at the Temple). However, "day of Preparation of the Passover" (RSV) may here be understood as "day of Preparation of Passover Week" (NIV). In John's

8. Josephus, *Antiquities* 18.2.2 (29).

9. A. T. Robertson, *A Harmony of the Gospels* (New York: Harper & Brothers, 1922), pp. 282-83.

time, "Preparation" was a term used for the day of the week we now designate as Friday. (This designation arose because every Friday was the day of preparation for the weekly Sabbath.) John's mention of the "Preparation of the Passover" would then refer to the Friday which fell during the seven-day festival.[10] Furthermore, if we assume the above interpretative scheme—that John is not necessarily in conflict with the Synoptic writers—the mention of "the evening meal" in John 13:2 would not be a fellowship meal with Jesus and his disciples but the Passover supper itself.

A different explanation from the above, but one which also seeks to bring the Synoptics and John into line, is based on the theory that the Jews may have used two different methods of reckoning time. Thus some scholars seek chronological harmonization by positing that two calendars were in use—one followed by the Synoptic writers, the other by John—and that Jesus celebrated Passover with his disciples a day ahead of the official Jewish date.[11] If it indeed was the case that the Jews ate their Passover meal on Friday evening as John's Gospel seems on first reading to imply, and that the Last Supper took place the evening before, it appears then, as Baruch Bokser points out, that "John is presenting Jesus as a Passover offering" since Jesus was slain during the time the Passover lambs were killed in the Temple.[12] Finally, in regard to chronology, we must point out that the above explanations, though possible, do not fully and satisfactorily reconcile the Johannine and Synoptic accounts.

Whatever chronology of the Last Supper one adopts, it seems clear that Jesus instituted the Lord's Supper by associating it with the third cup of wine, which came after the Passover meal was eaten (cf. 1 Cor. 11:25). It was known as the "cup of redemption," which rabbinic tradition linked to the third of the fourfold promise of redemption in Exodus 6:6-7, "I will redeem you." Jesus associated this cup of wine with his atoning death in saying, "This cup is the new covenant in my blood, which is poured out for you" (Luke 22:20; cf. 1 Cor. 11:25). He refused, however, to drink the fourth cup (Mark 14:25; cf. Mishnah, Pesahim 10:7),[13] referred to as the

---

10. Ibid., pp. 283-84.

11. Cf. I. Howard Marshall, *Last Supper and Lord's Supper,* pp. 57-75.

12. Baruch M. Bokser, "Was the Last Supper a Passover Seder?" *Bible Review* 3/2 (Summer, 1987): 33. In addressing the larger question raised by the title of his article, Bokser argues that the Last Supper was not a Passover meal but a traditional sacrificial meal.

13. See William L. Lane, *The Gospel According to Mark,* New International Commentary on the New Testament (Grand Rapids: William B. Eerdmans Publishing Co., 1974), pp. 508-509; also David Daube, *The New Testament and Rabbinic Judaism* (London: Athlone Press, 1956), pp. 330-31.

"cup of consummation" (cf. Exod. 6:7) based on the promise that God will take his own people to be with him.[14] The unfinished meal of Jesus was a pledge that redemption would be consummated at that future messianic banquet when he takes the cup and "drinks it anew in the kingdom of God" (Mark 14:25; cf. Matt. 26:29; Rev. 3:20; 19:6-9). The Lord's Supper concluded with the singing of a hymn (Matt. 26:30; Mark 14:26), doubtless the second half of the Hallel (Pss. 115–118).

In referring to his death as a sacrifice, Jesus was comparing himself to the Passover lamb (cf. Rev. 5:12, "Lamb who was slain"). John the Baptizer calls him "the Lamb of God" (John 1:29, 36). Paul reflects this same symbolism: "For Christ, our Passover lamb, has been sacrificed" (1 Cor. 5:7). Peter describes God's children as redeemed "with the precious blood of Christ, a lamb without blemish or defect" (1 Pet. 1:19). This blood-redeemed community is also described as "a new batch [of dough] without yeast" (1 Cor. 5:7). The prophetic significance of Jesus' death, "Not one of his bones will be broken" (John 19:36), is clear from those Old Testament passages which state that the bones of the Passover lamb were not to be broken (Exod. 12:46; Num. 9:12; cf. Ps. 34:20).

## Passover Today

Only the Samaritans, a small community of several hundred located near Shechem (modern Nablus), still observe annually the blood sacrifice of the Passover lamb. Unchangingly committed only to the Law of Moses (i.e., no other part of Scripture), and under the leadership of a high priest, the entire Samaritan community gathers on the slopes of the "chosen place" (cf. Deut. 16:2, 6-7), which in their tradition is Mount Gerizim, where they live during the entire festival.[15]

For the Jewish community, however, since Rome destroyed Mount Zion and the Temple, sacrifices have ceased. But this destruction did not mark the end of Jewish religious life. The rabbis began to teach that each

---

14. Vincent Taylor, *The Gospel According to St. Mark*, 2nd ed. (New York: St. Martin's Press, 1966), p. 547. For a contrary view which expounds the theory that Jesus abstained at the Passover, see Joachim Jeremias, *Eucharistic Words of Jesus*, pp. 84-88, 207-18.

15. The Samaritans have their own version of the Pentateuch, known appropriately as the Samaritan Pentateuch. This version is a recension of the Massoretic text (often abbreviated MT), the traditional Hebrew text of the Bible preserved and standardized by Jewish scholars known as Massoretes (literally "transmitters") prior to the 10th century A.D. The Samaritan Pentateuch contains numerous textual changes, including the identification of Mount Gerizim as the true location for Passover sacrifice, for it is the place where God's name dwells (Deut. 16:2).

person was to consider himself a temple; prayer, the sacrifice of one's lips, rather than the sacrifice of one's animal, was to be offered. *Tephillah* ("prayer"), *tzedaqah* ("righteousness," in the sense of charity), and *teshubah* ("repentance") became the new means by which atonement was sought.

## The Home Seder

When Passover ceased to be a sacrificial rite centered in the Temple, it again returned to the home. God, who brought Israel out of slavery into freedom, would be remembered as Redeemer by the praise and celebration of each family unit. In the contemporary ceremonial Passover meal (called a Seder), a shankbone and roasted egg are placed on the Seder plate to bring to mind the days of the Temple. These symbolize the roasted paschal sacrifice and the festival offering brought when the Temple was still standing.

The modern Passover Seder makes use of a written explanatory text called a *Haggadah.* In many Jewish communities it is traditional on the first night of Passover to hold a family Seder at home, and on the next night to hold a community Seder at the synagogue. On the Seder table is placed the "cup of Elijah," a goblet of wine poured but not drunk. According to scriptural tradition, Elijah, who ascended to heaven in a fiery chariot (2 Kgs. 2:11-12), would return as the herald and messenger of the coming Messiah (Mal. 4:5). Thus, in Jewish belief, messianic hope is kindled more strongly during Passover than at any other season, for it is the "season of redemption." According to the Midrash Rabbah (the most important collection of haggadic midrashim [i.e., homiletical commentaries written to inspire and admonish] on the Pentateuch), in Israel's history Nisan is the month of redemption: "When He [God] chose Jacob and his sons, He appointed for them a New Moon [i.e., month] of redemption in which Israel were redeemed from Egypt and in which they are *destined to be redeemed again*" (Exodus Rabbah 15:11; italics mine). Hence the "cup of Elijah" has been expectantly and faithfully filled in Jewish homes to greet the prophet when he visits on Passover night.

A custom arose to welcome the prophet in by going to the door and opening it at a set point in the Seder. This act, however, has had more than one interpretation. Some have held that the open door originated in the Middle Ages, when it was alleged that Jews butchered Christian children to get blood for the baking of matzot (unleavened bread), an allegation that came to be known as "blood libel." An open door at the Seder was intended to allay any suspicion on the part of Gentiles in the street that secret ritual torturings were being practiced inside. But the habit of opening the door may have originated in an earlier period when the head of the family made it a practice to step into the street to invite the poor and hungry to join in the holiday repast.

## Liturgy of the Synagogue

Synagogue liturgy at Passover includes several special emphases. On the first day of Passover a prayer for dew is recited, a reminder that in Israel the rainy season has now ended and the dry season is fast approaching. The second night of Passover begins the "Counting of the *Omer,*" literally "sheaf" (of barley). This period of seven weeks culminates in the festival of *Shabuot* ("Weeks"), often called Pentecost, which means fiftieth day.

Also during the Passover festival the Song of Songs is read. Since this book alludes to the beauty of springtime (Song of Songs 2:11-13), the very season of Passover, the rabbis interpreted it as a picture of God's love for his people Israel. Toward the end of Passover week, the Torah reading in the synagogue is the Song of Moses (Exod. 15:1-18), an ancient paean rehearsing the triumphant deliverance of Israel through the waters of the Red Sea.

## Hope of Future Redemption

Treating Passover as a festival of freedom, modern Jewry is not content to focus merely on the past fact of deliverance. Many contemporary Seders now include a fifth cup of wine to remember the enslaved Jews in the Soviet Union and other oppressed people elsewhere around the world. The Seder points beyond the present to the future as the song *"Addir Hu"* ("He [God] Is Mighty") is sung. *"Addir Hu"* concludes with a call for the Temple to be rebuilt: "Speedily, speedily, in our days soon, O God, rebuild, O God rebuild, rebuild Your Temple soon."

As the Jewish Seder points to a future day when God's redemptive work will be more fully realized, so for the Christian the repetition of the Lord's Supper is a constant reminder of a coming day that will climax redemption (1 Cor. 11:26). Finally, every Seder comes to a close on a note of hope; the ritual ends with the nostalgic and memorable prayer: *"Leshanah ha-ba'ah birushalayim!"*—"Next year in Jerusalem!" Thus for both Jew and Christian, Jerusalem remains the key city whenever the story of redemption is told. It is to Jerusalem that every Jew continues to look at Passover, anticipating the final day of redemption; and it is to this same city to which every Christian looks back to focus upon the death, resurrection, and ascension of Jesus in anticipation of his future return.

## Passover and Contemporary Christianity

In this chapter we have sought to shed light on one of the earliest and most pivotal aspects of Jewish heritage. The Synoptic Gospels clearly emphasize that the Passover provides the setting of the Last Supper for Jesus and the Twelve. Our study has emphasized not only the importance of the Old Testament as the foundation for the New, but also the usefulness of the writings of the Mishnah, Talmud, Midrash, and Josephus in establishing an important dimension of the *Sitz im Leben* (the cultural context or historical setting) for the first-century Church. To that extent, at least, our discussion has been intended to serve as a useful—though admittedly brief—paradigm for Christians on how they might profit from some of the linguistic, historical, and theological resources useful in illuminating the Jewish roots of the Christian faith. We also pointed to the celebration of Passover in the Jewish community today. We now focus particularly on this last area by making several practical observations relevant to today's Church.

First, in order for Christians to understand their own faith more fully, they should seek personally to experience Passover in a contemporary Jewish setting. One can learn much from books, films, and lectures, but one learns differently from personally experiencing Passover. Jews say that on Passover they "eat history." Therefore, to participate in a Seder within a Jewish home or synagogue, or to take part in an interfaith Seder, or even a model Seder specially conducted for Christians by some learned member of the Jewish community, will provide a creative and unforgettable dimension to the learning experience. By means of the Seder one becomes familiar with the Haggadah which, in connection with various symbolic foods on the table, recounts in a dramatic way the Exodus story. A simple, private reading of the Exodus account seems weak indeed compared with this dramatic celebration that engages the various senses— sight, sound, taste, and smell. Furthermore, the Seder allows one to become familiar with various songs which appropriately celebrate the grace of God in history and the joy of freedom from slavery.

Second, a serious study of the Passover will further enlighten Christians on the background of redemption, one of the key theological themes of Scripture. The Exodus event and the revelation at Mount Sinai are to the Jew what the crucifixion at Calvary is to the Christian—supreme events of deliverance, holy pillars of redemptive history. Unfortunately, many Christians tend to see the concept of redemption only in internal or spiritual terms, totally unrelated to its rich, external, this-worldly, Old Testament context. Accordingly, through the annual celebration of Passover, today's Jewish community provides the Church with a fitting reminder that God is also working out his plan of redemption in the concrete, historical world. As discussed above in chapter ten, the Hebrew Bible does not depict salvation essentially as some future escape to an invisible heavenly world, but as God's liberating involvement in the human predicament of this present world.

Third, by means of various liturgical emphases during Passover week, the Synagogue provides a useful reminder to the Church of some of the more unfamiliar aspects of its biblical heritage. How many Christians are familiar with the Hallel (Pss. 113–118)? Yet these psalms doubtless constitute the very core of hymns sung by Jesus and his disciples in the Upper Room. Furthermore, how often does today's Church expound the Song of Songs? Perhaps with its striking emphasis on aspects of human love and anatomy it has been deemed embarrassing, irrelevant, or even a joke by many in the Church. But this inspired—though widely neglected —biblical work, with its obvious mention of springtime love, holds a central place in the synagogue liturgy during Passover week.

Finally, from a study of the Passover contemporary Christians are led to reconsider the importance of joyful celebration in connection with the Hebraic background to the Last Supper. Today, when Christians take part for the first time in a Passover Seder conducted within the Jewish community, they are often taken aback. They are surprised that the mood of the evening is mainly one of lightheartedness and joy, the personal and corporate reliving of the Exodus in thankfulness to God for the priceless fact of freedom. It is not uncommon for Christians to expect that Passover will be a rather heavy and somber event, one of great solemnity and deep spiritual introspection. Still others, through vague associations, think the mood of Passover will be like that of a memorial service to a dead person. These types of preconditioning have largely come through an attempt, whether conscious or unconscious, to impose on the Passover Seder one's personal church experience of the Lord's Supper.

It is not our intention in any way to demean the death or atonement of Jesus, or to downplay the significance of self-examination in the conduct of the Lord's Supper (1 Cor. 11:28-29). Nevertheless, the note of joyful praise and celebration of life in the light of redemption—so much a part of the festival of Passover from Bible times to the present—has often become lost through the Church's singular focus on death. As central in Christian thought as the redeeming death of Jesus may be, it is of little consequence unless it leads directly to the joyful experience of life through resurrection. Is this not what the doxology in the introduction of the book of Revelation stresses when it exalts "him who loves us and has freed us from our sins by his blood" (Rev. 1:5; cf. Eph. 1:7)? The Israelites rejoiced at Passover, because their Liberator had miraculously redeemed them, freeing them from the bondage of Egypt. But they also rejoiced in anticipation of God's ultimate redemption (cf. Isa. 65:17-18; Mic. 4:1-5), when God's people would be redeemed from all remaining pharaohs and from that evil which dominates and disgraces this present world.

Doubtless, Jesus had this climax of redemption in mind when he abstained from the fourth cup in the Upper Room (see our discussion earlier in this chapter). At that Passover meal "Jesus *looked forward, beyond death* to the perfect fellowship of the consummated kingdom."[16] The Hebraic imagery for Jesus' teaching probably derives in part from "the little apocalypse" of Isaiah (chaps. 24–27). Here (especially 25:6-9) the prophet describes the consummation of God's kingdom in terms of the Lord preparing for all peoples a great banquet where "the best of meats and the finest of wines" are served (25:6). But also envisioned is a time when the Lord "will swallow up death forever . . . [and] will wipe away the tears from all faces" (25:8). In biblical terms, this is God's final act of deliverance, his ultimate outworking in history of that ancient promise, "When I see the blood, I will pass over you" (Exod. 12:13).

# UNDERSTANDING CHAPTER TWELVE

1. What major theological themes do Exodus and Sinai recall for the Jew, and the Upper Room and Calvary recall for the Christian? Why do Jews keep celebrating Passover, and Christians the Lord's Supper?

2. In the Hebrew Bible the term *Passover* is used in several different ways. What are they?

3. Passover appears originally to have combined two separate spring festivals. What are they? At what time of the month did each festival begin? By the end of the New Testament era and the time of Josephus (late first century), what change was taking place regarding the designation of these festivals?

16. Taylor, *Gospel According to St. Mark,* p. 547 (my emphasis).

4. From the account of Passover in Exodus 12:1–13:16, be able to define or explain the importance of the following: (a) full moon, (b) Abib and Nisan, (c) type and condition of the animal selected, (d) hyssop, (e) *merorim*, (f) matzot, (g) circumcision.

5. What does the term *Haggadah* mean? From the book of Exodus, explain how this term relates to the father of the family. What newer meaning does *Haggadah* carry today in connection with the celebration of Passover?

6. Why did the Law of Moses make provision for a second Passover or "minor Passover" to be celebrated a month later?

7. The Chronicler records two great Passover celebrations at the Temple in Jerusalem that followed revivals during the reigns of two of Judah's greatest kings. Who were these kings?

8. Which book of the Apocrypha is listed first? On what theme does its first chapter open? In what ancient source do we find the first mention of the drinking of wine in conjunction with Passover? Date this source.

9. Our understanding of the Passover during the New Testament era comes largely from three main sources. What are they?

10. When the Temple was destroyed in A.D. 70, Passover ceased being a pilgrimage festival at a central sanctuary. After this time, where did the celebration begin to center?

11. During the time of Jesus, at Passover, what payment did hosts entertaining pilgrims in their homes accept in lieu of rent?

12. When pilgrims would select an animal for purchase to sacrifice at the Temple, why was the size of the animal a matter of concern? Once a family group or company had sat down to eat the animal, what restriction were they required to observe?

13. In order to accommodate crowds of pilgrims at the Temple, how many divisions of priests were on hand instead of the usual one?

14. What was searched for by candlelight in each home the night before Passover? When it was found and then removed from the home, what became of it?

15. At the Temple in Jerusalem, the offering of the Passover sacrifice began mid-afternoon before Passover eve. What sound announced the beginning of the sacrifice? Who was responsible for slaughtering the lamb? What were the rows of gold basins and silver basins used for? What biblical selection constituted the *Hallel* sung by the Levites? What part of the lamb was burned as a sacrifice? Where did each offerer proceed after leaving the Temple? Where and how was the carcass of the lamb roasted?

16. What is meant by the term *Seder*? Why did each celebrant eat in a reclining position? At the Seder, how was each person required to regard himself? What symbolic foods were consumed? Who was responsible for asking the ceremonial question, "Why is this night different from other nights?" Who replied?

17. Was the Last Supper a Passover meal? What do the Synoptic Gospels

state? How does John's Gospel seem to conflict with the Synoptics on this matter? Briefly suggest two possible solutions for this conflict in chronology.

18. With which cup of wine does it seem that Jesus instituted the Lord's Supper? What term does rabbinic tradition use for this particular cup of wine? The refusal of Jesus to complete the meal by partaking of the "cup of consummation" may be understood as a pledge on Jesus' part. Explain.

19. To what in the Passover festival is Jesus likened by his early followers? (See John 1:29; 1 Cor. 5:7; 1 Pet. 1:19.) What does the Hebrew Bible say about the bones of the Passover lamb? How did the early Church understand the manner of Jesus' death in regard to the above passages dealing with the bones of the lamb (cf. John 19:33, 36)?

20. Who are the only people still observing annually the blood sacrifice of the Passover lamb? Where does this observance occur? What term is used for the Scripture of this people? (See footnotes to this chapter.)

21. Who were the Massoretes and what did they accomplish? What does the abbreviation "MT" stand for? (See footnotes to this chapter.)

22. After the Temple in Jerusalem was destroyed, what three actions did the rabbis prescribe as the means by which atonement should be sought? In comparison, how has the Church historically understood the concept of atonement and the place of the above three actions?

23. At the contemporary ceremonial Passover meal, what two items on the Seder plate symbolize the roasted pascal sacrifice and the festive offering brought when the Temple was still standing?

24. Explain the significance of the "cup of Elijah." What scriptural tradition is associated with Elijah? In Jewish tradition, what month is known as the "month of redemption"? Why, at a set point in the Seder, is the door opened?

25. What was the so-called blood-libel charge brought in the Middle Ages by Christians against Jews?

26. What special prayer is offered as part of the synagogue liturgy on the first day of Passover? Why did this prayer have particular existential meaning when offered within the land of Israel?

27. During the Passover festival, in the synagogue, which book of the Hebrew Bible is read that alludes to the beauty of springtime?

28. Why do contemporary Seders often include a fifth cup of wine? Discuss.

29. Every Seder comes to a close with a nostalgic and memorable prayer. What are these few brief words of hope?

30. Define *Sitz im Leben*. How does one go about seeking to establish the *Sitz im Leben* for the Last Supper?

31. On what occasion do Jewish people say they "eat history"? In what sense could this saying aptly describe today's Church in celebrating the Lord's Supper?

32. Why are Christians who take part for the first time in a Passover Seder conducted within the Jewish community often surprised or taken aback? Is the reason for this reaction only a "cultural/religious gap," or has there perhaps been

a lack of understanding or proper emphasis within the Church concerning the rich and joyful Hebraic legacy of redemption? Discuss.

33. Summarize the features of God's ultimate redemption envisioned by the Hebrew prophets (see Isa. 25:6-9; 65:17-18; Mic. 4:1-5).

## Chapter Thirteen

# Jews, Christians, and the Land

*The whole land of Canaan . . . I will give as an everlasting possession to you and your descendants after you*

Genesis 17:8

Nearly four thousand years ago God said to Abraham, "Go, walk through the length and breadth of the land, for I am giving it to you" (Gen. 13:17). The meaning of this promise, however, continues to be debated today by theologians, historians, and politicians. Both Jews and Christians often cite this scripture, and other portions of the patriarchal narratives like it, to support the fact that Zionism, the Jewish people's national liberation movement to "Zion," has deep roots in the Hebrew Bible. Certainly any discussion of the Jewish heritage of the Church cannot avoid facing the question of the Jewish people's, as well as the Church's, relation to the land. For indeed, the major witnesses of Jewish theology see "the Land as of the essence of Judaism."[1]

Considerable debate exists over what terminology should be employed in reference to the historic homeland of the Jewish people. Though terms such as *promised land* (cf. Gen. 12:1), *holy land* (cf. Zech. 2:12), and *land of Israel* (1 Sam. 13:19) have a scriptural basis during the biblical period, it is virtually impossible today to find a politically neutral term —granting the present nationalistic struggles in the Middle East—for that territory in which the Jewish people find their roots. Today, to many of the

1. W. D. Davies, *The Territorial Dimension of Judaism* (Berkeley: University of California Press, 1982), p. 53.

residents of the Middle East, the words *Palestine* and *Israel* are far from synonymous and often conjure up exceedingly different political connotations. Nonetheless, in the interest of establishing a reference point for the ensuing discussion in this chapter, and in keeping with the overall position upheld throughout this book, we have chosen to use mainly the historic words *Israel* or *Zion* (the latter was used early in Jewish history for Jerusalem) to refer to the present homeland to which the Jewish people have returned. By way of analogy, when an American says he is a citizen of the United States, he is not necessarily expressing full agreement with American political and military theory and practice. Nonetheless, one may assume that he not only recognizes the fundamental right of the United States to exist, but also does not hesitate to affirm support for that nation's survival. I view the legitimacy of using the words *Israel* and *Zion* throughout this chapter in somewhat the same vein.

The current struggle among nations in the Middle East forces us immediately to confront these substantive questions: What historical claims do the Jewish people have to the land? Does the Bible give evidence in support of a future for ethnic Israel? What role, if any, should biblical texts play in formulating a Christian understanding of the State of Israel? Should Christians today support the idea of a Jewish homeland? What are the prospects for peace between Arab and Jew, and what is the Christian's responsibility in face of this struggle? It will be our task in this chapter to seek to shed some light on these and other pertinent issues that center on Jews, Christians, and the land.

## Jews and the Land: An Overview

### Election and Preservation

In the mystery of the divine plan God chose the Hebrew patriarch Abraham. His election and the election of the land came together.[2] But this election to be an instrument of God's redemptive activity on this earth neither implied nor had its basis in superiority, innate giftedness, or spiritual elitism. Rather, the concept of chosenness surrounding Abraham was a matter of pure grace. It was human *ḥesed* ("loyal love") for God's *ḥesed*. With it, as with all those who followed this patriarch, came a summons to service, action, and responsibility. Abraham had a destiny to fulfill. The

---

2. See Abraham J. Heschel, *Israel: An Echo of Eternity* (New York: Farrar, Straus and Giroux, 1969), p. 100.

covenant promises made to him and his descendants intended that Israel would "be a blessing" to "all peoples on earth" (Gen. 12:2-3).

Throughout Israel's history—despite the people's sin and rebellious-ness—God never abandons his chosen. From Bible times to the present day, however, some have sought to dismiss the notion of Israel's election. Many of these have understood the Old Testament as essentially a pre-Christian document, long since annulled, having served its day. But the Bible is clear: the preservation of the people of Israel from generation to generation has reflected God's faithfulness, grace, and ultimate purposes in history, rather than Israel's own righteousness (Deut. 9:5-6). During the wilderness wanderings (Num. 14) God became so exasperated with Israel's rebellious spirit that he considered then and there to cancel the covenant; he thought of abandoning his people and starting over again with one man, Moses (v. 12).[3] Nevertheless, the account indicates that God did not abandon them, for his reputation and honor among the nations was at stake. Thus he kept his word—despite Israel's unbelief and failure—and remained faithful to those covenant promises he made to his own people (vv. 15-16). Through the Lord's great love, which the Scriptures assure us endures forever (cf. Ps. 138:8), he forgives his people (vv. 17-20), and they continue on their journey. The important point for us to remember in this account is that God's preservation of Israel is for his own honor and cause in the world, not a reward for any inherent human virtue.

We know how much this concept of divine election has cost the Jewish people. It has resulted in misunderstanding and resentment and has been used against the descendants of biblical Israel.[4] Tragically, many around the world have been blinded from experiencing this blessing. In-stead, they have turned against Jews, seeing them only as a problem, a threat—or, indeed, to some—a people cursed by God. Hence, Jews have been treated as eternal wanderers among the nations, an unwanted and homeless pariah people. The painful story of anti-Semitism with its Crusades, Inquisition, disputations, pogroms, and Holocaust bear grim testimony to this fact (see chapter seven above).

In this century, particularly since World War II, many have either questioned or strongly opposed the legitimacy of a Jewish state in the Holy Land. It should be pointed out, however, that most opponents of the modern Jewish State disavow any connection with anti-Semitism. Though it

3. I am grateful to Halvor Ronning of the Institute of Holy Land Studies in Jerusalem for calling this passage to my attention through his article, "Whose Promised Land?" *From Mt. Zion* 4/2 (June, 1984): 8.

4. Note the discussion of this point by Walter Harrelson, "The Land in Tanakh," un-published paper, National Conference of Christians and Jews, New York, 1985, p. 5.

may seem paradoxical, some even come from among the religious right within the Jewish community. But by far the largest and most vocal and persistent challenge to Israel's moral right to exist has come from the Arab nations, and particularly from members of the Palestine Liberation Organization within them. The words of the former president of Iraq, Abdul Mohammed Araf, are typical of this hostile stance: "The existence of Israel is a mistake that must be rectified. . . . Our goal is clear—to wipe Israel off the map."[5]

In response to their detractors and critics, Jews the world over point to certain pivotal dates in the establishment of the modern State of Israel. In 1897, the first Zionist Congress gathered in Basel, Switzerland, under the dynamic leadership of Austrian journalist Theodor Herzl, known today as the father of modern Zionism. The previous year Herzl had written his *Der Judenstaat (The Jewish State)* out of concern for the persecuted and disenfranchised Jews of the Diaspora who desperately needed a homeland. In 1917, the British government issued the Balfour Declaration in which it viewed favorably "the establishment in Palestine of a national home for Jewish people." In 1922, Britain was granted a mandate over Palestine. On November 29, 1947, the General Assembly of the United Nations adopted a Partition Plan, dividing Palestine into two sovereign states, one Jewish and the other Arab. The vote carried by more than the required two-thirds majority. Six months later, on May 14, 1948, the State of Israel was officially founded.

## Biblical and Historical Ties to the Land

As we have earlier emphasized (see chapter two above), the concept of *berit* ("covenant") within Judaism rests upon four foundational pillars: God, Torah, people, and land. Each interacts with and depends on the other. Far from the popular notion that Israel's covenant embraced only a spiritual dimension, it was in actuality "tied to earth, life, land."[6]

In the Tenakh, God's covenant faithfulness with his people guarantees their security, validity, and permanent existence (2 Sam. 7:24; Jer. 31:35-36). So, too, Israel understood God's "everlasting covenant" (Gen. 17:19) as a pledge that the land was to be an "everlasting possession" (Gen. 13:15; 15:18; 17:7-8). Many biblical passages concerning the

5. Quoted in Leo A. Rudloff, *Understanding Israel: A Christian View* (New York: Anti-Defamation League of B'nai B'rith, 1977), p. 5.
6. Seymour Siegel, "The Meaning of Israel in Jewish Thought," in *Evangelicals and Jews in Conversation,* ed. Marc H. Tanenbaum, Marvin R. Wilson, and A. James Rudin (Grand Rapids: Baker Book House, 1978), p. 105.

promise of land are in the form of an oath, with God himself offering the promise in the first person form of the verb. Furthermore, the Hebrew Bible describes this promised land as an actual piece of earthly real estate with specific geographical boundaries (Gen. 15:18-21; Num. 34:2-12; Josh. 15:1-12; Ezek. 47:13-20; etc.).

This point about the geophysical nature of the land is particularly important for Christians to understand. Unfortunately, the Church has often spiritualized the concept of land so that the earthly Canaan has evaporated into an ethereal heavenly Canaan. Krister Stendahl is correct in pointing out the inconsistency of Christians in this matter.[7] He notes that, on the one hand, Christians often have a problem accepting the literal, physical, this-worldly dimensions of the land and thus end up spiritualizing it, while, on the other hand, these same Christians usually emphasize greatly the incarnation and humanity of that One who became flesh.

The Hebrew Scriptures stress repeatedly that God is the true owner of the land. More than twenty-five passages in Deuteronomy (e.g., 1:20, 25; 2:29) emphasize that the land is a gift from the Lord. Israel was only to "possess" or "inherit" what rightly belonged to their Suzerain.

In time, however, Israel was "plucked off the land" and "scattered among all peoples." Israel's ongoing possession of the land was conditioned upon obedience. Moses and the prophets had warned Israel that disobedience to the Lord of the covenant would result in punishment by exile (Deut. 28:63-68; Isa. 7:17; Jer. 13:19; 16:13; 25:11). At the same time, Israel knew that exile would not be forever. Despite dispersion and persecution, God would "remember the land" (Lev. 26:42), fetch his people (Deut. 30:4), and bring them into the land that belonged to their fathers (v. 5). Indeed, "there is hope" for Israel's future (Jer. 31:17), "for the LORD has chosen Zion . . . for his dwelling . . . for ever and ever" (Ps. 132:13-14). The land covenant, therefore, was not cancelled or annulled; rather, "it was interrupted by the diaspora but not set aside forever by it."[8] In exile, the Jews found it difficult to "sing the songs of the LORD in a foreign land" (Ps. 137:4). Zion could not be forgotten; its remembrance became the Jews' "highest joy" (vv. 5-6). Accordingly, the words of the prophets sound continuously the note of return.

But when the seventy years of captivity had run their course, a comparatively small number of Jews actually returned to the land. Moreover, the descendants of those who did return would later find themselves driven

---

7. From a lecture by Krister Stendahl at Harvard University, December, 1978.

8. G. Douglas Young, "Israel: The Unbroken Line," *Christianity Today* (October 6, 1978): 22.

from the land by a worldwide second dispersion at the hands of Roman overlords. This return could hardly be the permanent one Jeremiah and Amos described: "I will plant them and not uproot them" (Jer. 24:6), "'I will plant Israel in their own land, never again to be uprooted from the land I have given them,' says the LORD your God" (Amos 9:15). In addition, the return from Babylonian captivity does not appear to be the universal in-gathering Isaiah mentioned (11:11-12; cf. Zech. 8:3-8). Likewise, prophetic literature pictures Israel's ultimate restoration to the land as a time of great peace and spiritual renewal affecting both Israel and all nations of the earth (Ezek. 36:24-28; Mic. 4:1-5). Was postexilic Israel *that* redeemed nation, a people who would yet be in bondage to Persia, Greece, and Rome?

The hopes and dreams of the Hebrew prophets were never fully realized. The triumph of God's kingly rule, the final earthly redemption of this covenant people, lay in the future. Accordingly, could it be that those who arranged the order of the Tenakh had something more in mind than purely historical concerns by ending it with 2 Chronicles? We believe so. For the last word in the Hebrew Bible (2 Chr. 36:23) is a prophetic word of hope pointing to a task that was not completed under Zerubbabel, Ezra, or Nehemiah. That word is, "Let him go up" *(ya'al)*. It is a call for Aliyah, a "going up" or return to Israel's homeland.

From biblical times to the present, the Jewish community never lost sight of this hope. As *Ha-Tiqvah* (The Hope), the national anthem of the modern State of Israel, affirms resolutely, "Our hope is not yet lost, the hope of two thousand years." Though there never was a time when all Jews left the land,[9] most Jews were scattered among the nations. Hence, rabbinic texts reflect an intense yearning to return to *Eretz Yisra'el* ("the land of Israel"). A certain mystique and aura now begins to be associated with the land. For example, a Jew was instructed to remember Zion by leaving a corner of the walls of his house unpainted, or by making jewelry with some part incomplete. The land of Israel was considered to be the "navel" or "center of the earth" (Ezek. 38:12; cf. also 5:5). Hence, it was a mitzvah to live there, for it brought one closer to God. Being buried in the land was thought of as being buried on an altar of atonement. The fruit of Israel was deemed better than that of any other country. Even the atmosphere of the land was thought to make people wise. Higher moral standards were believed to exist there. Furthermore, the Mishnah states that the land of Israel is holier than any other land. It is not surprising, then, as we pointed out in the last chapter, that year after year the Passover Seder concludes with the nostalgic yet hopeful proclamation, "Next year in Jerusalem!"

9. Davies, *Territorial Dimension of Judaism*, p. 50.

## The Spiritual-Secular Tension of Modern Zionism

When the modern State of Israel was born in 1948, it emerged as the product of a complex number of biblical, historical, political, economic, and social factors. Some scholars have argued that it was "due to the influence of (the Jewish) Scriptures more than a result of their persecution that they ultimately came home and built the nation again."[10] Though the question of the Scriptures' role has been continuously debated, it seems clear that the Bible was a factor—at the very least, in the collective existential conscience of world Jewry.

As we have already seen in chapters six and seven, in the early Christian centuries a triumphant and proud Church saw itself as superseder of Israel, arrogating to itself the title "new" or "true" Israel. Yet throughout all its history the Jewish community never relinquished to the Church the prophetic texts that held out hope of return. To the contrary, these very same biblical texts witnessed with conviction within the very depths of the Jewish being to an unending attachment to the land. Apart from some Orthodox Jews, most of world Jewry have not considered these texts as a kind of title deed to the land or proof which might be presented in a court of law. These texts have not been generally read and interpreted with any special exegetical acumen. Rather, these biblical passages have mainly served to foster Jewish historical self-awareness, an existential bonding to the land. Several decades before the founding of the State, this close attachment to the Hebrew Scriptures made Rav Kook the leading exponent of "religious Zionism." He established a talmudic academy in Jerusalem, insisted on the widespread use of Hebrew, and taught that all Jews who lived in Israel were preparing the land for "the final redemption . . . the coming of the days of the Messiah."[11]

But spiritual concerns did not dominate the earliest leaders of modern Zionism—Moses Hess, Leon Pinsker, and the aforementioned Theodor Herzl. Rather, they devoted most of their energies to the political dimensions of the movement. They stressed the need for a national Jewish homeland for the oppressed and persecuted Jews of the Diaspora at a time when other nations were undergoing national revivals. Ahad Ha-Am, another early Zionist leader, complemented the position of the political Zionists by emphasizing the need for a Jewish refuge where the religious ideals of cul-

10. See G. Douglas Young, "Christian and Jewish Understandings of the Word 'Israel,'" in *Prophecy in the Making,* ed. Carl F. H. Henry (Carol Stream, IL: Creation House, 1971), pp. 163-64.
11. Quoted in A. James Rudin, *Israel for Christians* (Philadelphia: Fortress Press, 1983), p. 35.

ture, learning, and history could develop freely. The complex diversity of the Zionist movement was enlarged even further by the socialist emphasis of David Ben-Gurion, the militant nationalism of Vladimir Jabotinsky, and the "Hebrew humanism" of Martin Buber, who called for a binational state that would recognize Jewish as well as Arab claims and rights.[12]

When the modern State of Israel was founded, this newborn entity was difficult for many Jews and Christians to accept. National rebirth of an ancient people did not come because God had sent his Messiah; rather, it came largely from secular, political, and naturalistic forces. These conflicting viewpoints in part explain why many within the Hasidic community in Israel today refuse to serve in the Israeli military. They do not recognize what they consider to be a largely secular state not established in connection with the Messiah's coming.

Though Israel often strove for power, especially from the time of the prophets Jews were taught as a nation to renounce military might, political alliance, and worldly power (Ps. 33:16-19; 147:10-11; Isa. 31:1; Zech. 4:6).[13] In exile, driven from their land, they became more spiritual, believing their powerlessness, victimization, and sufferings would hasten the Messiah's coming. This passive stance toward history, which resulted in the Jews responding to the action of others rather than initiating their own action, became a central emphasis in the teachings of Rabbinic Judaism. The early Zionists taught that Jews must seek to control rather than be controlled. This tension between traditional messianic thinking and modern secular thinking created the necessity for the former to be transformed or transmuted. There would be a radical break with the past. Now a so-called secular messianism had evolved in which "Jews would seek their own salvation, and at the same time await the Messiah . . . (they) would work and build instead of wait and sigh."[14]

## Christian Approaches to the State of Israel

In view of the complex mosaic of modern Zionism, how do contemporary Christians understand the State of Israel, and what role, if any, should the

12. Ibid., pp. 23-40.
13. See Jacques Ellul, *The Politics of God and the Politics of Man,* trans. Geoffrey W. Bromiley (Grand Rapids: William B. Eerdmans Publishing Co., 1972); idem, *False Presence of the Kingdom,* trans. C. Edward Hopkin (New York: Seabury Press, 1972); Vernard Eller, *Christian Anarchy: Jesus' Primacy over the Powers* (Grand Rapids: William B. Eerdmans Publishing Co., 1987).
14. Irving Miller, *Israel: The Eternal Ideal* (New York: Farrar, Straus and Cudahy, 1955), p. 71.

Bible play in response to this whole issue? A variety of perspectives may be found regarding Israel. Here we shall consider two main approaches to this problem, then a third alternative, which we espouse.

## *Replaced by the Church*

One Christian response has been to spiritualize and hence eliminate biblical promises made to the Jewish people. This response is based on the view that the Church has replaced ancient Israel. As the "new" Israel, the Church's "new covenant" has superseded the "old covenant" of Judaism. Thus the Jewish people and Jewish state have no theological legitimacy. According to this view, Jewish people today, having no living covenantal relationship to God, are the vestige of a biblically bankrupt and spiritually dead culture.

In his well-known work *American Protestantism and the Jewish State,* Hertzel Fishman has pointed out that American Protestant missionary work in Arab lands and the consequent political support toward Arab nationalism are no less significant theologically than support of Jewish nationalism. The return of modern Zionists to the land is but "a futile effort, not in harmony with God's ultimate purpose."[15] This theological delegitimizing of the Jewish people and the Jewish state, this cutting off of the Jews from the biblical promises concerning land and peoplehood, has unfortunately often contributed to the fostering of anti-Semitism on the part of the Church. In sum, this first approach argues that all geopolitical rights promised in the old covenant have been cancelled. The Jews, as a people, are permanently discarded. The best that world Jewry can now hope for is to be part of the new people of God, the Church—but without nationality, land, or statehood.[16]

## *Fulfillment of Prophecy—Divine Right*

A second position held by Christians, particularly by various evangelical and fundamentalist groups, affirms the State of Israel in a confident and enthusiastic manner. This view builds a case in support of Jewish restoration to the land primarily on the grounds that it fulfills prophecy. Israel's title to the land is prophetically decreed in the Bible, and hence the land is

15. Hertzel Fishman, *American Protestantism and the Jewish State* (Detroit: Wayne State University Press, 1973), pp. 27, 179.
16. See Uriel Tal, "Jewish Self Understanding and the Land and State of Israel," *Union Seminary Quarterly Review* 26 (1970): 353-54.

rightfully hers by divine sanction. In this connection, Jacques Maritain once stated, "It is a strange paradox to behold Israel being denied the only territory of which—considering the whole course of human history—it is absolutely, divinely certain that a people has a title to it."[17] As God's chosen people, Israel has a God-ordained claim to the land. One expression of this thinking appeared in a full-page advertisement in *The New York Times* entitled, "Evangelicals Concerned for Israel."[18] Underneath were the names of fifteen scholars and Church leaders who supported what they called "Israel's divine right to the land."

In an article entitled "Which Christians Can Israel Count On?" Church historian Martin Marty concludes that "premillennialism demands support of Israel" and is therefore the highest rung on his "ladder of sympathies."[19] Marty is correct in pointing to the strong support that fundamentalists of a premillennial persuasion have historically shown for Israel. But, unfortunately, this eagerness by premillennialists to back Israel has often been expressed in language which is highly deterministic and devoid of ethical and humanitarian considerations. Illustrations of this thinking abound in theological and Church literature. For example, consider the following response to the formation of the modern State of Israel: "The Jew will have Palestine with or without the help of Britain or any other nation on earth! . . . To oppose [Zionism] is to oppose God's plan."[20] This fatalistic statement is similar: "Of course the inhabitants of the land do not want them. Neither did the Canaanites of old want them . . . and yet they came and they are coming again. God has decreed it. It must be so."[21]

The premillennial method of biblical interpretation has usually taken a very literal approach to the fulfillment of prophecy. Thus, by searching for those biblical passages said to contain predicted details of forthcoming events, these Christians appear to infuse almost every move in the Middle East with some preordained eschatological significance. The result is that Israel seems to form the key piece to the end-times jigsaw puzzle of many premillennialists. Obviously, such deterministic thinking has some crucial implications and consequences for world history, especially in regard to such issues as anti-Semitism, the Holocaust, and the role of

17. Quoted in R. J. Zwi Werblowsky, "Jewish-Christian Relations," *Christian News from Israel* 24 (Autumn-Winter, 1973): 121.

18. *The New York Times,* November 1, 1977, p. 12.

19. Martin E. Marty, "Which Christians Can Israel Count On? A Ladder of Sympathies," *Christian Century* (March 8, 1978): 235.

20. Quoted in Dwight Wilson, *Armageddon Now!* (Grand Rapids: Baker Book House, 1977), p. 91.

21. Ibid., p. 130.

the Arabs (who are consigned a mainly demonic part in the last-days scenario).

In truth, no one has the privilege to lay claim to any land simply on the grounds of "divine right." The corridors of time are strewn with the wreckages of individuals and societies who have been tragic victims of those who had a "biblical mandate" or some "divine voice" giving approval to their inhumane acts. Witness, for example, the cruelty and bloodshed associated with a Church which supported such things as the Inquisition in Spain, the Crusades in Europe, black slavery in the American South, and the killing of witches in Salem, Massachusetts. Therefore, we argue that no solution to the problem of the land may be imposed on any people on the grounds that "it is willed by God." This also means that military conquest may not be used to prove a nation's right to a given land. For a nation to "misuse the Bible for political purposes is as blasphemous as to isolate it from the burning political and social questions of our day."[22] Wisely cautioning his fellow premillenarians, the historian Dwight Wilson describes the subtle deterministic trap often found in this eschatological system:

> When one analyzes the premillenarians' response to Israel, the inescapable conclusion is that their philosophy of history in many cases is equivalent to antinomian heresy. Antinomian means "against law"; if every action is preordained, then there is no need to measure one's actions by moral law, since the decision to obey or disobey the standard has already been made. If Israel is the elect, and Jewish history is predetermined by God and foretold by prophecy, then ordinary rules of international law (morality) do not apply to God's chosen people; and there is no absolute standard by which they can be judged. This is not implicit in the premillenarian view of prophecy, but it is what has worked out in practice in the response to Israel.[23]

The Church, in its frequent obsession with the future, must never forget that eschatology does not annul justice. "Indeed, the biblicist, no matter what his eschatological brand name—ought to view no particular world crisis as helpless. The Christian's God-assigned duty is . . . to pray and work for freedom, justice, and peace, doing everything he can within the limits of his opportunity."[24] The Christian community needs to give far more attention to the practical implications of premillennial thought on the concepts of history and social justice than they have given in the past.

22. R. J. Zwi Werblowsky, "Prophecy, the Land and The People," in *Prophecy in the Making,* ed. Carl F. H. Henry (Carol Stream, IL: Creation House, 1971), p. 353.

23. Dwight Wilson, *Armageddon Now!,* p. 143.

24. Vernon C. Grounds, "Evangelical Views of Today's Moral Crisis," in *Evangelicals and Jews in Conversation,* p. 263.

Upon close examination of Scripture, many of the details about Israel's future must remain obscure and uncertain for several reasons. First, the hermeneutic employed by the New Testament writers indicates that many Old Testament prophecies were fulfilled in ways totally unexpected by both the Old Testament authors themselves and the Jewish people of Jesus' day. Second, the language of prophecy has a certain indefiniteness about it. Prophecy may have a conditional element in it (cf. Jer. 18:7-10). Also, most prophecy is written in poetry rather than prose and so partakes of a certain measure of ambiguity with its numerous figures of speech. Third, some Christians frequently use unsound biblical exegesis to arrive at the supposed prophetic details about Israel's future. These questionable interpretations often derive from an eisegetical approach characterized either by sensationalism or sheer speculation. This approach often results in an unwarrantable attitude of arrogant anticipation and dogmatic certainty. Finally, Christians have seldom taken time to allow Jews the right to interpret their own Scriptures. Often the Church has been too anxious to tell Jewish people how to interpret their own Bible, which it received from them. How the Jewish community hears and understands biblical prophecy may be exceedingly instructive—if not revolutionary—to those Christians sage enough to inquire.

The New Testament seems to affirm a future for ethnic Israel; the nature of that future, however, deserves further comment. In Romans 9–11 Paul climaxes his theological discourse by addressing the theme of Jew and Gentile in the future plan of God. The main thrust of Paul's argument is that the destiny of Jew and Gentile is so intimately connected that the latter does not find God except through the former. As we emphasized in our introductory chapter, Paul describes the nature of this interdependence by the metaphor of an olive tree. In Romans 11, Paul is emphatic that despite Israel's unbelief God has not rejected his people (v. 1). Israel still belongs to God and is called a "holy" people (v. 16) and "loved on account of the patriarchs" (v. 28). Israel's historically unique preservation lends added support that it still has a vital role to play in the history of redemption (cf. v. 15). This divinely willed coexistence of God's ancient covenant people and the Church throughout the present age is, to Paul, a great "mystery" (v. 25). He is convinced, however, that God "does not change his mind about whom he chooses and blesses" (v. 29, TEV).

Paul's argument reaches its denouement when he refers to the future salvation of Israel, a time when "the deliverer will come from Zion" (vv. 26-27). The Old Testament context for Paul's composite quotation here is the salvation of Israel through the appearing of its divine Redeemer (cf. Isa. 59:20-21; 27:9). Thus "all Israel" (i.e., Israel as a whole) will be saved (v. 26). In Romans 11 Paul does not elaborate on how this deliverance from

Zion will take place, but it would seem from the other letters of Paul that he may have in mind the second coming of Jesus.

In the light of the precarious existence of the present Jewish state, Markus Barth seems correct in cautioning Christians not to consider the return of Jews to the land as a realization of eschatological promises in Scripture. He further points out that "Paul certainly does not prescribe for present-day Christians the stance they must take toward the new State of Israel. . . . Nevertheless, we may still ask for consequences and applications of his message, and we are in any case forced to take a position."[25] In my view, Barth is indeed right to oppose an ambivalence or vacillating uncertainty in regard to modern Israel, if for no other reason than that of consideration of the guilty silence of the Church during the Holocaust years. We would insist, in the very least, that the State of Israel is a remarkable sign of God's continuing love, preservation, and purpose for his people.

Moreover, as a people, Jews have an ongoing role in the furthering of God's ultimate redemptive purposes. But no matter what standard or position one adopts, Christians must not be blind to Joseph Klausner's objection that Christianity has sought to remove the national and political aspects of the prophetic hope.[26] God works through the sacred and the secular. James Parkes observes wisely that whenever the Church seeks to distinguish between the secular and the spiritual, in reality it negates its insistence on fulfilling the Old Testament.[27] Obviously, the modern State of Israel is significantly different from the idealized, perfected Israel of prophetic vision. The contrasts are striking and many. Nevertheless, if God can call a pagan Persian named Cyrus "his anointed" (Isa. 45:1), and another pagan king, Nebuchadnezzar, "my servant" (Jer. 25:9), and accomplish his holy purposes among the nations through both, who can say what plans God may yet have in store for those who from of old have been his people?[28]

We return to the main theme of this section by observing that "real estate" theology is, at best, precarious theology. It is always potentially dangerous when it seeks to make politics out of theology. Its theology, un-

25. Markus Barth, *The People of God* (Sheffield, England: JSOT Press, 1983), pp. 67, 69.

26. Joseph Klausner, *The Messianic Idea in Israel,* trans. W. F. Stinespring (New York: Macmillan, 1955), p. 10.

27. James Parkes, *The Foundations of Judaism and Christianity* (Chicago: Quadrangle Books, 1960), pp. 325-26.

28. For additional Christian works dealing with the future of Israel from a theological perspective, see Carl Edwin Armerding, "The Meaning of Israel in Evangelical Thought," in *Evangelicals and Jews in Conversation,* pp. 119-40; Hendrikus Berkhof, "Israel as a Theological Problem in the Christian Church," *Journal of Ecumenical Studies* 6/3 (Summer, 1969): 329-47; George E. Ladd, *A Theology of the New Testament* (Grand

less applied with great wisdom and sensitivity, usually hurts other people. It is therefore not willingly accepted. In a parallel vein, for centuries Jews suffered discrimination and victimization at the hands of Christians whose theological convictions seemed to permit—if not encourage—such unjust activity. In brief, it is exceedingly difficult to negotiate things from the "city of God" in relation to the "city of men." Therefore, we conclude, as long as Arabs and Jews argue from nonnegotiable theological absolutes, human beings can offer little hope for peace.

## A Homeland Rooted in Justice

This tension has led us to a different alternative in dealing with the problem of biblical claims. This third option, which I support, lies between the other two. It recognizes that this complex issue must be resolved neither by abandoning all theological concern of whatever stripe, nor simplistically on the grounds of divine right. Rather, in this view, one's understanding of the right of the Jewish people to a secure homeland is based primarily on the issues of justice, morality, and history.

We begin by recognizing that both Arabs and Jews seek the right to self-determination, national identity, and legitimate human rights. Arabs desire a homeland, and Jews desire a secure state with recognized borders. None of these goals will be fully realized until each group accepts the reality of the other with a spirit of mutual respect, humility, and trust. Though the Bible, as we have sought to demonstrate, bears witness to God's unceasing relation to his covenant people and their historic homeland, we must primarily pursue the prophetic concern for justice, righteousness, compassion, and peace. If Christians support the right of Israel to exist as a nation—and they should—they should do so on the basis that it is moral, just, and humane rather than simply on the grounds that "it fulfills prophecy." The creation of the State of Israel has allowed the Jew, once the "outsider of history," to reenter history. Christian encouragement and support of Israel today for juridical and moral reasons can be interpreted only as a giant step forward in seeking to right an ugly historical wrong. Built by the hands of survivors of a holocaust that claimed six million lives, Israel always has the issue of Jewish survival as a central concern.

---

Rapids: William B. Eerdmans Publishing Co., 1974), pp. 538-39; William S. LaSor, *Israel: A Biblical View* (Grand Rapids: William B. Eerdmans Publishing Co., 1976); Robert L. Saucy, "A Rationale for the Future of Israel," *Journal of the Evangelical Theological Society* 28/4 (December, 1985): 433-42; Marvin R. Wilson, "Zionism as Theology," *Journal of the Evangelical Theological Society* 22/1 (March, 1979): 27-44.

Modern Israel is not a theocracy. As a secular state, Israel was not, even during the time of the prophets, and is not now the kingdom of God. Therefore, today's Christian should not blindly condone all Israeli acts. Nevertheless, we object strongly to the practice of holding Israel to a different standard of morality from that applied to all other nation-states, especially to those committed to Israel's destruction. Israel's own prophets call the people to practice justice and compassion to those they consider "strangers" in the land. This term often means the displaced, homeless, and powerless. Justice, however, is a two-way street. Only when bitterness, hostility, and hatred give way to a spirit of compromise, friendship, and recognition will all residents of the land know peace.

While not dismissing specific biblical texts that point to both an historical and future relation of the people of Israel to the land, this third approach responds to Zionism from a different, yet not contradictory, point of view. We have argued that this perspective focuses on history and on the burning biblical issues of justice, compassion, and moral sensitivity. All too often the Church has been so intent on looking toward the future that it has failed both to deal with the present and to learn from the past. Our task is to "follow justice and justice alone" (Deut. 16:20), and then let God worry about whether this path, in any specific way, fulfills his future prophetic plan for Israel. Either way, it accomplishes that passion for justice which the prophets demanded (Amos 5:24; Mic. 6:8).

## Christians and Support of Israel

Throughout this book we have taken the position that the Church cannot afford to be passive, neutral, or aloof about laying claim to its full Jewish heritage. Accordingly, Christians, like Jews, have a Jerusalem connection. In this regard, the Church must come to grips with what W. D. Davies calls the "scandal of territorial particularity in Judaism." That is, Christians must recognize that "the Land is so embedded in the heart of Judaism . . . it is finally inseparable from it."[29] Consequently, the Church has no choice but to face this essential question: Can Abraham's spiritual seed really remain indifferent about Abraham's land? We believe that a sound rationale may be offered regarding Christian concern for the State of Israel, and we will now seek to spell out some of the implications of this rationale.

At the outset, it is crucial to insist (as we will again do at the conclusion of this chapter) that Christian solidarity with Israel does not imply the

29. Davies, *Territorial Dimension of Judaism*, p. 125.

negation of Palestinian Arabs. This is not an "us or them," "right or wrong" issue. Neither is it a "my-country-right-or-wrong" mentality. Indeed, in using the term *solidarity,* we are primarily concerned not about political agreement and unity but about an undergirding that is mainly identified with spiritual roots and about the survival of the people who have bestowed those roots. Palestinian Arab Christians, no less than American or European Christians, owe their spiritual heritage to the Jewish people. When disagreement over substantive territorial, political, economic, and military issues is allowed to turn into hatred, however, it becomes all the more difficult to affirm appreciation and indebtedness for our Jewish heritage—especially if one views the people who have imparted that legacy as oppressors. The political scene in the Middle East is important, but it must not sidetrack us from dealing with the central thrust of this book, namely, what the Christian faith owes to Judaism and the Jewish people. It is primarily from this recognition that solidarity with Israel derives. Alice and Roy Eckardt explain: "It is by virtue of [our] Christian existence that . . . Israel can never be just one more country. Christianity is devoid of spatial ties to the extent that it is on its own. But through its indissoluble bond with the Jewish people and the Jewish faith, the Christian faith is yoked spiritually to Eretz Yisrael."[30]

A relation to Israel based mainly on popularity polls, the ups and downs of politics, or biased or censored media coverage will certainly be swayed. But those who recognize in their innermost being that they are spiritual descendants of Abraham and are grafted into an all-Jewish organism will consider Christian support of Israel differently. It has something to do with family ties. Thus, on the deepest level, solidarity with Israel will not be swayed when grounded on a recognition of the very special relationship between the Church and Synagogue, on a renewed understanding of the roots of Christianity in Judaism, on a true encounter with the Jewish people and their teachings that have contributed immensely to the world in general and the Church in particular, and on an honest confrontation with the history of anti-Semitism and the Holocaust in the heart of so-called Christian Europe.[31] This type of critical solidarity and commitment to Israel comes from a profound spiritual awareness vitally linked to historical consciousness and brotherhood. Markus Barth describes further such Christian understanding of Israel: "Because of the Jew

30. Alice Eckardt and Roy Eckardt, *Encounter with Israel* (New York: Association Press, 1970), p. 262.

31. Isaac C. Rottenberg, "From Dialogue to Solidarity," unpublished paper (New York: The National Christian Leadership Conference for Israel, March, 1982), p. 3.

named Jesus Christ, and because salvation comes from the Jews, a Christian concerned for Jews will affirm and support this state. By God the Father, through Jesus Christ, and when only the slightest trace of the Holy Spirit moves them, Christians are called and enabled to say 'Yes' to it, and despite all its problems, to defend it against its ideological and political enemies. This state is a touchstone for anyone who is convinced that God's people does and will exist in tangible form, rather than in the shape of programmes, ideas, or dreams only."[32]

When Christians say that their roots run deep in Jewish soil, this is far more than a figure of speech. Let us take the city of Jerusalem as an example. The inspired prophets for us today are those ancient Israelite prophets who delivered their messages in and around Jerusalem. The Psalms, used in Temple worship in Jerusalem, became the primary source of early Christian hymnology. Jesus was born into a Jewish family near Jerusalem. Later, he taught there, died there, rose there, ascended there, and said he would return there. In addition, in the city of Jerusalem the Church was established by Jews, for Jews, on a Jewish festival. Furthermore, the first Jewish Christians —thousands in number—were baptized in Jerusalem. Thus a Christian's personal knowledge of Jerusalem, as well as the remainder of the land, is indispensable for understanding the origin of Christianity as well as the scope of biblical history, customs, languages, archeology, and geography. In brief, after personally being joined to the land of Israel, a Christian will never read the Bible the same way. But Israel is more than soil, tells, and artifacts; it is also people. Accordingly, after a visit to the Yad Vashem Memorial in Jerusalem, a Christian will never view anti-Semitism—and especially the Holocaust—the same way. Such experiences are characteristically at the very heart of Christian solidarity with Israel.

Christian interest in Israel may be expressed in many tangible ways.[33] A pilgrimage or interfaith study tour is a useful place to begin. But college and seminary students can especially benefit from a year of study in Israel. Furthermore, Christian biblical scholars are able to enhance their knowledge of Scripture and archeology by taking part in extended seminars with their Israeli Jewish counterparts. In addition, Christians have opportunity to contribute to the growth of the land through various social-action projects such as planting trees, volunteering in hospitals, and working on kibbutzim.

32. Markus Barth, *People of God*, pp. 69-70.
33. See Marvin R. Wilson, "An Evangelical Christian View of Israel," in *A Time to Speak: The Evangelical-Jewish Encounter*, eds. A. James Rudin and Marvin R. Wilson (Grand Rapids: William B. Eerdmans Publishing Co., 1987), pp. 170-76.

We have affirmed the importance of Christian support of Israel; but at the same time, several cautions are in order. First, Christians must never succumb to a line of thinking that suggests any criticism directed against Israel is tantamount to opposing God. People are not necessarily anti-Semitic or anti-Zionist if they oppose certain Israeli political policies or military actions. At times, we may need to express our strongest disapproval of the one whom we care about most deeply and love the most. Such is especially the case in family relationships. Irrational, blind, anti-Zionist hatred differs from constructive criticism offered out of true care by those who have had a strong record of interest in Israel's welfare.

Second, Church leaders must resist the temptation to say things about Israel that people want to hear rather than what they need to know. Some Christians seem to thrive on saying either romantic or sensational things about Israel. They seldom get beyond a prophecy-oriented mind-set. They should, however, be dealing with many of the harsh realities of day-to-day living in the land. Furthermore, Christians must refrain from placing Jewish people on a pedestal and thereby presenting an unrealistic or idealized picture of Israel. Sometimes this idealization has led Christians to turn against the Jewish community because their expectations have not been met. Christian friendship and concern shown to Jews—as to all people—must always be unconditional, not founded on prerequisites or any preconceived checklist of virtues.

Third, Christians must not impose their specific political or religious agenda upon Israeli Jews. The question of timing is always significant in the way God works. It is easy to become impatient with the slowness of peace talks or the bent toward secularism in much of contemporary Israeli society. God's sense of timing in accomplishing his purposes in history is often different from that of human beings. We must not forget that though the land was promised to Abraham as part of his call (Gen. 12:1), God's intention was to allow four generations to pass before Abraham's descendants were to take possession of it (15:16).

Finally, neither Christian nor Jew must absolutize the land or in any way idolize it. God alone is sovereign. He is Lord of life and Lord of land. We must not give our highest allegiance to anything but him or make anything of greater importance than him.

## Epilogue: Prospects for Peace

Many are presently concerned about a "Greater Israel" through militarism and other forms of expansionism. This issue must be seriously addressed.

Those who may have reason to push Israel's borders to their fullest biblical area should pause. The actual extent of Israel's boundaries specified in the Tenakh varies from passage to passage. Sometimes it includes land east of the Jordan, sometimes not. What the Bible emphasizes is not precisely defined borders but simply the land of Canaan. If Jews and Christians wish to study biblical texts to find support and inspiration for Jewish people living in the land, let them not, as some do, focus on the book of Joshua. That book relates the story of Israel's conquering and enslaving a people native to the land. These events happened in the earliest stages of Israel's history when rulership was by theocracy. Instead, let them find direction from Isaiah and his vision of servanthood and peace. In addition, rather than focusing on expansionism, one might gain more from studying the history of Zionism and reflecting on aspects of the binational proposal espoused earlier in this century by Judah Magnes and Martin Buber. These stalwarts sought a peaceful solution by attempting to have Jews share power with Arabs. Unfortunately, they could find no Arab partner willing to dialogue. It is, of course, improbable that the full concept of binationalism would be given serious consideration today. Nonetheless, it is important that peace talks be held directly between Arabs and Jews. In this connection, one can only admire the courage which prompted Anwar Sadat to step forward amid a sea of criticism. Let us hope for other leaders willing to be negotiating partners for peace in the days ahead.

Genuine security must come from good relations with one's neighbors, not from increased militarism. Some have argued that the main obstacle to peace between Arab and Jew is that an essential in each nationalism is the denial of the other.[34] This point is worth serious discussion. One of the obstacles for Arab recognition of Israel concerns the Holy City of Jerusalem. Though sacred to Jews for nearly three thousand years, Jerusalem has been occupied by an Islamic government most of the time since the seventh century. Furthermore, the racist extremism of those Israeli leaders who seek to expel all Palestinian Arabs from Judea and Samaria (the West Bank) fortifies the barrier of exclusivity represented within Israeli nationalism. From the Israeli side, it is difficult to understand why surrounding Arab nations have refused to absorb Palestinian refugees. A major refugee problem began in 1948 when Palestinian Arabs rejected the Partition Plan of the United Nations for a Palestinian Arab State. The partition lines were obliterated and most of the West Bank area was annexed to Jordan, an annexation only Britain and Pakistan recognized. Thus, in the thinking

34. Bert DeVries, "Beyond Nationalism—Israel and the Palestinians," *Reformed Journal* (December, 1984): 8.

of many Israelis today, in the area once known as eastern Palestine, the Arab-Palestinian State of Jordan serves as an independent, sovereign state. Thus they argue that another Arab Palestinian state is not needed.

Each group has stories of atrocity or terrorism to tell. But mere trading of these stories from the past has done little to advance the peace process in the present. The focus must now turn to both present and future and be conciliatory. *Shalom,* the well-known Hebrew word for "peace," carries with it the idea of wholeness, perfection, togetherness, integration, harmonization. For Arab and Jew, this healing and reconciliation cannot be imposed through peace talks. But, as Carl F. H. Henry rightly emphasizes, "International 'table-talk' does not . . . buy peace; it simply buys time, and that is a precious asset, for it includes time for repentance."[35] Even if peace talks lead to a two-state solution, the only real and lasting solution is reconciliation through forgiveness, accompanied by the respect and love each person owes the other.[36]

Christians must refrain from easy, quick-fix solutions to territorial and political disputes between the Israelis and Arabs. There are Israeli Jews and there are Palestinian Arabs; neither is going to leave the land. We do them an injustice if we seek to impose facile answers to complex, ancient problems. We must encourage each group jointly to negotiate a viable solution. The continuing conflict in the Mideast is not so much a struggle between right and wrong, good and evil; it is a conflict between two rights, between two peoples who have occupied with deep devotion the same territory for several thousand years.

God is on the side of justice. He loves all people. One cannot be pro-Arab and anti-Israel; neither can one be pro-Israel and anti-Arab. What, then, is our responsibility? It is to pray, to encourage, and to work for a permanent and fair sharing of the land between two peoples, Arabs and Jews, with a maximum of justice and a minimum of injustice.[37]

## UNDERSTANDING CHAPTER THIRTEEN

1. Give at least three different terms used in Scripture for the historic homeland of the Jewish people.

2. Today, to many of the residents of the Middle East, the words *Palestine*

---

35. Carl F. H. Henry, "Can Peace Come to the Mideast?" *Christian Life* (November, 1984): 72.

36. DeVries, "Beyond Nationalism," p. 12.

37. A. James Rudin, "Jewish Attitudes Toward Israel: A Precis," in *A Time to Speak,* p. 186.

and *Israel* are far from synonymous and often conjure up exceedingly different political connotations. Discuss some of the factors which lie behind this mixed response.

3. Give a brief definition of the term *Zionism*.

4. Some people have wrongly assumed that Abraham's chosenness was based on superiority, innate giftedness, or spiritual elitism. What does Scripture say? What destiny was Abraham called to fulfill?

5. Who was the "father of modern Zionism"? What well-known work did he publish in 1896? In brief, what was the Balfour Declaration?

6. Give the significance of the following dates associated with the history of the modern State of Israel: (a) 1897, (b) 1917, (c) 1922, (d) November 29, 1947, (e) May 14, 1948.

7. Krister Stendahl has pointed out an inconsistency on the part of Christians in regard to their failure to grasp the nature of the land. What is this inconsistency?

8. According to the Hebrew Scriptures, who is the true owner of the land? What was Israel's responsibility or right in this matter?

9. Upon what was Israel's ongoing possession of the land conditioned? Did Israel believe that the Exile would be forever and that the land covenant would be permanently set aside and cancelled? Explain.

10. In Babylonian exile, what became the "highest joy" of the Jewish people (see Ps. 137)?

11. What is the last book in the Hebrew Bible? What is the last word of the last book? Why is this term a focal point for the modern restoration of Israel to its ancestral homeland? In this present day, what term is used for "going up," i.e., the return of Diaspora Jews to Israel?

12. What is the name of the national anthem of the modern State of Israel? What is the translation of this title? Why was this an appropriate title on the part of the newly arrived Jewish settlers?

13. According to the prophet Ezekiel (and later Jewish teachers), what was the "navel" or "center of the earth"?

14. During the first half of the twentieth century, who was the leading exponent of "religious Zionism" who taught that all Jews who lived in Israel were preparing the land for "the final redemption . . . the coming of the days of the Messiah"?

15. In brief, point out the philosophy of Zionism that characterized each of the following leaders: (a) Theodor Herzl, (b) Ahad Ha-Am, (c) David Ben-Gurion, (d) Vladimir Jabotinsky, (e) Martin Buber. How has this complex mosaic of Zionist thinking affected unity within Israel among the Israelis? How has it affected the perception of Zionism by non-Jews living outside the land?

16. Why do many of the Hasidic Jews in Israel today refuse to serve in the Israeli military?

17. Prior to the rise of the modern State of Israel, Jews took a largely pas-

sive stance toward history. Explain what is meant by this stance. How did the early Zionists make a break from this earlier passive stance?

18. One Christian approach to the State of Israel argues that the Church has replaced the Jewish people. Thus any biblical promises made concerning the land to ethnic or national Israel are void. Give further explanation of this view. Discuss and evaluate.

19. A second position held by Christians concerning the land affirms the State of Israel on the basis of a "divine right." Give further explanation of this view. Discuss and evaluate.

20. Premillennialism, a viewpoint which holds that the second coming of Jesus will precede the millennium, makes a distinction between God's program for Israel and his program for the Church. Prophecy which is addressed to Israel as a people will be fulfilled by Israel. Which Christians does Martin Marty conclude Israel can count on the most? Why? Do you agree?

21. The eagerness of many premillennialists to back Israel has often been expressed in language which is highly deterministic and devoid of ethical and humanitarian considerations. Discuss the implications of this statement.

22. Why is it important to caution that no one has the privilege to lay claim to any land simply on the grounds of "divine right"?

23. Does eschatology annul justice? Discuss the relation of these two terms.

24. Note at least four reasons why Christians should be cautious to observe that the details in Scripture about Israel's future must remain obscure and uncertain.

25. Why is "real estate" theology, at best, precarious theology?

26. A third Christian approach to the State of Israel (and one argued for in this book) upholds the right of the Jewish people to a secure homeland, one based primarily on the issues of justice, morality, and history. Give further explanation of this view. Discuss and evaluate.

27. In this chapter, what is meant by Christian "solidarity" with Israel? Upon what is this understanding of solidarity based?

28. In what specific ways is a Christian's personal knowledge of Jerusalem indispensable for understanding the origin of Christianity?

29. Christian support of Israel necessitates that certain cautions be observed. What are they?

30. How precise is the Bible in defining the exact borders of the land of promise? What might modern theologians and politicians conclude from this?

31. It has been argued that the main obstacle to peace between Arab and Jew is that an essential in each nationalism is to deny the other. Cite examples of this philosophy and discuss its implications for both Arab and Jew.

32. What ought to be the Christian's responsibility in the light of the territorial and political disputes that have gone on between the Israelis and Arabs?

*Chapter Fourteen*

# A Life of Learning:
# The Heart of Jewish Heritage

*Hold on to instruction, do not let it go; guard it well, for it is your life*

Proverbs 4:13

Learning constitutes the very core of the heritage that Jewish civilization has bequeathed to the Church. An old rabbinic maxim states, "If you have knowledge, you have everything."[1] Historically, Jews have known the reality of this oft-repeated saying. They have long been called "the People of the Book." From Bible times to the present, Jews have been exiled from the homeland, and they have been victims of hostility and hatred (see chapter seven above). Nonetheless, out of all this tribulation, world Jewry learned one main thing: a Jew might be inhumanely stripped of all his earthly belongings, but if he possessed learning, no one could ever take that from him.

Since the biblical period, Jews have considered the quest for knowledge to be one of the great desiderata of life (cf. Phil. 3:4-11). "Learning —learning—learning: that is the secret of Jewish survival," Ahad Ha-Am once wrote.[2] Jews have long known that they and their religious heritage would perish from the earth if they neglected to pass its teachings on to their children. Such is reflected in the following sayings of the Talmud: "He who withholds a lesson from his pupils robs him of the heritage of his

1. Quoted from Henri Daniel-Rops, *Daily Life in the Time of Jesus,* trans. Patrick O'Brian (New York: The New American Library, 1962), p. 113.
2. Quoted from Tina Hacker, ed., *Shalom: The Heritage of Judaism in Selected Writings* (Kansas City, MO: Hallmark Editions, 1972), p. 21.

father" (Sanhedrin 91b); "He who teaches Torah to the child of another is as if he gave birth to him" (Sanhedrin 19b); "The world exists by the breath of school children" (Shabbat 119b). So strongly did the early rabbis feel about the priority of education that they said it may not be interrupted even for the rebuilding of the Temple. One modern Jewish scholar, Raphael Werblowsky, sums up the singular importance of education in these words: "Jewish learning has always been the root and fountainhead of Jewish life . . . without Jewish learning we cannot be Jews."[3]

## Education in Old Testament Times

The primary purpose of education in Bible times was to train the whole person for lifelong, obedient service in the knowledge of God (Prov. 1:7; Eccl. 12:13). The children of Abraham were to "keep the way of the LORD" (Gen. 18:19), and Torah was given to keep them on that path (Ps. 119:105). The aim of learning was holiness in living—to be set apart unto God in every dimension of life. This holiness required a knowledge of God's acts in history and a commitment to observe his mitzvot (commandments), which instructed one how to live. Israel was to acknowledge the Lord's authority in every circumstance and in every turn of the way (Ps. 16:8; Prov. 3:5-6). Thus the ultimate prophetic vision was that "all the peoples of the earth may know that the LORD is God and that there is no other" (1 Kgs. 8:60).

From early in Israel's history the center of education was the home. Both parents shared in this task (Prov. 1:8; 6:20), though the father bore chief responsibility for the instruction of the children (Deut. 11:19). Abraham Heschel has astutely underscored the current relevancy of this point: "Education is a matter which rests primarily with the parent, with the father. The teacher is but a representative of the father, according to Jewish tradition. Thou shalt teach them diligently, not vicariously. Now parents act as they please, commercialism and vulgarity blare from the loudspeakers—and little children are expected to listen to the voice of the spirit. Religious instruction, like charity, begins at home."[4]

The association of father with teacher may be traced back at least to Sumerian civilization. The headmaster of the Sumerian school was called

---

3. Raphael Z. Werblowsky, "Study or Action? Torah in Jewish Life," in *Jewish Heritage Reader,* ed. Lilly Edelman (New York: Taplinger Publishing Co., 1965), p. 155.
4. Abraham J. Heschel, *The Insecurity of Freedom* (New York: Schocken Books, 1972), pp. 54-55.

"school-father," and the pupil called "school-son."[5] In Egypt as well as in Mesopotamia instruction often took this "father-son" form. Furthermore, in the Hebrew Bible, teachers (priests) are called "father" (Judg. 17:10; 18:19), and the relationship between teacher and student (e.g., Elijah and Elisha) is expressed by "father" and "son" (2 Kgs. 2:3, 12). In addition, in the opening chapters of the book of Proverbs, the sage regularly addresses his student as "my son." Furthermore, in traditional Jewish homes today, when a child prays for his parents, he refers to them as "my father, my teacher; my mother, my teacher."

In Bible times the father—not textbooks, audiovisuals, or brightly colored classrooms—was the main instrument in the learning process. As teacher of his children, the father served as a living and dynamic communicator of divine truth. A Bible could not be substituted for him —there were no Bibles. Applying this principle to the challenge of biblical education today, Heschel has observed that "what we need more than anything else is not *textbooks* but text-people. It is the personality of the teacher which is the text that the pupils read; the text they will never forget."[6]

The fundamental goal of Jewish parental instruction was to transmit an historical and ethical heritage. The Talmud especially emphasizes this obligation of the father to teach his children: "The father is bound in respect of his son, to circumcise . . . teach him Torah, take a wife for him, and teach him a craft" (Kiddushin 29a). For a grandfather, the epitome of personal religious satisfaction was to hear a grandson recite a portion of the Torah (see Jerusalem Talmud, Shabbat 1:2). Thus, of all the 613 commandments[7] found in the Torah, none was more important for understanding the Jewish heritage of learning than these words: "Teach them to your children and to their children after them" (Deut. 4:9; cf. Ps. 78:1-8).

Education within the home also included acquiring an appropriate skill, craft, or trade for making a living. A son often learned as an apprentice of his father (Mishnah, Kiddushin 4:14). Sons were also instructed in the skills of farming and sheep tending (1 Sam. 16:11). A daughter usually remained with her mother to learn various domestic procedures such as

5. William Chomsky, "The Dawn of Jewish Education," in *Gratz College Annual of Jewish Studies,* ed. Isidore Passow and Samuel Lachs (Philadelphia: Gratz College, 1974), 3:20.

6. Abraham J. Heschel, "The Spirit of Jewish Education," *Jewish Education* 24/2 (Fall, 1953): 19.

7. Simlai, a rabbi of the 3rd century, numbered the commandments at 613. He divided them into 365 prohibitions and 248 positive concepts.

weaving and cooking (Prov. 31:13ff.). Because of the wide use of music and dance among the Hebrews, many parents must have provided instruction for their children in these areas as well (cf. Exod. 15:1-21; 32:19; Deut. 31:30–32:47; Luke 15:25; etc.).

Ancient Israel had no system or network of formal schooling, and professional education was not readily available to the masses. As a result, education tended to be quite diverse and mainly informal. The home remained the main source of learning, but other important educational authorities also influenced society. These included the priest, prophet, and wise man (cf. Jer. 18:18).

Priests were custodians and expounders of the Law (Deut. 31:9-13). Moses instructs the people to "act according to the law they [the priests] teach you" (Deut. 17:11). In Moses' blessings on the tribes, he says of Levi (the priestly tribe), "He teaches your [i.e., the Lord's] precepts to Jacob and your law to Israel" (Deut. 33:10). Periodically the priests would travel from town to town, gather people together, and teach them (2 Chr. 17:8-9). Ezra is described as a priest and "teacher well versed in the Law of Moses" (Ezra 7:6).

The prophets were champions of moral righteousness and social justice. They urged people to return to the ethical and spiritual teaching of Moses (Amos 5:21-24). Many prophets had disciples or "sons" who gathered about them to learn their teachings (Isa. 8:16, 18). These prophetic companies—sometimes called "schools"—passed on orally the sayings of the prophet before they were fully preserved in writing (2 Kgs. 8:4ff.).

A third recognizable teaching force was that of the wise men. A number of so-called wisdom schools attracted students seeking to be discipled by one of the sages of the day. Thus Koheleth (or Qohelet), the wise teacher, "imparted knowledge to the people" (Eccl. 12:9). It will now be our concern to discuss in greater detail the significance of the wisdom tradition and the place of wise man and fool.

## The Hebrew View of Wisdom

*Blessed is the man who finds wisdom,*
*    the man who gains understanding,*
*for she is more profitable than silver*
*    and yields better returns than gold.*
*She is more precious than rubies;*
*    nothing you desire can compare with her.*
*Long life is in her right hand;*

*in her left hand are riches and honor.*
*Her ways are pleasant ways,*
    *and all her paths are peace.*
*She is a tree of life to those who embrace her;*
    *those who lay hold of her will be blessed.*

Proverbs 3:13-18

The wisdom literature of ancient Israel is mainly found in the books of Proverbs, Ecclesiastes, Job, Song of Songs, and certain Psalms. In the gallery of Hebrew greats, Moses is recognized as the patron of law, David the patron of psalms and music, and Solomon the patron of wisdom literature. Scripture tells us that Solomon composed three thousand proverbs, and his wisdom was "greater than the wisdom of all the men of the East, and greater than all the wisdom of Egypt" (1 Kgs. 4:30). But the Gospels declare Jesus' wisdom, evident in his teachings and parables, to be greater than Solomon's (Luke 11:31; cf. 1 Cor. 1:30).

Sometimes the wise man reflected on perplexing issues of life and made prudent observations on them. This so-called speculative or contemplative aspect of wisdom is illustrated by the theme of the book of Job, namely, the justice of God in the face of innocent suffering. It is seen also in the book of Ecclesiastes, which struggles with the meaning of human existence.

But the most common function of the sage was to give wisdom *(hokhmah)* or counsel to people needing practical advice for living. We will focus on the book of Proverbs, a chief source for this kind of wisdom. Proverbs abounds in instructions and maxims for would-be learners. It appears to have been used as a kind of textbook for reciting the observations of the wise. Most of these sayings emphasize the success or well-being of the individual and stress reward in this life for following the proper course of action. The wise man had the ability to condense the wisdom of experience in pithy sayings. To the Greek, knowledge was the main way to virtue; the path to the good life was through the intellect. But to the Hebrew, wisdom went beyond intellectual pursuit; it was practical. Wisdom was established upon God-given principles of right and wrong. These principles had to be fleshed out in daily living, in the commonsense dimensions of interpersonal relationships.

Thus the Hebrews never viewed wisdom as mere factual information or as purely cognitive. Rather, it was skill in applying knowledge to a specific area. Wisdom began with the ability to see and evaluate all of life from God's point of view (Prov. 1:7). Wisdom had its seat in God.

Though all wisdom came from God, its ultimate source, the Hebrews tended to define wisdom empirically, in applied and rather concrete ways. That is, it usually implied the knack, know-how, or capacity to perform a particular task. Adroitness and cleverness might be called the handmaids of wisdom. God was concerned with the whole human being and the whole of life.

Hence, in Old Testament times, those endowed with wisdom included people with the capacity for leadership or administration (Gen. 41:33, 39; Deut. 34:9), the ability of a warrior (Prov. 21:22), the skill of a sailor (Ezek. 27:8), the technical know-how of garment making (Exod. 28:3), and the cleverness to make artistic designs in gold, silver, and bronze (Exod. 31:3-5). In short, wisdom was the practical ability to function successfully, to the best possible advantage, in one's chosen area of service. Thus *hokhmah*, "wisdom," properly meant to have good sense, aptitude, or technical skill.

## Young Fools and Old Fools

In biblical wisdom literature the pupils of the sages are the unwise, often termed "fools" (Prov. 1:7) or "simple ones" (1:22). We shall define various words for "fool" below, but at the outset of this discussion we must remember not to confuse *fool* or *simple one* with a person who is mentally defective. Rather, in wisdom literature the different kinds of fools—both young and old—are "the raw material on which the teacher had to work and they represent varying degrees of rawness."[8] Perhaps as much as anything else, the term *fool* is descriptive of an attitude, bent of mind, or direction in life which needs correcting.

The various Hebrew words for "fool" occur more than a hundred times in the book of Proverbs. This frequency demonstrates the intense passion of the wise men to increase wisdom, for in the presence of wisdom, folly begins to vanish. This push toward learning—lifelong learning —is poignantly captured in these inspired words of wisdom: "Hold on to instruction, do not let it go; guard it well, for it is your life" (Prov. 4:13).

Here is the general thrust of the proverbial teachings of the sages: wisdom leads to success in life; but folly, wisdom's antithesis, leads to failure. We must keep in mind, however, that proverbs represent a particular kind of literary genre. As such, proverbs are not ironclad promises guaranteed to work successfully, with no exceptions; rather, proverbs are

8. John Patterson, *The Wisdom of Israel* (Nashville: Abingdon Press, 1961), p. 64.

general observations on life that tend to hold true as a rule (i.e., in most situations). Certainly the book of Job represents an extended commentary on one of the not-so-uncommon "exceptions." As a work of wisdom literature, Job challenges the widely held maxim or belief that piety brings prosperity and success, that impiety leads to ruin and failure. Indeed, in Job's case, one of the world's truly righteous individuals experiences disaster after disaster (Job 1:13-19; 2:7).

One of the main reasons why there are exceptions to the proverbial teachings of Scripture is because the whole world is spiritually corrupt and displays a general disregard of God (1 Kgs. 8:46; Ps. 14:1-3; 130:3; cf. Rom. 3:10-18). In a sense, therefore, when we take all of Scripture into consideration, all human beings—in one way or another—are fools (cf. 1 Cor. 1:18-25). The Scriptures are filled with examples of people within the covenant community whose lives — at least from time to time — manifested the characteristics of one or more of the types of fools discussed below. Folly is indicative of those who disregard moral and spiritual values; this is a universal trait. Folly also characterizes those whose inept and inappropriate actions—if left uncorrected—bring downfall or destruction. The fool was the center of flawed relationships; the wise knew how to build successful ones. We must recognize that this type of polarity of thinking—those who are wise versus those who are fools—was common to the world of the Hebrews. It is fitting, therefore, to study some of the Hebrew terms used for "fool." These terms will provide further insight into the meaning of folly as the Israelite sages encountered it.

## The "Open" Fool

The Hebrew term *peti* (or *pethi*) is often translated "simple." For example, the prologue to the book of Proverbs speaks of giving "prudence to the simple" (1:4; also note 1:22 and elsewhere). The word derives from a root suggesting the idea of being "open, spacious, wide."[9] *Peti* is the term for "fool" which carries with it the greatest potential that one will welcome instruction and correction from a wise man. One who is "open" is accessible. Though often immature, inexperienced, and easily led into all kinds of enticement, the *peti* is, fortunately, teachable. A "simple" one might be naive, gullible, and easily fooled (see Prov. 7:7ff.), yet his mind is not barred to the entrance of wisdom. Openness has the potential of being turned into virtue as quickly as vice.

9. See Louis Goldberg, *"peti,"* in *Theological Wordbook of the Old Testament,* ed. R. Laird Harris, et al. (Chicago: Moody Press, 1980), 2:742.

Closemindedness, stubbornness, and fossilization were common marks of fools who stood before sages in Bible times. The same obstacles face teachers today. But, happily, God's pattern has been always to begin his work in people by meeting them where they are; if they are generally open to his leading, great possibility for growth exists. So, the *peti* type may have given the Hebrew sages reason to be somewhat encouraged. The *peti* is a person who is usually approachable and hence educable (cf. Prov. 7:21 for an example of the negative effects such approachability can have). These are essential and universal qualities for all would-be learners. Those giving instruction could usually work with the *peti;* he was young and flexible; his folly could be corrected. In sum, "the faults of the *pethi* . . . are the faults of youth. The sages had their chance here and they did not neglect it. The simple could be educated . . . — if the sages caught them early."[10] This is the "open" fool.

## The "Hardened" Fool

The words *kesil* and *ewil* are used of a second kind of fool that the sages encountered. The basic idea behind both these Hebrew terms seems to be similar, namely, "thickness" or "fatness."[11] A contextual study of these words indicates that they often refer to a person who is "thickheaded," "dullwitted," or "dense" in the sense of moral deficiency. The idea of thickness suggests a hardened, sluggish, and obstinate person, slow to change his ways. Calcified and seemingly impenetrable, these are fools who become mentally immune to the words of the wise, as the passages below demonstrate.

In the Hebrew Bible the *kesil* is a self-confident dullard (cf. the related word *kislah,* meaning "confidence"). The *kesil* is so self-confident that he is set in his ways. He is also strong-willed, refusing to learn readily. Hence, his propensity is to disregard moral ideals. He persists in evil: "As a dog returns to its vomit, so a fool *[kesil]* repeats his folly" (Prov. 26:11). He is full of braggadocio (12:23); he despises instruction (1:22; 18:2); and he is contentious (18:6). One who is a *kesil* finds pleasure in doing evil (10:23), is complacent (1:32), and brings bitterness and grief to his parents (10:1; 17:21, 25). In sum, he rejects the fear of the Lord (1:29).

---

10. Patterson, *The Wisdom of Israel,* p. 65.

11. See Brown, Driver, and Briggs, *Hebrew and English Lexicon of the Old Testament* (London: Oxford University Press, 1907), pp. 17, 492. Related to *kesil* is the Hebrew word *kesel,* "loins," the fatty muscles around the kidney area. Furthermore, Derek Kidner observes correctly that "the fact that the 'folly' of the *kesil* is almost always called *iwwelet* (from the same root as *ewil*) shows that these two names for 'fool' are virtually one" (*Proverbs,* Tyndale Old Testament Commentaries [Downers Grove, IL: InterVarsity Press, 1964], p. 41).

The *ewil* shares many of the same marks of senselessness and moral impropriety. This fool rejects instruction (12:15), babbles thoughtlessly (10:14), and is quick-tempered (14:29). Furthermore, the *ewil* quarrels (20:3) and rages (29:9). Coarse and hardened, he will not be broken (27:22). In his insolence, he mocks at sin (14:9). Such acts of folly reveal his wisdomless ways.

## The "Mocking" Fool

Teachers of wisdom also confronted the *letz*. This word means "scoffer" or "scorner." It is the term found in the familiar expression "seat of the scornful" in Psalm 1:1 (AV). The *letz* is a mocker. In modern Hebrew, the word for "clown," *letzan*, derives from the same root. The *letz* is "objectionable both to men and God. There is something of the highbrow in him: his folly savors of arrogant superiority."[12] Proud, sneering, disrupting, and deriding, the *letz* is a master of heckling. He ridicules and pokes fun at all that is good and holy. He is a debunker, an iconoclast, a troublemaker. He ignites controversy (Prov. 29:8), insults others (22:10), and acts haughtily (21:24). He knows all the answers; he turns his back to wisdom; he hates correction (9:7-8). The Lord, however, will not be outdone; he gets the last word with these repugnant "clowns," for he "mocks *[yalitz]* proud mockers *[letzim]*" (3:34). With his scurrilous, mocking attitude, the *letz* provided one of the greatest challenges for the sages of Israel.

## The "God-Denying" Fool

The final word for "fool" that we shall consider is *nabal*. It occurs but three times in the book of Proverbs, so we must look elsewhere in the Old Testament to grasp its meaning more fully. Perhaps the most pointed meaning of this word is found in Psalm 14:1: "The fool *[nabal]* says in his heart, 'There is no God.'" Such distorted thinking by this fool typifies that of the "wicked," of whom the psalmist says, "in all his thoughts there is no room for God" (Ps. 10:4). Devoid of spiritual perception, the *nabal* has a closed mind—at the moment—to the "God-idea." Thus the *nabal* is arrogant (Prov. 17:7); with an attitude that fails to reckon with God, he negates the foundational presupposition of Scripture, "In the beginning God . . ." (Gen. 1:1).

Isaiah indicates that this impiety of the *nabal* also includes moral de-

---

12. John Patterson, *The Book That is Alive* (New York: Charles Scribner's Sons, 1954), p. 58.

pravity (he is "busy with evil") and social insensitivity ("the hungry he leaves empty and from the thirsty he withholds water"—32:6). If one's theology is faulty, one's spiritual and social consciousness is blunted. And the reverse is equally true. Thus, God is not a live option to the *nabal.* We might call him a practical atheist. Through "vile deeds" (Ps. 14:1) the fool states, as it were, that the living reality of God is missing from human experience. But his viewpoint is spiritually defective. In his hubris and scorn he fails to acknowledge God for who he is. In doing so, the *nabal* declares himself to be a "God-denying" fool.

We have pointed out that wisdom is the daily ability to meet successfully the myriad of challenges along the road of life. Wisdom literature reveals that the Hebrew sages had one consuming desire in regard to fools of whatever stripe: to drive out folly and to teach wisdom. Whether young or old, fools left to their folly despised this call to wisdom. The wise men instructed their learners primarily in the practical realm, not the theoretical. Their concern was not with the world to come but with this world, with the here and now. They provided skillful advice in solving current problems common to the human condition.

Today's Church must remember this practical focus if it intends to grasp fully its Hebrew heritage. A good sermon is more than abstract theology or speculating about things to come. If it is to be authentic in the tradition of the Hebrew sages, it will be a pragmatic message that teaches people how to apply divine truth to daily life. For example, in the wisdom tradition of Israel use of the tongue is a major theme. Proverbs gives the practical principle: "A gentle answer turns away wrath, but a harsh word stirs up anger" (15:1). The New Testament letter of James, also a work containing wise sayings, states that "No man can tame the tongue. It is a restless evil, full of deadly poison" (3:8). "Out of the same mouth come praise and cursing. My brothers, this should not be" (3:10). In its proclamation of the wisdom of God today's Church must not lose sight of this emphasis upon clothing truth in loving deeds.

## The Hebrew View of Knowledge

Knowledge and wisdom are related concepts; both are rooted in God, and both share in the application of learning to life. In the Western world knowledge has often been limited in definition, confined to abstract concepts or theoretical principles. But in Hebrew thought to "know" something was to experience it, rather than merely to intellectualize it. To "know" someone was to share an intimate personal relationship with that one. Thus the Hebrew verb *yada,* "to know," means to encounter, experience, and share in an intimate way. So, a man may "know" a woman through sexual intercourse (Gen. 4:1, 17, 25), and a woman may "know" a man (Num. 31:17). In sum, in biblical Hebrew, the verb *yada* denotes "an act involving concern, inner engagement, dedication, or attachment to a person. It also means to have sympathy, pity, or affection for someone."[13]

The idea of knowledge thus embraced the whole human personality. A grasp of so much information was not enough; it also implied a response in the practical domain of life, in behavior and morals. For example, Proverbs 12:10 states literally that "a righteous man knows *[yode'a]* the life of his beast"; that is, he "cares for the needs of his animal" (NIV). The prophets also taught this idea of knowledge as action or involved concern for another. In Jeremiah 22:15-16, the Lord states through the prophet that to do "justice and righteousness" *(mishpat u-tzedaqah)* and to be concerned for the "cause of the poor and needy" is to "know" *(da'at,* a noun related to the verb *yada* but functioning verbally here) God. Thus, social action and good character result from a right relationship with God through his revelation. To "know" God is to walk faithfully in his ways and to live out the terms of his covenant. It included both the internalizing of truth and its outworking in the affairs of life. In short, for the Hebrew, to "know" was to "do."

Further evidence of the linking of both cognitive and affective elements in the sphere of knowledge is seen in a closer study of the verb *yada.* Though usually translated "to know," in seven passages the NIV translates it "to teach," "to instruct," or "to lead."[14] Of these passages, two deserve special consideration in that they signify a concrete action performed by the body rather than simply use made of the mind. In Judges 8:16, the verb *yada* means "to flail" someone with thorns and briers;[15] in 2 Chronicles 23:13, the same verb is used of singers with musical instruments who "lead" or "give signals for" songs of praise.[16] Therefore, "to know" or "to teach" went beyond mere intellectual activity; it was to act. It included down-to-earth activity or personal know-how applied to various realms and experiences of life.

As we have pointed out throughout this book, the Hebrew and Greek

13. Abraham J. Heschel, *The Prophets* (New York: Harper & Row, 1962), p. 57.

14. The NIV renders *yada* "to teach" in Deut. 4:9; Judg. 8:16; Job 32:7; Ps. 90:12; Prov. 9:9; "to instruct" in Isa. 40:13; and "to lead" in 2 Chr. 23:13.

15. See Robert C. Boling, *Judges,* Anchor Bible, Vol. 6A (Garden City, NY: Doubleday & Co., 1975), p. 157.

16. See Jacob M. Myers, *II Chronicles,* Anchor Bible, Vol. 13 (Garden City, NY: Doubleday & Co., 1965), p. 28.

attitudes toward life are not identical. In examining the concept of knowledge one of the main differences between these worldviews becomes perhaps most decisively pronounced. Norman Snaith has effectively summed up the issue:

> The object and aim of the Hebrew system is *da'ath elohim* (Knowledge of God). The object and aim of the Greek system is *gnothi seauton* (Know thyself). Between these two there is the widest possible difference. There is no compromise between the two on anything like equal terms. They are poles apart in attitude and method. The Hebrew system starts with God. The only true wisdom is Knowledge of God. 'The fear of God is the beginning of wisdom.' The corollary is that man can never know himself, what he is and what is his relation to the world, unless first he learn of God and be submissive to God's sovereign will. The Greek system, on the contrary, starts from the knowledge of man, and seeks to rise to an understanding of the ways and Nature of God through the knowledge of what is called 'man's higher nature'. According to the Bible, man has no higher nature except he be born of the Spirit.
>
> We find this approach of the Greeks nowhere in the Bible. The whole Bible, the New Testament as well as the Old Testament, is based on the Hebrew attitude and approach.[17]

## Education with a Difference

In comparison with other cultures, Jewish education was meant to be education with a difference. Accordingly, the great German Jewish leader Leo Baeck observed, "All education was directed to this end: to be different was the law of existence. . . . 'You shall be different, for I the Lord your God am different.'" Furthermore, he concluded, "The Jew was the great nonconformist, the great dissenter of history. That was the purpose of his existence."[18] Indeed, the world might describe the Jew as "the protestant of the centuries." On this point rests the quintessence of Jewish education: "the ideal of holiness, of separation from all other peoples in order to belong to God."[19]

In contrast, the Greek world did not understand education to be tied to holiness of life. Rather, teaching primarily involved the transference of

---

17. Norman H. Snaith, *The Distinctive Ideas of the Old Testament* (New York: Schocken Books, 1964), pp. 184-85.

18. Leo Baeck, *The Essence of Judaism* (New York: Schocken Books, 1948), p. 261.

19. William Barclay, *Educational Ideals in the Ancient World* (repr. Grand Rapids: Baker Book House, 1974), p. 47.

knowledge in the intellectual and technical areas, such as music, art, reading, or athletics. Thus, a teacher taught his pupil certain rules or procedures which, hopefully, would help to develop any aptitude that pupil might possess. If his reasoning powers needed development, then intellectual exercises were provided; if his body needed training, then sports and physical exercise were stressed; if greater manual dexterity was needed, then art or sculpturing might be taught.[20] In short, in secular Greek literature the *didáskalos* ("teacher") aimed mainly at developing the talents and potentialities of his pupil. Unlike the Jewish idea of teaching, Greek teaching did not usually concern itself with the development of the student's whole personality and his education in the deepest sense.[21]

Furthermore, in ancient Greek society, only the wealthy and leisure classes were enlightened through education.[22] Indeed, our English words *school* and *scholar* derive from the Greek verb *scholázō,* "to have leisure," "to have spare time," "to have nothing to do."[23] Accordingly, a "school" (Greek *scholé*) properly means "leisure employed in learning."[24] But we must emphasize that this Greek word has no counterpart in the Hebrew language. The ancient Jews considered it "idleness."[25] Judaism has always shunned the Greek idea that physical work is menial, hence only appropriate for slaves.[26] As William Chomsky has pointed out, "The Aristotelian lofty aloofness, which regarded manual labor as degrading, and those engaged in it as inferior people, who are unworthy and incapable of education, was utterly alien to the Hebrew mind."[27]

In contrast with the Greek concept of education, Jewish education

20. J. Leuba, "Teaching," in *A Companion to the Bible,* ed. J. J. Von Allmen (New York: Oxford University Press, 1958), p. 414.

21. K. Rengstorf, *Theological Dictionary of the New Testament* (Grand Rapids: William B. Eerdmans Publishing Co., 1964), 2:137.

22. Among the wealthy, the *paidagōgós,* "child-guide," "tutor" (cf. 1 Cor. 4:15; Gal. 3:24-25), played a special role. While his pupil was between 7 and 18, the *paidagōgós* accompanied the boy to school, carrying his books and seeing that he arrived there safely. He was also concerned with his conduct, teaching the boy all that was implied in the Greek term *eukosmía,* "good deportment, good manners, pleasantness of life." See William Barclay, *New Testament Words* (Philadelphia: Westminster Press, 1974), pp. 206-209.

23. Henry G. Liddell and Robert Scott, *A Greek-English Lexicon,* ed. Henry S. Jones (Oxford: Oxford University Press, 1940), p. 1747.

24. Among the meanings of *scholé,* Liddell and Scott (ibid.) give these: "leisure, spare time, ease"; "that in which leisure is employed"—especially a learned discussion or lecture; "a group to whom lectures were given, school."

25. Morris Kertzer, *What Is a Jew?* (New York: Collier Books, 1960), p. 50. It should also be noted that Liddell and Scott (ibid.) give "idleness" as one of the meanings of *scholé.*

26. See Abba Hillel Silver, *Where Judaism Differed* (New York: Macmillan Co., 1956), pp. 64-67.

27. William Chomsky, "The Dawn of Jewish Education," p. 26.

was for all people and concerned the whole person. A careful study of the biblical materials reveals that in the majority of instances teaching had to do primarily with the communication of the Law or will of the Lord by God himself, by the father of the family, or by a religious leader within the community. The aim of the Jewish teacher was not so much to develop certain intellectual or practical faculties in his disciple but rather to summon his learner to submit to the authority of the divine message of the Scripture upon which he was commenting. Here the Jew's whole personality is involved; to be taught called for radical obedience to that higher divine reality outside oneself.[28] To sum up this point, we may state the contrast no clearer than this: "The Greeks learned in order to comprehend. The Hebrews learned in order to revere."[29]

## The Sweetness of Learning

One of the most frequently quoted biblical texts dealing with education is Proverbs 22:6: "Train a child in the way he should go, and when he is old he will not turn from it." The Hebrew verb translated "train" is *hanakh*. The Old Testament use of this word deserves particular comment in that *hanakh* has become part of modern Hebrew terminology for learning. In modern Hebrew, the word *hinukh* means "education," and a *mehannekh* is an "educator."

In the Old Testament the verb *hanakh* and its derivatives occur mainly in contexts suggesting the sense of "to begin, initiate, inaugurate."[30] For example, the root is used for the formal opening of a building (e.g., Solomon's Temple, 1 Kgs. 8:63), for an initiation gift for an altar (Num. 7:10), and for the time one starts to live in a new house (Deut. 20:5). Since cult sacrifices, consecration rites, or prayers were often connected with the inauguration or formal opening of a structure, the meaning "to dedicate" eventually became extended to *hanakh* (see English translations of the above passages). This rendering, though not inherent in the root itself, accounts for *Hanukkah* being translated in John 10:22 as "Feast of Dedication."[31] Following

---

28. J. Leuba, "Teaching," p. 414.

29. Abraham J. Heschel, *Insecurity of Freedom*, p. 41.

30. See S. C. Reif, "Dedicated to Hnkh," *Vetus Testamentum* 22 (1972): 495-501. See also Victor P. Hamilton, *"hānak,"* in *Theological Wordbook of the Old Testament*, ed. R. Laird Harris, et al., 1:301-302.

31. The Hebrew noun *hanukkah* is properly a rite of inauguration, an event often associated with joyful celebration and sacrifice. Thus the word is most often used in reference to the ceremony of "dedication" or "consecration" of some structure. The origin of the Jewish holiday Hanukkah goes back to the 25th of the month Kislev, 165 B.C., when the Maccabees rededicated the Temple after Antiochus IV Epiphanes had desecrated it.

this apparent root meaning of "begin," the NEB renders the first part of Proverbs 22:6: "Start a boy on the right road" (cf. NIV margin, "Start").

In practice, over the centuries, however, it is evident that the Jewish community understood *hanakh* as derived from a different root. The verb *hanakh* has customarily been linked with a root meaning "rub the palate or gums"; hence the cognate *hekh*, "palate, roof of the mouth, gums."[32] The Semitic scholar T. H. Gaster states that the original meaning is suggested by the Arab custom of immediately smearing date juice on the gums and palates of newborn children. He also points out that Calvin, the sixteenth-century Reformer, indicates that the Jews of his time used to apply honey in a similar way.[33]

Whatever the etymology of *hanakh*, the custom of using honey deserves special mention in any study of Jewish education. Rabbinic tradition informs us that it was the Jewish practice to use honey in a special ceremony on the first day of school. The young child was shown a slate which had written on it the letters of the alphabet, two verses of Scripture (Lev. 1:1; Deut. 33:4), and one other sentence: "The Law will be my calling." The teacher next read these words to the child, and the child repeated them back. Then his slate was coated with honey, which he promptly licked off, being reminded of Ezekiel, who said after eating the scroll, "I ate it; and it tasted as sweet as honey in my mouth" (Ezek. 3:3). After this ceremony, the child was given sweet cakes to eat with Bible verses from the Law written on them.[34]

Why did the rabbis tie study and honey together? The answer appears to be due, at least in part, to the linguistic connection they made between the use of *hekh* ("palate, gums") and *hanakh* ("to educate") in certain biblical texts. The rabbis found *hekh* in passages comparing the sweetness of honey to the sweetness of the wisdom and words of God which one spiritually ingests. Two passages are of special note: "Eat honey, my son, for it is good; honey from the comb is sweet to your taste *[hekh]*. Know also that wisdom is sweet to your soul" (Prov. 24:13-14a); "How sweet are your words to my taste *[hekh]*, sweeter than honey to my mouth!" (Ps. 119:103). In addition, the Midrash Rabbah states that the study of Torah "is compared to milk and honey: just as these are sweet throughout, so are the words of the Torah, as it says, *Sweeter also than*

32. Brown, Driver, and Briggs, *Hebrew and English Lexicon of the Old Testament*, p. 335.

33. Theodor H. Gaster, *Customs and Folkways of Jewish Life* (New York: William Sloane Associates Publishers, 1955), p. 14.

34. For further details of this procedure see William Barclay, *Educational Ideals in the Ancient World*, pp. 12-13.

*honey* [Ps. 19:10]" (Song of Songs Rabbah 1:2, 3). Thus, in the rabbis' view, education came to involve the task of causing people to enjoy the sweetness of studying divine truth.

One other major point is in order before leaving Proverbs 22:6, "Train a child in the way he should go." Today, this text is frequently taken to be a command directed to parents, an exhortation for them to instruct their child in the teaching of Scripture and in the way of godly living. Although the Bible gives a mandate for parental instruction of children,[35] the above proverb does not appear to be one of those texts.

The Hebrew of Proverbs 22:6 is *hanokh la-na'ar al-pi darko*, literally "Train [start] a child according to his [the child's] way." There is a great difference between the training of a child according to the *child's* way (i.e., encouraging him to start on the road that is right for him), and training him according to a way chosen, prescribed, and imposed by the parents. The former is in keeping with the child's unique God-given bent, disposition, talents, and gifts. It is considerate of the uniqueness of the child; it does not treat all developing personalities the same. As Derek Kidner has correctly observed, since the training prescribed in the verse is "according to the child's way," this verse implies "respect for his individuality and vocation."[36] In short, "the instruction of youth, the education of youth, ought to be conformed to the nature of youth."[37]

The above translation and interpretation put the onus on the child to choose the right path. It is one thing for a parent to encourage, nurture, guide, and inform a child so that the child *himself* is prepared to choose the path that is right for him; it is something else for a parent to choose that path for the child. This point is the crux to understanding this verse. Again, we must emphasize that this rendering does not negate the parents' role as teachers of biblical tradition. But it does provide some additional insight into the Hebrew educational process, which, parenthetically, corresponds well with certain modern schools of progressive education. The "training" process begins by seeking to conform the subject matter and

35. See Deut. 4:9; 6:7; 11:19; Ps. 78:5-6; Prov. 1:8; Eph. 6:4.

36. Derek Kidner, *Proverbs*, Tyndale Old Testament Commentaries (Downers Grove, IL: InterVarsity Press, 1964), p. 147.

37. Franz Delitzsch *Proverbs*, trans. M. G. Easton (repr. Grand Rapids: William B. Eerdmans Publishing Co., 1976), 2:86. Walter C. Kaiser, Jr., expands this point further: "It [instruction] ought to regulate itself according to the stage of life, evidence of God's unique calling of the child and the manner of life for which God is singling out the child. This does not give the child a carte blanche to pick and choose what he or she wishes to learn. It does, however, recognize that the training children receive must often be as diverse and unique as the number of children God has given to us" (*Hard Sayings of the Old Testament* [Downers Grove, IL: InterVarsity Press, 1988], pp. 180-81).

teaching methods to the particular personality, needs, grade level, and stage in life of the child. (The word *na'ar,* "child," in Proverbs 22:6 does not necessarily mean infant or small boy; its more than two hundred occurrences in the Old Testament reveal a wide range of meanings from childhood to maturity.) Thus, the ability of a "child" to exercise more and more his individual freedom by personal choice—albeit one informed by his parents—is certainly not ruled out.

By way of application, the above understanding of Proverbs 22:6 places a special responsibility upon every parent. The parent must carefully observe each child and seek to provide opportunities for each child's creative self-fulfillment. In addition, the parent must be sensitive to the direction in life to which the child would naturally conform. For it is only by walking in *that* path that the child will come to realize his God-given potential and find his highest fulfillment. Elizabeth O'Connor effectively grasps how this proverb may apply: "Every child's life gives forth hints and signs of the way that he is to go. The parent that knows how to meditate, stores these hints and signs away and ponders over them. We are to treasure the intimations of the future that the life of every child gives to us so that, instead of unconsciously putting blocks in his way, we help him to fulfill his destiny. This is not an easy way to follow. Instead of telling our children what they should do and become, we must be humble before their wisdom, believing that in them and not in us is the secret that they need to discover."[38] This is a tall order. But when parents see that their responsibility is primarily to facilitate, to teach the *child* to choose the right path, only then will the child be enabled to "fulfill his destiny." And herein lies an important educational key to making learning a sweet and palatable adventure.

## Hebraic Insights on the Task of Teaching

The Hebrew Bible uses a variety of terms for describing or characterizing those whose task it is to impart wisdom and knowledge. We shall consider some of the more important terms in order to gain further insight into the different roles and responsibilities of the teacher. What was true of teachers in Bible times is equally true today. In this section we will also focus upon how this material may apply as a brief outline of some of the duties incumbent upon Christian teachers.

38. Elizabeth O'Connor, *Eighth Day of Creation* (Waco, TX: Word Books, 1971), p. 18.

## Edifying the Learner

The Hebrew verb *ra'ah* means "to tend" or "to feed the flock." The noun *ro'eh*, "shepherd," derives from this verb and occurs over sixty times. God is the *ro'eh* of his people (Ps. 23:1). Jeremiah uses this term for the leaders that God will give to instruct Israel when the people return to him: "Then I will give you shepherds *[ro'im]* after my own heart, who will lead you with knowledge and understanding" (3:15). In Proverbs 10:21 (NEB), the verb *ra'ah* is translated "to teach": "The lips of a good man teach many." This term suggests the edification, care, and guidance that one who would impart knowledge must have for his flock. But it also implies the need to provide food and nourishment for growth.

In the New Testament, the office of "pastor" is literally that of "shepherd" (Greek *poimēn*), and embraces two roles in one—pastor-teacher (Eph. 4:11). Much so-called teaching today is little more than jokes, drivel, and human-interest stories. Good teaching has solid content and substance. Like shepherds, teachers must spend more time feeding and sustaining the learner. In the Hebraic view, teaching and nourishment go together.

## Explaining Ideas

A second Hebrew verb, *bin,* comes from a Semitic root meaning "distinguish, separate." A cognate is the Hebrew preposition *ben,* "between."[39] In most contexts the verb *bin* is translated "to understand, discern, distinguish." But it is also rendered "teach" or "instruct" in several passages,[40] including 1 Chronicles 25:8, where the participle is used as a noun, "teacher," in the expression "young and old alike, teacher *[mebim]* as well as student."

Behind this word is the idea of separating, evaluating, or distinguishing one thing from another, in the sense of taking an idea or argument apart. It often carries the nuance of being able to think critically by explaining something. Hence the verb *bin* in Daniel 8:16 means "to explain," as Gabriel tells Daniel the meaning of a vision. A teacher has the ability to separate and explain issues and to solve problems. In Hebrew education, one of the roles of the teacher was to bring understanding, as well as knowledge, to his students. He taught them to think by evaluating arguments and sorting out the questions.

39. For a discussion of *bin,* see Helmer Ringgren, *Theological Dictionary of the Old Testament,* trans. John T. Willis, rev. ed. (Grand Rapids: William B. Eerdmans Publishing Co., 1977), 2:99-107.

40. Note 2 Chr. 35:3 and Neh. 8:9.

In this connection we would do well to ponder Heschel's thought-provoking words regarding modern education: "We evaluate the student by his ability to answer questions rather than to understand problems. Cribs and ponies become a major source of edification." He concludes by calling for a reverse of the traditional Socratic method: "The truth, however, is that the valid test of a student is his ability to ask the right questions. I would suggest that we evolve a new type of examination paper, one in which the answers are given—the questions to be supplied by the students."[41]

## Impressing the Mind

One of the more graphic words translated "to teach" is the verb *shanan.* It appears to derive from a root meaning "sharpen, whet." The Hebrew noun *shen,* "tooth," also derives from this root, giving force to the idea "to be sharp," "to pierce," or "to prick." *Shanan* is used of sharp instruments such as swords (Deut. 32:41) and arrows (Isa. 5:28); in Psalm 73:21 it is translated "to feel sharply stabbed" (in the kidneys, i.e., to be "pricked in heart" [RSV]). In the well-known prayer called the Shema (see chapter eight above), *shanan* is translated "to impress," that is, to teach diligently: "Impress them [God's words] on your children" (Deut. 6:7).

For the teacher God's Word is to be an instrument which "cuts" or "pierces" as he drills his points home to his pupils. The very finest points of Scripture are to be imprinted upon the life of the learner. In this vein, the writer of the letter to the Hebrews states, "For the word of God is living and active. Sharper than any two-edged sword, it penetrates even to dividing soul and spirit, joints and marrow" (Heb. 4:12). Biblical teaching—if it is to be in the Hebraic mode—will make points and impress them firmly on the mind.

## Giving Guidance

The word *torah,* commonly translated "law," derives from the verb *yarah,* "to cast, throw, shoot." The word *yarah* is frequently used for the "shooting" of arrows (1 Sam. 20:36-37), and its plural participial form *(morim)* is translated "archers," literally "the ones who shoot" (1 Sam. 31:3). In time, *yarah* took on the extended meaning "to teach," as is attested in more than forty Old Testament passages. In addition, of special note is the noun *moreh,* "teacher" (Gen. 12:6; Isa. 30:20), also from the same root.

The historical development of the term *yarah* suggests that, like an

41. Abraham J. Heschel, *Insecurity of Freedom,* pp. 46-47.

archer, a teacher has something to shoot out or project, guiding it toward a specific target. He has an aim and a goal. Accordingly, sometimes *yarah* is translated "to direct" or "to point out," as in showing one the way (providing directions) to a specific place (e.g., Goshen, Gen. 46:28). Hence, *torah* in many contexts properly means "direction, instruction, teaching" (see our discussion above in chapter eleven). The Torah "points out" by giving guidance and direction for life. The teacher must project God's teaching with sufficient precision so as to direct his students toward their destination on the road of life. As it is written, "I will instruct you and teach [the verb *yarah*] you in the way you should go" (Ps. 32:8).

## Training and Disciplining

The most common Hebrew term translated "to teach" is the verb *lamad.* In nearly fifty passages it is rendered "teach," while in other contexts it is often translated "learn." The basic meaning of *lamad* is "get accustomed to," "exercise in," or "train." The training or teaching often involves specific content or a particular subject such as song (Deut. 31:19), warfare (Isa. 2:4), commandments (Deut. 4:5), or a foreign language (Dan. 1:4).

Early in the historical development of *lamad* the term seems to have conveyed the idea of "to practice" or "to discipline." In this connection, a forceful, visual reminder to every Hebrew student that learning requires discipline is found in the Hebrew alphabet: the letter *l* is named *lamed,* and it is formed in the shape of a goad used for urging or prodding the one being trained. Indeed, the Hebrew word for "oxgoad," *malmad,* an instrument fitted with a pin or nail, means literally "the thing which teaches" (see Judg. 3:31). God's people, Israel, is called a "trained *[melummadah]* heifer" (Hos. 10:11).

Toward the close of the Old Testament period, the term *talmid* was used for a "scholar" in the sense of a "pupil" or "student" (1 Chr. 25:8). During the rabbinic period, the teacher of the Law was known as the *talmid,* and his pupils or apprentices as the *talmidim.* These pupils underwent rigorous training at the feet of the rabbi discipling them. The Oral Law, a large compendium of Jewish learning that became codified between A.D. 200 and 500, is known as the *Talmud*—literally "learning" or "study."

All training, study, and teaching requires discipline. Accordingly, the book of Proverbs advocates use of the rod as part of ancient Hebrew training: "He who spares the rod hates his son, but he who loves him is careful to discipline him" (Prov. 13:24; also see 22:15; 23:14). During their sojourn of four hundred years in Egypt, the Israelites had to be impressed by the Egyptian emphasis upon discipline in learning. In the Egyptian language, the word *sebayet* may be translated either "teaching" or "punishment." In the pictographic Egyptian language, part of the word "to teach" is the picture of a man hitting with a stick. An Egyptian inscription from the biblical period records the words of a teacher in Egypt: "The ear of the boy is on his back, and he listens when he is beaten."[42] Certainly few Westerners today would advocate beating as an important component in the learning process. Nevertheless, discipline is essential to all learning; and the centrality of this point throughout Hebrew tradition must not become lost in our modern world.

## Education in New Testament Times

During the intertestamental period the institution of the synagogue emerged. In addition, newly established scribal schools gave their attention to studying, interpreting, and copying the Scriptures (cf. Ezra 7:10; Neh. 8:8). Before the New Testament period began the scribes held a recognized position as the official teachers of Israel's spiritual heritage.

The first use of the word *school* occurs in Sirach (or Ecclesiasticus; ca. 180 B.C.), a manual of ethical maxims and the oldest book in the Apocrypha. Sirach invited students to come and learn in his *bet midrash*, "house of study" (Sir. 51:23). Other scholars established their own "houses" for instruction in the Law. The synagogue gradually became the center for study in the community, however, and following New Testament times it became known as the "house of study."

The Jerusalem Talmud credits the Pharisees with establishing the first district school system for youths. Simeon ben Shetach (ca. 75 B.C.) enacted that children should attend school, literally *bet sepher,* "house of the book" (Jerusalem Talmud, Ketubot 8:11). In this expression "book" obviously means the Torah. The next significant educational development came under Joshua ben Gamla, high priest about A.D. 65. The Babylonian Talmud indicates that he was responsible for appointing teachers for boys six to seven years of age in every province and town of Palestine (Baba Batra 21a).

The Jewish historian Josephus (late 1st century A.D.) indicates that education was taken most seriously: "Above all we pride ourselves on the education of our children."[43] Up to the start of their teen years youths at-

---

42. Quoted in *Everyday Life in Bible Times* (Washington, D.C.: National Geographic Society, 1967), p. 111.
43. Josephus, *Against Apion* 1.12 (60).

tended elementary school, an institution attached to the synagogue.[44] The earliest years were spent in the *bet sepher,* where the reading of the written Law was taught. The next stage of schooling was the *bet talmud,* "house of learning," where by the age of ten study of the Oral Law (later codified in the Mishnah) began (cf. Mishnah, Abot 5:21). The Jerusalem Talmud states that before A.D. 70, 480 synagogues existed in Jerusalem, each with its own *bet sepher* and *bet talmud* (Megillah 3:1).

Around the age of thirteen, gifted and diligent pupils might continue their studies in their spare time at a *bet midrash,* "house of study." These "academies" were conducted by teachers of the Law, some of considerable repute (c.g., Hillel and Shammai). The substance of many of the discussions held in the academies was eventually reduced to writing and used by the rabbis in the formulation of the Talmud.

The biblical curriculum for the earliest phase of schooling *(bet sepher)* seems to have consisted in the Shema (Deut. 6:4-9; 11:13-21), the law of the tzitzit (or zizith, Num. 15:37-41), the Hallel (Pss. 113–118), the Creation Story (Gen. 1–5), and the essence of the levitical law (Lev. 1–8).[45] It was customary to begin biblical study with the book of Leviticus. The Midrash Rabbah states that children begin with Leviticus rather than Genesis "because young children are pure, and the sacrifices are pure; so let the pure come and engage in the study of the pure" (Leviticus Rabbah 7:3). Other scholars suggest Leviticus was used because in Bible times the priests were teachers, and they needed to acquaint their own sons with the Torah that would deal with their future priestly service around the Temple.[46] A beautiful tradition later developed in the *heder,* the elementary Hebrew school, conducted in Eastern Europe. When a child was taken for the first time to meet his teacher and classmates, he was wrapped in a prayer shawl like a scroll.[47]

During New Testament times the landscape was also dotted with itinerant teachers and their disciples. Jesus was one such teacher in the scribal tradition (cf. Matt. 13:52). The Gospels refer to Jesus as *didáskalos,* "teacher," forty-one times and as "rabbi" sixteen times. Like a scribe, he teaches in synagogues (Mark 1:21), sits to teach (Luke 5:3), and expounds Scripture (Luke 4:16-21). In Jesus' day the word *rabbi* was a popular term

---

44. For a useful, scholarly discussion of first-century schooling, see S. Safrai, "Education and the Study of the Torah," in *The Jewish People in the First Century,* ed. S. Safrai and M. Stern (Philadelphia: Fortress Press, 1976), 2:945-70.

45. William Barclay, *Educational Ideals in the Ancient World,* p. 42.

46. S. Safrai, *The Jewish People in the First Century,* p. 951.

47. See Abraham J. Heschel, *The Earth Is the Lord's* (New York: Harper & Row, 1950), p. 47.

of honor meaning "my master," "my great one." Only later (2nd century), at the time of Johanan ben Zakkai, with the rite of ordination (the laying on of hands), did "rabbi" become an official title and term of formal address (see chapter six above).

The Mishnah states that no one should use the Torah as a "spade" for the digging of wealth (Abot 4:5). Hence, teachers and sages are often linked with various occupations and trades. These include that of woodchopper (Hillel), surveyor (Shammai), blacksmith (Joshua), tanner (Ishmael), and water-carrier (Huna) (cf. Abot 2:2). Paul's activity as a leather-worker (Acts 18:3) reflects this custom of not receiving payment for religious teaching (cf. Acts 20:34; 2 Cor. 11:7-8; 1 Thess. 2:9; 2 Thess. 3:8).

## Everyone a Student

We have pointed out that the quest for learning held center stage in the Jewish community from early in the biblical period. Postbiblical Judaism later built upon this foundation from the Hebrew Bible. Accordingly, the Mishnah asks, "Who is wise? He who learns from all men" (Abot 4:1). The Mishnah also instructs, "Let your house be a meeting-place for the sages, and sit in the very dust at their feet, and thirstily drink in their words" (Abot 1:4). It further states, "If you have learned much, do not think highly of yourself for it, since for this you were created" (Abot 2:8). In this vein, Jacob Neusner observes aptly, "Other traditions had their religious virtuosi whose virtuosity consisted in knowledge of literary tradition; but few held, as does Judaism, that everyone must become such a virtuoso."[48]

The great twelfth-century philosopher Maimonides reflected this rabbinic attitude that every Jew should be devoted to Torah study: "Every man in Israel is obliged to study the Torah, whether he is firm of body or a sufferer from ill health, whether a young man or of advanced age with his strength abated. Even a poor man who is supported by charity and obliged to beg at doors, and even one with wife and children to support, is obliged to set aside a period for Torah study by day and by night, as it is said: Thou shalt meditate therein day and night."[49]

This community-wide dedication to learning advocated by Maimonides is presently modeled in America in a remarkable way by the

48. Jacob Neusner, *The Way of Torah: An Introduction to Judaism* (Encino, CA: Dickenson Publishing Co., 1974), p. 44.
49. Cited from Theodore Friedman, "Study," in *Encyclopedia Judaica* (Jerusalem: Keter Publishing House Ltd., 1971), 15:456.

Hasidic community. Among the Hasidim in Brooklyn, New York, boys begin their study of Hebrew at age three. In their fourth year, they start learning the Torah. Here is a snapshot view of their ongoing rigorous training: "For an adolescent, the Torah is all. Six days a week, boys rise at 3 or 3:30 in the morning to go to the *mikveh* [the ritual bath], are in school from 5:30 or 6 a.m. until nearly sundown, and then return to synagogue. After supper, they return to synagogue for the nightly study session. On Saturday, the sabbath, they are in synagogue all day."[50]

Large segments of today's Church may well be amazed at this contemporary Hasidic example of commitment to learning. But the Church should be inspired to rethink its commitment to a program of Christian education which is serious in its goals of learning. Too often the Church's attitude toward learning amounts to little more than passive satisfaction with its seemingly superficial Sunday scanning of the Scriptures.

As an outgrowth of Judaism, the New Testament supports the idea that both learning and teaching should be the concern of every Christian. The Great Commission (Matt. 28:18-20) is a command incumbent upon the entire Church. It includes both a responsibility—to "make disciples of all nations"—and a method—"teaching them" to obey all that the Lord commanded. In this passage, the term "make disciples" (Greek *mathēteúsate*) is grammatically an imperative, stressing the obligation entailed. The centrality of learning to New Testament thought is also borne out by the fact that the noun *mathētēs,* "disciple" (from the same Greek root as above), occurs nearly 250 times.

The making of disciples results in the training of others to teach. Good teaching produces a chain reaction. The task Paul outlined to Timothy embraces four groups of teachers: "And the things you have heard me say in the presence of many witnesses entrust to reliable men who will also be qualified to teach others" (2 Tim. 2:2). This same Timothy from infancy knew the "holy Scriptures," that is, the Old Testament (2 Tim. 3:15). Doubtless, Timothy's knowledge of Scripture in his early years, and his "sincere faith" that grew from this knowledge, came largely through the chain of godly family teachers to which he was linked: his grandmother Lois and mother Eunice (see 2 Tim. 1:5).

The New Testament states clearly that a special gift of teaching has been given to *some* within the Church, for teaching is listed among the *charísmata,* "gifts" (see Rom. 12:7; 1 Cor. 12:28). Further, as alluded to earlier, the New Testament combines the office of pastor with that of

50. Steven Isaacs, "Hasidim of Brooklyn," *The Washington Post,* Sunday, Feb. 17, 1974, p. B4.

teacher (Eph. 4:11).[51] The pastor-teacher has a rich Hebraic background to inform this pattern of ministry. Indeed, when Paul states that the Lord's servant must be "able to teach" (2 Tim. 2:24), he is drawing on a tradition that extends back to the patriarchs themselves.

Reflecting on biblical scholarship in the history of his own Jewish people, Leo Baeck confronts the modern Church with these poignant words:

> When men realized that the teaching of God was no heritage that one accepts passively but rather a heritage that has to be won, they began to see this relationship to the Bible as a religious obligation. It became a supreme commandment to "study," to explore the Scriptures. To explore means to consider the Bible as a challenge rather than a gift. . . . The duty to "explore" requires further thinking; each end becomes a new beginning and each solution a new problem. . . . Hence Judaism's desire to comprehend the ancient word ever afresh . . . the feeling of never having finished with it but ever pursuing it in the search for its true meaning.[52]

Once today's Church is fully aware of the vast importance of learning, it too will realize that it cannot afford to be passive about the matter. Each new generation of Christians must renew its commitment in action to personal rediscovery of the great historical sources of the faith.

## Teaching Methods and Priorities

### *By Word of Mouth, Not Books*

The first Bible to come off the printing press was the Gutenberg in 1453. Since scrolls had to be laboriously copied by hand—it took a scribe the greater part of a year to copy just the five books of Moses—they were not widely available during the biblical period. Therefore, the Old Testament emphasizes that teaching was conducted by word of mouth: "Tell your son" (Exod. 13:8); also, "Talk about them when you sit at home" (Deut. 6:7).

The lesson consisted entirely of repetition. It should be remembered that the word *mishneh,* a term which refers to the Oral Law, means "repetition, review." The Talmud has much to say about the need for reviewing one's lesson. "He who studies the Torah and does not review is like one who plants and does not harvest" (Sanhedrin 99a). And again, "He

---

51. I have further elaborated on this point in "A Question for Rabbis, Pastors, and Teachers," *Christianity Today* (Feb. 14, 1969): 5-7.
52. Leo Baeck, *The Essence of Judaism,* pp. 24-25.

who repeated his chapter a hundred times is not to be compared with him who repeated it a hundred and one times" (Hagigah 9b). Peoples of the ancient Near East have always relied a good deal on oral tradition. The Old Testament itself is a collection of early Hebrew sources which were meant to be read *aloud*. It is quite likely that much of it was originally handed down by word of mouth. Often the traditions were passed along in a melodious manner—words were chanted or at least rhythmically recited.[53]

## Memorizing the Lesson

We live in a day when educators tend to de-emphasize and even depreciate the importance of memorization. Rather, they stress concepts, principles, and relationships. In Bible times, however, the mechanics of learning required that the teacher listen to the student repeat the lesson back to him verbatim. The most important quality for being a good scholar was a trained and retentive memory.[54]

The importance of memorization can be well illustrated by the writing of the Gospels. A number of years elapsed—many scholars think two decades or more—between the death of Jesus and the writing of the first Gospel. During this time the early Church (primarily Jews at this point) kept alive and preserved many of the sayings of Jesus by means of the Jews' keenly trained memories. These sayings of Jesus (and the record of his deeds) were subject to the scrutiny of various independent eyewitnesses. It is often asked whether the Hebrew reliance on memory for the transmission of tradition necessarily led to wide-scale corruption of the accounts being handed down. To the contrary: the late William Foxwell Albright, for many years doyen of American biblical archeologists, argued convincingly for the reliability and trustworthiness of oral tradition. He stated summarily that "writing was used in antiquity largely as an aid or guide to memory, not as a substitute for it."[55]

The Jewish people employed various aids to memory. About one-third of the Hebrew Bible is poetry. Poetry's extensive use of parallelism, balance of thought, and figures of speech made the memorization of collections like the Psalms much easier. In addition, teachings were tightly and tersely worded. It should not seem incredible that those chosen for the highest order of Christian clergy in the fifth century A.D. were required to

53. Birger Gerhardsson, *The Origins of the Gospel Traditions,* trans. Gene J. Lund (Philadelphia: Fortress Press, 1979), p. 21.

54. William Barclay, *Educational Ideals in the Ancient World,* p. 40.

55. William F. Albright, *From the Stone Age to Christianity,* 2nd ed. (Garden City, NY: Doubleday & Co., 1957), p. 64.

commit to memory all one hundred fifty Psalms. One aid to memory is the so-called alphabetic acrostic, a section of Scripture structured by using the twenty-two letters of the Hebrew alphabet as the first letters of the verses. Examples of such acrostics are Psalm 119, which focuses on the Law of the Lord; Proverbs 31:10-31, on the wife of noble character; and most of the book of Lamentations, a dirge that concerns the destruction of Jerusalem.

As further aids to memory, historical poems and songs such as the Song of the Crossing of the Red Sea (Exod. 15) and the Song of Deborah (Judg. 5) were set to music and accompanied by dancing to the tune of musical instruments.[56] Repetition, alliteration, tautology, onomatopoeia, and wordplays were also widely used as teaching techniques (see chapter nine above).

## Scheduled and Spontaneous Learning

Rabbinic literature emphasizes that each member of the community should be diligent to maintain a study schedule. This was a mitzvah, a religious duty. Indeed, the rabbis taught that in the life to come, when a person is led in to be judged, one of the first questions that person must answer is, "Did you fix times for learning?" (Babylonian Talmud, Shabbat 31a). In more precise terms this question means: "Have you set yourself regular periods to study the Torah?" [57] Though set times were doubtless arranged throughout the biblical period, they became more important during the talmudic period. This study might involve a scheduled time at home with one's child: "Rabbi Hiyya did not eat breakfast until he reviewed the previous day's lesson with the child and added another verse" (Babylonian Talmud, Kiddushin 30a). But the synagogue became the communal study hall where young and old alike engaged in the study of Torah and Talmud. The rabbis considered the synagogue's role as a house of study more important than its role as a house of prayer.

Spontaneous times of teaching are reflected throughout the Bible, particularly in the ministry of Jesus of Nazareth, an itinerant teacher. Early in Hebrew tradition, at the time of the Exodus, Moses spoke of the need for the Hebrew people to be prepared for spontaneous question-and-answer teaching times within their own families: "In the days to come, when your son asks you, 'What does this mean?' say to him . . ."

---

56. William Chomsky, "The Dawn of Jewish Education," p. 22.

57. Nahum N. Glatzer, ed., *Hammer on the Rock: A Short Midrash Reader* (New York: Schocken Books, 1962), p. 102.

(Exod. 13:14). In short, each father had to be ready to give a haggadah (literally a "telling, narration, story") about the Exodus to his questioning son. This method of teaching is still beautifully dramatized today as part of the annual Passover Seder celebration (see chapter twelve above). In the New Testament, this spontaneous question-and-answer method of teaching is illustrated in Philip's encounter with the Ethiopian eunuch who was sitting in his chariot reading Isaiah 53 (Acts 8:26-40). The eunuch asks Philip, "Tell me, please, who is the prophet talking about, himself or someone else?" (v. 34). Philip then "explains" (cf. v. 31) the meaning of the Scripture (v. 35), and the eunuch responds by entering the waters of baptism (vv. 36-39).

## A Major Commitment of Time

Several years ago a rabbi commented to me that he was compelled to send his three teenage children out of state to attend a private Jewish day school: "My children need a minimum of twenty hours each week of study in the Bible, Jewish history, and Hebrew language. There is no place around here where they can get that." He concluded, "The best preventative against assimilation is a solid Jewish education."

There is no short-cut method to a sound education. If one wants to make spiritual training a priority, one must make a major commitment of time. Thus the psalmist says of the righteous man: "His delight is in the law of the LORD, and on his law he meditates day and night" (Ps. 1:2). The Qumran community, which produced the now famous Dead Sea Scrolls around the time of Jesus, made a very deep commitment of time for learning. According to the Manual of Discipline discovered at the community, the laws of Scripture had to be continuously studied, day and night, throughout the year. In order to accomplish this task, the membership was divided into three shifts. Thus, hundreds in the community were reading, studying, and worshiping all night long.

The Talmud records one scholar who told his students: "The words of Torah are firmly held [i.e., established] only by one who kills himself (in study) for it" (Berakhot 63b). In Judaism, one maintains self-respect through study. This unrelenting pursuit of wisdom by people of all ages was a vital part of the pre-Holocaust Jewish community of Eastern Europe. Consider this vivid description of these committed people:

> In almost every Jewish home in Eastern Europe, even in the humblest and the poorest, stood a bookcase full of volumes; proud and stately folio tomes together with shy, small-sized books. Books were neither an asylum for the frustrated nor a means for occasional edification. They were furnaces of

living strength, timeproof receptacles for the eternally valid coins of spirit. Almost every Jew gave of his time to learning, either in private study or by joining one of the societies established for the purpose. . . .

Poor Jews, whose children knew only the taste of "potatoes on Sunday, potatoes on Monday, potatoes on Tuesday," sat there like intellectual magnates. They possessed whole treasures of thought, a wealth of information, of ideas and sayings of many ages. When a problem came up, there was immediately a host of people, pouring out opinions, arguments, quotations. . . . The stomachs were empty, the homes barren, but the minds were crammed with the riches of Torah.[58]

## Visual Aids and Object Lessons

The Bible gives many examples of visual aids and concrete symbols which were effective tools in the learning process. When describing how covenants were made, the teacher could provide a vivid illustration. A covenant was a contract or agreement between two parties whereby each pledged to bind himself to the other with certain obligations and responsibilities. The covenant was usually sealed with some symbolic action, thus dramatizing the terms of the agreement. As we have previously pointed out, in Hebrew, "to make a covenant" is literally "to cut a covenant" *(karat berit)*. When God sealed his covenant with Abraham, animals were taken, cut in two, and the halves arranged opposite each other (Gen. 15:9-10). This was a covenant of blood. It dramatized in a moving way that the contract was inviolable. As a smoking firepot with a blazing torch (symbolizing God's presence) passed between the halves (v. 17), the blood served as an object lesson. In ancient Near Eastern covenants of this type, if either party went back on his word, his blood would be shed. The covenant partners were bound by blood. Thus covenant making was serious business; breaking the covenant could mean death for the offender.

Other covenants made use of a different kind of visual aid than the blood of an animal. Sometimes the hand was placed under the thigh so as to grasp the genitals (Gen. 24:2, 9). Since this vital area was the seat of reproductive power, to touch it in this formal manner might convey the threat that the offending party would become sterile or that his offspring would be destroyed. In any case, the servant Eliezer makes this gesture to Abraham as he is about to leave on a mission that will assure the patriarch of the descendants God had promised to him. This graphic act finds its counterpart in a Roman practice that provided the etymological root of our

58. Abraham J. Heschel, *The Earth Is the Lord's,* pp. 42-44.

English word "testify." A witness would take the preliminary oath with his hands clutching his own testicles.[59] Such gestures underscore the seriousness of the ancient concept of witnessing. More than reputation was at stake when one pledged his word about a matter. The very existence of one's children—and even grandchildren—was potentially in jeopardy.

The Passover provides another set of concrete symbols used since Bible times in the learning process. Each item on the Passover Seder table represents something from the life of tyranny that Jews experienced in Egypt. The matzot recalls the unleavened bread they ate before their hasty departure. The *maror* ("bitter herb") is a reminder of the bitterness of slavery. The *haroset*, a pasty mixture of nuts, cinnamon, apples, and wine, symbolizes the mortar used for the making of bricks. After Israel had come out of Egypt and entered the promised land, twelve stones were set up in the Jordan River (Josh. 4:20-23) as objects for teaching future generations that "Israel crossed the Jordan on dry ground."

In the New Testament period visual aids were also used. In his discourse on humility, Jesus took a little child and placed him in the midst of the disciples (Mark 9:36). In answering the question posed by Jews concerning paying taxes to Caesar, Jesus called for a coin and asked, "Whose portrait is this?" (Mark 12:13-17). Likewise, Paul employs a visual object lesson by relating believer's baptism to the burial and resurrection of Jesus (Rom. 6:4).

## Respect for the Word

The New Testament refers to the Hebrew Bible as the "sacred writings" or "holy Scriptures" (2 Tim. 3:15). They were considered sacred and worthy of respect because the prophets of old "spoke from God as they were carried along by the Holy Spirit" (2 Pet. 1:21). The Scriptures were upheld as God's Word; in them he had spoken. The most sacred cult object in ancient Israel was the *aron qodesh*, "holy ark." In it were stored the two tablets of the Law given to Moses on Sinai. Today, the holy ark of the synagogue is a cabinet which contains copies of the full Torah, the five books of Moses. When the ark is opened, the congregation rises to its feet in respect. In Bible times it was the custom to rise as the Torah was read (Neh. 8:5). Today, when the Torah is paraded throughout the congregation, it is the custom for congregants located near the aisle to touch their prayer

---

59. Daniel Polish, "Witnessing God After Auschwitz," in *Issues in the Jewish-Christian Dialogue: Jewish Perspectives on Covenant, Mission, and Witness*, ed. Helga Croner and Leon Klenichi (New York: Paulist Press, 1979), p. 134.

shawls to the Torah. The shawls are then brought to the lips in a gesture of love and honor. If a Torah scroll accidentally drops to the floor, those present are required to fast. God's Law brings life, so a Torah scroll is dressed as if it were a living person; it has a covering, a breastplate, and a crown. If a fire were to break out in the sanctuary of a synagogue, after saving all human lives, the very next items in priority for rescue are the sacred Torahs. When a Torah scroll becomes old or irreparably damaged, it is buried in a grave, like a human being.

The Bible is not just any book; it is the Book of Books. Today, educational programs in the Church must teach the sacredness of Holy Writ. One way to begin is by having the congregation stand for Scripture readings. The Bible is one of the main channels through which God's voice may be heard today. Christians must continue to think of new and creative ways to teach respect and honor for the Word of God.

## Music and Song

When Jacob's wife Leah had borne her fourth son, she said, "'This time I will praise the LORD.' So she named him Judah" (Gen. 29:35). Both the word *Judah* (Hebrew *Yehudah*) and the word *Jew* derive from the verb *yadah*, "to praise." Hebrew praise and prayer often involved music. The Psalms were poems written to be sung to musical accompaniment. So David writes, "I will give thanks to him *[ahodenu]* in song" (Ps. 28:7). The place of song is crucial to a correct understanding of Jewish prayer. As Heschel has observed, "Let us not misunderstand the nature of prayer, particularly in Jewish tradition. The primary purpose of prayer is not to make requests. The primary purpose is to praise, to sing, to chant. Because the essence of prayer is a song, and man cannot live without a song."[60] Holocaust survivor Elie Wiesel agrees that song is crucial: "Who is a Jew? A Jew is he—or she—whose song cannot be muted, nor can his or her joy be killed by the enemy . . . ever."[61]

Moses began his forty-year trek through the wilderness with a song of praise for God's deliverance at the Red Sea (Exod. 15). Forty years later Moses ended his ministry on the same note with another hymn of joy (Deut. 32). These songs were memorized by the Israelites and passed on to future generations. Why? Because "man cannot live without a song."

60. "A Conversation with Doctor Abraham Joshua Heschel," *The Eternal Light,* NBC/TV transcript (New York: National Broadcasting Company, 1973), p. 4.
61. Elie Wiesel, *Four Hasidic Masters* (Notre Dame, IN: University of Notre Dame Press, 1978), p. 95.

This is precisely what Moses taught all Israel after he had recited his final song while overlooking the promised land: "They are not just idle words for you—they are your life. By them you will live" (Deut. 32:47).

The Israelites learned of their history and traditions through music. After defeating the Canaanites, Deborah and Barak sang a song of praise (Judg. 5). David played the harp (1 Sam. 16:16-17; cf. Amos 6:5) and taught the men of Judah a "lament of the bow" (2 Sam. 1:17-27). A thousand and five songs are attributed to Solomon (1 Kgs. 4:32). Like other ancient Near Eastern love poetry, the Song of Songs was chanted from an early time within the covenant community. During the reign of King Hezekiah, in the Temple, a large choir was accompanied by those playing cymbals, harps, lyres, and trumpets (2 Chr. 29).

The New Testament shows an extensive use of music, reflecting the same Hebraic tradition. Luke records various songs of Jesus' birth. At Corinth, psalms were sung as part of the worship service (1 Cor. 14:26). These psalms had been taught and passed on from generation to generation as the heart of Jewish learning. Paul is able to instruct the Ephesian believers to draw on that same rich tradition when he commands, "Speak to one another with psalms, hymns and spiritual songs" (Eph. 5:19). In Revelation, the final book of the New Testament, we return to the Mosaic theme of deliverance (15:3-4). Here John depicts a heavenly scene where, with harps, the Song of Moses (Exod. 15) and the Song of the Lamb—a single song—are sung.

Much Christian music today seems shallow. It is not worship in the Hebrew tradition. It often focuses almost exclusively on human problems, experiences, and needs, rather than extolling and praising the greatness of God. Though the Hebrews did not eliminate the human dimension from their songs, their songs usually had motifs that inspired faith and deeper commitment to the teachings of God's truth. The Hebrews learned much of their knowledge of theology and Hebrew history from reciting in song the great redemptive acts of God. Today's Church would do well to rethink its concept of hymnology and music in the light of the songs of Scripture.

## Study as Worship

The question of motivation for learning has been a problem from time immemorial. People seek education for many worthy reasons: some desire to broaden horizons; others wish to develop skills; still others want to satisfy their intellectual curiosity. The Bible, however, teaches that study ought to be, above everything else, an act of worship,[62] one of the highest ways by which a person can glorify God. Again, it is important to emphasize that the Hebrew word *abodah* has a double meaning, embracing two actions that are normally viewed as mutually exclusive or contradictory to each other: work and worship. Thus, in Jewish tradition, "Study as well as prayer, is worship, like it called by the name of the service of the altar (*'abodah*)."[63] For this reason, in the Talmud, the synonym for "education" is "heavenly work."[64]

As a Pharisee, Paul was a learned product of Judaism, a man well versed in Jewish thought and biblical theology (see Phil. 3:4-6). Yet, as we mentioned earlier in this volume, Paul makes no distinction between the so-called sacred and secular areas of life. He taught—as his Hebrew forebears did—that all of life was God's domain of activity. Every detail of life, therefore, must be set aside and consecrated to the glory of God. So, Paul writes to the Corinthians, "whatever you do, do it all for the glory of God" (1 Cor. 10:31). He later writes to the Colossians, "whatever you do, whether in word or deed, do it all in the name of the Lord Jesus, giving thanks to God the Father through him" (3:17). As David Hubbard reminds us, "There is an intimate connection between work and worship, for to work is to give glory to God. . . . We [like the Hebrews] work with God's goods, and we use God's talents to perform that work, and we serve God's people through our work."[65]

Paul knew nothing of the teaching prevalent in some Christian circles today which claims that the Devil controls the minds of men, and therefore knowledge is sinful or at least suspect.[66] To the contrary, in every aspect of life the Christian is called to acknowledge the lordship of Christ and to recognize that something sacred is at stake. All of life must be seen as a unity (see chapter ten above). The commonplace activities, like studying, must be elevated to the realm of spiritual experience. Such is affirmed in the words of Paul: "For everything God created is good, and nothing is to be rejected if it is received with thanksgiving, for then it is consecrated by the word of God and prayer" (1 Tim. 4:4-5).

---

62. For a study of this theme based on the mishnaic tractate Abot and the New Testament see Benedict T. Viviano, *Study As Worship* (Leiden: E. J. Brill, 1978).

63. George Foot Moore, *Judaism in the First Centuries of the Christian Era* (Cambridge: Harvard University Press, 1927), 2:240; cf. 217ff.

64. See Abraham J. Feldman, *Contributions of Judaism to Modern Society* (New York: The Union of American Hebrew Congregations, n.d.), p. 18.

65. David A. Hubbard, *The Wisdom of the Old Testament*, Messiah College Occasional Papers, no. 3 (Grantham, PA: Messiah College, August, 1982), p. 23.

66. For an excellent critique of this unbiblical position, see Virginia R. Mollenkott, *Adamant & Stone Chips* (Waco, TX: Word Books, 1967), pp. 11-30.

The Hasidim have long taught—and rightly so—that a person worships and serves God not simply from the depths of his spirit or soul but with his body and mind as well.[67] In short, a person worships with his whole being. The Hasidim often cite two passages in support of this teaching: "I have set the LORD always before me" (Ps. 16:8), and "In all your ways acknowledge him" (Prov. 3:6). In this vein, Heschel, a rabbi of Hasidic ancestry, has poignantly observed: "Genuine reverence for the sanctity of study is bound to invoke in the pupils the awareness that study is not an ordeal but an act of edification; that the school is a *sanctuary,* not a factory; that study is *a form of worship.*"[68]

## "Guard It Well, for It Is Your Life"

In today's Church, excuses abound from the lips of adults as to why they have no set time for study. Some of the more common ones are these: "I'm too busy, but when I get the time. . . ." "I'm too old, and besides, it's for kids." "It's for scholars and teachers." "I'm not a bookworm; I'm a practical person." "I already have a college degree." "I'd rather watch TV; you can learn from it." "I went to Sunday school when I was young." "Education corrupts! I'd rather be a fool on fire than a scholar on ice!" Anyone proffering one of these excuses has yet to understand and take seriously the legacy of learning bequeathed to Christians through their Jewish roots.

The German Jewish theologian Franz Rosenzweig once compared modern Jewry to a diver in the ocean whose life is maintained by the previously stored oxygen he finds in his tank; once it is used up, he dies. Only by returning to the historical sources found in the Bible and its life-giving air can each new generation be sustained.[69] Or, using a different analogy, the Talmud states, "As the fishes in the sea immediately perish when they come out of the water, so do men perish when they separate themselves from the words of Torah" (Abodah Zarah 3b). Learning is no less optional for the Christian. Without it, he too will die.

In this chapter we have sought to offer correctives to many of the fallacies and myths that relate to the Christian and learning. But one final misconception remains. Heschel, a biblically wise Jewish scholar, brings it to our attention: "It is wrong to define education as *preparation* for life.

---

67. See Martin Buber, *Hasidim and Modern Man* (New York: Harper & Row, 1958), pp. 84-95.

68. Abraham J. Heschel, *Insecurity of Freedom,* p. 42.

69. Recounted in Leo Trepp, *Judaism: Development and Life* (Belmont, CA: Dickenson Publishing Co., 1966), p. 196.

Learning *is* life, a supreme experience of living, a climax of existence."[70] Learning is life, and life is for learning. Accordingly, a Christian has only two options. The first is to profess an identity with "the People of the Book" while remaining largely ignorant about what that identity entails. The other—and only viable—option is to dedicate oneself to learning, a life-sustaining adventure in worship. Then will be realized the inspired wisdom of the ancient Hebrew sage who taught, "Hold on to instruction, do not let it go, guard it well, for it is your life" (Prov. 4:13).

# UNDERSTANDING CHAPTER FOURTEEN

1. In Jewish tradition, why was the quest for knowledge one of the great desiderata of life? According to the Talmud, by what does the world exist?

2. In Bible times, what was the aim of learning?

3. From early in Israel's history, who bore chief responsibility for the instruction of the children?

4. Who was responsible for numbering the commandments at 613? Were there more negative commandments or positive?

5. What was the fundamental goal of Jewish parental instruction? What was the secondary goal of education within the home?

6. In ancient Israel, in addition to the home, name three other important educational influences that circulated throughout society. To which of these three groups did Koheleth belong?

7. What biblical books constituted the wisdom literature of ancient Israel? Who was the patron of wisdom literature? Why?

8. Briefly describe the two main functions of the wise man or sage. What books of the Hebrew Bible best illustrate each of these functions?

9. What book appears to have been used as a kind of textbook for reciting the observations of the wise?

10. Define wisdom *(hokhmah)* from a Hebraic perspective. In what sense does wisdom go beyond certain views of knowledge? In the Hebrew Bible, what areas of practical ability or service are associated with those endowed with wisdom?

11. In what sense is folly the antithesis to wisdom?

12. What are the characteristics or qualities of the *peti*? Why may the *peti* have given the Hebrew sages reason to be somewhat encouraged?

13. What terms in general reflect the character of the *kesil* and *ewil*? How does the book of Proverbs describe the life-style of these fools?

14. Describe the character and attitude of the *letz*. Why did this type of fool provide one of the greatest challenges for the sages of Israel?

70. Abraham J. Heschel, *Insecurity of Freedom*, p. 42.

15. Describe the character and life-style of the *nabal*. Does the term *atheist* correctly describe the *nabal*? Explain.

16. What is distinctive about the Hebrew view of knowledge? How does a study of the verb *yada* in its biblical setting shed light on the Hebrew view of knowledge? The Western world often limits the definition of knowledge. Explain. Norman Snaith points out that a comparative study of the Hebrew and Greek approaches to knowledge reveals that they are "poles apart in attitude and method." What does Snaith mean?

17. According to Leo Baeck, what was the purpose of Jewish existence? How did the idea of "being different" relate to the need to educate for a life of holiness?

18. The Greek world, unlike the Hebrew world, did not understand education to be tied to holiness of life. What was the aim of teaching among the Greeks? In general, who received education in ancient Greek society? What was the role of the *paidagōgós*, "child-guide," "tutor" (see footnote)? How does the origin of our word *school* shed light on the question of who was educated? In sum, where did the Jewish concept of education differ from the Greek?

19. Give two possible roots from which the Hebrew verb *ḥanakh*, "to train," "to educate," may derive.

20. Explain the origin of Hanukkah or "Feast of Dedication" (see footnote).

21. According to rabbinic tradition, how was honey used in a special ceremony on the first day of school? Why did the rabbis tie study and honey together?

22. Answer the following questions concerning Proverbs 22:6: (a) What has been the common way of interpreting this verse? (b) How is this verse worded when translated literally? (c) What alternative interpretation does this above rendering seem to imply? (d) Assuming the above interpretation concerning the way of instruction to be correct, what is the role or responsibility of the parent and/or teacher to the child?

23. What insight on the task or responsibility of the teacher in Bible times may be gained from a study of various Hebrew verbs meaning "to teach"? In regard to the subject of teaching, answer the following questions: (a) What is the literal meaning of the New Testament term *pastor*? How may this meaning shed some light on the function of the pastoral office? (b) In what way does Abraham Heschel call today for a reverse of the traditional Socratic method of education? What are your reactions to Heschel's proposal? (c) How does the letter *l* in the Hebrew alphabet shed light on the subject of learning among the Hebrews? (d) Define or give the English equivalent of the following common Hebrew terms associated with learning: *moreh, talmidim, Talmud.* Summarize the significance of each of the main points as reflective of a brief outline detailing some of the duties incumbent upon Christian teachers.

24. Immediately prior to the New Testament period, who held a recognized position as the official teachers of Israel's spiritual heritage?

25. How did the meaning of the term *bet midrash*, "house of study," evolve

from its original usage in the second century B.C.? Who is the earliest person on record to invite students to come and learn in his house of study?

26. What is the importance of Simeon ben Shetach (ca. 75 B.C.) and Joshua ben Gamla (ca. A.D. 65) in the history of Jewish education?

27. In the educational system for children during New Testament times, especially in regard to age and subject matter, distinguish the following terms: (a) *bet sepher,* (b) *bet talmud,* (c) *bet midrash.*

28. Outline the basic biblical curriculum for children attending a *bet sepher.* Why did the book of Leviticus seem to be of such major importance? Why is Leviticus virtually unknown among many Christians today?

29. What evidence from the New Testament points to the fact that Jesus was recognized as an itinerant teacher in the scribal tradition? In Jesus' day, what did the word *rabbi* mean? By the second century, how had this meaning changed?

30. Why did teachers of religious tradition and sages usually have a secular occupation or trade? How does the life of Paul reflect this practice?

31. Why did the rabbis insist, "If you have learned much, do not think highly of yourself for it"?

32. According to Maimonides, who was obliged to study Torah? What exemptions were made on the basis of age, health, or economic status?

33. Compare the Hasidic approach to the religious education of youth with that of various Christian denominations. What factors account for the differences in approach?

34. How is the theme of "a life of learning" related to the heart of the Great Commission incumbent upon the Church? In what way does good teaching produce a chain reaction? Use Paul's second letter to Timothy to explain or illustrate your answer.

35. Give two lines of New Testament evidence that point to the fact that some people have been given a special gift of teaching within the Church.

36. Discuss Leo Baeck's observation that the teaching of God is "no heritage one accepts passively but rather a heritage that has to be won."

37. What evidence is there that teaching was conducted primarily by word of mouth, not by studying books? What clue is found in the meaning of the term *mishneh?*

38. Today's Church has the Bible in English translation. The Old Testament, however, is a collection of early Hebrew sources which were meant to be read *aloud* (in the original language). Discuss the advantages and disadvantages of reading the Bible silently in translation as opposed to reading it aloud in the original.

39. In Bible times, what was the most important quality for being a good scholar?

40. Since memory played such a major role in the transmission of Hebrew thought, did this normally lead to wide-scale corruption of the accounts being handed down? What is William F. Albright's observation on this issue?

41. What aids to memory were employed by the writers of the Hebrew Bible? Define and give several biblical examples of "alphabetic acrostic."

42. The rabbis taught that in the life to come the fulfilling of a certain mitzvah regarding learning would be one of the first questions to which a person must answer. What is this mitzvah?

43. What commitment of time did the Jewish community at Qumran make for study and learning? How do we know?

44. What graphic object lesson involving covenant, widely practiced in the ancient Near East, later finds its counterpart in a Roman practice that provided the etymological root of our English word *testify*? Cite a biblical example of this practice from the book of Genesis. Among the Hebrews, what serious meaning was associated with this type of dramatic act?

45. At Passover, various items on the Seder table symbolize the life of tyranny Jews experienced in Egypt. Describe the following foods and indicate what each symbolizes: (a) matzot, (b) *maror,* (c) *haroset.*

46. What was the most sacred cult object in ancient Israel? Why? In modern synagogues, where are copies of the Torah kept? How are respect and reverence for the Torah demonstrated in synagogues today?

47. What is the linguistic origin of the words *Judah* and *Jew*? According to Abraham Heschel, what is the primary purpose of prayer in Jewish tradition?

48. Illustrate the important role that music played in the life of Israel and the early Church. What song of deliverance from Israel's experience in Egypt reappears as a heavenly song of praise in the book of Revelation?

49. What double meaning is found in the Hebrew word *abodah*? How has Platonic dualism influenced the Church in such a way as to believe that the above meanings are mutually exclusive or contradictory to each other? (See chapter ten.) Discuss.

50. In the Talmud, what synonym is used for "education"?

51. Cite or paraphrase some of the Scriptures which lend support to the teaching that study is a form of worship.

52. Discuss various reasons why people today find it difficult to address study in a serious manner as a lifelong commitment.

53. To what foolish activity that causes men to perish does the Talmud compare fishes in the sea that immediately perish when they come out of the water?

54. Do you agree with the observation that "It is wrong to define education as *preparation* for life. Learning *is* life"? Discuss.

*Part V*

# Toward Restoring Jewish Roots

## Chapter Fifteen

# If Not Now . . . When?

*Let us not love with words or tongue but with actions and in truth*

1 John 3:18

Our focus in this concluding chapter is upon the question of contemporary relevance. How does this entire book fit together as a call to action for today's Church? How can it, and other works that deal with Christian-Jewish relations, become useful rather than merely informative? How do Christians, especially those relatively new to the world of Hebrew thought, go about acquiring an even deeper appreciation of Jewish heritage? How may sensitive and lasting links with the Jewish community be established? Such issues will now be our concern.

Throughout this volume we have stressed that the essence of biblical faith is relationship. In scriptural terms, the ethical command to love God and one's neighbor is more important than burnt offerings and sacrifices (Mic. 6:1-8; Mark 12:28-34). It would be wrong, however, to refer to this undertaking as *religion,* in the modern sense of this word. The popular use of "religion" distorts how the Jewish biblical writers define a godly life. We must, therefore, look at this concept more closely.

Our English word *religion* most likely derives from the Latin *religare,* "to bind." Accordingly, religion is commonly thought to be a state of life to which one is bound by certain vows, duties, rites, or obligations. By definition, the *Christian religion* thus came to mean—particularly as the Church strayed more and more from its Jewish roots—a particular system of doctrine. In brief, religion was primarily seen as a body of beliefs governing worship and behavior.

To be sure, theological truths are important in biblical teaching. Nevertheless, the Hebrews did not view a life of true piety and godliness as an impersonal relationship to a structure of thought, but as a personal relationship renewed each day with the living God. Its true locus was not found in an array of dogmas or cultic regulations, but in the response of one's whole person in love and total obedience to the Creator.

In today's Church a similar danger exists. It is sometimes labeled "bibliolatry." Christians must take heed that they do not so esteem the written truth of Scripture that they become blind to the actual worship of the living Word behind that Scripture. The biblical heroes of the faith did not live primarily to extol a creed; they sought to walk daily in close fellowship with their omnipresent Lord.

Judaism bequeathed its relational and pragmatic emphases to the Church. Hence our task in the following pages is to develop a modus operandi or practical outworking for the Church in regard to Jewish heritage. The process of restoring the withered Jewish roots of the Christian faith involves far more than learning about Jewish values, history, and culture in the abstract. Rather, at its very core, it involves the restoring of relationships. Revitalization through ideas can carry one only so far. Knowledge must also be transmuted into concrete action through personal contact with the Jewish community. True growth comes by encountering people as well as concepts; it is nourished as much through the wisdom of practical experience and concrete action as through the world of thought.

We might, therefore, entitle this chapter, "A Call to Reflection and Action." Our attempt is to make this study utilitarian by synthesizing and interweaving a number of practical threads. Here we invite the reader to become personally involved in the contemporary Christian-Jewish encounter. In brief, our aim is to explore the question: Now that we have been introduced to the world of Hebrew thought, where do we go from here?

Perhaps the above query can best be answered by first posing another question (a traditionally Jewish manner of reply; cf. Luke 20:1-8). In the Mishnah, the great sage Hillel confronts his students by asking, "If not now . . . when?" (Abot 1:14). These probing and timeless words are a call to avoid procrastination, not to put off to another day what should be acted on today. They are words for us. We must seize the present moment to apply what we know—now.

In getting started, we offer here no pat formula or instant, ready-made plan to acquire a deep appreciation and understanding of the Jewish roots of the Christian faith. What works for one will not necessarily work for another. We are dealing with a personal issue. Each person who embarks on this road is at a different starting point. Therefore, our immediate concern is to take a broad look at the dynamics of Christian-Jewish relations and present a wide range of considerations, practical guidelines, and avenues of exploration. Many of these suggestions grow out of my own experience in the field of Christian-Jewish relations. But what is presented below is not an exhaustive treatise; rather, it is primarily a series of personal reflections and pragmatic observations on how some of the themes from this book might be implemented in the experience of individual Christians and in the life of the Church. Our plan is to detail some useful steps and new directions that may enable Christians to begin to restore the more important aspects of Jewish heritage. But we also wish to convey something of the style of openness and the spirit of sensitivity needful for those committed to this rewarding task.

## Preliminary Considerations for Christians

### A Jewish Heart

If one approaches the subject at hand in a purely academic manner, it will not take hold. One cannot be involved in this discipline in an impersonal or detached way. There must be something deeper at work on the subjective or personal level. Perhaps we might call this orientation "having a Jewish heart." One must acquire a personal, living feel for the world of Judaism. A fire must be burning within (cf. Jer. 20:9). This feeling cannot be imparted in a solely objective or programmed manner. In brief, it must be caught; it cannot be taught.

A profound and abiding Christian appreciation for Jewish culture and the Jewish people comes from sensing inwardly that one's deepest spiritual identity is with a Jewish Lord, and that "salvation is from the Jews" (John 4:22). It is being cognizant that one has received a spiritual heart transplant, of being changed from the inside out. It is the existential realization that spiritually one is "grafted into Israel," a Jewish people. It is to recognize that through father Abraham one enters a new family and new world of relationships (Gal. 3:29). This personal perception is particularly fed by a consciousness that one owes an enormous debt of appreciation to the Jewish people. One of the most gratifying, self-imposed responsibilities is not merely to acknowledge that debt, but also to seek meaningful and constructive ways to repay it.

## A Humble Spirit

Pride and arrogance on the part of Christians have probably proved over the centuries to be the greatest barriers to positive relations with the Jewish community. Though Paul warned gentile believers about this problem (Rom. 11:17-24), it still persists. It is all too easy for one to become enslaved by prejudice. Humankind is stubborn. No one likes to admit being wrong. It takes moral courage to face the truth and to be willing to change.

Nothing inherent in Christianity makes one individually, or Christians corporately, better than Jews. It is indeed to the Church's shame that Christians have openly displayed this proud and elitist spirit, particularly in situations that seem to have little respect for the concept of religious pluralism within a democratic society. Such attitudes of superiority have often resulted in the negation of Judaism to the point that the ground has been prepared for the sowing of the seeds of anti-Semitism.

The general condition of the Church's relation to the Synagogue may be likened to the soil of Israel in the month of September. During the hot summer months most of the land receives no rain. By fall, the ground is hard-packed and parched, the roots of much vegetation withered. This lifeless setting anxiously awaits the early October rains to revive withered roots and to enable the unploughed ground to be broken up and become productive again (see Hos. 10:11-12). So is the Church in need of restoration. Its roots long for reviving. But the drought of pride, which has left its ground hard and virtually impenetrable, must first be broken by the rain of humility. For as Scripture says, "God opposes the proud but gives grace to the humble" (Jas. 4:6; 1 Pet. 5:5; cf. Prov. 3:34).

Though the attitude of individual Christians toward Jews differs, the overall stance of the Church, since near its inception, has been adversarial. Before the Church can hope to revive its Jewish roots, it must first reexamine its own way of thinking. Ungodly attitudes must be purged. Denigration, stridency, and insensitivity must be checked; scapegoating and berating must be eliminated. We are not speaking of a polite toleration of Jewish people, but of a new spirit whereby a different Christian image emerges. Instead of Christians arrogantly claiming truth, they should live the truth in a convincing manner. The sole passion of certain Christians to overcome Jews by argument needs to be replaced by a spirit of humility and servanthood. In addition, one must be open to reordering priorities, rewriting agendas, and redirecting energies.

Christians must take the initiative in the righting of wrong attitudes toward others. Jesus teaches, "If you are offering your gift at the altar

322

and there remember your brother has something against you. . . . First go and be reconciled to your brother; then come and offer your gift" (Matt. 5:23-24). Without a genuine spirit of repentance within one's group for past wrongs and failures, there can be little prospect for healing and ultimate reconciliation.

In order to change our attitude, we must examine our theological views and change those which are faulty. Unlike God's immutable Word, theology is a human and fallible discipline. Thus it is always open to fresh statement and revision; one must be prepared to write theology with pencil and eraser, not indelible ink. Theology may change or mature as one grows to perceive God's teachings and his work in history more clearly. Furthermore, no single theologian or theological tradition has all truth contained within a distinct system. The body of believers is diverse, and we must learn from one another. God still has more insight and correction to bring to his people from his Word. In recent years many Christians have been open to rethinking and revising unbiblical assumptions they may have earlier entertained concerning such subjects as the gifts of the Spirit, the "health-wealth" gospel, and the role of women. Is it not also time that Christians reexamine their attitudes concerning the Synagogue and the rich Hebraic heritage undergirding the Christian faith?

## A Long-term Venture

Christian-Jewish relations may best be described as a venture or experiment. The road is long and not easy; surprises and risks await along the way. It is essential, therefore, that one be fully committed and prepared for the various challenges that may be encountered. Some Christians may become weary or fainthearted on the way, and others lost. Some may sense discouragement or even devastation, and others give up from frustration. Some may become battle-scarred or suffer disillusionment. Some may find something they never expected; and others may expect what is never to be found.

Interfaith relations is a new world for most Christians, and numerous unanticipated adjustments have to be made. Commitment and patience, therefore, are indispensable. The very idea of change may be unsettling or threatening. Change involves a process and normally comes slowly. We must be prepared to work with people for an extended period of time, and they with us. We should not expect instantaneous results.

Furthermore, as individual Christians begin to come closer to the Jewish community in search of their Jewish roots, they may encounter misunderstanding or opposition from the Christian community. In certain situations resistance may be so harsh that one may feel challenged or set upon by his own people. Some Christians seem to wonder why other Christians take an interest in Jewish things, especially since "Jewish" often betokens to them the opposition or "other side." Depending on one's theological and denominational background, inquisitiveness—even outright criticism—may come from various angles. Certain clergy may caution their parishioners against embracing any new teaching (probably only a euphemism for their lack of appreciation for Jews or Judaism from seminary days to the present). Some Christians may argue that the Church is the "new Israel," and thus Christians can learn nothing from Jews. Others may bluntly claim that Jews are a secular people, devoid of any spiritual vocation. Some in the Church may say that since Jews have turned their back on Jesus as Messiah, Christians have no valid reason to associate with them. Yet others may be critical of any Christian who supports the right of the people of Israel to live securely in their historic homeland on the grounds that a Christian must be neutral out of fairness to the Arab cause. It is important that one deal honestly and patiently with such issues, recognizing that nineteen hundred years cannot be fully rethought in a day.

The "us-them" syndrome that has created an isolationist attitude on the part of Christians toward Jews must be broken down. Certainly, the Jewish roots of Christianity cannot be explored in a vacuum. Christians may no longer pretend that Jewish people do not exist. Indeed, Christians have an obligation to reach out thoughtfully, humbly, and caringly to Jews and others around them. Christians who oppose such concern betray a fundamental lack of biblical understanding. Indeed, the Church is expected to "show true humility toward all men" (Tit. 3:2), and to "do good to all people" (Gal. 6:10). In addition, Christians have the responsibility to "entertain strangers" (Heb. 13:2). Jesus teaches, "If you love those who love you, what reward will you get?" (Matt. 5:46). Here is a mandate to reach out to embrace even one's potential enemies.

We have seen that preparation for contact with the world of Jewry requires a Jewish heart and a humble and teachable spirit. But Christians must also count the cost. Even though the road at times gets rough, one must have a commitment to stick with it. For if the Scriptures teach that Christians have an obligation to build bridges of humble service to all people, how much more ought they to be concerned for those in whose spiritual debt they stand.

Many avenues and resources are available and useful in fostering a Christian appreciation of Jewish roots. In the remainder of our discussion we will focus primarily on three main areas: personal understanding through interfaith dialogue, educational activities, and social action.

## Face-to-face in Dialogue

Interfaith dialogue provides opportunity for Christians to examine the commonalities and differences that Judaism has with Christianity. Dialogue is not merely a forum for self-definition; it also has the advantage of permitting inquiry through personal interaction. One learns from listening to the practitioners of another faith rather than only reading its theoreticians. Christians frequently discover a great gap in perception as they engage Jews face-to-face in discussion. Stereotypes and misperceptions rapidly begin to vanish. A picture of Jews and Judaism that is up-to-date and authentic starts to emerge. Thus it is again crucial for us to stress that the quest for Jewish roots must pay attention not only to what the tradition teaches but also to those who interpret it in the context of everyday life.

## *The Purpose of Dialogue*

Christians approach dialogue with differing motives. For this reason Jews often have a certain apprehension and wariness about making themselves vulnerable in a dialogue. Too frequently in the past dialogues have exposed hidden Christian agendas and tactics. Interfaith dialogue must establish some guidelines to assure its integrity.

First, let us look at some objectionable approaches. Dialogue must never be viewed as an opportunity to overcome the "opposition." Dialogue is not an arena wherein people assemble in order to choose sides, and then cheer their team to victory as they score verbal points. Christians and Jews are not rivals locked in a bitter, unending conflict. Any dialogue will be short-lived if approached merely as a chance to outduel the "other side" with militant words. Dialogue is not a stage for angrily venting one's frustrations or blaming others for the sins of the past. It is also not a platform to exploit one's neighbor in order to promote one's own program. Dialogue is not a setting to abolish one's enemy by making truth claims arrogantly. It is no place for one seeking greatness for himself.

Furthermore, the object of dialogue is not to convert one's partner from one faith and tradition to another. Conversion is the work of God, not of human beings. Though dialogue provides each community with a format for witness to one another, we must recognize that we cannot impose our faith on another. Unfortunately, the horrendous history of Christian-Jewish relations indicates that the Church has not always understood this point.

In addition, the purpose of dialogue is not the seeking of reconciliation through theological compromise. It is not to melt down Judaism and

Christianity to their lowest common denominators. Our definition of dialogue does not call for the development of some symbiotic world religion through the cross-fertilization of Judaism and Christianity. In brief, the object of dialogue is not homogenization of belief.

What then is the purpose of dialogue? It is an invitation to learn. Dialogue is a means for enhancing personal growth and understanding through a mutual search for truth. Neither Christian nor Jew must be content with mutual toleration of each other's errors and caricatures. Dialogue provides the context whereby Christians and Jews can achieve a new rapprochement as they explore ancient sources and forge new links together. Dialogue gives occasion to broaden and enrich one's spiritual capacity without need to compromise or relinquish one's deepest faith commitments. Dialogue allows Christians the format to reveal a new image—that of a winsome and open spirit—while exploring the Jewish foundations of Christianity. It gives opportunity not only to enhance one's knowledge through personal encounter, but also to demonstrate by true humility and servanthood an attitude conducive to further growth through mutual trust.

The New Testament sets some broad guidelines for Christians who engage in dialogue. James, a book filled with aphoristic bits of practical wisdom, states, "Everyone should be quick to listen, slow to speak" (Jas. 1:19). To listen and to seek to understand—not necessarily acceding to the other's viewpoint—is perhaps the most important quality necessary in dialogue. The book of 1 Peter carries this point a step further by indicating that a Christian must earn the right to be heard: "Always be prepared to give an answer to everyone who asks you to give the reason for the hope that you have. But do this with gentleness and respect" (1 Pet. 3:15). In any conversation it is easy to pose and answer questions that one's partner has never asked. Peter indicates that a different rule should prevail. When one's partner in dialogue initiates interest in hearing about the Christian hope, then one should be prepared to give an answer. And that answer must not be presented arrogantly or thoughtlessly, but with sensitivity to and respect for the inquirer.

## Dealing with Differences

In Christian-Jewish dialogue —especially with Christians in search of common roots—it is all too tempting to ignore differences. Judaism and Christianity are, however, two different faiths. Part of constructive and mature dialogue is to look honestly at these disagreements rather than to avoid them. It is not essential in dialogue that both sides agree totally on every issue. But both Christian and Jew should make a sincere effort to understand, seeking to perceive each other's position accurately.

Let us look briefly at three areas where differences are frequent. First, in dialogue, Christians and Jews often use the same words but with different meanings. Hence, those in dialogue must be careful to define their terms. For example, to a Jew the word *Bible* does not normally imply the New Testament, whereas to a Christian it does. To a Jew, the word *Gentile* often suggests "Christian." But in the Church's eyes, the words are far from synonymous. A Christian may hear the word *Pharisee* and think "hypocrite," whereas a Jew thinks of his respected, spiritual forebears. A Christian may use the word *crusade* for a large, modern, gospel-preaching rally. When a Jew hears this word it usually brings to mind the Church's several military expeditions, starting in A.D. 1096, that brought forced baptism or death to thousands of Jews.

A second area where differences often appear is in the inaccurate assumptions that one group holds of the other. Let us note several common Jewish misunderstandings of traditional Protestant Christianity. (a) Christians are often said to worship three gods rather than one God. But Christians, like Jews, are monotheists. (b) Many Jews view significant portions of the New Testament as anti-Semitic. Christians, however, should see the whole Bible as a book written by Jews and about Jews. Regrettably, sometimes Gentiles have taken its most bitter parts out of context and used them to justify hatred against Jews. (c) Jews commonly characterize Christianity as a religion of faith, with good deeds more or less of secondary importance or optional. But the New Testament teaches that "faith without deeds is dead" (Jas. 2:26) and that "a person is justified by what he does and not by faith alone" (2:24).

A third area of difference centers on Jesus of Nazareth and the perception each group has of him. Christianity sees Jesus as Messiah and God; Judaism does not. For the Jew, the concept of Messiah is understood in purely human terms. For the Christian, the Messiah is the God-man Jesus. This christological factor lies at the foundation of the great divide between Christianity and Judaism. Modern Judaism holds that the Church deified Jesus. What is more, Jesus failed to measure up to Jewish messianic expectations, for the world remains unredeemed. Christians, however, argue that the claim to the divinity and messiahship of Jesus—though ultimately based on faith—is firmly rooted in Scripture and history, and is based on the uniqueness of Jesus, on the empty tomb, on the appearances to eyewitnesses, and on the rapid growth of the Church.

Both faith communities must recognize honestly why there is an impasse over Jesus. The principal reason is that Jews and Christians operate from different presuppositions. The former hold to an authoritative canon of thirty-nine books, the latter to a canon of sixty-six. Jews extend authority to the Talmud, the Codes, and the Responsa; Christians do not. Christians generally hold the Gospels to be sacred history, and the miracle accounts of the New Testament as actual events rather than legend. Jews, however, do not.

Though Jesus and the faith that developed around his teachings remain the major obstacles in the split between Judaism and Christianity, the divorce is not permanent. In the New Testament Paul stresses that the coexistence of both faiths is in keeping with God's mysterious plan. Eventually, however, there will be a breakthrough, and the "ultimate transcendence of the divorce."[1] This final barrier only God can remove. In the meantime, however, it should not obscure the profound contribution Jews can make to Christians in helping them understand the Jewishness of Jesus in his first-century setting. Finally, in the dynamics of dialogue, it behooves both Christians and Jews to face this watershed difference, and less important differences as well, with utmost honesty, candor, and respect.

## Education and Personal Growth

"Learning" is the name of the gate one must enter to find the way back to one's Jewish roots. In the previous chapter, we dealt in some detail with the biblical and rabbinic teaching on this theme. We shall now go on to point out some of its practical implications for today's Church.

Humankind tends to rationalize sin and categorize its various types. Sins of the flesh are usually viewed as being far more serious or evil than sins of the tongue or sins of the spirit. The Bible, however, makes no such classifications or distinctions. In the Ten Commandments, the bearing of false witness is placed in the same list of prohibitions as adultery and murder.

One finds a direct relevance in the above conception of sin when confronting the appalling lack of education in the area of Christian-Jewish relations. As we mentioned earlier, Christians have frequently defamed or discredited their Jewish neighbors unknowingly by perpetrating inaccurate teaching about Jews and Judaism.[2] Any Christian may seek to rationalize such culpable activity, but this rationalization cannot assuage the guilt of misrepresenting, injuring, or vilifying his neighbor. Moses

---

1. Jean Radermakers, "The Meaning and Purpose of a Jewish-Christian Dialogue" (trans. Olga Prendergast), *Lumen Vitae* 30 (June, 1975): 251.
2. See Carl D. Evans, "The Church's False Witness Against Jews," *Christian Century* (May 5, 1982): 530-33.

condemns the spreading of slander (Lev. 19:16), and Paul commands, "Put off falsehood, and speak truthfully" (Eph. 4:25). Christians are responsible for insuring that what they learn and teach about the Jewish experience is correct. Whenever the Jewish faith is distorted, or its people wronged by the words of Christians, the very integrity of the Christian message is jeopardized.

## Drinking from the Sources

Christians who desire to deepen their knowledge of Jews and Judaism may do so in a variety of ways. Some will have opportunity to take formal courses in educational institutions or in special programs sponsored by synagogues or churches. Others will opt to study on their own. Those in the latter group may consult the selective bibliography at the end of this volume for suggested titles.

But whatever the avenue of study, it is essential that Christians place a decisive emphasis upon Jewish sources, so that the history of the Church may be studied from the roots up.[3] A return to the Hebraic soil of early Christian thought will reveal various foreign teachings that the Church has picked up over the years. Contemporary Christian-Jewish relations do not begin in a vacuum; they have a history of nearly two millennia behind them. Throughout this time-span the Church has undergone spiritual dehydration. It must go back and drink from the sources so its perspective may both be revived and revised.[4]

Each generation should expect new truth to emerge from a fresh study of Scripture. As we emphasized above in chapter eight, the Church must take a new look at its foundation and give greater priority to a study of the Old Testament and other early Jewish sources. One of the major reasons Christians misunderstand certain basic Jewish teachings is because they do not start with the Old Testament. Many Christians study the Old Testament *only* through the eyes of the New Testament. But if Christians *began* with the Old Testament before moving to the New, they would come to understand the rich historical, linguistic, and cultural background which this part of Scripture constitutes on its own. The Old Testament must be read as more than a pre-Christian bridge to the New, a mere propaedeutic

3. I am in strong agreement with Stuart Rosenberg, who develops this point in his epilogue, "If I Were a Christian," in *The Christian Problem: A Jewish View* (New York: Hippocrene Books, 1986), p. 222.

4. For the terminology of "drinking from the sources," I am indebted to the work of Jacques Doukhan, *Drinking at the Sources* (Mountain View, CA: Mountain Press Publishing Association, 1981).

to the Christian faith. Sound biblical exegesis insists that a text first be heard in its original setting.

Finely tuned, systematic categories of Christian thought have too often been imposed deductively upon the Old Testament, thus obscuring its original meaning. In Jewish thinking, however, "not system but *commentary* is the legitimate form through which truth is approached."[5] Because Christians have been overly anxious to systematize Jewish thought, they have left themselves open to misinterpreting the text. In addition, the search for truth can be unsettling, especially if the interpreter is willing to go wherever the text leads him. Seeking to bring forth the meaning of Scripture inductively — which is precisely the task of the commentator—sometimes results in a diversified and fragmented understanding of truth. But it is more honest and wiser to handle the text in this manner than to construct an artificial system that in the end fails to let truth speak clearly in its own terms.

## *Affective Learning*

Understanding Jews and Judaism is more than a cerebral exercise. It is also vital that an individual become personally involved in the educational process. Learning must be applied to the concrete world; it must be pragmatically oriented. For example, in a particular way Jewish history comes alive to any Christian visiting Israel for the first time. An existential awareness is bound to grip him and declare viscerally, "This is not just Israel's homeland, but I too have something personal and tangible at stake here."

In a similar vein, whenever a sensitive Christian pays a visit to a death camp such as Dachau or Auschwitz, the term *Holocaust* is suddenly transformed. No longer is it a vague word dimly associated with the Nazis. Rather, the Holocaust becomes an unspeakable event, unparalleled in history. This catastrophe must never be trivialized, for, though not all victims were Jews, all Jews were victims. In view of the Church's guilty silence, Christians can no longer simplistically consider the Holocaust as a Jewish problem. One sight of the barbed wire and crematoria speaks volumes: we must never forget; we are all involved, accountable to one another and responsible for imparting the lessons of this atrocity to future generations.

The learning process entails both input and output. Knowledge that has been acquired should be used, built into the lives of others. Study about the Jewish roots of the Christian faith becomes reinforced and solidified when passed on in either formal or informal settings. Christians must avail

---

5. Gershom Scholem, *The Messianic Idea in Judaism* (New York: Schocken Books, 1971), p. 289.

themselves of opportunities to meet with prospective learners—whether one-on-one, in small groups, or in scheduled classes. The ultimate challenge is to reproduce in others that which is burning within you. For many Christians, contacts within the local church provide a good place to begin.

A number of programs and projects relevant to church groups may be designed in consultation with the Jewish community. Many of these may be set up to focus on active rather than passive learning. Each of these interfaith activities is likely to fall into one of the following broad areas: faith and traditions, culture, or history. Let us note several workable examples of each.

Jewish faith and traditions may be effectively grasped through a series of visitations to nearby synagogues. Here one may learn of such areas as Jewish worship, prayer, symbolism, education, holidays, and synagogue architecture. Opportunity to participate in a community Passover Seder may also be available. In addition, one may learn from taking courses in conversational Hebrew or introduction to the Talmud at a local Jewish community center, or by attending a lectureship series sponsored by a synagogue. Visitation to a Jewish funeral establishment (for a study of the rites of death and burial) or to a day school (for a study of how the Bible, the Hebrew language, and Jewish tradition are taught) will also prove very informative. Furthermore, Christian clergy should be urged to schedule regular teaching or lecturing exchanges with local rabbis. Also, Christian women's groups should seek to hold one of their monthly meetings each year with a nearby Jewish Hadassah chapter. An illustrated lecture on Jerusalem would provide a worthwhile topic of mutual interest.

The world of Jewish culture provides a second area where Christians may deepen their appreciation of Jewish heritage. Visitation at Jewish museums and traveling exhibitions will visually broaden one's understanding of both ancient and modern Judaism. In addition, an archeological presentation on the Holy Land, illustrated by artifacts, allows a wide range of cultural exposure. A community-produced (and discussed) version of the play *Diary of Anne Frank* or *Fiddler on the Roof* will provide great insight into the Jewish experience. An evening of Jewish music or folk dancing, or a jointly sponsored class on traditional Jewish cuisine, will give additional cultural enrichment.

Finally, one's personal understanding of Judaism may be expanded in the area of history. A joint Christian-Jewish study mission to Israel, which would allow for interaction with national political and religious leaders, would produce direct insight into the ancient and modern history of the land. Interfaith discussion groups on historical topics may also be established at a local church or synagogue. These discussions may include areas of current interest such as the literature of the Holocaust (e.g., the works of Elie Wiesel), the history of anti-Semitism, or the Arab-Israeli conflict. In addition, a long-term research project by a group of churches within the same denomination may be profitably undertaken on the theme of what and how Christians teach about Jews and Judaism. Such a study, confined to the educational literature of that denomination, will often shed considerable light on how the Jew has been portrayed throughout history.

## Social Action

A third major avenue that can bring a deepening appreciation of the Jewish roots of the Christian faith is that of social action. Orthodoxy (correct or straight thinking) must lead to orthopraxy (right doing). In Judaism and Christianity, theory is always wed to practice. The concept of election in Scripture is not a summons to self-contemplation but a call to service. Christianity, in particular, must be careful that it does not allow *dogma* (the way to believe, prescribed by creed) to overshadow *halakhah* (the way to walk or live).[6] Both concepts must be held in balance.

### A Covenant of Caring

As we have previously emphasized, Christians have a biblical mandate to show concern for all people. Indeed, even the feeding of one's enemy is obligatory for Christians (Rom. 12:20-21). It is almost inconceivable how the Church reversed this theology for centuries, looking upon the Jewish world as its adversary, with little compassion or care. Today, however, more and more Christians feel a particular responsibility to stand beside Jewish people in matters of social justice. These Christians acknowledge a special historical tie to Jews, a unique sense of spiritual bonding, and a deep realization of the need to redress tangibly some ugly wrongs from the past. Rather than remain indifferent, the Church must send a new message of action to the world: "To attack Jews is to attack Christians, and we will not stand idly by." The so-called religion of love, which permitted hate and even sometimes was permeated by it, must be transformed into a covenant of caring.[7] Jesus taught that the hallmark of true faith is revealed

6. Cf. W. D. Davies, "Torah and Dogma," *Harvard Theological Review* 61 (1968): 88.
7. This point is effectively developed by Kenneth S. Kantzer in "Concerning Evangelicals and Jews," *Christianity Today* (April 24, 1981): 13.

in deeds. Thus he warned, "Not everyone who says to me, 'Lord, Lord' will enter the kingdom of heaven, but only he who does the will of my Father in heaven" (Matt. 7:21).

The Scriptures make highly ethical demands. They urge God's people to act justly, to show mercy, and to pursue peace. "Follow justice and justice alone," cries Moses (Deut. 16:20). Christians are to be clothed with compassion and kindness (Col. 3:12; cf. Eph. 4:32). "Blessed are the merciful," teaches Jesus, "for they will be shown mercy" (Matt. 5:7). Later, the rabbis also paralleled this attitude: "He who is merciful to others, mercy is shown to him by Heaven" (Babylonian Talmud, Shabbat 151b). Christians are also to "seek peace and pursue it" (1 Pet. 3:11). Indeed, "peacemakers" are declared "blessed" (Matt. 5:9). The Bible's vital humanism teaches us to regard God's passion for human beings. It calls God's people to bear responsibility and care for each other. The Hasidic masters taught that the eventual goal of social justice is the fullest realization of the concept of *tikkun olam,* "repairing [or fixing] the world." It is that day toward which we continue to press and of which the prophets dreamed, when "the earth will be full of the knowledge of the LORD as the waters cover the sea" (Isa. 11:9).

## Revising Agendas

Today's Church has a prophetic function. This responsibility—like that of the prophets of Israel—is not primarily to focus on the future but to address actively and constructively the social and spiritual ills of the present. Christians have an obligation to speak out against those who would deal unjustly with the Jewish community. In the past, Jews have been vehemently denounced and vilified, the victims of bigotry and myths. If the Church's ministry is truly prophetic, it will bring a corrective influence against the proponents of such teachings and deeds. The refutation of propaganda and protestation of evil acts must also be accompanied by a concerted effort to rid Christian textbooks of negative teaching and inaccurate stereotypes about Jews and Judaism.

This task may best be accomplished if several considerations are kept in view. First, local church calendars should be carefully reviewed. All too often the Church has reacted slowly — if at all — to crises affecting the Jewish community. Therefore, it must take the leadership and design an annual calendar that places importance upon bridge building and preventative education. Throughout the church year creative and instructional programs may be presented on Sundays, or on other occasions, that focus on social issues such as Holocaust awareness, Soviet refuseniks, Israel's present and future, and brotherhood building. Since the horrendous event of the Holocaust, considerable Jewish energy has been concentrated on the simple concern for survival. It is expedient, therefore, that the Church assume an active role in addressing that concern.

Second, the leaders of local churches may find it beneficial to band together to form a task force against racism and anti-Semitism. This social-action body would be responsible for conducting educational workshops on anti-Semitism for local clergy. But it would also function, in consultation with Jewish leadership, in response to anti-Semitic incidents in the local area. Appropriate action may include repair of defaced property, reimbursement for loss, or condemnation and exposure of the offending parties through the media.

Third, to assist the Church in accomplishing its agenda, a network of relationships and a pool of resources should be established that reaches beyond the local community. Selected newspapers, periodicals, and films dealing with current problems and events that affect the Jewish community are useful. But, very often, problems are complex and need the collective wisdom and insight of others more knowledgeable in this field. Through the assisting of the inexperienced by the experienced, through the sharing of both advice and resources, not only will Christians come to understand their Jewish heritage better, but they will also become more effective doers of the Word.

## "The Greatest of These Is Love"

Throughout this chapter we have presented a wide range of concrete measures vital for bringing renewed life to the withered Jewish roots of the Christian faith. We pointed out in the earlier chapters that the main reason these roots became dry and lifeless is because the gentile Church became not only boastful but also hostile to the Jewish olive tree that had first nurtured it. Consequently, the history of anti-Judaism and anti-Semitism is virtually as long as the history of the Church. After nineteen hundred years, it is time for a new relationship between Church and Synagogue.

The biblical antidote to indifference, alienation, and hostility is love. Drawing upon the precepts of the Torah, Jesus taught that no commandment is greater than that of loving God and one's neighbor (Mark 12:28-34; cf. Deut. 6:4-5; Lev. 19:18). Christians are instructed to "live a life of love" (Eph. 5:2), to "walk in love" (2 John 6), and to "love with actions" (1 John 3:18). "Love covers over a multitude of sins" (1 Pet. 4:8). Indeed, of all the godly virtues a person may possess, "the greatest of these is love" (1 Cor. 13:13).

Love, however, may be a dangerous word. Over the centuries, much so-called Christian love has brought anger and anguish to Jewish people. A person may do the wrong thing though having the right motive. For instance, during the time of the Inquisition, Christians wanted so much for Jews to accept the "love" which they had to share that thousands of Jews were put to death for not accepting that "love." But how, we ask, is it possible to say one loves another without first inquiring what gives that person pain?

The only love that is worthy of the name "Christian" is free, spontaneous, and accepting of others, with no preconditions attached. As God loves us, so we must love people for who they are, in and of themselves — with all their imperfections and weaknesses. People are not to love others for what they may become, for their potential. Suppose a person one loves very much never changes. Human love, like God's, must know no prerequisites or bounds. Genuine love is "not proud," is "not rude," is "not self-seeking," is "not easily angered," and "keeps no record of wrongs" (1 Cor. 13:4-5).

The time has come for the Church to light the lamp of love. Darkness has separated Christian and Jew too long. Change, however, is often a long and arduous journey. Yet it is not our responsibility to complete this task. God will remove the final darkness. But in the meantime, we must not desist from our labors, for "love is patient, love is kind" (1 Cor. 13:4). We must not lose hope or begin to despair. The day will yet come when "the LORD will be king over the whole earth. On that day there will be one LORD" (Zech. 14:9).

Christians and Jews need each other. The Church stands in great debt to the Jewish community, and the Church's ongoing support of the Jewish community is crucial to the outworking of God's own purposes and to the establishing of his own name. In the words of Markus Barth, "With the complete physical extinction of all Jews from the face of the earth the demonstration and proof of God's existence would collapse and the church would lose its *raison d'être:* the church would fall."[8]

Every Christian should desire a greater knowledge and strengthening of the Jewish roots of his faith. In this lifelong search and endeavor, loving concern for Jewish people is not optional. Indeed, Christians are commanded, "Love your neighbor as yourself" (Matt. 22:39; Gal. 5:14). Passive love is not enough, however. A person cannot claim to love his neighbor if he has not yet made a sincere effort to reach out to get to know and understand his neighbor. And so, Hillel again compels us to reply by asking, "If not now . . . when?"

8. Markus Barth, *The People of God* (Sheffield, England: JSOT Press, 1983), p. 72.

*335*

# UNDERSTANDING CHAPTER FIFTEEN

1. The essence of biblical faith is relationship—the fulfilling of the ethical command to love God and one's neighbor. Granting this to be the case, what is the place of the Law and its demands?

2. Define the word *religion* in the most basic terms. If theological dogmas and cultic regulations do not constitute the true locus of biblical godliness and piety, wherein does it lie?

3. God's people are always in danger of falling prey to "bibliolatry." Define this term. What makes some Christians more prone than others to this distortion of the faith?

4. The process of restoring the withered Jewish roots of the Christian faith involves far more than learning about Jewish values, history, and culture in the abstract. What else, at the very core, does this process involve?

5. What great sage of Judaism asked his students, "If not now . . . when?" What was he asking them?

6. Summarize what is implied by the expression "having a Jewish heart."

7. How have pride and arrogance on the part of Christians over the centuries probably proved to be the greatest barriers to positive relations with the Jewish community? What correctives must the Church now offer?

8. Discuss the meaning of the following statement: "One must be prepared to write theology with pencil and eraser, not indelible ink." Why is this statement of particular importance when applied to Christian-Jewish relations?

9. What challenges and potential opposition require that Christians be committed to a long-term venture in the field of Christian-Jewish relations?

10. A number of New Testament texts encourage Christians to reach out thoughtfully, humbly, and caringly to all other peoples around them. Paraphrase several of these texts.

11. Christians approach dialogue with differing motives. What four guidelines are offered to assure the integrity of interfaith discussion? Discuss how each of these points, when not observed, can become a stumbling block to effective dialogue.

12. Summarize the purpose of dialogue in four or five sentences.

13. The New Testament sets some broad guidelines for Christians who engage in conversational dialogue. What two main points emerge from a study of James 1:19 and 1 Peter 3:15?

14. In dialogue, Christians and Jews often find themselves using the same words but with different meanings. Explain the potential differences of perception associated with the following words: (a) Bible, (b) Gentile, (c) Pharisee, (d) Crusade.

15. Summarize the major differences between the Jewish people's historical perception of Jesus and that of Christians. What is the principal reason for this impasse over Jesus? Is the "divorce" between Judaism and Christianity permanent? Discuss.

16. How does the prohibition in the Ten Commandments concerning the bearing of false witness relate to the area of Christian-Jewish relations? Discuss.

17. Define what is meant by the expression "drinking from the sources."

18. Why must today's Church stress that the Old Testament be read as more than a pre-Christian bridge to the New, a mere propaedeutic to the Christian faith?

19. How has the systematic emphasis of Christian thought sometimes led to an obscured meaning of the biblical text?

20. In Jewish thinking, according to Gershom Scholem, what is the "legitimate form through which truth is approached"?

21. For a Christian, how is learning about the Jewish experience by personal visitation of places such as Dachau, Auschwitz, or Israel bound to differ greatly from reading books about them?

22. What is the "ultimate challenge" in the learning process?

23. Give several examples of interfaith activities by which Christians may deepen their appreciation of Jewish heritage in the following areas: (a) faith and traditions, (b) culture, (c) history.

24. Distinguish *dogma* from *halakhah*.

25. Though the Church has a biblical mandate to show concern for all people, why do informed, sensitive Christians often feel a particular responsibility to stand beside Jewish people in matters of social justice?

26. Develop from the Scriptures a basis for "a covenant of caring."

27. What did the Hasidic masters mean by the expression *tikkun olam*?

28. If the Church's ministry today is truly prophetic, how should it focus positively on the Jewish community?

29. In order to accomplish its agenda of social action in relation to the Jewish community, what three practical considerations must the Church keep in view?

30. The biblical antidote to indifference, alienation, and hostility is love. Why, however, may love be a dangerous word? Give a negative example from the history of Christian-Jewish relations.

31. Outline some of the characteristics of genuine love that have direct bearing on Christian-Jewish relations.

32. Respond to this statement of Markus Barth: "With the complete physical extinction of all Jews from the face of the earth the demonstration and proof of God's existence would collapse and the church would lose its *raison d'être:* the church would fall."

33. A person cannot claim to love his neighbor if he has not yet made a sincere effort to reach out to get to know and understand his neighbor. Do you agree? Discuss.

# A Selective Bibliography

Achtemeier, Paul, and Elizabeth Achtemeier. *The Old Testament Roots of Our Faith.* Nashville: Abingdon Press, 1962.

Adler, Morris. *The World of the Talmud.* New York: Schocken Books, 1963.

Agus, Jacob. *Dialogue and Tradition.* New York: Abelard Schuman, 1971.

Alon, Gedaliah. *The Jews in Their Land in the Talmudic Age.* 2 vols. Jerusalem: Magnes Press, 1980.

Aron, Robert. *The Jewish Jesus.* New York: Orbis Books, 1971.

Baeck, Leo. *The Essence of Judaism.* New York: Schocken Books, 1948.

————. *Judaism and Christianity.* New York: Harper & Row, 1966.

Bamberger, Bernard. *The Search for Jewish Theology.* New York: Behrman House, 1978.

Bammel, E., C. K. Barrett, and W. D. Davies, eds. *New Testament Studies in Honour of David Daube.* New York: Oxford University Press, 1977.

Barclay, William. *Educational Ideals in the Ancient World.* Repr. Grand Rapids: Baker Book House, 1974.

Baron, Salo. *A Social and Religious History of the Jews.* 16 vols. Philadelphia and New York: Jewish Publication Society and Columbia University Press, 1952.

Barr, James. *The Semantics of Biblical Language.* New York: Oxford University Press, 1961.

Barth, Markus. *Israel and the Church.* Richmond, VA: John Knox Press, 1969.

————. *Jesus the Jew.* Atlanta: John Knox Press, 1978.

————. *The People of God.* Sheffield, England: JSOT Press, 1983.

————. *Rediscovering the Lord's Supper.* Atlanta: John Knox Press, 1988.

Baum, Gregory. *Is the New Testament Anti-Semitic?* Glen Rock, NJ: Paulist Press, 1965.

Bea, Augustin. *The Church and the Jewish People.* New York: Harper & Row, 1966.

Ben-Sasson, H. H., ed. *A History of the Jewish People.* Cambridge: Harvard University Press, 1976.

Berger, David. *The Jewish-Christian Debate in the High Middle Ages.* Philadelphia: Jewish Publication Society, 1979.

Bevan, Edwyn R. and Charles Singer, eds. *The Legacy of Israel.* Oxford: Clarendon Press, 1944.

Bivin, David, and Roy B. Blizzard. *Understanding the Difficult Words of Jesus.* Austin, TX: Center for Judaic-Christian Studies, 1984.

Boadt, Laurence, and Helga Croner and Leon Klenicki, eds. *Biblical Studies: Meeting Ground of Jews and Christians.* New York: Paulist Press, 1980.

Boman, Thorleif. *Hebrew Thought Compared with Greek.* Trans. Jules L. Moreau. Repr. New York: W. W. Norton & Co., 1970.

Bright, John. *The Authority of the Old Testament.* Repr. Grand Rapids: Baker Book House, 1975.

Bruce, F. F. *Jesus and Christian Origins Outside the New Testament.* Grand Rapids: William B. Eerdmans Publishing Co., 1974.

Buber, Martin. *Hasidism and Modern Man.* New York: Harper & Row, 1958.

————. *Two Types of Faith: The Interpenetration of Judaism and Christianity.* New York: Harper & Row, 1961.

————. *Israel and the World.* 2nd ed. New York: Schocken Books, 1963.

Callan, Terrance. *Forgetting the Root: The Emergence of Christianity from Judaism.* New York: Paulist Press, 1986.

Carlson, Paul. *O Christian! O Jew!* Elgin, IL: David C. Cook, 1974.

Carson, D. A., ed. *From Sabbath to Lord's Day.* Grand Rapids: Zondervan Publishing House, 1982.

Cohen, A. *Everyman's Talmud.* New York: Schocken Books, 1949.

Cohen, Arthur A. *The Myth of the Judeo-Christian Tradition.* New York: Harper & Row, 1970.

Cohen, Martin A., and Helga Croner. *Christian Mission—Jewish Mission.* New York: Paulist Press, 1982.

Cohen, Shaye J. D. *From Maccabees to the Mishnah.* Philadelphia: Westminster Press, 1987.

Collins, John J. *Between Athens and Jerusalem.* New York: Crossroad, 1983.

Croner, Helga, ed. *Stepping Stones to Further Jewish-Christian Relations.* New York: Stimulus Books, 1977.

————, ed. *More Stepping Stones to Jewish-Christian Relations.* New York: Paulist Press, 1985.

Croner, Helga, and Leon Klenicki, eds. *Issues in the Jewish-Christian Dialogue.* New York: Paulist Press, 1979.

Dalman, Gustaf. *Jesus-Jeshua.* Trans. P. L. Levertoff. Repr. New York: Ktav, 1971.

Danby, Herbert, ed. *The Mishnah.* London: Oxford University Press, 1938.

Daniélou, Jean. *Dialogue with Israel.* Baltimore: Helicon Press, 1968.

Daube, D. *The New Testament and Rabbinic Judaism.* London: Athlone Press, 1956.

Davies, Alan T., ed. *Anti-Semitism and the Foundations of Christianity.* New York: Paulist Press, 1979.

Davies, W. D. *Christian Origins and Judaism.* Philadelphia: Westminster Press, 1962.

―――. *The Setting of the Sermon on the Mount.* Cambridge: Cambridge University Press, 1964.

―――. *The Gospel and the Land.* Berkeley, CA: University of California Press, 1974.

―――. *Paul and Rabbinic Judaism.* 4th ed. Philadelphia: Fortress Press, 1980.

―――. *The Territorial Dimension of Judaism.* Berkeley: University of California Press, 1982.

―――. *Jewish and Pauline Studies.* Philadelphia: Fortress Press, 1984.

De Lange, Nicholas. *Judaism.* New York: Oxford University Press, 1986.

De Sola Pool, David. *Why I Am A Jew.* Boston: Beacon Press, 1957.

De Vaux, Roland. *Ancient Israel.* Trans. J. McHugh. Repr. New York: McGraw-Hill, 1965.

Dimont, Max. *Jews, God and History.* New York: American Library, 1964.

Dix, Dom Gregory. *Jew and Greek: A Study in the Primitive Church.* London: Dacre Press, 1953.

Donin, Hayim H. *To Be a Jew.* New York: Basic Books, 1980.

Doukhan, Jacques. *Drinking at the Sources.* Mountain View, CA: Mountain Press Publishing Association, 1981.

Eban, Abba. *Heritage: Civilization and the Jews.* London: Weidenfeld and Nicolson, 1984.

Eckardt, A. Roy. *Elder and Younger Brothers.* New York: Scribner, 1967.

―――. *Your People, My People.* New York: Quadrangle, 1974.

Eckstein, Yechiel. *What Christians Should Know About Jews and Judaism.* Waco, TX: Word Books, 1984.

Edelman, Lily, ed. *Jewish Heritage Reader.* New York: Taplinger Publishing Co., 1965.

Epstein, I., ed. *The Babylonian Talmud.* 35 vols. repr. in 18. London: Soncino Press, 1961.

Falk, Harvey. *Jesus the Pharisee: A New Look at the Jewishness of Jesus.* New York: Paulist Press, 1985.

Fasching, Darrell J., ed. *The Jewish People in Christian Preaching.* New York: Edwin Mellen, 1984.

Feldman, David M. *Marital Relations, Birth Control, and Abortion in Jewish Law.* New York: Schocken Books, 1968.

Fisher, Eugene. *Faith without Prejudice.* New York: Paulist Press, 1977.

Fishman, Hertzel. *American Protestantism and the Jewish State.* Detroit: Wayne State University Press, 1973.

Flannery, Edward H. The *Anguish of the Jews.* Rev. ed. Mahwah, NJ: Paulist Press, 1985.

Flusser, David. *Jesus.* New York: Herder and Herder, 1969.

―――. *Judaism and the Origins of Christianity.* Jerusalem: Magnes Press, 1988.

Förster, Werner. *Palestinian Judaism in New Testament Times.* Trans. Gordon E. Harris. London: Oliver & Boyd, 1964.

Fuller, Daniel. *Gospel and Law.* Grand Rapids: William B. Eerdmans Publishing Co., 1981.

Gade, Richard E. *A Historical Survey of Anti-Semitism.* Grand Rapids: Baker Book House, 1981.

Gager, John G. *The Origins of Anti-Semitism: Attitudes toward Judaism in Pagan and Christian Antiquity.* New York: Oxford University Press, 1983.

Gaster, Theodor. *Customs and Folkways of Jewish Life.* New York: William Sloane Associates Publishers, 1955.

———. *Festivals of the Jewish Year.* New York: William Sloane Associates, 1953.

Gerhardsson, Birger. *The Origins of the Gospel Traditions.* Trans. Gene J. Lund. Philadelphia: Fortress Press, 1979.

Gittelsohn, Roland B. *My Beloved Is Mine: Judaism and Marriage.* New York: Union of American Hebrew Congregations, 1969

Goldstein, M. *Jesus in the Jewish Tradition.* New York: Macmillan, 1950.

Gordis, Robert. *Judaism in a Christian World.* New York: McGraw-Hill, 1966.

———. *The Root and the Branches.* Chicago: University of Chicago Press, 1962.

———. *Sex and the Family in the Jewish Tradition.* New York: Burning Bush Press, 1967.

Gordon, Cyrus H. *The Common Background of Greek and Hebrew Civilizations.* 2nd ed. New York: W. W. Norton & Co., 1965.

———. *The World of the Old Testament.* Garden City, NY: Doubleday & Co., 1958.

Grant, F. C. *Ancient Judaism and the New Testament.* New York: Macmillan, 1959.

Hagner, Donald A. *The Jewish Reclamation of Jesus.* Grand Rapids: Zondervan Publishing House, 1984.

Hare, Douglas R. A. *The Theme of Jewish Persecution of Christians in the Gospel According to St. Matthew.* Cambridge: Cambridge University Press, 1967.

Harrington, Daniel. *God's People in Christ: New Testament Perspectives on the Church and Judaism.* Philadelphia: Fortress Press, 1980.

Harshbarger, Luther H. and John A. Mourant. *Judaism and Christianity.* Boston: Allyn and Bacon, 1968.

Hedenquist, Göte, ed. *The Church and the Jewish People.* London: Edinburgh House Press, 1954.

Hengel, Martin. *Judaism and Hellenism.* Trans. John Bowden. Philadelphia: Fortress Press, 1974.

Herford, R. Travers. *Judaism in the New Testament Period.* London: Lindsey Press, 1928.

———. *Christianity in Talmud and Midrash.* Repr. Clifton, NJ: Reference Book Publishers, 1966.

———, ed. *The Ethics of the Talmud.* Repr. New York: Schocken Books, 1962.

Hertz, Joseph H., ed. *Authorized Daily Prayer Book.* Rev. ed. New York: Block Publishing Co., 1948.

Heschel, Abraham J. *The Earth Is the Lord's.* New York: Farrar, Straus & Giroux, 1950.

————. *God in Search of Man.* New York: Farrar, Straus & Giroux, 1955.

————. *The Prophets.* New York: Harper & Row, 1962.

————. *Israel: An Echo of Eternity.* New York: Farrar, Straus & Giroux, 1969.

————. *The Insecurity of Freedom.* New York: Schocken Books, 1972.

————. *The Sabbath.* New York: Farrar, Straus & Giroux, 1975.

Hill, David. *Greek Words and Hebrew Meanings.* Cambridge: Cambridge University Press, 1967.

Hooker, Morna. *Continuity and Discontinuity: Early Christianity in its Jewish Setting.* London: Epworth Press, 1986.

Idelsohn, A. Z. *Jewish Music in Its Historical Development.* New York: Schocken Books, 1956.

Isaac, Jules. *The Teaching of Contempt.* New York: Holt, Rinehart and Winston, 1964.

————. *Jesus and Israel.* New York: Holt, Rinehart and Winston, 1971.

Jacob, Walter. *Christianity Through Jewish Eyes.* Cincinnati: Hebrew Union College Press, 1974.

Jocz, Jakob. *The Jewish People and Jesus Christ.* 3rd ed. Repr. Grand Rapids: Baker Book House, 1979.

Johnson, Paul. *A History of the Jews.* New York: Harper & Row, 1987.

Juster, Daniel. *Jewish Roots.* Rockville, MD: Davar, 1986.

Kaufman, Harriet. *Jews and Judaism Since Jesus.* Cincinnati: Kaufman House Publishers, 1978.

Kirsch, Paul J. *We Christians and Jews.* Philadelphia: Fortress Press, 1975.

Kitov, A. E. *The Jew and His Home.* New York: Shengold Publishers, 1963.

Klausner, Joseph. *Jesus of Nazareth.* Trans. W. F. Stinespring. New York: Macmillan, 1945.

————. *The Messianic Idea in Israel.* Trans. W. F. Stinespring. New York: Macmillan, 1955.

Klein, Charlotte. *Anti-Judaism in Christian Theology.* Philadelphia: Fortress Press, 1978.

Klenicki, Leon, and Richard John Neuhaus. *Believing Today.* Grand Rapids: William B. Eerdmans Publishing Co., 1989.

Klenicki, Leon, and Geoffrey Wigoder, eds. *A Dictionary of the Jewish-Christian Dialogue.* New York: Paulist Press, 1984.

Koenig, John. *Jews and Christians in Dialogue: New Testament Foundations.* Philadelphia: Westminster Press, 1979.

Köhler, Ludwig. *Hebrew Man.* Trans. Peter R. Ackroyd. Repr. Nashville: Abingdon, 1957.

Küng, Hans, and Walter Kasper, eds. *Christians and Jews*. Trans. John Maxwell. New York: Seabury Press, 1975.

Ladd, George E. *The Pattern of New Testament Truth*. Grand Rapids: William B. Eerdmans Publishing Co., 1968.

Lamm, Maurice. *The Jewish Way in Love and Marriage*. New York: Harper & Row, 1980.

Lapide, Pinchas. *Three Popes and the Jews*. New York: Hawthorn Books, 1967.

———. *Israelis, Jews and Jesus*. Trans. Peter Heinegg. Garden City, NY: Doubleday & Co., 1979.

———. *Hebrew in the Church: The Foundations of Jewish-Christian Dialogue*. Trans. Erroll F. Rhodes. Grand Rapids: William B. Eerdmans Publishing Co., 1984.

Lapide, Pinchas, and Ulrich Luz. *Jesus in Two Perspectives: A Jewish-Christian Dialogue*. Trans. Lawrence W. Denef. Minneapolis: Augsburg, 1985.

Lapide, Pinchas, and Peter Stuhlmacher. *Paul: Rabbi and Apostle*. Trans. Lawrence W. Denef. Minneapolis: Augsburg, 1984.

LaSor, William S. *Israel: A Biblical View*. Grand Rapids: William B. Eerdmans Publishing Co., 1976.

———. *The Dead Sea Scrolls and the New Testament*. Grand Rapids: William B. Eerdmans Publishing Co., 1972.

Littell, Franklin. *The Crucifixion of the Jews*. New York: Harper & Row, 1975.

Longenecker, Richard N. *Paul: Apostle of Liberty*. New York: Harper & Row, 1964.

———. *The Christology of Early Jewish Christianity*. Repr. Grand Rapids: Baker Book House, 1981.

Marcus, Jacob. *The Jews in the Medieval World*. New York: Atheneum, 1972.

Marshall, I. Howard. *Last Supper and Lord's Supper*. Grand Rapids: William B. Eerdmans Publishing Co., 1981.

Martin, Bernard. *A History of Judaism*. Vol. 2: *Europe and the New World*. New York: Basic Books, 1974.

Martin-Achard, Robert. *An Approach to the Old Testament*. Trans. J. C. G. Greig. Edinburgh: Oliver & Boyd, 1965.

Montefiore, Claude G., and H. Locwe. *A Rabbinic Anthology*. New York: Schocken Books, 1974.

Moore, George Foot. *Judaism in the First Centuries of the Christian Era*. 3 vols. Cambridge: Harvard University Press, 1927-30.

Nash, Ronald H. *Christianity and the Hellenistic World*. Grand Rapids: Zondervan Publishing House, 1984.

Neuhaus, Richard John, ed. *Jews in Unsecular America*. Grand Rapids: William B. Eerdmans Publishing Co., 1987.

Neusner, Jacob. *Invitation to the Talmud*. New York: Harper & Row, 1973.

———. *Judaism in the Beginning of Christianity*. Philadelphia: Fortress, 1984.

———. *Judaism in the Matrix of Christianity*. Philadelphia: Fortress Press, 1986.

Newman, Louis I., ed. *The Talmudic Anthology.* New York: Behrman House, 1945.

Olson, Bernhard E. *Faith and Prejudice.* New Haven: Yale University Press, 1963.

Opsahl, Paul, and Marc Tanenbaum, eds. *Speaking of God Today: Jews and Lutherans in Conversation.* Philadelphia: Fortress Press, 1974.

Parkes, James. *The Conflict of the Church and the Synagogue.* New York: Hermon Press, 1974.

―――. *The Foundations of Judaism and Christianity.* Chicago: Quadrangle Books, 1960.

Patai, Raphael. *The Jewish Mind.* New York: Scribner, 1977.

Patte, Daniel. *Early Jewish Hermeneutic in Palestine.* Missoula, MT: Scholars Press, 1975.

Pawlikowski, John T. *Sinai and Calvary: A Meeting of Two Peoples.* Beverly Hills: Benziger, 1976.

―――. *What Are They Saying about Christian-Jewish Relations?* New York: Paulist Press, 1982.

Peck, Abraham J., ed. *Jews and Christians after the Holocaust.* Philadelphia: Fortress Press, 1982.

Rahner, Karl, and Pinchas Lapide. *Encountering Jesus—Encountering Judaism: A Dialogue.* Trans. Davis Perkins. New York: Crossroad, 1987.

Rausch, David A. *A Legacy of Hatred.* Chicago: Moody Press, 1984.

Richardson, Peter. *Israel in the Apostolic Church.* Cambridge: Cambridge University Press, 1969.

Riches, John. *Jesus and the Transformation of Judaism.* New York: Seabury Press, 1982.

Rivkin, Ellis. *What Crucified Jesus?* Nashville: Abingdon Press, 1984.

Robinson, H. Wheeler. *Corporate Personality in Ancient Israel.* Rev. ed. Repr. Philadelphia: Fortress Press, 1980.

Rosenberg, Stuart E. *The Christian Problem: A Jewish View.* New York: Hippocrene Books, 1986.

Rosenstock-Huessey, Eugen. *Judaism Despite Christianity.* University, AL: University of Alabama Press, 1969.

Roth, Cecil. *The Jewish Contribution to Civilization.* London: Horovitz Publishing Co., 1956.

Rudin, A. James. *Israel for Christians.* Philadelphia: Fortress Press, 1983.

Rudin, A. James, and Marvin R. Wilson, eds. *A Time to Speak: The Evangelical-Jewish Encounter.* Grand Rapids: William B. Eerdmans Publishing Co., 1987.

Ruether, Rosemary. *Faith and Fratricide.* New York: Seabury Press, 1974.

Runes, Dagobert, ed. *The Hebrew Impact on Western Civilization.* Secaucus, NJ: Citadel Press, 1976.

Safrai, S., and M. Stern, eds. *The Jewish People in the First Century.* Vol. 2. Philadelphia: Fortress Press, 1976.

Sanders, E. P. *Paul and Palestinian Judaism.* Phildelphia: Fortress Press, 1977.

————. *Paul, the Law, and the Jewish People.* Philadelphia: Fortress Press, 1977.

————, ed. *Jewish and Christian Self-Definition.* Vol. 1: *The Shaping of Christianity in the Second and Third Centuries.* Philadelphia: Fortress Press, 1980.

Sandmel, Samuel. *We Jews and You Christians.* Philadelphia: Lippincott, 1967.

————. *Anti-Semitism in the New Testament?* Philadelphia: Fortress Press, 1978.

————. *Judaism and Christian Beginnings.* New York: Oxford University Press, 1978.

————. *We Jews and Jesus.* New York: Oxford University Press, 1978.

Schechter, Solomon. *Some Aspects of Rabbinic Theology.* New York: Schocken Books, 1961.

Schoeps, Hans-Joachim. *The Jewish-Christian Argument: History of Theologies in Conflict.* Trans. David E. Green. New York: Holt, Rinehart & Winston, 1963.

————. *Jewish Christianity: Factional Disputes in the Early Church.* Trans. Douglas R. A. Hare. Philadelphia: Fortress Press, 1969.

Schürer, Emil. *The History of the Jewish People in the Age of Jesus Christ (175 B.C.-A.D. 135).* 3 vols. Rev. ed. G. Vermes, et al. Edinburgh: T. & T. Clark, 1979-87.

Shiel, James. *Greek Thought and the Rise of Christianity.* Harlow: Longmans, 1968.

Silberman, Charles E. *A Certain People: American Jews and Their Lives Today.* New York: Summit Books, 1985.

Silva, Moises. *Biblical Words and Their Meaning.* Grand Rapids: Zondervan Publishing House, 1983.

Silver, Abba Hillel. *Where Judaism Differed.* New York: Macmillan, 1956.

Silver, Daniel Jeremy. *A History of Judaism.* Vol. 1: *From Abraham to Maimonides.* New York: Basic Books, 1974.

Silverman, William B. *Rabbinic Wisdom and Jewish Values.* Rev. ed. New York: Union of American Hebrew Congregations, 1971.

Snaith, Norman H. *The Distinctive Ideas of the Old Testament.* New York: Schocken Books, 1964.

Spong, John Shelby. *This Hebrew Lord.* New York: Seabury Press, 1974.

Spong, John Shelby, and Jack Daniel Spiro. *Dialogue: In Search of Jewish-Christian Understanding.* New York: Seabury Press, 1975.

Steinberg, Milton. *Basic Judaism.* New York: Harcourt, Brace & World, 1947.

Steinsaltz, Adin. *The Essential Talmud.* New York: Bantam Books, 1976.

Stendahl, Krister. *Paul Among Jews and Gentiles.* Philadelphia: Fortress Press, 1976.

Strack, Hermann L. *Introduction to the Talmud and Midrash.* New York: Atheneum, 1974.

Strack, Hermann L., and Paul Billerbeck. *Kommentar zum Neuen Testament aus Talmud und Midrasch.* 4 vols. Munich: C. H. Beck'sche Verlagsbuchhandlung, Oscar Beck, 1928.

Swidler, Leonard. *Women in Judaism.* Metuchen, NJ: Scarecrow Press, 1976.

Talmage, Frank E., ed. *Disputation and Dialogue.* New York: Ktav, 1975.

Tanenbaum, Marc H., Marvin R. Wilson, and A. James Rudin, eds. *Evangelicals and Jews in Conversation on Scripture, Theology and History.* Grand Rapids: Baker Book House, 1978.

—————. *Evangelicals and Jews in an Age of Pluralism.* Grand Rapids: Baker Book House, 1984.

Trepp, Leo. *Judaism: Development and Life.* Belmont, CA: Wadsworth, 1982.

Tresmontant, Claude. *A Study of Hebrew Thought.* Trans. M. F. Gibson. New York: Desclee Co., 1960.

Tuchman, Barbara. *Bible and Sword.* New York: Minerva, 1968.

Van Buren, Paul. *Discerning the Way.* New York: Seabury Press, 1980.

Van den Haag, Ernest. *The Jewish Mystique.* New York: Stein and Day, 1969.

Vermes, Geza. *Jesus the Jew: A Historian's Reading of the Gospels.* Philadelphia: Fortress Press, 1981.

—————. *Jesus and the World of Judaism.* Philadelphia: Fortress Press, 1984.

Viviano, Benedict T. *Study As Worship.* Leiden: E. J. Brill, 1978.

Wigoder, Geoffrey, ed. *Encyclopaedia Judaica.* 16 vols. Jerusalem: Keter Publishing House, 1971-72.

Williamson, Clark M. *Has God Rejected His People?* Nashville: Abingdon Press, 1982.

Wouk, Herman. *This Is My God.* New York: Pocket Books, 1970.

Yaseen, Leonard C. *The Jesus Connection.* New York: Crossroad, 1985.

Young, Bradford H. *The Jewish Background to the Lord's Prayer.* Austin, TX: Center for Judaic-Christian Studies, 1984.

—————. *Jesus and His Jewish Parables.* Mahwah, NJ: Paulist Press, 1989.

Zeik, Michael, and Mortin Siegel, eds. *Root and Branch: The Jewish-Christian Dialogue.* New York: Roth, 1974.

Zimmerli, Walther. *The Old Testament and the World.* Trans. John J. Scullion. Atlanta: John Knox Press, 1976.

# Index of Biblical Texts

# INDEX OF BIBLICAL TEXTS

# Index of Rabbinic Literature

# Index of Other Early Extrabiblical Literature

# Index of Authors

# INDEX OF AUTHORS

# Index of Subjects

# Index of Hebrew Words

(Several Aramaic terms are also included in this index.)

# Index of Greek Words

66 RUST HOUSE  MAIN ST.
House TO THE LEFT.
Abandoned.

Joe Eaton (Talked w/)


Bill THAYER
Architect MAIN
on Historical Commission